MONETARY ECONOMICS IN DEVELOPING COUNTRIES

Monetary Economics in Developing Countries

Second Edition

Subrata Ghatak

St. Martin's Press

First edition 1981
Second edition 1995

Published in Great Britain by
MACMILLAN PRESS LTD
Houndmills, Basingstoke, Hampshire RG21 2XS
and London
Companies and representatives
throughout the world

A catalogue record for this book is available
from the British Library.

ISBN 0–333–57224–6 hardcover
ISBN 0–333–57225–4 paperback

10 9 8 7 6 5 4 3 2 1
04 03 02 01 00 99 98 97 96 95

Printed in Great Britain by
Mackays of Chatham PLC
Chatham, Kent

Second edition first published in the United States of America 1995 by
Scholarly and Reference Division,
ST. MARTIN'S PRESS, INC.,
175 Fifth Avenue,
New York, N.Y. 10010

ISBN 0–312–12496–1

Library of Congress Cataloging-in-Publication Data
Ghatak, Subrata, 1939–
Monetary economics in developing countries / Subrata Ghatak.
p. cm.
Includes bibliographical references and index.
ISBN 0–312–12496–1
1. Money—Developing countries. 2. Monetary policy—Developing countries. I. Title.
HG1496.G44 1994
332.4'91724—dc20 94–36053
CIP

Contents

Preface to the first edition ix
Preface to the second edition xi
Acknowledgements xii

Chapter 1 The role of money in a less developed country **1**
1.1 Money in a barter economy 1
1.2 The definition of money: money and credit creation 2
1.3 Money markets in less developed countries (LDCs) 5

Chapter 2 The Keynesian and monetarist views on the importance of money **8**
2.1 The classical view 8
2.2 The Keynesian theory 12
2.3 Money and the interest rate 16
2.4 A general equilibrium approach: the Hicksian IS–LM curves 18
2.5 Monetary and fiscal policy 21
2.6 The monetarists' case 22
2.7 Special characteristics of LDCs 24
2.8 Recent developments in the demand for money studies in LDCs 27
Appendix to Chapter 2: A2.1 35
Appendix to Chapter 2:A2.2: Demand for money in India: 1950–86: a cointegration analysis by *Anita Ghatak* 37

Chapter 3 The demand for money in LDCs: empirical results by (*D. F. Deadman*) **47**
3.1 Conventional demand for money studies 47
3.2 Stability testing of conventional demand for money studies 50
3.3 Error-correction models of demand for money functions for developing countries 53

Chapter 4 Monetary institutions in LDCs **63**
4.1 The central bank: its functions in the LDCs 63
4.2 The commercial banks: the creation of bank deposits 65
4.3 The changing pattern of commercial banking in the LDCs 69
4.4 Rural money markets in LDCs 71
4.5 Currency boards in Africa 73

Chapter 5 Theories of money and economic growth **75**
5.1 A simple Harrod–Domar growth model 75
5.2 The neo-classical growth model 76
5.3 Money in a neo-classical growth model: the Tobin model 78
5.4 Problems in the application of neo-classical monetary growth theory to LDCs 81
5.5 Economic growth and the role of financial intermediaries 84
5.6 The Gurley–Shaw model 84
5.7 Economic development and 'financial accumulation' 86
5.8 Financial repression and economic growth: the McKinnon and Shaw model 87
Appendix to Chapter 5 91

Chapter 6 Money, inflation and growth (*with Peter Ayre*) **94**
6.1 Characteristics of inflation in LDCs 94
6.2 The causes of inflation 96
6.3 The effects of inflation on growth 103
6.4 Financial repression and the case against inflation 115
6.5 Major problems and policies for stabilisation in LDCs 118
Appendix to Chapter 6: A model of inflation generation and stabilisation 125

Chapter 7 The Polak model: its application to the LDCs **133**
7.1 The Polak–Boissonneult (PB) model 133
7.2 The application of the PB model 135
7.3 The PB model within the Keynesian income analysis 136
7.4 The empirical results 137
7.5 Policy implications of the PB model 140
7.6 Limitations of the PB model 141

Chapter 8 Monetary policies in developing countries **143**
8.1 Objectives of monetary policies in the LDCs 143
8.2 The theory of monetary policy 144
8.3 The instruments of monetary policy 148
8.4 The role of monetary policy in LDCs 155

Chapter 9 International liquidity, LDCs and Special Drawing Rights **157**
9.1 The need for international monetary reserves 157
9.2 The exchange rate and the need for reserves 158
9.3 The Bretton Woods system and the dollar standard 159
9.4 Problems of international liquidity 159
9.5 The nature and role of SDRs 162
9.6 The Extended Fund Facility 170
9.7 The Trust Fund 171

Chapter 10 Rural financial institutions in LDCs **176**
10.1 Unorganised money markets in LDCs and some consequences 176
10.2 Determination of rural rates in LDCs 179
10.3 An evaluation 186
10.4 Policies for an integrated development of rural financial markets in LDCs 187
10.5 Rural money markets and implications for monetary policy 191
Appendix to Chapter 10: Grameen Bank of Bangladesh 193

Chapter 11 The international debt crisis **194**
11.1 LDC borrowing before 1973 195
11.2 Debt problems after 1973 196
11.3 Benefits and costs of default theory 197
11.4 Application of the model to the debt crisis of 1982 199
11.5 Managing the debt crisis 200
11.6 Policy responses to the debt crisis of 1982 202
11.7 The International Monetary Fund (IMF), adjustment policies and LDCs 205
11.8 Criticisms of the IMF action 206
11.9 Response of the International Monetary Fund 206
11.10 New critiques of the International Monetary Fund 209
11.11 How effective are the International Monetary Fund programmes? 210
Appendix to Chapter 11 (with Paul Levine) 212

Chapter 12 Exchange rate policies in developing countries (*by Kate Phylaktis*) **224**
12.1 The role and influence of exchange rates in the economy 224
12.2 Alternative exchange rate regimes 226
12.3 Exchange rate arrangements in developing countries 227
12.4 The choice of exchange rate regimes 231
12.5 The real target approach to exchange rate policy 235
12.6 The nominal anchor approach to exchange rate policy 237
12.7 Summary and conclusions 240

References 243

Index 262

For
Churni

Preface to the first edition

This book is intended as an up-to-date undergraduate text for students taking a course on monetary economics in less-developed countries (LDCs). Since monetary economics is a vast subject, I had to be selective in my choice of topics. However, the important issues confronting the LDCs in the use of monetary and theory policy have been discussed carefully and rigorously. Some basic knowledge of micro- and macro- economics, elementary math-ematics and statistics has been assumed. A major aim of writing this book is to 'ease the constraint' on the supply of introductory textbooks on monetary economics in the LDCs. In this respect, I hope that this book may be useful. The text highlights some of the major areas of interest in current teaching and research in monetary economics in LDCs. After a brief introduction in which an attempt has been made to familiarise the readers with the special characteristics of the financial market and institutions in the LDCs, the focus of attention has been the theoretical contributions to the literature by the 'Keynesians' and the 'monetarists'. Next, the relevance of such theories to the LDCs has been discussed. Of particular interest to the readers could be the section on the empirical estimation of stability in the demand for money in the LDCs which has kindly been written by colleague Derek Deadman, to whom I remain very thankful. Chapter 3 describes the monetary institutions in the LDCs. However, given the availability of a significant amount of literature on the institutional side, no attempt has been made to discuss their activities in detail. In chapter 4, the important relationship between money and economic growth has been discussed. Special emphasis has been given to the Tobin and McKinnon–Shaw models and the theory of financial repression in the LDCs. These models are then evaluated in the light of recent empirical findings. The scope of inflationary financing and growth in the LDCs has been the subject of thorough investigation in chapter 6. I am grateful to Peter Ayre who has kindly written this chapter with me. The Polak model and its empirical relevance to the LDCs has been the subject of careful analysis in chapter 6. Chapter 7 examines the role of monetary policy in the LDCs. The chapter on international liquidity and Special Drawing Rights has been written jointly by Peter Ayre and myself. I remain thankful to my colleague, Tony Jennings, who has kindly written the last chapter on the international monetary systems and the LDCs. He has indicated the need for international monetary reform in the 1980s, from the point of view of the LDCs, through the setting up of a new international economic order.

The issues raised in the book are mainly discussed within a framework of analytical economics. I am fully aware of the omissions that have taken place.

However, I hope that the book will provide a concise and fairly comprehensive account of a number of key issues in monetary economics in the LDCs.

The book has been written during 1978 and 1979 while I have been teaching development economics at Leicester University. During the period of my writing, I have received constructive criticisms from many people. I am chiefly indebted to Peter Ayre, who has been kind enough to comment on various drafts of a number of chapters. I am also grateful to Michael Howard, Derek Deadman and Paul Herrington for their comments on different chapters. I also remain very thankful to Jeanne Cretney, Dorothy Logsdon, Joan Cook, Mavis Johnson, Heather Hopper and Janet Marks, for their skill and patience in typing the successive drafts of the manuscript.

University of Leicester SUBRATA GHATAK

Preface to the second edition

The major objective in the second edition has been to achieve a reasonable balance between the recent monetary growth theories and policies and the realities of economic development in less developed countries (LDCs). Many chapters have been completely revised. Since readers may be particularly interested in understanding the basic concepts of the 'financial repression' and economic liberalisation, I have added a short section on the theories and applications of such concepts and their practical evaluations in LDCs. Chapters on 'Money, Inflation and Economic Growth and 'International Liquidity', originally with Peter Ayre, have been extensively revised in the light of of changes that occurred in the 1980s. New chapters on exchange rate policies and the debt crisis in LDCs have been added. The chapter on rural financial institutions and their role in macroeconomic stabilisation is also new. Sections on structural adjustments and financial liberalisation in the 1980s in many LDCS have been revised. A number of case studies have been discussed to analyse the relationship between money and prices in developing countries. To facilitate easy reading, I have relegated some technical and mathematical sections as appendices to the different chapters. Many new tables have been used to provide recent information of the recent events in the LDCs.

In the preparation of this edition, I am grateful to many colleagues and students. I am particularly grateful to Dr Anita Ghatak, Professor Paul Levine, Dr Kate Phylaktis, Ziggy MacDonald, Churni Ghatak, Nursen Albayrak and Steve Wheatley-Price for their help. I am also indebted to Stephen Rutt of Macmillan for his patience and excellent cooperation.

University of Leicester SUBRATA GHATAK

Acknowledgements

The author and publishers wish to thank the following who have kindly given permission for the use of copyright material:

Chapman & Hall and John Wiley, publishers of the journal *Applied Economics* and *Journal of International Development*, relatively.

International Monetary Fund for tables and graphs from *Annual Report of the International Monetary Fund*, 1978, and figures and tables from *Finance and Development*, September 1978, December 1978, July 1979.

McGraw-Hill Book Company for a diagram from *Estimating Foreign Resource Needs for Economic Development*, 1967, by J. Vanek.

Organisation for Economic Co-operation and Development for tables from *The OECD Observer, Development Co-operation*, 1977 Review, and *Borrowing by Developing Countries on the Eurocurrency Market*, 1977, by P. Wellons.

The World Bank for tables from *Borrowing in International Capital Markets, and Private Direct Foreign Investment in Developing Countries: Policy Issues for Host and Home Governments and for International Institutions* by K. Billerbeck and Y. Yasugi, World Bank Staff Working Paper No. 348, July 1979; World Bank, IMF, *The Debt Tables*, 1992–3, Washington, DC.

Every effort has been made to trace all the copyright-holders, but if any have been inadvertently overlooked the publishers will be pleased to make the necessary arrangement at the first opportunity.

1. The role of money in a less developed country

1.1 Money in a barter economy

The introduction of money in a barter economy is regarded as a very important phenomenon for several reasons. In a barter economy, goods are usually exchanged against goods. But to facilitate exchanges of goods among their producers, it is necessary to have 'a double coincidence of wants'. For instance, a man from the plains may wish to exchange some cloth against some wood; if a man from the hills brings some wood which he wants to exchange against cloth in a common market at a mutually agreeable time and *if* the amount of cloth and wood to be exchanged are acceptable to both the parties, then exchange would take place. Such a barter system may operate in many villages of less developed countries (LDCs). But the defects of such a system are well known

First, it is not easy to envisage a double coincidence of wants which could be easily satisfied without a common unit of measurement. In the example given above, it has been assumed rather boldly that the size of the cloth and the length of the wood are quite satisfactory to the parties concerned. This is unlikely to occur in practice.

Secondly, the barter system restricts the number of transactions that could take place. The system could work when exchanges are very limited. But once trade and exchange grows, and the number of transactions increases, the barter system would be an inefficient way to facilitate such exchanges.

Thirdly, it is possible to confuse the use value and exchange value of goods and services in a barter economy. Such a confusion precludes a rational allocation of resources and promotion of economic efficiency.

Fourthly, when exchanges take place over time in a barter economy, it is necessary to store goods for future exchange. If such goods are perishable by nature, then the system will break down.

Fifthly, the development of industrial economies usually depends on a division of labour, specialisation and the allocation of resources on the basis of choice and preferences. Economic efficiency is achieved by economising on the use of most scarce resources. Without a common medium of exchange and a common unit of account which is acceptable to both consumers and producers, it is very difficult to achieve an efficient allocation of resources to satisfy consumer preferences.

In the light of the above discussion it is now possible to understand easily the traditional role of money.

Money as a medium of exchange

In a non-monetised economy, the introduction of money as a medium of exchange has the clear advantage of facilitating exchanges in a manner which is mutually satisfactory to all parties. The scope of exchange enlarges, division of labour increases, and a greater efficiency is achieved in the allocation of resources. As the market expands with the issue of money, factors can be used to make goods which they most efficiently produce. Therefore, these factors are no longer needed to produce as much for their own use. As a result, the production possibilities of the economy will expand.

Money as a unit of account or measurement

Money serves a very useful purpose as a unit of measurement. In a primitive economy, the introduction of money develops a sense of accounting and commercial calculations in economic activities. The principle of rational allocation of resources cannot be applied in the absence of a common unit of measurement. Hence, a barter economy is clearly inefficient in obtaining such a rational allocation. It is also important to point out for a LDC that the issue of money in a subsistence economy has a salutary effect on the development of those business habits which are necessary for achieving a higher rate of economic growth.

Money as a store of value

Before the introduction of money, a society is likely to save in real terms. Such savings would then consist of food grains, livestock, etc. This would obviously involve a high cost to the society, i.e. the cost of storing. There is also an additional cost of damage to the saved stock. Clearly, once money has been introduced, members of the society can hold money at a zero cost. Also, the risk of holding money is practically nothing (assuming, of course, stability in the level of prices). Thus, the introduction of money can raise the rate of return from savings which, in its turn, promotes the overall savings of the society necessary for growth. Notice that the presence of money relaxes the constraints on the acquisition of real resources which can now be productively used for the creation of more wealth. As Friedman points out: 'Money is something more basic than a medium of transactions; it is something which enables people to separate the act of purchase from the act of sale. From this point of view, the role of money is to serve as a temporary abode of purchasing power,' (Friedman, 1964).

1.2 The definition of money: money and credit creation

Money is generally defined as a medium of exchange. Thus anything that could act as a *common medium of exchange* because it is acceptable as an instrument of debt settlement could be regarded as money. To settle legal payments, money has been conferred the status of legal tender. Such legal tender usually takes the form of token money or paper note which has no commodity value, but which is acceptable as a medium of exchange. On the other hand, commodity money – a commodity which is used as a medium of exchange – may have some commodity value, but it is not generally acceptable as an instrument of exchange to settle all claims, Bank deposits could be regarded as money if they are acceptable to the payee (Newlyn, 1978). It is now easy to see how bank deposits, if *lent* to borrowers, could create additional money. Thus the credit-creating activity of the banks can increase the amount of money in the economy as long as a part of bank deposits are lent and circulated outside the vaults of banks. Notice that the creation of credit by banks can change the supply of money even when banks cannot issue money. When a bank decides to grant credit to a borrower after examining his credit-worthiness it creates an 'account' or 'deposit' in his favour. The borrower can now draw on his account to settle payments in bank money. However, there is a limit to the banks' ability to create credit. Such a limit is usually set by the central bank of the country. The other limit is obviously set by the proportion of deposits that banks can lend without losing the confidence of the members of the public in meeting claims when bank cheques are issued to settle the payments. A further limit to credit creation is set by the desire of the people to hold currency rather than convert it into bank deposits. The ability and the scope of the banking system to create credit will be discussed more fully in chapter 4.

The definition of money, then, includes (a) cash; (b) coins; (c) deposits with the commercial banks. Demand deposits, i.e. money payable on demand, are clearly included in the concept of money. As regards time deposits, there is some controversy whether they should be regarded as money since these deposits cannot be withdrawn on demand to meet outstanding claims. Clearly, in a narrow definition of money, which may be termed M_1, time deposits are excluded. However, in a broader definition of money, time deposits are included as they have all characteristics of money except for the fact that they could be used as a medium of exchange only after a short time-lag. Let M_2 be denoted as money which includes time deposits. There are other types of financial institution which accept deposits from the public. These include insurance companies, building societies in Britain, and co-operative societies in many LDCs. These societies are generally known as *non-banking financial intermediaries*. They do not perform the usual commercial banking activities. Nevertheless, their activities affect the total volume of liquidity. The Radcliffe Committee in Britain greatly emphasised the role of the 'structure of liquidity' in the economy (Radcliffe, 1959). It is, however, true that there always exists a variety of financial assets (e.g. government securities, bonds) in an economy and such assets are close substitutes for money as stores of value. Even so, the essential property of money as a medium of exchange should not be neglected. A wider definition of money, say M_3, should include deposits with the building societies etc. But the presence of near-money assets does not eliminate the distinction between money and liquidity. As Yeager points out, 'One does not need to blur the distinctions between supplies of and demand for assets and between influences on supply and influences on demand. We can define the supply of money narrowly, as a measurable quantity, and see it confronted by a demand for cash balances – a demand influenced, to be sure, by the availability and attractiveness of other assets' (Yeager, 1968). However, people's desire to alter their holdings of other financial assets and cash may have important consequences on the level of aggregate demand.

To distinguish money from other assets which serve as a generally acceptable medium of exchange, it has been suggested that money should be considered uniquely a medium of exchange because it does not offer any interest to induce people to hold it. On the other hand, to induce people to hold other forms of financial assets it is necessary to offer positive interest rates (Pesek and Saving, 1968). Money would then consist of notes, coins and bank demand deposits. Travellers' cheques have also been regarded as money, as they are a mixture of bank deposits and private bank notes. Assets which are accepted as media of exchange but offer interest to their holders are considered as joint products. However, difficulties arise in the classification of assets as money because of differences in interest rates paid on different types of assets. Pesek and Saving argue that the 'moneyness' would then be given by the difference between rate of interest on the asset and the market rate of interest.

Clearly, judgements regarding the 'moneyness' of an asset made simply by examining an *arbitrary* interest rate is very subjective. Another criticism of the Pesek–Saving argument is that 'it confuses price with quantity and marginal with average'. Let us assume that bank deposit rates are equal to market interest rates. Therefore, in line with the Pesek–Saving analysis, the value of such deposits as money is nil. Clearly, such a value is neither the average nor the total, but

> the marginal value of the money services provided by the deposits... Similarly, because price, which corresponds to marginal value, is zero, it does not mean that the quantity is zero. In other words, the equilibrium quantity of bank deposits could still provide a positive amount of medium of exchange services and consequently a positive amount of 'moneyness' even though, at the margin no medium of exchange services are provided and no'moneyness' exists. (Pierce and Shaw, 1977)

To avoid these difficulties, it is suggested that 'perfect acceptability and fixity of value in terms of the unit of account are together necessary and sufficient conditions for an asset to qualify as money' (Morgan, 1969). But, according to this definition, bank deposits will be excluded from the concept of money. Hence, it is contended: 'The further condition we need for the deposits and/or notes of commercial banks to qualify as money is the existence of a mechanism which provides offsetting action whenever the volume of notes or deposits of a bank is altered by the actions of transactors who are not issuers of money. In general this condition is met by banks who keep a reserve with a central bank, and only by such banks.' Thus, any increase of bank reserves, for example, can be neutralised by the open market operations of the central bank.

The above analysis shows the difficulties which are inherent in the definition of the concept of money. That is why some economists have suggested empirical investigations of the roles of different types of assets which operate as mediums of exchange. Others have favoured an empirical definition of money 'a definition that will enable us most readily and accurately to predict the consequences for important economic variables of a change in the conditions of demand for or supply of money' (Friedman and Schwartz, 1969; see also Laidler, 1969). Notice that if the consequences of alterations of money supply are to be predictable with a fair degree of accuracy, then the demand function for money must be reasonably stable. The monetary authorities will then be able to control the level of output, employment and prices by changing the money supply, which now consists of a class of financial assets that include notes and coins. Whether such a demand function is empirically stable or not in both developed and LDC's will be examined in Chapter 3.

1.3 Money markets in LDCs

At this stage, it may be useful to have some knowledge about the money markets of LDCs. It is important to distinguish between money and capital markets at the outset. While the money market deals with short-term money capital, the capital market deals with long-term money capital. It may, however, be difficult to distinguish between the short and long term since there may be overlap between the two. A money market usually caters for the demand for and supply of short-term loanable funds.

Functions of a money market

The functions of a money market can be summarised briefly:

(a) It allocates savings into investment and tends to obtain an equilibrium between the demand for and supply of loanable funds. Such an action of the money market leads to a more rational allocation of resources.

(b) A money market promotes liquidity and safety of financial assets and thereby it encourages savings and investment. This is important in LDCs, where savings and investment habits are rather poor. In many rural areas of LDCs, savings too often comprise land- and gold-holdings rather than the holdings of financial assets which could channel savings into productive investment.

(c) A money market promotes financial mobility by enabling the transfer of funds from one sector to the other. Such flow of funds is regarded as being essential for the growth of the economy and commerce. Elasticity in the flow of funds is thus provided by a money market.

(d) A well-developed money market is essential for the successful implementation of the monetary policies of the central bank.

Financial 'dualism' in LDCs

The money markets of most LDCs are generally characterised by what has been called financial 'dualism'. In simple terms, it means that the money market in LDCs may be divided into two broad categories: (a) organised; (b) unorganised. The organised sector usually consists of (i) the central bank; (ii) the commercial banks; (iii) the co-operatives; (iv) other financial institutions, e.g. development banks, agricultural and industrial financial corporations; and (v) the insurance companies. While the organised sector is amenable to financial control, the unorganised sector is not.

The unorganised sector chiefly consists of (i) the moneylenders; (ii) the indigenous bankers; (iii) the pawnbrokers; (iv) traders and merchants; (v) friends and relatives; and (vi) landlords. Division of labour and specialisation does not always exist and it is thus sometimes possible to find moneylenders who are landlords and merchants as well.

The main features that differentiate the unorganised money market from the organised money market are as follows:

(a) flexibility in loan transactions;
(b) personal dealings with borrowers;
(c) simple and sometimes crude system of maintaining accounts;
(d) blending of money-lending with other types of economic activities;
(e) informal dealings with customers; and
(f) utmost secrecy about financial dealings (indeed, the accounts of the moneylenders in the unorganised sector are hardly open to inspection).

It is important to point out that in most LDCs the unorganised sector still controls a significant section of the money market, chiefly because of its hold over agriculture, which is usually the predominant sector in LDCs. The flow of funds between the organised and the unorganised sector is very small, though attempts are being made to promote integration of the two types of money markets, as the dichotomy in the money has had the following harmful effects.

First, it has restricted the use of bank cheques. Secondly, by reducing the volume of monetary transactions, it has helped to perpetuate non-monetary transactions. Thirdly, it has deprived the society of an array of financial assets through which savings could have been more effectively mobilised and converted into investment for promoting economic growth. Finally, the dichotomy has perpetuated some age-old practices, such as gold-hoarding and investment in land and buildings, which have prevented the use of available resources for productive investment. All these factors make the task of central banks' use of monetary policies very difficult. Clearly, the policy objective should be for the organised sector to bring the unorganised sector within its fold. A detailed analysis of rural money markets will be made in chapter 10. Let is suffice for the present to state that for an efficient system for allocation of resources and for mobilising savings into investment the case for an integration of a dual money market cash can hardly be over-emphasised.

2. The Keynesian and monetarist views on the importance of money

In this chapter we shall discuss the classical, the Keynesian and the 'monetarist' theories regarding the role of money in economic activity. Briefly, in the classical theory the role of money has been relegated to the background. It is argued that monetary forces do not affect the movements of the real variables, that is, output and employment, in the economy. In the Keynesian theory it is suggested that a change in the money supply may change the level of output via changes in interest rates. The 'monetarist' school, headed by Milton Friedman, contends that the classical rather than the Keynesian theory would be valid as long as money can affect real variables in the short run, but only nominal magnitudes in the long run. We shall first discuss the classical theory.

2.1 The classical view

The classical theory of income and employment is usually built around Say's law which states, 'supply creates its own demand'. If this were true, the economy could never experience either unemployment or underconsumption. Since there would be no dearth of demand, total expenditure within an economy would always be adequate to match total production at a full employment level, given the profit motive (for something is needed to induce the output to be supplied).

The classical argument could be stated in a simple way. Let us assume that there is a market for goods and services as well as for labour. Assume also a production function which states that given the existing technology, a given output could be produced by a certain amount of labour, fixed capital and equipment. All prices and wages are flexible and they respond to the forces of demand and supply.

Now, should there be unemployment, the real wage rate, W/P (that is, money wage rate, W, divided by prices, P) would decline, as there is an excess supply of labour. A fall in W/P will reduce the labour supply under the assumption of a normally upward-rising supply curve of labour. But a fall in W/P will increase the demand for labour since the demand curve of labour slopes downward. Hence, employment will tend to rise. Eventually, full employment will be restored at a point like E in figure 2.1. It can be checked very easily from figure 2.1, where W/P is measured vertically and employment (N) is measured

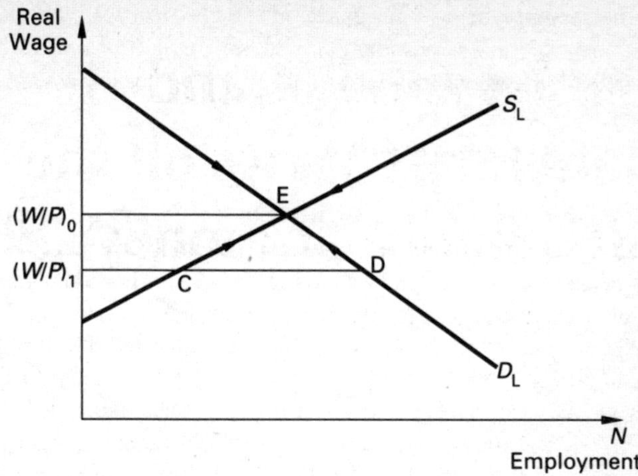

Figure 2.1

horizontally, that in case of an excess demand for labour (for example, C–D), the situation of over-full employment will be rectified again because the economy will eventually move towards E, the point of full employment equilibrium, where the demand for labour is exactly equal to the supply of labour and resources are fully utilised.

We can use the same analysis to explain how a disequilibrium situation will be corrected in a goods market. If there is an excess demand for goods, prices will rise. This will lead to a rise in supply (assuming a normal supply curve which slopes upwards) and a fall in demand, assuming a downward-sloping demand curve. Eventually the economy will reach equilibrium. Similarly, given an excess supply of goods, prices will fall, demand will rise and supply will fall. The 'invisible hand' has once again played the trick in adjusting supply to demand. All the markets are now being cleared with flexible wages and prices and full employment prevails. Unemployment is then a phenomenon of dynamic disequilibrium. Notice that money does not play any role in the determination of employment and output.

A digression on the classical view

The above mechanism looks simple and elegant but one of the important 'classical' economics remained unconvinced. His name was Thomas Malthus. He took a rather critical view of the classical analysis. According to Malthus, although the production of goods plus services in an economy will create income which will be equal to the value of the output, this does not mean that total *expenditure* in the economy will be equal to total production. In other words supply may create its own income but it may not be able to create enough *expenditure*. Such a shortfall in expenditure could take place when people save a part of their income. A deficiency in demand could result which might lead to the accumulation of inventories and a fall in production. This could result in unemployment. The 'crack' in the classical wall can now be seen clearly. This idea of under-consumption and its implications have been given considerable attention in Keynesian economics, which will be discussed later.

Classical savings, investments and interest rate

It should be pointed out that the classicist were well aware of the possibility of saving. Classical economists argued that saving is generally invested as a result of the interest rate mechanism. Let S stand for saving, I stand for investment and r denote the interest rate (which can be a proxy for a range of interest rates). More formally, we can write

$$S = S(r) \tag{2.1}$$

$$I = I(r) \tag{2.2}$$

$$S = I \tag{2.3}$$

By equation 2.1 we have S as a function of r, If r rises, S rises as people are induced to save more. According to equation 2.2, I is a function of r. But this relationship is inverse. Therefore, as r rises, I falls since the cost of borrowing rises. These relationships are shown in figure 2.2, where r is measured on the vertical axis and S and I are measured on the horizontal axis. The equilibrium r is r_o where $S_o = I_o$. Notice that the equilibrium is stable because if there is any excess saving (for example, GF) at r_1, r will fall and this will lead to a fall in S and a rise in I; eventually, the equilibrium will be reached at E. It should be mentioned here that the 'propensity to invest' depends on the investor's evaluation of the rate of return at the margin and r. If

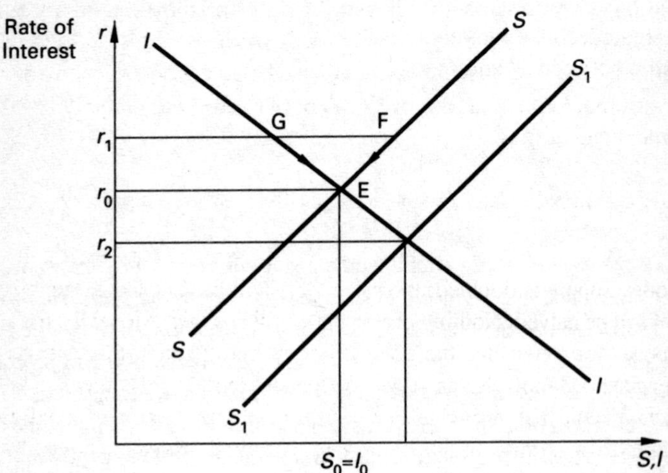

Figure 2.2

r is low, then the projects which were marginal before may now be undertaken as the rate of return is greater than r. Following the Malthusian lesson, if people decide to save more, the saving curve will shift to the right as indicated by the movement of SS to S_1S_1. Obviously, to the misery of Malthus, the end of the world has not been reached as the new equilibrium is restored at a lower r – that is, r_2.

In the above analysis, money does not play any role in the determination of output and employment. In fact, output and employment are determined by labour, capital, saving behaviour, existing technology. The interest rate is given by saving habits and capital productivity. The classicists thus argued that the sole function of money is to determine the general level of prices at which goods and services will be exchanged. Money is a 'veil' and this has been demonstrated most clearly in the quantity theory of money.

The classical quantity theory of money

The classical quantity theory of money is best illustrated with the help of Irving Fisher's (1911) equation of exchange. Let M indicate the average stock of money over a period, V its velocity, P the price level and Q the real income or output of that period. Then we have

$$MV = PQ \tag{2.4}$$

The above equation is basically an identity which simply states that when the money stock is multiplied by V or the number of times money is used to buy final output, we obtain total expenditure which must be equal to the product of P and Q or the value of output bought. In the original writing, T, i.e. total transactions, and not Q was used. Here Q has replaced T because there are some transactions which are not included in the estimation of gross national product.

Assume now that V is relatively fixed because payments patterns and habits could be regarded as relatively constant. Q also is fixed. We then obtain a direct relationship between M and P since

$$M = \frac{PQ}{V} \tag{2.5}$$

$$\text{or } P = \frac{MV}{Q} \tag{2.6}$$

If the money supply is doubled, the price level will be doubled; contrawise, if M is halved, P will be halved. Nothing else in the world changes. Money is just a 'veil'. Its sole purpose is to determine the general price level at which transactions of goods will take place. Money 'burns holes' in the pockets of individuals. The classical economists assume that individuals are rational and wish to maximise utility. Money, *per se*, fails to maximise utility. It is only as a medium of exchange that money enables people to acquire goods and services. Therefore, a rational individual should not demand money for its own sake. That is why the idea of a demand for money has been neglected in the classical quantity theory. However, the Cambridge economists viewed the matter rather differently!

The 'Cambridge' demand for money: the cash balance approach

According to the 'Cambridge' school, it is necessary to pay attention to the fraction of income that could be held in cash. But equation 2.4 can now be written as a behavioural equation given a stable velocity and fixed Q (see later):

$$M = kPQ \tag{2.7}$$

where k is the fraction of income that is held in cash. Notice that

$$k = \frac{1}{V} \tag{2.8}$$

and formulated in this way, the difference between equation 2.4 and 2.7 is insignificant. Nevertheless equation 2.8 can now be regarded as the one which shows the *demand for money* that enables people to carry out transactions.

It is necessary to point out here that equation 2.4 is an identity which can be transformed into a casual mechanism. A direct relationship can be established between M and P if Q is fixed and V remains stable since the demand for money is dictated by habits which are unlikely to change much. It naturally follows that M and P will be directly related. If M rises for some reasons, let us say, by the actions taken by the central bank, people will accumulate excess cash balances; this will lead to more spending and could only result in a rise in prices, as output or Q cannot be raised beyond the level of full employment. Analytically, the effect of changes of money supply on prices will be identical, no matter whether one follows the basic equation of Fisher or the Cambridge demand-for-money theory. According to the Cambridge theory, in the equilibrium situation the demand for money must be equal to the supply of money. If M rises there would be more money than people would wish to hold. In other words, *ceteris paribus*, the demand for money will be less than the money supply. This will raise the level of expenditure and prices, as output cannot change. Additional expenditure will come to an end when people wish to hold rather than spend money, i.e. when the demand for money is equal to the supply of money. Notice that although money income changes, real income remains the same. The Cambridge version of the quantity theory thus underlines the real (M/P) rather than nominal money holdings of the people.

If the classical quantity theory is viewed as a long-run analysis, then it is not difficult to understand the assumptions regarding fixed Q and a stable V. But Keynes was not convinced by the classical analysis. In any case, it may be quite interesting to look at the short-run behaviour of the economy because 'in the long-run we are all dead'.

2.2 The Keynesian theory

Keynes argued that the classical mechanism might fail to guarantee full employment equilibrium because of several reasons. For one thing, wages and prices may not be flexible; for another, income, rather than the interest rate, may determine savings and if the (speculative) demand for money (which Keynes called the liquidity preference schedule) is infinitely elastic with respect to changes in the interest rate (i.e. the 'liquidity trap'), then no extra investment would be forthcoming from a further rise in saving and the economy would end up in an unemployment *equilibrium.* To understand these points, we will have to discuss several parts of the Keynesian theory.

The Keynesian 'building blocks'

One of the most important points to be borne in mind is that although *ex-post.* saving and investment are equal to one another, in the equilibrium *planned* saving must be equal to *planned* investment. But suppose planned saving is greater than planned investment. In a classical world, this should not pose much of a problem because such a phenomenon would lead to an increase in inventory accumulation and prices will continue to fall. Supply will fall because production in plans will be cut back; with a fall in production the equality between demand for and supply of goods will be restored.

A fall in production will lead to a fall in employment and wages. But such a fall in wages will maintain the equality between demand for and supply of labour in the labour market. The interest rate will also fall as saving exceeds investment. But such a fall will reduce the desire to save and increase the desire to invest until the saving and investment plans are brought to equality.

Keynes pointed out that these results are unlikely to occur in practice. First, wages could be inflexible downwards. So whenever saving exceeds investment, production plans are cut back and unemployment follows. It is very difficult to restore full employment by reducing the level of wages because of trade-union resistance. Secondly, the interest rate may not determine the equilibrium level of saving and investment. The process of interest-rate determination was regarded by Keynes as a monetary phenomenon. The rate of interest is determined in the money market where the demand for money is equal to the supply of money and the equilibrium between saving (S) and investment (I) determines the level of income (Y). Hence output will continue to fall as long as planned saving exceeds planned investment. Eventually the equilibrium is restored where $S = I$. In the Keynesian analysis the theory of the consumption function plays an important role. Keynes contended that at the macro level, expenditure (E) determines income (Y). Total expenditure is the sum of consumption expenditure (C) and investment expenditure (I), i.e.

$$Y = C + I \tag{2.9}$$

Consumption depends on income, i.e.

$$C = a + bY \tag{2.10}$$

where $b = \Delta C/\Delta Y$ or marginal propensity to consume or the slope of the consumption function. Keynes argued that $0 < b < 1$. The term 'a' in equation 2.9 denotes the fixed level of consumption which is independent of Y. This is often known as autonomous consumption. The process of income generation can then be described as follows:

$$Y = C + I \tag{2.11}$$

$$\Delta Y = \Delta C + \Delta I \tag{2.12}$$

Dividing by ΔY

$$\Delta Y / \Delta Y = \Delta C / \Delta Y + \Delta I / \Delta Y \tag{2.13}$$

or $$1 - \frac{\Delta C}{\Delta Y} = \Delta I / \Delta Y \tag{2.14}$$

$\therefore$ $$\frac{\Delta Y}{\Delta I} = \frac{1}{1 - \Delta C / \Delta Y} \tag{2.15}$$

or $$\frac{\Delta Y}{\Delta I} = \frac{1}{1 - MPC} \text{ or } \frac{1}{1 - b} \text{ or } \frac{1}{MPS}$$

where MPS = marginal propensity to save.

Thus $$\Delta Y = \frac{1}{1 - b} \Delta I \tag{2.16}$$

Equation 2.15 defines the multiplier (m) which is the inverse of the marginal propensity to save. Clearly, the value of the m will be positively related to the value of b or MPC and inversely to the MPS. It is now easy to see why savings constitute a leakage in the stream of income generation. The whole process is summarised in figures 2.3(a) and (b).

In figure 2.3(a) the equilibrium between S and I now determine the level of Y rather than the interest rate. Saving in the Keynesian theory is assumed to vary directly with income. That is why we have $S(Y)$. Investment or I is assumed to be autonomous. In figure 2.3(b) it has been shown that total expenditure or $E(= C + I)$ determines Y_o.

Unlike the classical theory, there is no reason to assume within the Keynesian analysis that equilibrium Y will also be a full employment level of income. The investment function could be unstable as it depends on investors' expectations regarding future demand (or planned savings). If investment prospects are gloomy, then I may fall and this will reduce equilibrium Y to a less than full-employment level. This is shown in the movement of II to I_1I_1 and a fall in income from Y_o to Y_1 in figures 2.3(a) and (b). To restore full employment, it may be necessary to stimulate expenditure by using fiscal policies, e.g. an increase in government expenditure (G) or a cut in taxes, to stimulate demand, or both. These are usually regarded as the 'Keynesian' remedies to cure recession or depression.

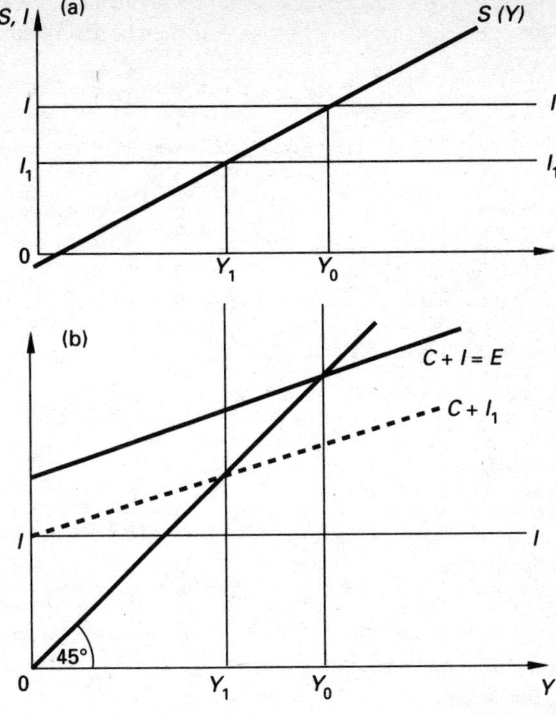

Figure 2.3 (a) and (b)

The above analysis, which has been christened as 'Keynes without money' (Ritter), suggest that money does not play any role in determining output and employment. This is not quite so in full Keynesian model of a situation of unemployment. According to Keynes, an increase in money supply would increase the cash balances held by economic agents. People will then be confronted with the following three choices: (1) to keep money idle; (2) to buy plant and machinery; (3) to buy bonds. The first alternative is unacceptable given the principle of utility maximisation. Most people would not like to follow the second option. They are, according to Keynes, most likely to buy bonds with excess cash balances. This will raise the bond prices and drive down the interest rate. A fall in the interest rate will stimulate the level of investment and an increase in investment will raise the level of income via the workings of the multiplier. Thus, an increase in money supply could increase the level of output particularly at a less than full-employment level without affecting prices. There could be secondary effects on prices but these are more likely to be important when the economy moves closer to the zone of full employment. Any increase in money supply beyond the level of full employment will raise the price level in the classical fashion. This has been shown in figure 2.4. Output (*Q*) is measured

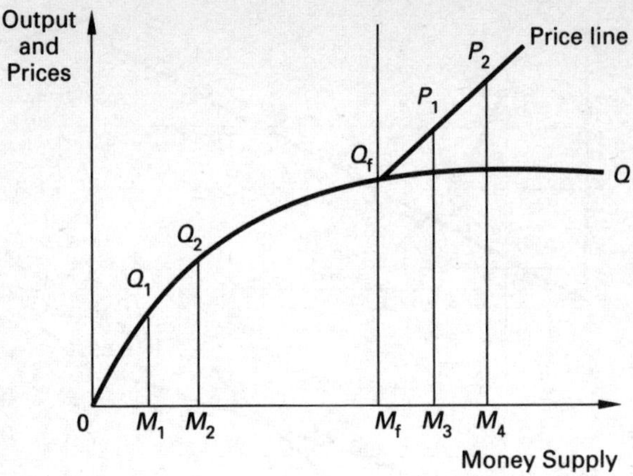

Figure 2.4

on the vertical axis and money supply (M) is measured on the horizontal axis. Full employment output is given by $M_f\,Q_f$ on an output growth curve OQ and M_fQ_f is consistent with a full employment money supply of OM_f. Before M_f any increase in money supply, for example, OM_1 to OM_2 raises production from M_1Q_1 to M_2Q_2. Beyond full employment, a rise in money supply from OM_3 to OM_4 simply bids up the prices to P_1 and P_2 as has been indicated by the price line.

The interest rate is, however, determined in the money market and this will be discussed next.

2.3 Money and the interest rate

In the Keynesian model, the rate of interest (r) is determined by the demand for money (M_d) and supply of money (M_s). Money supply is usually treated as fixed in the short-run and as such M_s is invariant to changes in r and this is shown by S_1S_1 in figure 2.5. The demand for money or M_d consists of three parts: (a) transaction demand for money, that is, M_t (b) precautionary demand for money i.e. M_p; and (c) speculative demand for money i.e. M_{sp}. Thus we have

$$M_d = M_t + M_p + M_{sp} \tag{2.17}$$

The demand for money for day-to-day transaction purposes usually depends upon the level of income or Y. The precautionary demand for money also depends upon Y and it stems from the necessity to hold cash balances for the 'rainy days'. The speculative demand for money is the real Keynesian invention. If money could be regarded as a financial asset in the portfolio, then such an asset could be held in the portfolio along with 'other' assets. Keynes lumped together these 'other' assets and called them 'bonds'. People may wish to hold 'bonds' rather

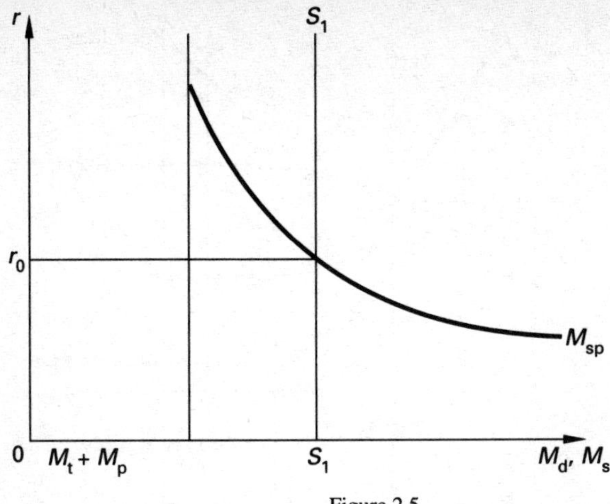

Figure 2.5

than liquid money because interest is paid to the bondholders. The bond prices could change and thus bond holding involves some risks. Also, on different bonds different rates of interest are paid. The average of such interest rates may be regarded as 'the' interest on bonds. Keynes argued that the demand for money or 'liquidity preference' is an inverse function of r (see figure 2.5).

$$M_{sp} = f(r) \tag{2.18}$$

Let r be measured on the vertical axis and M_d and M_s be measured on the horizontal axis as shown in figure 2.6. It is shown by the line KN that $M_t + M_p$ remain completely inelastic with respect to changes in r. The M_{sp} is inversely related to changes in r. The reason is simple. When r is low, people expect that it will rise soon in the future. Since the bond price and r are inversely related, people would like to avoid the capital loss which accompanies a rise in r. Hence, they would wish to hold more money. The reverse happens when r is high. People part company with their liquid money and hold bonds as they speculate that r will fall and bond prices will rise. Hence, r can be regarded as a price paid for parting with liquidity. In terms of the portfolio analysis of Tobin (1958), we can say that since people are not risk-lovers, therefore a higher r must be paid to seduce them into holding a greater proportion of bonds in their wealth 'portfolios'. The equilibrium r is determined at r_o where $M_d = M_s$. The interest rate could change with a change in M_d of M_s or both. Thus if the money supply increases from M_d to M_{s1}, r falls from r_o to r_1. Notice that if M_s increases further (with no change in M_d, of course) r does not fall any more. This is precisely what happens when the money supply rises from M_{s1} to M_{s2} as the economy is caught in the 'liquidity trap'. As r ceases to fall, there would not be any effect on investment and income. The Keynesian 'liquidity trap', then clearly shows the limitation of monetary policy in curing recessions. The liquidity trap could

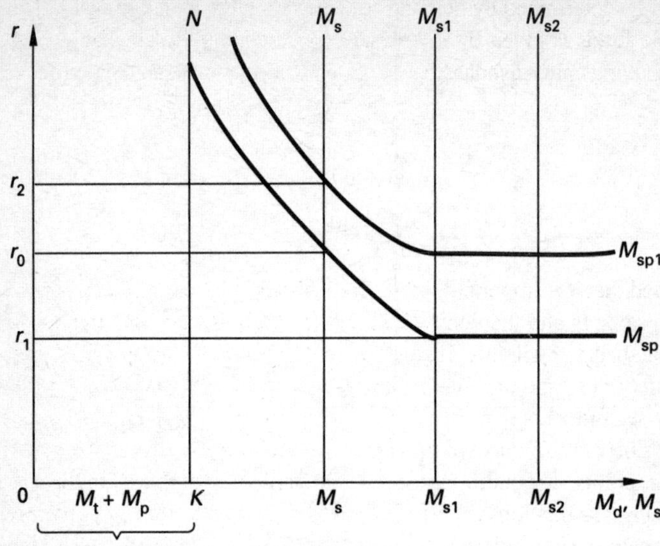

Figure 2.6

operate at a very low r when the demand for money is infinitely elastic since everybody expects a rise in r and a consequent fall in bond prices. Therefore, nobody wants to hold bonds. It also follows that the efficacy of monetary policy would decline when the demand for money is more elastic. It is also implied that if the investment function is interest-elastic, then there will be a stronger impact on output or income. Obviously, the strength of monetary policy will diminish considerably if the investment function is interest-inelastic. In figure 2.6, it has also been shown that if the M_{sp} rises, the liquidity preference schedule shifts to the right ($M_{sp} \rightarrow M_{sp1}$). Assuming that M_s is the supply of money, r rises to a new equilibrium, r_2.

2.4 A general equilibrium approach: the Hicksian *IS–LM* curves

Although Keynes claimed that the interest rate is purely a monetary phenomenon, it has been argued by Hicks that a truly 'general' theory of interest rate determination should be stated in a framework of a general equilibrium analysis (Hicks, 1937). In a more general version of the determinants of the demand for money, we should include both income (Y) and the rate of interest. Thus we have,

$$M_d = f(r, Y) \tag{2.19}$$

This could also be stated as

$$M_d = kY + f(r) \tag{2.20}$$

Also, r can be determined by demand for and supply of loanable funds. The demand for loanable funds is given by investment and the supply of loanable fund is given mainly by savings plus dishoardings. Following Hicks, we can then write

$$M_d = f(r, Y) \tag{2.21}$$

$$S = S(r, Y) \tag{2.22}$$

$$I = I(r, Y) \tag{2.23}$$

Hicks argued that it is important to look at the basic relationships between r and Y via changes in savings and the demand for money. If Y rises, S will rise and, following the classical theory, r will fall. This is shown in figure 2.7. When Y rises from Y_o to Y_1, S rises from S_o to S_1 and the S curve shifts to the right. The interest rate r falls from r_o to r_1. If Y rises further, say from Y_1 to Y_2 S rises further, i.e. from S_1 to S_2 as shown in the further shift of the S curve to the right. The equilibrium r thus falls to r_2. If we then join all the points of equilibrium between S and I, we obtain an IS curve which depicts an *inverse* relationship between r and Y. It is clear that every point on the IS curve is a point of equilibrium between I and S. This is shown in figure 2.9.

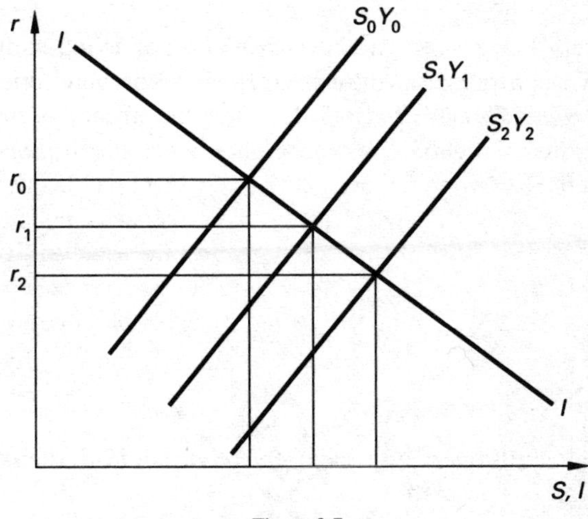

Figure 2.7

In the money market, following Keynes, let us assume that the equilibrium interest rate, r_o, is determined where $M_d = M_s$ as shown in figure 2.8. Let us think that this M_d is given by income Y_o (says Rs. 100 billion). If Y rises from Y_o to Y_1, M_{do} also rises and this is shown by the shift of the M_d curve from M_{do} to M_{d1}. The equilibrium r now rises from r_o (say 4 per cent) to r_1 (say 5 per cent). If Y rises further to Y_2 ($Y_2 = 300$ billion rupees), M_{d1} shifts upwards to M_{d2} and equilibrium r rises from r_1 to r_2 (i.e. say, from 5 per cent to 6 per cent). If we now join all the points of equilibrium between M_d and M_s with a rise in income, we trace out an upward sloping curve which has been called LM. Once again, the LM curve

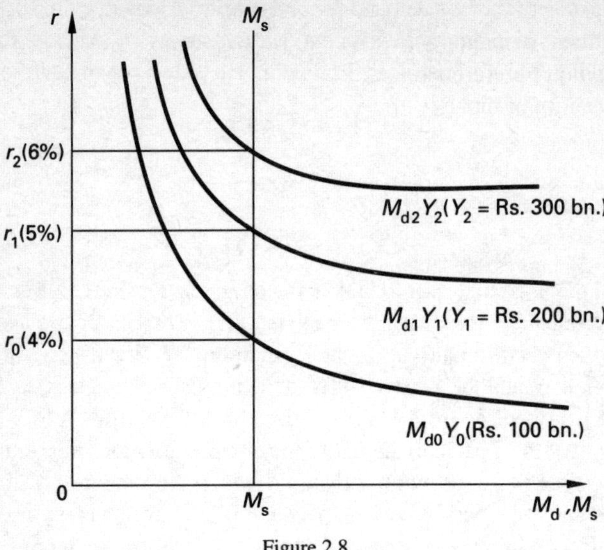

Figure 2.8

depicts the relationship between r and Y when the money markets is in equilibrium (i.e. $M_d = M_s$). If we now combine the two curves together, as in figure 2.9, we obtain 'the' equilibrium rate of interest, r^* (say, 5 per cent). It can be checked easily that the equilibrium r^* is stable.

In simple terms, a general equilibrium theory of interest rate determination should include the following factors:

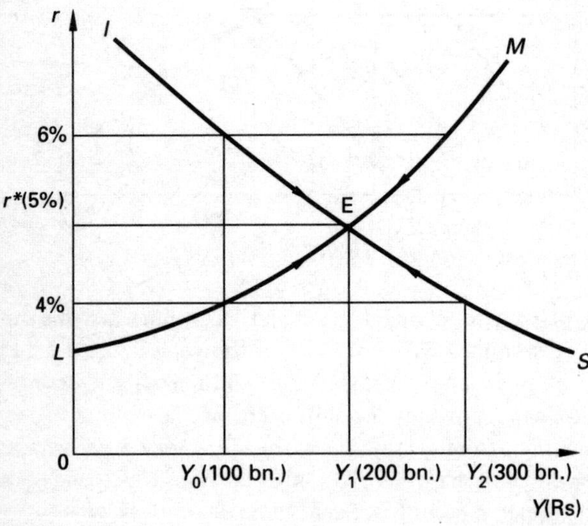

Figure 2.9

1) savings;
2) investment-demand;
3) the liquidity preference;
4) the quantity of money.

2.5 Monetary and fiscal policy

The *IS* and *LM* curves are powerful analytical tools to describe the workings of monetary and fiscal policies. In figure 2.10, we discuss some theoretical situations.

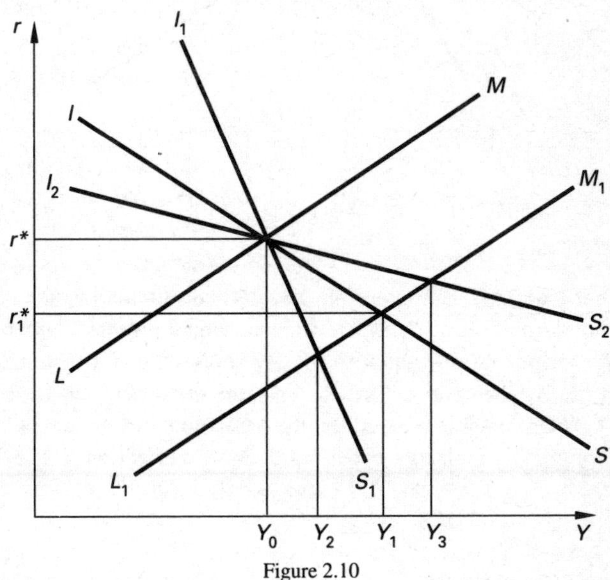

Figure 2.10

The equilibrium interest rate is given by r^* as before where the *IS* curve intersects the *LM* curve. If the monetary policy is expansionary, the *LM* curve shifts to the right to L_1M_1 and this leads to a fall of r^* to r^*_1. Income rises from Y_o to Y_o. Recall our previous comment on the interest-inelasticityof the investment function. Given such interest inelasticity of investment (i.e. I_1S_1 rather than I_2S_2) the effect on income generation would be much less (check that $Y_oY_2 < Y_oY_3$; check also that given an interest-inelastic demand for money schedule, i.e. a steeper *LM* curve, an expansionary monetary policy will have a greater impact on *Y* with an interest-*elastic IS* curve).

The effect of *fiscal policy* can also be shown easily with the help of *IS* and *LM* schedules. In figure 2.11, an expansionary fiscal policy, e.g. an expansion of government expenditure, shifts the *IS* curve to the right to I_1S_1 and income rises from Y_o to Y_1 while r rises from r_o to r_1. If the *LM* curve is more interest-inelastic

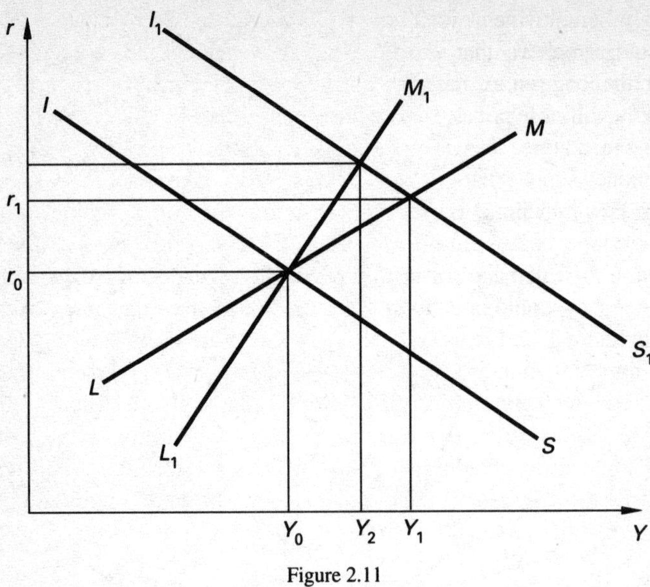

Figure 2.11

i.e. L_1M_1 rather than *LM*, the increase in *Y* would be smaller, i.e. $Y_0Y_2 < Y_0Y_1$. The reason is simple. An interest-inelastic *LM* curve would require a larger rise in *r* to make the demand for money equal to money supply. Such a large rise in *r* will reduce significantly the level of private investment, which will lead to a small increase in *Y*. This impact is now called the 'crowding out' effect. When the *LM* schedule is completely inelastic, fiscal policy has no effect on *Y*. The shift of the *IS* curve to the right on a vertical *LM* curve simply raises the *r*.

2.6 The monetarists' case

The monetarists' case is advocated strongly by a number of economists, the most prominent of whom is Professor Milton Friedman of Chicago University. Friedman has stated a 'modern' quantity theory which has its roots in the 'ancient' quantity theory but is broader than its predecessor. Stated in a very simple way, the 'modern' quantity theory states that a change in money supply will change the price level as long as the demand for money is stable; such a change also effects the real value of national income and economic activity but in the *short-run* only. For Friedman, the stability in the demand for money is just a behavioural 'fact', 'proven' by empirical evidence. As long as the demand for money is stable it is possible to predict the effects of changes of money supply on total expenditure and income. The monetarists argue that if the economy operates at a less-than-full-employment level, then an increase in money supply will lead to a rise in output and employment because of a rise in expenditure, but only in the short-run. After a time, the economy will return to a less-than-full-employment situation which must be caused by other, 'real' factors. The monetarists believe that changes in money supply cannot affect the 'real' variables in the long run. At near-full-employment point or beyond it, an increase in money supply will raise prices. Before full employment, Y rises with a rise in money supply and expenditure. The rise in Y will, then, crucially depend upon the ratio of income to money supply, that is Y/M or velocity. With an increase in spending during a recession, Y will continue to rise until it has reached a limit where it stands in its previous ratio to M because at that point output can no longer be increased. People will now raise their demand for money rather than spend it and the supply of and demand for money would once again be equal to one another. These arguments are illustrated in figure 2.12. Let us assume that Y is measured vertically and demand for (M_d) and supply of money (M_s) are measured horizontally. Assume that money supply is fixed (and therefore that the M_s line is completely inelastic with respect to changes in Y). The M_d varies with income, but this relationship is proportional since $M_d = k\,Y$ (people always hold a given fraction, k, of their income). The monetarists thus emphasise the *transactions demand for money.* The equilibrium Y is given by Y_o where $M_d = M_s$. If $M_d < M_s$, as at Y_1, total expenditure rises and Y rises from Y_1 to Y_o.

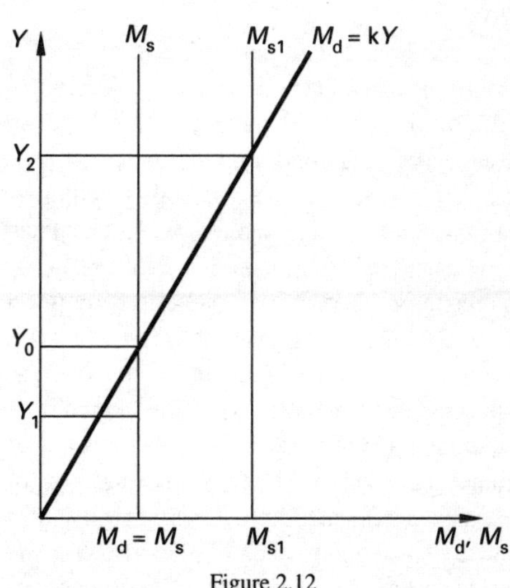

Figure 2.12

If M, rises, the M_s curve shifts to the right to M_{s1} and Y rises to Y_2 because $M_s > M_d$ and spending rises until $M_s = M_d$ at a higher level of income, i.e. Y_2. In contradistinction to the Keynesian analysis, note that nothing is known about changes in r when M_s changes. It is also assumed that the demand for money remains stable; in other words , $1/k$ is fixed. Given the stability in the velocity, the central bank can control the volume of spending by controlling the money supply. The stabilisation policy should then concentrate only on monetary policy, that is, controlling the volume of the money supply.

The central issue that one faces in the above analysis is whether the demand for money is stable or not. It is, however, possible to be a Keynesian and still accept that there is stability in the demand for money. The recent debate between the monetarists and the Keynesians centres round the question of changing aggregate demand by monetary or fiscal policies. The so-called 'Keynesians' point out that only fiscal policies can change the level of income by changing aggregate demand, whereas the 'Monetarists' argue that aggregate demand can be changed only by monetary policies. It is not certain, whether Keynes actually held such views. Nevertheless, it seems that the monetarists' case rests on the working of a vertical or near-vertical *LM* curve. This implies that the demand for money is very inelastic to changes in the interest rate. Similarly, the 'Keynesian' case rests on the working of a vertical or near-vertical *IS* schedule with a normal *LM* curve. This implies a very low elasticity of the investment function with respect to changes in the interest rate. We now turn to the empirical evidence, which will largely determine the validity of one theory or the other.

2.7 Special characteristics of LDCs

It is important to note that in LDCs, a substantial proportion of consumption and income originate through non-monetary transactions. This is chiefly due to the fact the economics of LDCs are usually characterised by 'dualism'. That is why we observe the co-existence of organised and unorganised markets side by side. Although the organised market could be fairly competitive, modern and sophisticated, the unorganised market is marked by the characteristics of barter trade whether goods are exchanged against goods. In other words, we have two different markets in LDCs: (1) monetised and (2) non-monetised. With economic growth, it is reasonable to suppose that the proportion of non-monetarised transactions will decline. Hence, one would expect a rise in the transaction demand for money because of the increase in economic growth and a rise in the degree of monetisation (see the Appendix). It may be argued that for LDCs, the relevant concept of income in monetary analysis is a monetised component of income and not total national income. However, this point has been neglected in many empirical studies on the demand for money in LDCs because of the paucity of data. Bhattacharyya (1974) has shown how the estimated demand for money function with monetised income data has been different from the estimated with national income data. Clearly, estimates of non-marketed output are beset with great difficulties but none the less are normally included in estimates of GNP for LDCs.

The other important feature of the money market of LDCs is what Myint called the 'financial dualism' (Myint, 1971). It implies the co-existence of heterogeneous interest rates in the organised and unorganised money markets. The former market is quite sophisticated where one expects the speculative demand for money to vary with interest rates. In the latter, i.e. the unorganised market (usually dominated by the shopkeepers, moneylenders, landlords, merchants or the combination of some of them which may ultimately create a monopoly situation), the interest rates are expected to change with the risks and returns on real assets. Under such circumstances, the supply of money may not affect the rates of interest significantly. Hence, the Keynesian theory may not be very applicable to the LDCs. There is some evidence to suggest that there are some links between the organised and unorganised money markets. Until now, the evidence suggests that these links are weak.

The nature of interest rate in LDCs

It may be further argued that in many LDCs, the interest rate is administered rather than market determined in the organised sector. This would imply that the effects of normal operations of the laws of demand and supply will not be fully reflected in the observed interest rates. In the unorganised markets, the interest rate could be determined by a number of both economic and institutional variables. The determination of the rural rate of interest is usually viewed from the supply side, given the paucity of information on the demand side. It has been argued that on the supply side, the rural interest rate (r) could be determined by the risk premium (α), administrative costs (β), opportunity cost (γ) and the degree of monopoly power of the moneylenders (θ), (Bottomley, 1971).

$$r = \alpha + \beta + \gamma + \theta$$

There is evidence to suggest that such rural interest rates are mainly determined by the premium for risk and uncertainly due to default in repayments rather than the monopoly power of the money lenders (Ghatak, 1975). However, the power of the moneylenders should not be discontinued altogether, given the lack of specialisation and the complex nature of the socio-economic relationships between the farmers/landlords/merchants/moneylenders (Bhaduri, 1977; Bottomley, 1971; Ghatak, 1976, 1979). Under such circumstances, it is difficult to see how the interaction between the demand for and supply of money could determine the rate of interest. It remains the case that the empirical estimates of the demand for money in the rural money markets of LDCs in one of the most under-researched topics in this area.

It may be pointed out, however, that some writers have found *short-run* fluctuations in their estimates of income velocity of money for LDCs (e.g. Park, 1970), use of observed interest rate as the opportunity cost of holding money). It is worth noting that in the face of unstable income velocity, the use of the Quantity theory of money to explain the demand for money will not be suitable. This is the reason for investigating the opportunity cost of holding money in LDCs and in most case studies, the *expected rate of inflation* is observed as a major variable in influencing the demand for money in LDCs (Deaver, 1970; Campbell, 1970; Hynes, 1967). The main reason for using the expected rate of inflation is that wealth holders in LDCs can hold either real commodities (e.g. buildings, land, etc) or money. Hence, the opportunity cost of money holding is given by the expected rate of inflation. The foregoing suggests that the use of interest rates in the money demand function for LDCs is not regarded as particularly appropriate for the following major reasons:

(a) limited size of the organised financial market;
(b) the institutional pegging of interest rates;
(c) limited array of financial assets, and
(d) limited degree of substitution between money and financial assets in comparison with the economically developed countries.

Under such circumstances it is possible to understand why the demand for money in LDCs has usually been regarded as more a function of income and expected rate of inflation rather than the interest rate. It is also clear why the transaction motive for holding money is supposed to dominate other motives for money holding. The empirical measure of the expected rate of inflation is usually given by the weighted average of all post rates of inflation with geometrically declining weights.

It is possible to argue that to the extent borrowing plays a role in financing economic activity and in so far as there is some relationship between the organised and unorganised money markets (Ghatak, 1976, chapter 6), the rate of interest could be used as an explanatory variable in the demand for money function (Adekunle, 1968; Park, 1970; Polak, 1957). Others have argued that in many LDCs, the interest rates in the rural money market may not be observed, although they would reflect the degree of credit restraint itself. An appropriate estimate of credit restraint could now be considered as a proxy variable for the interest rate in the money demand function for LDCs (Wong, 1977). Thus, Wong suggested the use of the following money demand function for LDCs:

$$M_t^d = g\left(Y_t^e, CR_t^e, \left(\Delta P_t / P_{t-1}\right)^e, U_t\right) \tag{2.24}$$

where

M_t^d = long run demand for money at time t
Y_t^e = expected nominal GNP at t
CR_t^e = the expected index of the degree of credit restraint at t
$(\Delta P_t / P_{t-1})^e$ = expected percentage change in the rate of inflation
U_t = disturbance term.

Wong argues that given the institutional pegging of interest rates, observed interest rates are likely to be the linkage variables between holdings of alternative assets.

The rationale behind such an argument is easy to understand once it is recognised that borrowings in LDCs are the major sources of finance of many economic activities. Hence, the *availability* rather than the cost of credit is more likely to influence demand. If a stringent monetary policy is pursued in LDCs, there will be a greater tendency towards economising on available money balances and to depend more on the moneylenders in the unorganised money market to meet the target expenditures. This will push up the interest rates even if they may not be observed. Obviously, the income velocity will tend to rise. In

DCs, such a situation will lead to expansion of financial securities and a rise in interest rates. The demand for money will thus tend to fall. Wong has suggested many ways to measure the degree of credits restraint, e.g. the discount rate of the Central Bank, the negative of the ratio of domestic credit to income ($-DC_t/Y_t$) and the negative of the rate of domestic credit expansion ($-\Delta DC_t/DC_{t-1}$).

It should be remembered that the different methods for estimating the demand for money in LDCs actually try to analyse more clearly the actual nature of 'transmission mechanism' of monetary policy in the developing countries and to provide an empirical basis to the formulation of more appropriate money and credit policy.

Lags in demand adjustment

In view of high risks and uncertainties in LDCs stemming from the dominance and the fluctuations in the production cycles of the agrarian economy, it has been suggested that lags could be ignored in LDCs (Adekunle, 1968, e.g. he has found small income expectation lag for LDCs). On the other hand, if it is assumed that a large number of people are risk averters there could be an expectation lag since risk averters take time in adjusting their portfolios (Wong, 1977). If this is true, then it is possible to introduce lagged money into a short term money demand function. Such lags could be useful to analyse both demand adjustment and expectation lags with respect to income, prices, etc. The nature and length of such lags could, of course, vary from country to country and they can be estimated only empirically.

2.8 Recent developments in demand for money studies in LDCs

Most traditional studies on the demand for money in LDCs use domestic interest rates or the actual or expected rate of inflation as a measure of the opportunity cost of holding money. However, if the economy of a LDC is 'open' and domestic residents have access to foreign financial assets, then *foreign* interest rates could be an argument in money demand functions. For example, for Hong Kong and Singapore, it is easy to see the importance of foreign interest rates as factors influencing money demand, particularly when these countries are fairly well-integrated with global capital markets.

Given the presence of large unorganised/informal financial markets in some LDCs, it may be necessary to consider interest rates in informal money markets ('curb' market rates) as the appropriate opportunity cost of holding money. Some investigators have tried to use rates in unorganised money markets as arguments in money demand functions, and have achieved some success (see Chapter 3). Indeed, given the dominance of the agricultural sector in some economies of LDCs, it may be useful to have disaggregated money demand functions for the rural sector. The estimation of such a money demand function will obviously depend upon the availability of relevant data on annual/seasonal agricultural income and the type of rural assets available to farmers and their rates of return (Page, S., 1993).

The *stability* of the demand for money has been at the heart of economic research and policy analysis. The discussion about the relative merits of orthodox, buffer-stock and more recently error-correction models (explained later) of money demand have concentrated on parameter stability. Indeed, such stability and the homogeneity in prices have recently been cited as the key tests of money demand specifications (Hendry and Ericsson, 1991). In the context of LDCs, the scope for remonetisation following the programmes of stabilisation (as advocated by the International Monetary Fund (IMF) and the World Bank) crucially depends on the upward shift in money demand and the subsequent predictability of higher money demand with lower inflation (Asilis, Honohan and McNelis, 1991). In particular, Dornbush and Fischer (1986) underline the 'need to print money' after stabilisation, describing it as 'the most overlooked lesson of stabilisation'. They argue that any policy that makes a 'fetish' out of lower monetary growth is 'headed for trouble' in the form of high real interest rates. In the case of Bolivian stabilisation, it has been shown that remonetisation has been very slow since no provision was made for a sharp rise in money demand after stabilisation. An increased money demand makes further credit expansion following stabilisation programmes non-inflationary.

Inflation *uncertainty* has an important impact on money-price correlation. Note that high inflation uncertainty would make money a risky asset, leading to a reduction of both long-term and (possibly) short-term money demand. Thus, policies affecting inflation will have an extra impact via their effect on inflation uncertainty as well as on expected inflation. In DCs, some investigators have examined the effect of *interest rate uncertainty* on money demand (Baba, *et al.*, 1992). Khan (1977) measured inflation uncertainty by the absolute value of the change in inflation. In Khan's model, inflation uncertainty *indirectly* influences money demand by altering the adaptive expectations parameter in the adjustment of inflation expection.

During the 1980s, Bolivia experienced severe macroeconomic instability as hyperinflation raged at 20 000 per cent annum and monetary disequilibrium was quite evident. After the introduction of a stabilisation programme in Bolivia in 1985, the annual rate of inflation came down to 25 per cent during the late 1980s. The use of sophisticated econometric techniques (for example, error-correction, time-varying parameter estimation with Kalman filtering and GARCH models, that is, generalised auto-regressive conditional heteroskedasticity) by Alisis, *et al.* (1993) show that in Bolivia during the 1980s both expected inflation, and inflation uncertainty affect the demand for money. The time-varying parameter analysis reveals that the reaction to monetary disequilibrium was significantly more rapid during hyperinflation. More precisely, the model assumes that the long-run equilibrium money demand (M – P)* depends on the expected inflation rate and inflation uncertainty σ^2. The long-run money demand is given as follows:

$$(M - P)^* = b_0 + b_1 TR + b_2 \Pi + b_3 \sigma^2 \qquad b_2 < 0, b_3 < 0 \qquad (2.25).$$

All the variables, such as, money (M) and prices (P), are expressed in their logarithms and Π = rate of inflation, σ^2 = the variance of inflation and TR = trend. A distinction is made between short- and long-run money demand.

The empirical results of money demand functions in Bolivia suggest the role of inflationary adjustments in a complex dynamic process, showing changing beliefs of private agents regarding future government actions. They also underline the role of inflation variance as well as expected inflation in the money demand function. The results also show a dramatic change in the speed of cash balance accumulation after 1985, highlighting the belief of private agents in a credible government stabilisation programme. This was made possible partly by reducing fiscal deficits gradually but mainly by 'front-loading' its stabilisation effect with a massive cut of the government pay-roll and public-sector salaries. The important lesson is that the inclusion of inflation variance and expected inflation in money demand functions can substantially increase the predictability of money demand in those LDCs which suffer from high inflation.

Short- and long-run demand for money

In the late 1970s and 1980s, although the theory of the long-run money demand remained in an 'oasis of tranquillity'. the short-run money demand function received considerably more attention (see Gordon, 1984; Laidler, 1993). The distinction between short- and long-run money demand is important in the light of the 'Goldfield Puzzle' of too little money and too much velocity in the mid-1970s and the reverse puzzle of the 1980s of too much money and too little velocity in the DCs.

In the empirical estimates of money demand functions in both DCs and LDCs before 1973, a small coefficient on the lagged dependent variable was observed frequently. The strong inertia in the adjustment of real money balances was generally explained as resulting from portfolio adjustment costs. However, Laidler (1993) and Gordon (1984) argue that the short-run function may be partly 'a Phillips curve in disguise'. Slow adjustments in real balances may show inertia in overall price adjustments, as well as inertia in portfolio adjustment. The instability in the short-run money demand function witnessed after 1973 and in the early 1980s could be the by-product of shifts of the Phillips curve which occurred because of supply shocks in 1973–5. The existence of inertia in the process of inflation has led to reasons for doubting the identification of a short-run money demand function. The orthodox money demand function accounts for changes in real balance in terms of current output, interest rates and lagged real balances; i.e.

$$(M/P) = f\left[Y, r, (M/P)_{t-1}\right] \qquad (2.26)$$

But with sticky prices, the burden of adjustment to changing output and interest rates must be borne by the nominal money supply. If the central bank wants to fix interest rates, money supply must change quickly to changes in output and interest rates and these changes in money supply should pick up the short-run money demand schedule. But if the central bank targets nominal money supply growth (and not the interest rate), then output and interest rates are endogenous variables and will respond to changes in such money supply.

The long- and short-run concepts of money demand are made on the grounds of the absence of adjustment costs in the former and their presence in the latter. With upper case letters to stand for log level (and lower case letters for growth rates), the *desired long-run* real money demand function in logs ($M_t^* - P_t$) depends on vector of variables (X) (Gordon, 1984):

$$M_t^* - P_t = f(X_t) \tag{2.27}$$

or

$$M_t^* = f(X_t) + P_t \tag{2.28}$$

Such a long-run function assumes that agents can adjust their holdings instantly and costlessly to any change in the (X_t) that determine money holdings. Such a function is homogenous of degree one in prices.

Because of adjustment costs ($M_t - P_t$) (that is, actual) $\neq$ ($M_t^* - P_t$) (i.e. desired). A part (λ) of the difference is closed in any one discrete period, i.e. current level of real balances is a weighted average of desired and lagged real balances, that is,

$$M_t - P_t = \lambda(M_t^* - P_t) + (1-\lambda)(M_{t-1} - P_{t-1}) 0 \leq \lambda \leq 1 \tag{2.29}$$

Hence,

$$M_t - P_t = \lambda f(X_t) + (1-\lambda)(M_{t-1} - P_{t-1}) \tag{2.30}$$

The short-run function then captures the adjustment of the observed values of real balances in response to the more fluctuating vector of X_t as a result of changes in portfolio adjustment costs, with 1 minus the estimated coefficient of the lagged dependent variable as the portfolio adjustment coefficient $[1-(1-\lambda)] = \lambda$ and $(1-\lambda)/\lambda$ as the mean adjustment lag.

Dynamic specification of the money demand function and error-correction

A simple equation case

The standard partial adjustment model is one of several cases of a class of ADL (autoregressive distributed lag) models:

$$d_0(L)Y_t = \sum_{i=1}^{N} d_i(L)X_{it} + \epsilon_t$$

Where $d_i(L)$ = is a polynomial in the lag operator (L) such that $L^jY_t = Y_{t-j}$.

An alternative dynamic specification based on the works of Hendry, Pagan, Sargan (HPS) could be the following structural relationship in levels:

$$Y_t = \beta_0 + \beta_1 X_t + \beta_2 X_{t-1} + \beta_3 Y_{t-1} + \epsilon_t \tag{2.31}$$

where
X_t = exogenous variable, ϵ_t = error term (white noise).

The usual partial adjustment model in the money demand literature is written as follows:

$$Y_t = \beta_0 + \beta_1 X_t + \beta_3 Y_{t-1} + e_t \qquad \beta_2 = 0 \tag{2.32}$$

A serious potential weakness of the partial adjustment model is the possibly incorrect exclusion of X_{t-1}, which could result in the erroneous conclusion that speeds of adjustment are slow even it they are not. Besides, if e_t is autocorrelated, β_3 is biased upwards in the face of positive serial correlation. The mean adjustment lag would then be overstated, i.e. $\beta_3/(1-\beta_3)$.

If $\beta_3 = 1$, and $\beta_2 = -\beta_1$ we can write equation (1) as:

$$y_t = \beta_0 + \beta_1 x_t + e_t \tag{2.33}$$

where
x_t and y_t = differences in logs.

Such differencing is supposed to achieve 'stationarity' of time series data and to avoid spurious regression. However, data differencing leaves the equilibrium solution in (2.33) indeterminate, and it has been shown that if $\beta_o = 0$ and e_t is white noise, there is no long-run relationship between the levels of Y and X.

This is an unattractive feature of estimating models in terms of differences in data only. Such problems of differencing may be removed with the aid of the use error correction method (ECM) (see Chapter 3 for further details). The ECM uses equation (1) with restriction $\beta_1 + \beta_2 + \beta_3 = 1$.

$$y_t = \beta_0 + \beta_1 x_t + (1-\beta_3)(X-Y)_{t-1} + \epsilon_t \tag{2.34}$$

Equation (2.33) is a special case of (2.34) with the extra restriction that $\beta_3 = 1$, that is, since

$$\sum \beta_i = 1, \; \beta_1 = -\beta_2$$

Let g denote the steady state growth rate of both X and Y. We then have, from (2.34):

$$g = \beta_0 + \beta_1 g + (1-\beta_3)(X-Y)$$

$$\Rightarrow \qquad Y = X + \frac{\beta_0 - (1-\beta_1)g}{1-\beta_3}$$

Here, the assumption of proportionality could be appropriate for some relations that display a unitary elasticity with stable velocity, for example, demand for M_2. However, to explain the demand for M_1, such an assumption may be erroneous and the ECM model should be written as:

$$y_t = \beta_1 x_t + (1-\beta_3)(X-Y)_{t-1} + (\beta_1+\beta_2+\beta_3-1)X_{t-1} + e_t$$

$$= c_0 x_t + c_1(X-Y)_{t-1} + c_2 X_{t-1} \tag{2.35}$$

and the restriction $c_2 = 0$ can be tested directly. If such a restriction is invalidated, the long-run relation can be written as:

$$Y = \frac{(\beta_1+\beta_2)X + \beta_0 - (1-\beta_1)g}{1-\beta_3} \tag{2.36}$$

Short-run demand for real balances could respond with different lags to changes in prices and output. In this sense the ECM tries to capture the complex adjustment process of dynamic behaviour. However, the ECM is a method of describing statistically short-run dynamics, 'not of discovering the nature of the economic process generating them' (Laidler, 1993).

If the short-run money demand function is not properly identified and suffers from specification error, then the estimated parameters of a long-run money demand function will be seriously misleading. Recently, cointegration techniques have been used to estimate long-term relationships more accurately without taking a rigid attitude towards the modelling of the short-run dynamics. Let

$$V - \alpha r_t = e_t$$

where:

e_t = error term unrelated to r; r_t =the interest rate; V = velocity of income.

If $E(e_t) = 0$ and always tends to be so, then V and r are said to be co-integrated. If V and r are causally related, α becomes a structural parameter of the long-run money demand function. The argument is valid as long as the value of e tends to be zero, correcting the error at the end.

Clearly, the co-integration technique is a new and interesting way to get rid of spurious regression. On the other hand, it is important to remember that co-integration does not imply causality. Such causality comes from economic theory.

Demand for money in a dual-currency, quantity-constrained economy

Many LDCs experience excess demand for goods – for example, the centrally planned economies (CPEs) of Eastern Europe. Such excess demand in goods market can affect the demand for money in the money market.

In a number of empirical money demand analyses of a centrally planned economies (Portes and Winter, 1978; Portes and Santorum, 1987) attempts have been made to fit a Keynesian-type model to money data, with or without a restriction on the interest rate. Little attention has, however, been paid to the analysis of the impact of other constraints traditionally associated with a CPE, such as consumption and private investment constraints.

In fact, a typical CPE is usually under a financially repressed regime (FRR) (see chapter 5). This regime is characterised by suppressed nominal *r* and prices, which lower the real rate of growth and retard the development process (see Shaw, 1973). In a FRR, private investment is saving-constrained, while savings are distorted by an administratively fixed interest rate, often below the equilibrium level. In these circumstances, an increase in the real deposit rate of interest (nominal rate minus the expected rate of inflation) may raise savings, investment and, as a result, the rate of economic growth (McKinnon, 1973, pp. 71–7).

On the other hand, the savings process in these economies is subject to influences arising from goods shortages. In the presence of consumption shortages money could, in fact, be a forced asset demand. This could develop into a 'parallel' market for goods trading either in the official currency (for a thorough review see, for example; Davis, 1988) or, in the case of a relatively open private market, in foreign convertible currencies (see Chapter 12).

The model and market-clearing hypothesis

We start with a common Keynesian-type transaction, precautionary and asset money demand function for a cash economy in a CPE (for applications see, for example; Portes and Winter, 1978).

$$\left(\frac{M}{P}\right)^d = L\left(\frac{Y}{P}\right) \tag{2.37}$$

where M = total money stock; P = price level; Y = income.

In (2.37) we assume that price and income also include the unofficial sector of the economy, that is, the price level term reflects both official and black market prices while income includes unofficial (illegal) earnings. Moreover, we assume that the total money stock is heterogeneous, i.e. two currencies and two money stocks exist: official, which constitutes the domestic, 'soft currency' emission of a central bank, denoted hereafter as OM (official market) money, and unofficial, being usually a currency of one of the Western countries, BM (black market) money. In Poland, the US dollar has the role of the latter while in East Germany it was the West German Deutsche Mark. We allow for perfect and free exchange between the unofficial and official currencies. Consequently, the total of real money is given by

$$\frac{M}{P} = \frac{OM + XBM}{P} \tag{2.38}$$

where X is the black market rate of exchange of the *BM* into the *OM* currency. The following additional hypotheses are then formulated to derive the official money and black market money demand functions:

(i) The existence of a financially repressed regime. Interest-bearing savings deposits of the official currency are available but the nominal interest rate is controlled by the central financial authorities and changes in it are not usually related to changes in the money market. This is an indirect consequence of the commonly used assumption that the state financial market is institutionally separated from the private one.

(ii) The indivisibility of private investment activities. Following McKinnon (1973) it is asserted that a consequence of the FRR is that economic units (private enterprises) are restricted to self-finance. In fact in the CPEs, credit facilities for the private sector are limited and credit institutions are highly inefficient (for a detailed description of financial institutions in Eastern Europe see, for example, Zwass, 1979). Because of the relatively high-risk nature of the second-economy activities, unofficial credit is also scarce. Consequently, a private investor usually has to accumulate his own finance investment purposes.

(iii) A spillover effect from the quantity-constrained market on to the money market. If the private sector is constrained on commodities, this creates a divergence of the effective (constrained) demand from the notional (non-constrained) demand (see Barro and Grossman, 1976, pp. 74–5). In the OM market, the quantity constraints may lead to forced savings and/or to substitution into the 'parallel' market. The medium of exchange on the parallel market is often a foreign currency; hence consumer shortages increase demand for foreign currencies.

With these hypotheses, the OM and BM money demand function can be formulated as

$$\left(\frac{OM}{P}\right)^d = L_M\left(\frac{Y}{P}, \frac{I}{Y}, \frac{\overline{C}}{Y}, d - \dot{P}^e\right) \tag{2.39}$$

$$\left(\frac{XBM}{P}\right)^d = L_X\left(\frac{Y}{P}, \frac{I}{Y}, \frac{\overline{C}}{Y}, d - \dot{P}^e\right) \tag{2.40}$$

where I = private investment; $\overline{C}$ = fixed personal consumption; d = nominal interest rate on deposits; $\dot{P}^e$ = expected future rate of inflation.

We define P as a price averaged over both state-controlled and 'parallel' markets. Hence, $\dot{P}^e$ reflects also the expected BM exchange rate. With a negative real exchange rate, a consumer acts rationally if he/she withdraws demand for the official currency and increases it for foreign currencies.

Some of the parameters in (2.39) and (2.40) may be symmetric and represent the hypothesis formulated above. In particular, if the parameters of the $(d - \dot{P}^e)$ variable have identical arguments but opposite signs then, for a negative real interest rate, the effect on the demand for official money of suppressing the interest rate is fully substituted by the increase of asset demand in the secondary currency. If, however, the sum of the coefficients of the real interest rate in equations (3) and (4) is negative and $(d - \dot{P}^e)$ is non-positive then the financial repression effect (*FR* effect) holds.

The McKinnon 'conduit' effect occurs if the relationship between the investment/income ratio and total demand for money is positive. If there is a self-finance motive for accumulating money ahead of investment expenditure, the coefficient of the I/Y variable in the OM equation is positive, but, if there is a symmetry of the coefficients of I/Y in (3) and (4) the aggregate effect of investments on money demand can be zero. If this is the case, the McKinnon 'conduit effect' (McKinnon hypothesis hereafter) does not hold.

Finally, there can be an analogous symmetric relation with respect to the quantity constraints, that is, for the coefficients of $\bar{C}/Y$ in both equations. If such a symmetric relation holds, spillover effects from the quantity-constrained consumption market on to the official and unofficial money markets cancel each other. Official currency unspent on the fix-price quantity-constrainted consumption market is withdrawn from the OM and fully transferred into the BM. Consequently, aggregate money demand does not change. This led Nuti (1986) to hypothesise the equilibrating role of the flexible-price 'parallel' market in a CPE. The sysmmetry of the coefficients of $\bar{C}/Y$ inequations (3) and (4) is called the Nuti hypothesis (for a detailed application, see Charemza and Ghatak, 1990).

Appendices to Chapter 2

A.2.1

In a growing economy, it can be shown that the rate of increase in the money supply should equal the rate of growth of real income. The size of rise in money supply could be stated if changes in the demand for money are known.

Let

$$M_d = KPQ \tag{2A.1}$$

where

M_d = the amount of money demanded,
K = the fraction of income held as money in the economy,
P = the price level, and
Q = the volume of total output in the economy.

If we differentiate (2A.1) with respect to time (t), we obtain

$$\frac{dM_d}{dt} = PQ\frac{\delta K}{\delta t} + QK\frac{\delta P}{\delta t} + KP\frac{\delta Q}{\delta t} \tag{2A.2}$$

or,

$$\frac{1}{M_d}\frac{dM_d}{dt} = \frac{1}{K}\frac{\delta K}{\delta t} + \frac{1}{P}\frac{\delta P}{\delta t} + \frac{1}{Q}\frac{\delta Q}{\delta t} \tag{2A.2a}$$

Let the lower-case letters denote proportional growth rates. Thus we may write (2A.2a) as

$$m_{\text{d}} = k + p + q \tag{2A.2b}$$

which implies that the rate of change in the demand for money is equal to the sum of the rates of change in the fraction of income held in the form of money, the level of price and real output. If it is assumed that K and P are constant, we obtain the familiar result that rate of growth of output or real income should be equal to the rate of growth of money supply. Note that throughout the analysis, we have assumed that P is equal to unity.

Under a hundred per cent reserve system, the size of the non-inflationary deficit financing could be shown as follows. Let the rise in M_{d} equal the stock of money (M) times its growth rate. Thus, we have

$$\Delta M_{\text{d}} = M \cdot m = M(k+q) \tag{2A.3}$$

$$\Delta M_{\text{d}}/Q = \frac{M}{Q}(k+q) = K(k+q) \tag{2A.3a}$$

Given the incremental capital-output ratio (v) and the target rate of growth of income, the necessary ratio of investment (I) to national income is

$$I/Q = vq \tag{2A.4}$$

If we divide (2A.3a) by (2A.4), we obtain

$$\Delta M_{\text{d}}/I = K(k+q)/vq \tag{2A.5}$$

Under a fractional reserve system, the rise in the demand for money given by (2A.3) will not be equal to the surplus released to the government for investment. But this need not pose a problem. Let C denote the supply of 'currency' which consists of notes, the amount of commercial banks' reserves with the Central Bank and the money created by the commercial banks. The relationship between money supply (M) and currency will then be given by

$$M = \alpha C \tag{2A.6}$$

where $\alpha = 1/1 - d$ and d stands for the proportion of the total deposits that banks retain in the form of currency. If we differentiate (2A.6) with respect to time, we obtain,

$$\frac{dM}{dt} = C\frac{\delta\alpha}{\delta t} + \alpha\frac{\delta C}{\delta t} \tag{2A.7}$$

or

$$\frac{1}{M}\frac{dM}{dt} = \frac{1}{\alpha}\frac{\delta\alpha}{\delta t} + \frac{1}{C}\frac{\delta C}{\delta t} \tag{2A.7a}$$

Once again, using lower case letters to denote proportional growth rates, we have

$$m = a + c \tag{2A.7b}$$

where $$a = \frac{1}{\alpha}\frac{\delta\alpha}{\delta t},\ c = \frac{1}{C}\cdot\frac{\delta C}{\delta t}$$

Clearly, (2A.7b) implies that the rate of change in money supply is equal to the sum of the rates of change of currency and the bank multiplier. If we assume constant prices and equate changes in supply of money (2A.7b) to demand for money (2A.2b), we obtain the following equilibrium condition for the rate of change in currency:

$$c = k + q - a \tag{2A.8}$$

The rise in the demand for currency in this case will be equal to the release of real resources. Within a given (short) period, this is given by the stock of currency times its growth rate, so that

$$\frac{\Delta C}{Q} = \frac{C}{Q}\cdot c = \frac{K}{\alpha}(k + q - a) \tag{2A.9}$$

The proportion of investment which could be financed by non-inflationary deficit financing is now obtained by dividing (2A.9) by (2A.4).
Hence

$$\frac{\Delta C}{I} = \frac{K(k + q - a)}{\alpha\, vq} \tag{2A.10}$$

For details see Bhambri, R. S. (1968). 'Demand for Money and Investible Surplus', *Nigerian Journal of Economic and Social Studies*, **10** (1), 87–93.

A.2.2 *Demand for money in India, 1950–86: a cointegration analysis (by Anita Ghatak)*

The present study, unlike the previous studies, uses time-series modelling techniques and applies them to different definitions of money supply for deriving reliable estimates of demand for money equation for India. The recent development of time-series modelling in econometrics emphasises the need for verfying the existence of long-run equilibrium relations, which the conventional approach takes for granted, and the need for consequent re-estimation if such relations are found to exist. Tests for stationarity and cointegration of various time-series and estimation of error-correction models (ECM) of conintegrated time-series are the standard diet of modern time-series modelling. Reliable estimation of demand for money is important as the success of anti-inflationary stabilisation policy depends on a stable demand for money function. Dornbusch and Fischer (1986) have underlined the 'need to print money' after 'liberalisation' of an economy. Thus, stability in the demand for money function is essential for an analysis of the effects of monetary expansion during the process of 'economic liberalisation' experienced in India during the period under consideration. The rationale behind applying time-series modelling to different components of money supply is to check which components should be chosen as policy instruments. The time-series data for India are available for two definitions of money, narrow and broad. The former includes cash and demand deposits and the latter includes time deposits as well. If these different time-series do not all have the same stationarity properties and are not cointegrated with all the explanatory variables under consideration, stabilisation policy should aim at only those components of money which are cointegrated with the variables explaining the desired demand for money.

The standard single-equation approach to the estimation of a demand for money function for a less developed country (LDC) has been familiarised by Gujarati (1968). Real demand for money is assumed to be a function of real income, real interest rates, rate of inflation, inflation uncertainty, etc. In addition, some kind of adaptive behaviour or adjustment of actual to desired demand is assumed to distinguish between the short and long-run demand for money. Inflation uncertainty could be measured by absolute value of the change in inflation. Inflation uncertainty has an important impact on money-price correlation. High inflation uncertainty would make money a risky asset leading to a reduction of both long-term and possibly short-term money demand. The LDCs usually experience high inflation rates in the early stages of development. The variation of interest rates is, on the other hand, within a narrow margin. Accommodating these explanatory variables, demand for money equations can be written in the forms discussed later in the equations (2A2.3)–(2A2.8). The advantage of introducing additional explanatory variables gradually is that one can note their relative contribution to the explained sum of squares through the F-test or towards achieving cointegration among variables. The latter objective is highlighted in the present section.

The main objective here is to determine a *long-run* stable relationship between money demand and its determinants on the basis of annual data for the period 1950–86. Monetary targeting based on such a *long-run* association may (a) reduce short-run instability in monetary aggregates; and (b) control the rate of inflation through control over the money supply. Thus, monetary targeting is a necessary condition to control inflation and obtain stable output growth in the Indian economy (Karfakis, C. and Parikh, A. 1993).

Data and symbols

The data for the period 1950–86 on money supply variables, M_1 defined as currency with the public plus demand deposits with banks and M_3 defined as M_1 plus time-deposits with banks, GDP, interest rates and the price deflator have been taken from *International Financial Statistics* (IFS) and those on population have been taken from *Economic Survey* (India), 1991 (Government of India).

The symbols, Y_t, M_t and R_t stand for real per-capita GDP, real per-capita money supply and nominal interest rates respectively. The real rate of interest being defined as nominal rate minus the rate of inflation was negative for a few years under study. So the logarithm of real interest rates would not have been available. The rate of inflation, p, has been measured by the first difference of the logarithm of the price level and inflation uncertainty by the first difference of p. The lagged logarithm of money demand has been added to indicate an adjustment mechanism. If real desired money demand (M^*) is a function of a few variables like real income, interest rate, etc., and if actual demand adjusts to desired demand at a speed, $0<\lambda<1$, then the coefficient of lagged money demand will be included as an additional explanatory variable as shown in equation (2A2.2). If $\lambda = 1$, then adjustment is instantaneous. The closer the value of λ is to unity, the lower the proportion of any discrepancy between actual and desired balances that is made up in the course of any given time period.

$$\log M_t^* = f(\log Y_t,\ \log R_t,\ p, \Delta p) \tag{2A2.1}$$

$$\log M_t = \log M_{t-1} + \lambda\left(\log M_t^* - \log M_{t-1}\right) \tag{2A2.1}$$

$$\log M_t = \lambda \log M_t^* + (1-\lambda)\log M_{t-1} \tag{2A2.2}$$

The existence of an adjustment mechanism like (2A2.2) has been tested along with demand for money equations given in (2A2.3)–(2A2.8) below. The interest rate has been taken in its logarithm and arithmetic form. The latter is preferred for it distinguishes between elasticities at the same percentage change on different initial rates (Haache, 1974). Each of the six equations has been tested with and without the lagged dependent variable as an additional regressor and for both definitions of money supply. Such modified equations have been denoted by primes over the respective original equation numbers:

$$\log M_t = b_0 + b_1 \log Y_t + b_2 \log R_t + u_t \tag{2A2.3}$$

$$\log M_t = b_0 + b_1 \log Y_t + b_2 R_t + u_t \tag{2A2.4}$$

$$\log M_t = b_0 + b_1 \log Y_t + b_2 \log R_t + b_3 p_t + u_t \tag{2A2.5}$$

$$\log M_t = b_0 + b_1 \log Y_t + b_2 R_t + b_3 p_t + u_t \tag{2A2.6}$$

$$\log M_t = b_0 + b_1 \log Y_t + b_2 \log R_t + b_3 p_t + b_4 \Delta p + u_t \tag{2A2.7}$$

$$\log M_t = b_0 + b_1 \log Y_t + b_2 R_t + b_3 p_t + b_4 \Delta p + u_t \tag{2A2.8}$$

Cointegration analysis

Before estimating regression equations like (2A2.3)–(2A2.8), we ensure that the variables are cointegrated. In a multiple regression, the order of integration of the dependent variable cannot be higher than that of any of the explanatory variables and the latter should preferably be integrated of the same order (Charemza and Deadman (CD, 1993). The order of integration of each variable has been checked by the standard Dickey-Fuller (DF) and/or the augmented DF(ADF) tests. Such tests check for the presence of unit roots in the relevant series. The type of equation used to check for a unit root in a series X_t can be written as:

$$\Delta X_t = \alpha + \beta_1 \Delta X_{t-1} + \beta_2 \Delta X_{t-2} + \gamma X_{t-1} + \delta_t \tag{2A2.9}$$

Where t stands for the time trend variable and where only two period lags have been used to save on degrees of freedom.

The ADF t-value tests for the statistical significance of the coefficient, γ. A negative, significant ADF t-value rejects the hypothesis of a unit root in the series X_t implying that the series is stationary or integrated of order zero. To check for higher order of integration, the equation (2A2.9) has to be written in the appropriate order of difference of the series. Table A2.2.1 gives the ADF t-values of the logarithms of various time-series of our analysis. Logarithm of real money supply, M_1, is stationary at 1 per cent and that of M_3 is integrated of order one at 5 per cent levels. Logarithm of nominal interest rate and rate of inflation and first difference of rate of inflation are all stationary at 5 per cent and 1 per cent levels respectively. Interest rate and logarithm of per-capita GDP deflated by consumer price index are integrated of order one at 10 per cent and 5 per cent levels respectively. After checking for order of integration, in the next stage, cointegration tests were made following Engle and Granger (1987) (EGC). Such tests run in two stages. In the first stage, each regression equation, e.g. (2A2.3)–(2A2.8) is estimated by least squares adding a linear time trend to the respective equation. In the second stage, residuals, $\hat{e}_t$ from such regressions are tested for stationarity, using DF t-values as above. The DF t-values for coefficient of $\hat{e}_{t-1}$ in case of each regression are given in table A2.2.2. These DF t-values are larger for all the equations for the narrower definition of money supply. As already stated, the broader definition of money supply is integrated of a higher order in its real per-capita logarithmic form. The definition M_3 includes time deposits with banks which contributes to the non-stationarity of the series. Using McKinnon critical values only the variables in the equations (2A2.3) and (2A2.4) in case of M_1 are cointegrated at 10 per cent significance level. Using other critical values, e.g., those simulated by CD (1993), these variables along with lagged dependent variable are cointegrated at 5 per cent significance level and the variables in the equations (2A2.5)–(2A2.8) and those in (2A2.4)–(2A2.6) with lagged dependent variable are cointegrated at 10 per cent level for M_1. For M_3 the variables are not cointegrated in any of the demand equations. Lack of cointegration results in 'spurious regression', typical symptoms of which are high $\bar{R}^2$ and low Durbin Watson Statistic (DWS) – at least DWS < $\bar{R}^2$ (Hendry, 1986). So we derived the least squares estimates for cointegrated and non-cointegrated cases to check on $\bar{R}^2$ and DWS, table A2.2.3 gives these results.

The results given in table A2.2.3 indicate that the DWS is lower than $\bar{R}^2$ in four cases and they are all with the broader money supply as the dependent variable and they all correspond to the cases when cointegration was not achieved. Judged by lack of cointegration, the estimates of demand for money

Table A2.2.1 Results of testing for unit roots

Series	*ADF t-values for coefficients of*	
$\log M_1$	$\log M_{t-1}$	–4.73*
$\log M_3$	$\Delta \log M_{t-1}$	–4.5054*
$\log Y_{t-1}$	$\Delta \log Y_{t-1}$	– 3.8105**
$\log R_t$	$\log R_{t-1}$	– 3.6605**
p_t	P_{t-1}	– 3.8518**
Δp_t	ΔP_{t-1}	– 4.6577*

* significant at 1 per cent level.
** significant at 5 per cent level.

equations for the broader definition are unreliable. So only brief comments will be given on them. The real-income elasticities are all greater than unity, implying that M_3 is a luxury asset. This result is in agreement with Gujarati's based on Indian data for 1948/9–1964/5. Gujarati (1968) found an estimated value of the adjustment coefficient equal to 0.47, significantly less than unity. In our estiamtes, the value of $(1 - \lambda)$ when significant, ranges between 0.57 to 0.95 for M_3 and between 0.61 to 0.65 for M_1implying an adjustment lag well below unity in all cases. While statistical insignificance of interest rates in money demand is a

Table A2.2.2 EGC tests for variables in the demand for money equations

Equation number	*DF t*-values for $\log M_1$	$\log M_3$
(2A2.3)	–4.63***	–1.55
(2A2.4)	–4.66***	–2.13
(2A2.5)	–3.87	–1.38
(2A2.6)	–3.81	–1.88
(2A2.7)	–3.38	–1.66
(2A2.8)	–3.42	–1.99
(2A2.3) with lagged dependent variable as a regressor	–4.13	–2.27
(2A2.4) with lagged dependent variable as a regressor	–3.96	–2.44
(2A2.5) with lagged dependent variable as a regressor	–3.77	–3.39
(2A2.6) with lagged dependent variable as a regressor	–3.76	–3.35
(2A2.7) with lagged dependent variable as a regressor	–3.39	–3.28
(2A2.8) with lagged dependent variable as a regressor	–3.44	–3.30

*** significant at 10 per cent level.

Table A2.2.3 Estimates of demand for money equations for India: 1950–86

Equation number and coefficients		For M_1	For M_3	t-values for M_1	t-values for M_3	$\bar{R}^2$, DWS for M_1	$\bar{R}^2$, DWS for M_3
(2A2.3)	b_0	–0.97	–3.55	–2.8578	–7.099	0.6059	0.90
	b_1	0.717	1.7618	4.0853	6.8315	1.3444	1.02
	b_2	–0.047	0.1879	–0.6628	1.7984		
(2A2.4)	b_0	–0.9499	–3.00	–2.5277	–5.83	0.604	0.91
	b_1	0.689	1.5629	4.0124	6.65	1.3414	1.06
	b_2	–0.0056	0.045	–0.4989	2.9473		
(2A2.5)	b_0	–0.9822	–3.55	–3.4249	–8.408	0.728	0.931
	b_1	0.69	1.718	4.6694	7.889	1.087	0.85
	b_2	–0.3775	0.2688	0.11	2.97		
	b_3	–0.377	–0.6112	–2.553	–2.806		
(2A2.6)	b_0	–1.0515	–3.11	–3.311	–7.199	0.728	0.94
	b_1	0.726	1.60	5.017	8.136	1.093	0.91
	b_2	–0.0016	0.0518	–0.172	3.987		
	b_3	–0.37	–0.6032	–2.528	–3.0239		
(2A2.7)	b_0	–0.691	–3.4018	–2.43	–7.6339	0.74	0.93
	b_1	0.5289	1.6115	3.59	6.9813	1.18	0.8297
	b_2	0.09	0.354	1.39	3.4999		
	b_3	–0.8289	–1.1911	–3.44	–3.154		
	b_4	0.418	0.351	2.809	1.503		
(2A2.8)	b_0	–0.74	–2.91	–2.30	–6.3988	0.73	0.9425
	b_1	0.586	1.507	4.011	7.296	1.177	0.9410
	b_2	0.009	0.063	0.958	4.5214		
	b_3	–0.755	–1.1453	–3.238	–3.475		
	b_4	0.38	0.3799	2.577	1.8135		
(2A2.3′)	b_0	–0.919	–1.603	–2.87	–2.695	0.686	0.9464
	b_1	0.6259	0.7696	3.546	2.577	1.207	1.4356
	b_2	–0.03	–0.0749	–0.463	0.8787		
	b_5	0.188	0.6277	1.1879	4.3511		
(2A2.4′)	b_0	–0.97	–1.5769	–2.7496	–2.6978	0.687	0.94
	b_1	0.64	0.79	3.64	2.744	1.2107	1.410
	b_2	–0.0058	0.018	–0.57	1.35		
	b_5	0.1865	0.5729	1.18	3.77		
(2A2.5′)	b_0	–0.5696	–0.44	–2.32	–1.929	0.8293	0.993
	b_1	0.3359	0.17	2.376	1.513	1.6944	
1.07599							
	b_2	0.0166	0.089	0.34	2.896		
	b_3	–0.775	–1.1049	–5.27	–14.517		
	b_5	0.655	0.9496	4.472	16.66		
(2A2.6′)	b_0	–0.63	–0.493	–2.341	–2.065	0.8287	0.992
	b_1	0.37	0.233	2.66	1.971	1.6898	1.0137
	b_2	0.000016	0.012	0.002	2.288		
	b_3	–0.7663	–1.081	–5.231	–13.583		
	b_5	0.6532	0.933	4.447	14.534		
(2A2.7′)	b_0	–0.36	–0.2527	–1.523	–1.20	0.8381	0.994
	b_1	0.239	0.0759	1.7723	0.723	1.7532	1.3972
	b_2	0.0668	0.1276	1.2939	4.108		

Table A2.2.3 *continued*

Equation number and coefficients		For M_1	For M_3	*t*-values for M_1	*t*-values for M_3	$\bar{R}^2$, DWS for M_1	$\bar{R}^2$, DWS for M_3
	b_3	–0.979	–1.291	–5.0346	–12.10		
	b_4	0.286	0.215	2.3389	3.24		
	b_5	0.6097	0.9556	4.294	18.65		
(2A2.8′)	b_0	–0.3895	–0.2965	–1.45	–1.309	0.8336	0.994
	b_1	0.2739	0.1459	2.00	1.31	1.7529	1.3268
	b_2	0.0072	0.0177	0.916	3.21		
	b_3	–0.9295	–1.2156	–4.90	–11.07		
	b_4	0.2586	0.1895	2.136	2.67		
	b_5	0.6202	0.9350	4.322	15.54		

well-established contention for many LDCs (Gujarati, 1968; Fan and Lun, 1970–71; Fry, 1988), the positive but significant nominal interest elasticity in case of M_3 can be explained by real interest rates being consistently negative in the 1970s and the first half of the 1980s. Gujarati's estimates were confined to only conventional econometric methods without any cointegration analysis. On the same ground, our OLS estimates based on M_3 will have to be rejected as well for lack of cointegration among the variables.

The results in table A2.2.2 demonstrate that the real demand for M_1, real income, nominal interest rate and lagged money demand are cointegrated in the log-linear form. So the respective estimates in table A2.2.3 can be regarded as reliable and not based on spurious regression results. The estimated equations (2A2.3) and (2A2.3^1) both turn out significant real-income elasticities below unity implying that real cash balances is a necessary asset. The logarithm of nominal interest has the expected negative sign. Its statistical insignificance can be explained by the fact that M_1 does not include interest-bearing deposits and, therefore, can be insensitive to interest-rate changes. The statistical insignificance of previous year's demand throws doubt on the existence of an adjustment mechanism. The significant negative constant term means a financially 'repressed' money market which is expected in a LDC like India. In the demand for M_1 cointegration was achieved by CD critical values in all cases but two. So, the corresponding regressions deserve further comments. The rate of inflation expectedly influences money demand inversely. Inflation uncertainty as measured by change in inflation rates also influences money demand, M_1, significantly. Inflation uncertainty raises demand for M_1 as people anticipating worse time to come raise their demand for cash and demand deposits with easy convertibility. Judged by the DF *t*-values in the second column of the table, error correction models were estimated only for equations (2A2.3)–(2A2.6) with and without the adjustment mechanism. For all cointegrated variables, there exists an error-correction mechanism (ECM) which combines the long-run equilibrium relationship with short-run dynamics. The parameters of the ECM are the short-run parameters. A simple ECM in this context can be written as:

$$\Delta\log M_t = \rho\hat{e}_{t-1} + \beta_1 \Delta\log Y_t + \beta_2 \Delta\log R_t + \beta_3 \Delta p_t \qquad (2A2.10)$$

where the lagged residuals from the respective cointegration regressions (2A2.3)–(2A2.6) represent the EC term. If it is negative and statistically significant, then the short-run deviations around the long-run equilibrium relation (2A2.3)–(2A2.6) will fade away in the long-run. If, in any period, the amount of money balances were above the equilibrium level, the holder will reduce his demand in the next period meaning that the coefficient ρ should be negative. This idea is similar to that of partial adjustment mechanism used in the conventional estimation of demand for money functions but the idea of EC is more general and it allows for a wider pattern of dynamic adjustment (Deadman and Ghatak, 1994). In more general forms ECM can also include lagged first differences of the dependent and of all the independent variables (Miller, 1991). We have chosen form (2A2.10) to save on degrees of freedom. Table A2.2.4 summarises the results of estimation of the ECM of form (2A2.10) with and without the lagged dependent variable. The error correction term is significant and negative in all cases. The real-income elasticities are all positive and significantly less than unity.

The nominal interest rate is statistically insignificant but has the correct negative sign in five out of eight cases. The rate of inflation is significant and negative in all cases. The lagged dependent variable in the first difference form improves the explanatory power of equations with inflation rate as an additional explanatory variable. The coefficient of the former implies a very speedy adjustment of actual to desired demand in a given time period. As already noted, $\Delta\log M_{t-1}$ can be viewed as an explanatory variable of a more general formulation of ECM (Miller, 1991).

Conclusions

In India, the real demand for money defined to include cash and demand deposits exhibits a long-run equilibrium relationship with real income, nominal interest rate and the rate of inflation. Any deviation from this equilibrium relation or 'error' is corrected. This error has been separated from the speed of adjustment by estimating ECMs with the lagged dependent variable. The coefficient of the latter in the ECM implies a very rapid adjustment of actual to desired demand. The short-run income elasticities ranging between 0.25 and 0.68, as obtained from the ECM, are lower than the long-run elasticities ranging between 0.34 and 0.72 as obtained from the respective static forms with and without the partial adjustment mechanism. They are all significantly less than one implying real cash balances as a necessary asset. The rate of inflation has a very significant negative influence on money demand, a conclusion similar to that obtained for developed countries.

The real demand for money defined in the broader sense to include cash, demand as well as time depostis is not only non-stationary but also non-cointegrated with the real income, interst rate and inflation. So the estimates of static equilibrium demand for money equations for the broader definition, M_3 are less reliable.

Table A2.2.4 Error-correction models for cointegration regressions India 1950–86

ECM of equation no for M_l only	Coefficient estimates	*t*-values	$\bar{R}^2$, DWS respectively
(2A2.3)	$\rho = -0.7333$	–4.5493	0.457
	$\beta_l = 0.6849$	3.229	1.3234
	$\beta_2 = -0.1814$	–1.2117	
(2A2.4)	$\rho = -0.7535$	–4.7738	0.4601
	$\beta_l = 0.6791$	3.1966	1.2894
	$\beta_2 = -0.0269$	–1.1358	
(2A2.5)	$\rho = -0.5794$	–3.6229	0.4172
	$\beta_l = 0.6149$	3.5818	1.6618
	$\beta_2 = 0.0249$	0.1890	
	$\beta_3 = -0.2209$	–2.3157	
(2A2.6)	$\rho = -0.5635$	–3.5321	0.4146
	$\beta_l = 0.6053$	3.4747	1.6531
	$\beta_2 = -0.0057$	–0.2816	
	$\beta_3 = -0.2159$	–2.2566	
(2A2.3[1])	$\rho = -0.821$	–3.6313	0.3212
	$\beta_l = 0.599$	3.0574	1.8955
	$\beta_2 = -0.085$	–0.6188	
	$\beta_5 = 0.3487$	2.1501	
(2A2.4[1])	$\rho = -0.8112$	–3.6105	0.3294
	$\beta_l = 0.5811$	2.9563	1.8679
	$\beta_2 = -0.0232$	–1.0943	
	$\beta_5 = 0.3458$	2.1499	
(2A2.5[1])	$\rho = -1.1658$	–5.3811	0.6129
	$\beta_l = 0.2491$	1.667	1.9946
	$\beta_2 = 0.1132$	1.0291	
	$\beta_3 = -0.7988$	–6.3025	
	$\beta_5 = 0.946$	5.5488	
(2A2.6[1])	$\rho = -1.1379$	–5.1675	0.6011
	$\beta_l = 0.265$	1.7434	1.9901
	$\beta_2 = 0.0108$	0.6230	
	$\beta_3 = -0.7885$	–6.0967	
	$\beta_5 = 0.9319$	5.3675	

In the context of India, therefore, stabilisation policy should primarily aim at the narrower money, M_1 as the latter displays stability and it very consistently predicts 'higher money demand with lower inflation' (Asilis, Honohan and McNelis, 1993).

Future direction of research could proceed in terms of capturing the effects of expected rate of inflation with a better proxy than the actual rate, and of structural change, e.g., with variables like urbanisation and monetisation (see, e.g., Yi, 1993). The analysis of the impact of such structural factors on the different components of money supply, e.g., M_1 and M_3 could be useful for designing more appropriate monetary stabilisation policy instruments.

3. The demand for money in LDCs: empirical results

D. F. Deadman

Generally speaking, the empirical literature on money-demand functions in LDCs has provided little that is new in the way of approaches to the problem of estimation compared to the (large) amount of equivalent work undertaken for developed countries. (For a summary of this work for DCs see Laidler, 1993.) However, studies relating to the LDCs have yielded useful additional evidence on the role of the expected rate of inflation in demand for money functions, and of the influences and effect of varying monetary frameworks and degrees of monetisation of different countries. In part, these two features of the studies outlined below are interrelated. Countries with an underdeveloped monetary system may reflect this with lesser importance of interest rates and greater importance of expected inflation in demand for money functions compared with DCs. Expected inflation rather than interest rates may provide a more realistic guide to the opportunity cost of holding money balances in such societies. In other respects, including the process of adjustment to equilibrium positions in the money market, the marked importance of some measure of income, the evidence of economies of scale in money holdings and the homogeneity in prices for demand for money functions, the findings tend to confirm those already noted for DCs.

The empirical evidence for the LDCs reflects the developments made over time in applied econometric methodology. Early work started from a conventional single equation relating some measure of real money balances to a set of variables (for example, interest rates, income and the expected rate of inflation) with possibly some adjustment being made for money market disequilibrium in the short run. In such studies, the primary applied estimation problems were seen to be those of measuring expected values and the joint presence of multicollinearity, serially correlated errors and lagged dependent variables in the estimated equation. Subsequently, empirical work has concentrated on the stability aspects of such equations, and to reconsider the estimation of such equations from the point of view of new ideas in time series econometrics. Modern studies which concentrate on error correction forms of demand for money functions and on exogeneity testing are direct outcomes of such new ideas.

3.1 Conventional demand for money studies

The standard single equation approach to the estimation of a demand for money function for a developing country may be exemplified by the model of Gujarati (1968) for India. A simple demand function is assumed, namely:

$$M_t = f(R_t, Y_t) \tag{3.1}$$

where

$M_t = M_t^n / P_t$ are aggregate real cash balances demanded at time t;
R_t is a nominal (short- or long-term) rate of interest;
Y_t is aggregate real national income;
M_t^n are nominal cash balances; and
P_t is the price level.

A distinction is made between long- and short-run behaviour in the money market with a long-run function defined in terms of aggregate desired real cash balances, M_t^*,

$$M_t^* = A \cdot R_t^b \cdot Y_t^c \tag{3.2}$$

and a partial adjustment model of actual (real) cash balances (M_t) towards this desired level of the form:

$$\log M_t - \log M_{t-1} = \lambda\left(\log M_t^* - \log M_{t-1}\right) + \epsilon_t \quad 0 \leq \lambda \leq 1 \tag{3.3}$$

This can be used in conjunction with the long-run function to give a general short-run function used for estimation:

$$M_t = A^\lambda \cdot R_t^{b\lambda} \cdot Y_t^{c\lambda} \cdot M_{t-1}^{(1-\lambda)} \tag{3.4}$$

If $\lambda = 1$, there is no lag in adjustment. The closer to unity the value of λ, the greater the proportion of any discrepancy between actual and desired balances that is made up in the course of any given time period. In Gujarati's empirical results, based on annual data from 1948–9 to 1964–5, the estimated value of λ was about 0.47. This value is similar to that found by Chow (1966) for the United States. Income proved to be the most significant determinant of the demand for real cash balances, the (long-term) interest rate being a statistically insignificant variable. In contrast to developed economies, Gujarati comments that 'the Indian money market is comparatively under-developed' and hence the finding on interest rates supports the contention of Kaufman and Latta (1966) that the interest elasticity of the demand for money function would be more significant in countries with well-developed money markets. Gujarati also found evidence that the long-run income elasticity was greater than unity, a result that may be interpreted as indicating that money can be viewed as a luxury asset.

A more extensive analysis, covering Japan, Taiwan, Korea, India, Pakistan, Burma, Sri Lanka, the Philippines and Thailand, was undertaken by Fan and Liu (1970/71). Essentially the same model as that used by Gujarati was adopted, with broadly similar results. Estimation using annual data from 1953 to 1968 indicated very low interest elasticities (Taiwan excepted). All income elasticities were significantly different from zero, and nearly all were inelastic, including India. Burma provided an unconvincingly high income elasticity, however. This was discounted largely on the grounds that over the period considered, the growth in the money stock had been extremely irregular compared to the other countries, reflecting a state of severe disequilibrium in the Burmese money market.

Abe *et al.* (1978) have provided a study that had as a central aim the re-estimation and re-evaluation of an earlier one for Pakistan by Akhtar (1974). In contrast to Akhtar's use of the current rate of inflation as a proxy for the expected rate, Abe *et al.* (1978) estimated the expected rate using weights derived from an Almon lag scheme involving both current and lagged values of the actual rates of inflation. (For details of the Almon approach, see Johnston, 1984). In this way, the authors found a significant role for expected inflation in the demand for money function for Pakistan. Akhtar's finding that income was the primary determinant of the demand for money was reinforced, and when a narrow definition of money was employed, the rate of interest also appeared as a statistically significant variable. Later studies on Pakistan include those by Mangla (1979) and Nisar and Aslam (1983). Mangla used permanent rather than current income as the scale variable to explain the demand for real narrow money balances, and found the Gujarati formulation to be suitable for Pakistan, confirming in the process that such a function was homogeneous of degree zero in prices. Nisar and Aslam attempted to use the whole term structure of interest rates but multi-collinearity problems led to the use of just two parameters to represent this, namely the intercept and slope of the yield curve. Both parameters were significant, confirming the importance of interest rates in determining the demand for money in Pakistan. Doe (1982/3) considered the demand for money between 1960 and 1977 for a wide range of countries (Colombia, Costa Rica, Egypt, Gabon, Ghana, Ivory Coast, Malaysia, Nicaragua, Nigeria, Thailand, Togo and Tunisia) from the point of view of the appropriate income and opportunity cost variables to be included in the function. The inflation rate was statistically significant in only two of the countries considered.

The question of which variable best represents the opportunity cost of holding money in developing countries – interest rates or the expected rate of inflation – has also been usefully addressed by a series of papers on Latin America. These papers include those by Hynes (1967) and Deaver (1970) for Chile; Diz (1970) for Argentina; and Cardoso (1983) and Darrat (1985a) for Brazil. The use of data from these countries is attractive as, compared with developed countries, they have a greater experience of long-run inflation. Asset substitution is likely to be between money and real assets rather than between money and financial assets, so that the expected rate of inflation represents the more appropriate opportunity cost variable.

Hynes (1967) based estimates of both the expected rate of inflation and expected income on weighted sums of current and past observations. When combined with an adjustment mechanism for disequilibrium in the money market, the resulting demand for money equation related the actual quantity of real money balances per capita to these measures of expected inflation and expected income. A shift variable was also included to allow for differences between wartime and peacetime periods. The model was estimated from annual data, from 1935 to 1960. Preliminary tests indicated that the demand for nominal money balances could be taken as being homogeneous of the first degree in the price level, thus allowing the later results to be presented in terms of an explanation of real rather than money cash balances. Like the Almon scheme mentioned above in relation to the study by Abe *et al.*, the weighting pattern generating estimates of both the expected inflation rate and expected income is allowed to rise and fall (if the data justifies this) rather than simply fall geometrically from the current value, as would be implied from the use of simple exponential weights. Hynes excluded interest rates from the study as necessary data were unavailable, but since it was believed that the major changes in the money rate of interest were due to alterations in the expected inflation rate, the latter variable could be taken as representing the opportunity cost of holding money. The long run 'interest' elasticity was calculated to be about –0.36 and was significant. The evidence on the long-run income elasticity was surprising, however, in that it was found that a narrow definition of money had a higher elasticity than a broader definition. This reverses the pattern found for most developed countries (for example, Fisher, 1968; Meltzer, 1963; see also Bank of England, 1970).

The demand for money in Chile has also been investigated by Deaver (1970). Like Hynes, Deaver recognised that Chile provided an intermediate case between countries whose demand for money had been dominated by the expected inflation rate during periods of hyperinflation, and other countries (such as the USA) where changes in income have outweighed alterations in the cost of holding money over the long run. Thus, as Deaver stated, 'what would be the result if the cost of holding money were high and variable relative to that occurring in the United States, yet low by comparisons with the hyperinflations? And what if, at the same time, income were changing substantially, so that according to the experience in the United States, it should have an effect on money holdings also?' Demand for real cash balances was taken to be a function of the expected rate of inflation and income. Higher income elasticities were obtained when permanent income (a weighted sum of past incomes) was used rather than measured income, though generally the income elasticity was found to be less than unity. Time deposits were found to be more sensitive (elastic) to changes in the cost of holding money than demand deposits or other kinds of money. However, in contrast to Hynes' approach, exponentially declining weights were used to define expected inflation. Deaver's conclusion was that the tests 'show that a stable demand function can be defined for Chile that explains most of the variations that took place in the real money stock between 1878 and 1955'.

Cardoso (1983) questioned the emphasis placed on the role of expected inflation in demand for money functions, particularly for Brazil. Her conclusion was that interest rates rather than expected inflation rates affected the demand for real cash balances, suggesting either that inflation effects had been captured by movements in the nominal rate of interest, or that physical goods did not provide an alternative to holding money. The rate of inflation was identified as affecting only nominal cash balances. However, Darrat (1985a) argued that Cardoso was incorrect in rejecting the inflation rate for Brazil. Using Almon weights rather than the Koyck (geometrically declining) weights implied by the partial adjustment process for cash balances as used by Cardoso, Darrat found both interest rates and inflation rates significant in a demand for money equation for Brazil. Darrat also concluded that Cardoso's estimated equations exhibited structural instability (some other evidence on structural stability of demand for money equations in developing countries is reviewed below) but that equations involving both interest rates and inflation rates were structurally stable over the sample period (1966 to 1979). Gerlach and Nadal de Simone (1985) confirmed that the inflation rate should not be excluded as an explanatory variable for Brazil. They adopted an approach similar to that of Darrat in that lags longer than one period were use for the explanatory variables but their model also involved several lagged values of the dependent variable (technically, they used an autoregressive distibuted lag model).

Cardoso (1983) also considered whether the empirical evidence was in favour of the adjustment of actual to desired money holdings to be in real terms (as was the case in the Gujarati model presented above) or in nominal terms.

Using the same notation as above, the latter adjustment process would imply the estimation of the model

$$M_t = A^{\lambda} \cdot R_t^{b\lambda} \cdot Y_t^{c\lambda} \cdot \left(M_{t-1}^{n} / P_t\right)^{1-\lambda} \tag{3.5}$$

so that the lagged money term involves division by P_t rather than P_{t-1}, as was the case for adjustment in terms of real cash balances. This distinction has been the focus of attention in studies by Fair (1987) for twenty-seven countries (including Colombia, Peru, India, Pakistan and the Philippines), and Gupta and Moazzami (1990) for eleven Asian countries. The results of both studies are strongly in favour of the nominal adjustment hypothesis.

3.1 Stability testing of conventional demand for money studies

Within the conventional approach, considerable attention has been paid to the structural stability aspects of estimated demand for money equations. One operational consequence of parameter instability in a demand for money equation is that predictions about the effects of alterations in monetary policy would become more hazardous. Indeed, such instability could in itself be a source of disturbance to an economy. Work on stability aspects on demand for money equations for developed countries became widespread in the mid-1970s (for example, see Leventakis and Brissimis (1991) for a survey of studies relating to the USA, and Boughton (1981) for a more geographically extensive analysis). Structural stability has usually been interpreted as being equivalent to parameter constancy over time. Evans (1988) has pointed out that one reason for the finding of evidence for structural breaks in conventional demand for money studies might be traced to the pervasive use of the partial adjustment hypothesis in such studies. More sophisticated assumptions about the dynamics of the adjustment process (for example, as adopted in the studies of Darrat (1986a) or Gerlach and Nadal de Simone (1985)) seem to exhibit a greater degree of stability. The most widely used tests for structural stability in the empirical literature on demand for money functions for LDCs where there is a prior belief as to the potential structural break point or points have been the Chow (1960) test, the Goldfeld (1973) test for predictive power, and the Gupta (1978) test. Typically, where the point of potential break is unknown, the Quandt (1960) procedure, the Farley and Hinich (1970) or the Brown–Durbin–Evans (1975) cusum or cusum of squares approaches have been used.

Darrat (1986a) has investigated structural stability for three OPEC members (Saudi Arabia, Libya and Nigeria) for the period 1963 to 1979. He adopted conventional (Gujarati-type) demand for money equations but used an Almon lag process to represent the lag structure in the money demand equation in a similar fashion to that he adopted for Brazil (Darrat (1985a) and for Kenya (Darrat (1985b)). The open-economy nature of the OPEC countries implied the possible importance of foreign rather than domestic interest rates as relevant opportunity cost variables in the demand for money equations. Darrat concluded that permanent real income, inflationary expectations and foreign interest rates were all significant factors in determining real money demand in each economy. Moreover, the equations appeared to require the presence of foreign interest rates to achieve structural stability, judged here on the basis of the predictive power, Chow, Gupta, and Farley and Hinich tests mentioned above. Metwally and Rahman (1990) also used a foreign interest rate (the Eurodollar rate) in their study of the demand for money for Saudi Arabia. Specific dummy variables were used in conventional demand for money equations, for both the whole economy and for the non-oil sector, to account for structural shifts engendered by the oil embargo of 1973. The structural break dummies were not significant for the non-oil sector.

The first oil embargo of 1973 also provided the hypothesised break point for Kallon (1992), who analysed the stability of the demand for money in Ghana. Interestingly, rather than using official interest rates as an explanatory variable, Kallon computed an unofficial inflation-adjusted rate to represent the rate that would be paid to moneylenders in rural societies. Kallon investigated the question posed above as to whether cash adjustments are made in a real or nominal sense, but did so via conventional models with an implied Koyck adjustment process. The stability tests adopted were those of Chow, and Farley and Hinich. Structural stability for the period 1966 to 1986 was accepted. The unofficial interest rate variable was statistically significant while, as was expected by Kallon given the limited access of a rurally-based people to foreign assets, foreign interest rates were not.

Arize *et al.* (1990) have also stressed the importance of taking account of a large non-monetised sector in their demand for money studies of seven African countries (Egypt, the Gambia, Mauritania, Morocco, Niger, Nigeria and Somalia) for the period 1960 to 1987. However, in contrast to Kallon (1992), foreign interest rates and a measure of capital mobility (defined as the foreign interest rate plus the expected exchange rate) were hypothesised as being directly important to the LDCs they investigated. Equations allowing for adjustments of money balances in both real and nominal terms were modelled and tested using a partial adjustment process in each case. The estimated models were found to be structurally stable using both the Chow and the Farley–Hinich tests. External influences reflected in foreign rates and/or the capital mobility variable were found to be statistically significant at the 10 per cent level. Also in an African context, Arize (1984–5) examined whether the expected rate of inflation and permanent or measured incomes played a significant role in money demand functions for Nigeria between 1960 and 1977. Three alternative specifications were tested for stability using a Chow test. The subperiods into which the sample period was broken up were selected on the basis of the start of the oil boom in Nigeria in 1970. As is not uncommon with studies for LDCs (for example, Fry, 1973; Aghevli *et al.*, 1979; Perera, 1988; and Arize, 1989), long-run income elasticities were found to be in excess of unity, and to be larger the broader the definition of money adopted. The tests indicated stability for conventional money demand functions, for both narrow and broad definitions of money.

Partly as a result of its bank nationalisation programmes and the growth of financial intermediation in the 1970s and 1980s, India has reasonably well-developed money and financial markets, especially when compared with many African countries. Indeed, Darrat and Webb (1986) used India explicitly as an example of the effect of the deepening of financial markets on the demand for money of an LDC. As India also possesses a relative abundance of readily available data, unsurprisingly there has been more work done on the demand for money there than for any other developing country. Kamath (1984) provides an extensive study which incorporates a survey of some of this empirical work. However, despite a developed monetary sector, India also has a large non-monetised sector, which was one of the reasons put forward by Kamath to argue for the use of expected inflation rather than interest rates as the variable to represent the opportunity cost of money balances in his equations. Most results pertain to models incorporating a partial adjustment mechanism for desired money balances, but Almon lag schemes were also investigated. In common with many other studies for India, the demand for both narrow and broad definitions of money were investigated. Kamath concludes that there exists a stable demand for money function for India, despite also finding evidence of structural breaks for both definitions of money when the sample period was broken up into periods of low (1952 to 1963) and high (1964 to 1976) inflation. Kamath (1985) has extended his model to incorporate an index of credit restraint in the demand for money (a variable used by Wong (1977) in his study of five Asian developing countries), and to consider the possibility of simultaneous equation bias by examining also the supply of money. Using the same sample periods, Chow tests were used to test for stability in the demand for money equations, with some narrow money equations being unstable but with all the broad money equations tested exhibiting structural stability. This conclusion reinforces the findings of Deadman and Ghatak (1981), who used the Brown–Durbin–Evans test to investigate the structural stability of conventional demand for money equations for India for the period 1948 to 1976. Other studies of structural stability for Indian demand for money functions include those of Ram and Biswas (1983) and Kulkarni (1986).

In general, studies of demand for money functions for LDCs indicate that stable functions can be estimated on the same lines as constructed for DCs. Exceptions to this conclusion are provided by Darrat (1986b) for a number of South-American countries (Brazil, Chile and Peru) for the period 1950 to 1981. The estimation of conventional functions which incorporate a partial adjustment mechanism remains an active research area, as exemplified by the demand for money studies of four Asian developing countries (Pakistan, the Philippines, South Korea and Thailand) by Arize (1989), and those of Sri Lanka by Perera (1988) and of Kenya, Ghana, the Ivory Coast, Indonesia, Bangladesh and China in Page (1993).

3.3 Error-correction models of demand for money functions for developing countries

Almost without exception, the studies reported above have adopted models for estimation formulated in terms of the levels of the variables concerned. Typically, the level of real money balances is regressed on the level of a scale variable (measured or permanent income), the level of a variable representing the opportunity cost of holding money (foreign or domestic interest rates, or the rate of inflation) and the lagged dependent variable. Moreover, in several of these studies, model specification was determined on the basis of a combination of 'best fit' (the value of the adjusted or unadjusted coefficient of determination) and the statistical significance or otherwise of individual coefficients judged by *Student-t* tests. Modern econometrics would question the usefulness of such approaches. (For an account of recent developments in econometrics relating to these approaches and to a more formal discussion of many of the points below, see Charemza and Deadman, 1992.)

Contemporary econometrics places great emphasis on the time series properties of the variables involved in an econometric model. The statistical properties of ordinary least squares estimators of coefficients of models relating the levels of variables together where such variables exhibit systematic tendencies to change over time are complicated and non-standard. This means that in such cases, standard inference procedures such as determining 'statistical significance' from conventional t-tests are generally untrustworthy. Variables exhibiting systematic tendencies to change (and this is the case for many of the variables used in demand for money studies) are termed 'nonstationary'. Systematic changes in the mean, variance or autocovariances of a variable over time would constitute nonstationary behaviour in that variable. Although rarely stressed by econometric texts, conventional regression analysis presupposes the variables considered in a regression to be stationary.

Hence, variables need to be tested for stationarity, and if found to be non-stationary, need to be transformed in some way before models are estimated. For many economic variables (namely those termed integrated variables) the transformation is simply that of taking differences an appropriate number of times. For most economic variables, first differencing is sufficient to achieve stationarity, and the variables are described as being integrated of order one. This does not imply, however, that demand for money studies are best estimated solely in terms of the first differences of the variables rather than the levels, as such dynamic models will fail to reproduce in an equilibrium context the generally accepted long-run equilibrium theory of the demand for money. Loosely, what is required are models in which the variables are stationary and which also simplify to the accepted long-run economic theory in a steady state. One formulation of models with such properties are termed 'error-correction' models and are usually discussed in the closely related context of 'co-integration'.

Consider a postulated long-run equilibrium relationship between the logarithm of real money balances and a scale variable (say the logarithm of current real income):

$$\log\left(M_t/P_t\right) = \alpha + \beta \cdot \log\left(Y_t\right) \tag{3.6}$$

If this relationship really does represent a long run equilibrium relationship between these variables, then the short run discrepancies or errors

$$\mu_t = \log\left(M_t/P_t\right) - \alpha - \beta \cdot \log\left(Y_t\right) \tag{3.7}$$

should not show any tendency to increase systematically over time. If this is the case and, more precisely, if μ_t is stationary, the variables (the logs of real money balances and real income), are said to be co-integrated. It is only possible for these two variables to be co-integrated if they are integrated of the same order, as it is only then that μ_t can be stationary. In addition, if the two variables are co-integrated, there will only be single values of the parameters α and β that makes them so (technically, there is a unique cointegrating vector).

If the model is extended to a multivariate case, say to include an interest rate variable, R_t:

$$\log\left(M_t/P_t\right) = \alpha + \beta \cdot \log\left(Y_t\right) + \gamma \cdot R_t \tag{3.8}$$

then, as above, for this model to represent a co-integrating relationship between these variables, the errors from this long-run model should be stationary. One method used in practice for the testing of co-integration involves the estimation of the postulated long-run model and the testing of the residuals from this model for stationarity. There are alternative views about how static long-run relationships should be estimated (see Charemza and Deadman (1992, pp. 156–8)), although estimation by ordinary least squares of the parameters (but not their standard errors) may still retain some desirable statistical properties despite the nonstationarity of the regressors (for example, see Banerjee *et al.*, 1993, p. 158). In the multivariate case, it is not necessary for the variables to be integrated of the same order for this relationship to be a co-integrating relationship. Moreover, in this case there is the possibility of multiple co-integrating vectors.

If the variables can be accepted as being co-integrated, there is an error correction representation of these variables. An error-correction model is a short-run model that incorporates a mechanism by which money balance holders will attempt to restore their balances to the long-run relationship should they be in a disequilibrium position in any period. For example, if in the first model above the money balances and income variables (in logs) were both integrated of order one, then a short-run model incorporating an error correction term could be written as (see Charemza and Deadman, 1992, pp. 58–9)

$$\Delta \log \left(M_t/P_t\right) = \otimes_1 \cdot \Delta \log \left(\mathrm{Y}_t\right) + \otimes_2 \cdot \left(\log \left(\mathrm{M}_{t-1}/P_{t-1}\right) - \alpha - \beta \cdot \log \left(Y_{t-1}\right)\right)$$

where

$$\Delta x_t = x_t - x_{t-1} \tag{3.9}$$

For a static equilibrium, where money and income are unchanging period by period, the model above simply solves to the long-run equilibrium relationship. For a stable equilibrium, where real money balances and income are growing at a constant rate g, the model solves as

$$g = \otimes_1 \cdot g + \otimes_2 \cdot \left(\log \left(\mathrm{M}_{t-1}/P_{t-1}\right) - \alpha - \beta \cdot \log \left(Y_{t-1}\right)\right)$$

or for period t;

$$\log \left(M_t/P_t\right) = \alpha + \beta \cdot \log \left(Y_t\right) + \frac{g(1-\otimes_1)}{\otimes_2} \tag{3.10}$$

which is a sensible form for the long-run function in the presence of growth. If, in any period, the money balances holder considered real money balances to be above that desired for the given level of income, the holder will attempt to restore money balances to the long run equilibrium relationship by running down money balances in the next period. Hence, the sign of the parameter on the error correction term, $\otimes_2$, is expected to be negative.

The important aspect of the short-run model is that all variables, including the error-correction term, are now integrated of order zero. That is, all variables are stationary, and methods based on classical regression analysis are appropriate for the estimation of this short-run model. These ideas extend directly to multivariate models, such as the second model above.

Clearly there is a similarity between the conventional partial adjustment mechanism for money balances discussed earlier, which has been so widely used in empirical demand for money studies, and the idea of error correction of money balances. In fact, the error-correction approach is more general than that of the partial-adjustment mechanism in that it allows for a wider pattern of dynamic adjustment. This can be seen quite easily through a simple example.

Suppose desired real money balances at time t (M_t^*) are proportional to money income (Y_t), and actual money balances (M_t) are subject to simple partial adjustment behaviour, so that:

$$M_t^* = \alpha \cdot Y_t, \tag{3.11}$$

with

$$M_t - M_{t-1} = \lambda \cdot \left(M_t^* - M_{t-1}\right) + u_t, \quad 0 \leq \lambda \leq 1$$

This yields an estimating equation:

$$M_t = (1 - \lambda) \cdot M_{t-1} + \alpha \lambda \cdot Y_t \tag{3.12}$$

If both money balances and income are integrated of order one and the long-run co-integrating relationship is

$$M_t = \alpha \cdot Y_t + v_t, \tag{3.13}$$

then a simple error-correction model can be written as

$$\Delta M_t = \beta_1 \cdot \Delta Y_t + \beta_2 \cdot (M_{t-1} - \alpha \cdot Y_{t-1}) \tag{3.14}$$

or

$$M_t = (1 + \beta_2) \cdot M_{t-1} + \beta_1 \cdot Y_t - (\beta_1 + \beta_2 \cdot \alpha) \cdot Y_{t-1}$$

If this equation is compared with the estimating form for the demand for money equation incorporating a partial adjustment mechanism, it is evident that the two equations will coincide only if the lagged income term can be omitted from the demand for money equation. Technically, the partial-adjustment model is said to be 'nested' within the more general error-correction model – that is, it imposes more severe constraints on the equation for money demand in that a lagged income term is excluded. The partial-adjustment model may be adapted to allow for forward-looking behaviour (for example, see Nickell, 1985; Domowitz and Hakkio, 1990; or Alogoskoufis and Smith, 1991) which generates models of an error-correction form. However, the application of such models to demand for money equations (for example by Domowitz and Hakkio) do not support the use of conventional partial-adjustment behaviour. In relation to such assumed behaviour, Gordon (1984) and Hendry *et al.* (1984) have pointed out that the invalid exclusion of lagged values of explanatory variables from demand for money models may result in implausibly long estimated speeds of adjustment for money balances (as were found, for example, by Killick and Mwega, 1993). Gordon (1984, pp. 414–16) also points out that if the price level fails to adjust immediately to its equilibrium level in each period, this would be likely to manifest itself in the widespread finding of autocorrelated errors in conventional demand for money functions. Both these aspects of conventional studies may be usefully addressed by considering models which allow for a more general dynamic structure, of which error-correction forms have been the most widely adopted.

Banerjee *et al.* (1993, p. 60) provide two generalised forms of equivalent error correction models with p exogenous variables. These are useful for discussing the empirical studies available on developing and newly industrialised countries which have adopted error-correction approaches. These equivalent models may be written (for $r = \min(n, m)$) as either

Model 1

$$\Delta y_t = \alpha_0 + \sum_{i=1}^{r} \delta_i \cdot \left(y_{t-i} - \sum_{j=i}^{p} x_{jt-i} \right) + \sum_{j=1}^{p} \beta_{j0} \cdot \Delta x_{jt} + \sum_{j=1}^{p} \sum_{i=1}^{r} \xi_{jt} \cdot x_{jt-i}$$

$$+ \sum_{j=1}^{p} \sum_{i=r+1}^{n} \psi_{jt} \cdot x_{j\,t-i} + \sum_{i=r+1}^{m} \alpha_i \cdot y_{t-i} + \epsilon_t$$

or as

Model 2

$$\Delta y_t = \alpha_0 + \sum_{i=1}^{r} n_i \cdot \left(y_{t-i} - \sum_{j=i}^{p} \gamma_j \cdot x_{jt-i} \right) + \sum_{j=1}^{p} \beta_{j0} \cdot \Delta x_{jt} + \sum_{j=1}^{p} \sum_{i=1}^{r} \xi^{*}_{jt} \cdot x_{jt-i}$$

$$+ \sum_{j=1}^{p} \sum_{i=r+1}^{n} \psi_{jt} \cdot x_{jt-i} + \sum_{i=r+1}^{m} \alpha_i \cdot y_{t-i} + \epsilon_t \qquad (3.15)$$

where in each case there are r error-correction terms, and where the models contain lags of lengths n and m on the levels of the p endogenous variables (the x_j variables) and the level of the dependent variable (y_t) respectively. In practice, a single error-correction term at lag r is usually employed, generally where r is equal to one. The long-run equilibrium relationship is envisaged as being of the form

$$y_t = \sum_{j=1}^{p} \gamma_j \cdot x_{jt} + v_t \qquad (3.16)$$

The error-correction terms in Model 1 appear as

$$\left(y_{t-i} - \sum_{j=1}^{p} x_{jt-i} \right)$$

rather than as

$$\left(y_{t-i} - \sum_{j=1}^{p} \gamma_j \cdot x_{jt-i} \right)$$

but one term in each x_{jt-i} $(i \leq r)$ is also allowed for in this equation. This allows the equilibrium relationship to take the form above, with the γ_i coefficients not necessarily being equal to one. Testing the statistical significance of the lagged x_{jt-i} variables $(i \leq r)$ thus becomes a test of whether the long-run function is homogeneous in the p explanatory variables. Studies which have adopted models in the form of Model 1 for estimation include those by Domowitz and Elbadawi (1987) for Sudan, Calomiris and Domowitz (1989) for Brazil, and Gupta and Moazzami (1990) for eleven Asian countries.

Model 2 incorporates the non-homogeneity ($\gamma_i \neq 1$) aspect of the equilibrium relationship directly. Banerjee *et al.* (1993) show that the estimated coefficients on the error-correction terms (the δ_i and η_i coefficients in the two models above) will be equal for all i and arbitrary γ_i in these formulations. If the γ_i coefficients in the long-run model were assumed to be known (as would be the case if the long-run model had been previously estimated), the lagged x_{jt} variables could be omitted from Model 2. Studies using this formulation thus include the lagged residual from the estimated long-run function (say $\hat{v}_{t-1}$) in the short-run dynamic model for estimation. Studies adopting a Model 2 form include Margaritis and Maloy (1990), Manning and Mohammed (1990), Arestis and Demetriades (1991), Asilis, *et al.* (1993), and Psaradakis (1993).

Given what was indicated above about the problems involved in estimating models that include explanatory variables which are nonstationary, estimation of error-correction models might seem to pose difficulties. Models 1 and 2 presented above include variables measured in both differences and levels. Typically in demand for money studies, real money balances, real income and interest rates will be found to be integrated of order one, and hence their first differences rather than their levels will be stationary. In fact, the dynamic specifications represented by these error-correction models may still be estimated sensibly by ordinary least squares as the inclusion of several variables and their lags as explanatory variables increases the chance that the variables will be co-integrated (see Banerjee, *et al.*, 1993, chapter 6).

Arestis and Demetriades (1991) used an error-correction model to investigate the demand for broad money in Cyprus. The political history of Cyprus suggested that a major structural break could be expected to be present in the estimated relationship. A permanent increase in the income eleasticity of demand at the time of the shock was allowed for by a variable introduced into the co-integrating regression, and in the presence of this, structural stability was not rejected. Tests for the orders of integration of the variables employed in this study revealed real per capita money balances, real per capita GDP, real per capita consumers' expenditure; interest rates, and the expected rate of inflation (measured by the current rate), all to be integrated of order one. The lagged residuals from the estimated long-run relationship were included in a short-run error-correction model and found to be statistically significant with the expected negative sign. Non-nested tests (see Charemza and Deadman, 1992, chapter 8) indicated that consumers' expenditure was a better scale variable than GDP for the demand for money in Cyprus. An earlier study by Arestis (1988) also considered Cyprus, along with Mauritius and Malta, using error-correction models. In all cases, the error-correction term was significant. Exchange-rate variables performed unimpressively in each country, though marginally better for the more open economies of Mauritius and Malta, indicating some substitutability between real money balances and foreign balances in these countries. All three countries have relatively unsophisticated financial markets.

Greece has also been described as having a financial system that 'remains rather underdeveloped and inadequate' (Psaradakis, 1993). Margaritis and Maloy (1990) have also considered the demand for money function for this economy. Margaritis and Maloy adopt a model of money demand formulated by Domowitz and Hakkio (1990) which nests generalised versions of both partial adjustment and error-correction models within it. Because capital markets are relatively undeveloped, interest rates were not expected to measure expected inflation adequately, and accordingly the inflation rate was added to the set of regressors to explain the demand for narrow money balances between 1975 and 1987 (quarterly data). A measure of expected currency depreciation was also included among the opportunity cost variables, to allow for possible substitution of foreign for domestic money. This study provides an example of testing (and rejecting) the hypothesis of a unitary elasticity of income by including a lagged income term on the lines discussed above. Various combinations of pairs of the opportunity cost variables were tried. In each case, the error-correction term was highly significant. A model using all the opportunity cost variables was found to be superior to any model using only a subset of them, contradicting previous findings of other researchers based on conventional partial adjustment studies. A conventional model was estimated for comparative purposes, and this indicated the finding mentioned above of an implausibly long adjustment lag. Lags estimated from the error-correction forms were more reasonable.

Psaradakis (1993) also looked at the demand for narrow money in Greece (1960 to 1989, quarterly data) but started from an unconstrained vector autoregressive VAR model (see Charemza and Deadman, 1992, chapter 6). In contrast to Margaritis and Maloy (1990), formal tests were reported on the orders of integration of the variables used in the study, namely real money, real income, interest rates and inflation. First differences of each of these variables were found to be stationary using standard tests, results which were confirmed for all variables apart from inflation by the use of more extensive testing. The hypothesis that the money demand equation had a unitary income elasticity was not rejected. A structural error correction model incorporating the lagged error term from the long-run equation had statistically significant coefficients. The change (first difference) of inflation strongly influenced money balances, and adjustment of money balances to income changes was found to be quite rapid (a mean lag of 3.6 quarters). A conventional partial adjustment model was not found to be an adequate representation of the demand for money function compared with the error correction form employed in this study.

It was noted earlier that Gupta and Moazzami (1990) used conventional partial-adjustment models to test whether the empirical evidence was in favour of money balances adjustment being in nominal or in real terms. They also considered this problem using error-correction models for ten of the eleven Asian developing countries in their study for which the error-correction form seemed appropriate. In all ten cases, the error-correction term carried the expected negative sign, and was statistically significant in nine cases. Generally, adjustment in nominal terms received further support from the results of these models. Of the ten countries studied, one (Singapore) has received detailed examination by Manning and Mohammed (1990). Although the role of interest rates in the demand for money is considered, the main relationships examined in this paper are between nominal narrow money balances, real GDP and the consumer price index from 1967 to 1985. The logarithms of these three series were all found to be integrated of order one, and a long-run co-integrating vector between the three transformed series using money as the dependent variable was established as it was found to have stationary residuals. The lagged residuals were used as an error-correction term in an error-correction model for money balances, and determined to be statistically significant. The model also passed a Chow structural stability test. Some evidence was found for multidirectional causality between money, GDP and prices, a problem that is explored more fully in Chapter 6. The lending rate was not found to be a significant variable in the demand for money in Singapore, but this seems to have been the only opportunity cost variable introduced into the regression analysis despite the openness of the Singapore economy.

The homogeneity of money demand with respect to income and prices has been tested for directly by Domowitz and Elbadawi (1987) for Sudan. Using an error-correction model in the form of Model 1 above, lagged income and price terms were statistically insignificant. The implication of a unitary long-run income elasticity of demand runs counter to the widespread belief that LDCs would tend to have elastic income effects of income changes on money balances. As with other countries with a lack of financial assets to act as substitutes for money, the rate of inflation was found to be a significant explanatory variable over the sample period (1956 to 1982). Stability of the estimated model was checked by a number of tests, including the Chow test. The implied speed of adjustment from the error-correction term was lower than that found for DCs, but about the same as that noted for Brazil, a country with an intermediate state of development and relatively sophisticated financial markets (Cardoso, 1983). Brazil has also been studied by Calomiris and Domowitz (1989). who used monthly data from 1972 to 1981 to fit an error-correction model for real money balances as a function of income, expected inflation and treasury bill velocity. This last variable was a proxy variable to capture the increased use of treasury bill repurchase agreements as money substitutes. The rate of exchange-rate depreciation was also used to test for the effect of foreign currency substitution which, as was noted above, could be an important variable for countries that have experienced high rates of inflation. The long-run income elasticity of money demand was insignificantly different from unity. In common with other studies, the mean adjustment lags were found to be smaller than those estimated from conventional partial adjustment models. The results indicated a smaller elasticity (around –0.16) for expected inflation than those reported in other studies.

Bolivia experienced both years of extremely high annual inflation rates (over 20 000 per cent) as well as several years of steady moderate rates (around 25 per cent) during the 1980s. Asilis *et al.* (1993) have investigated the demand for money in Bolivia, concentrating on the role of inflation uncertainty that could result from such marked variations. A generalised autoregressive conditional heteroscedastic (GARCH) random walk model for inflation (where the rate of inflation is measured by Δp_t with p_t being the logarithm of the consumer price index) was used to estimate the conditional variance of inflation (σ_t^2)as:

$$\Delta p_t = \Delta p_{t-1} + \epsilon_t, \quad \text{with} \quad \epsilon_t \sim N\left(0, \sigma_t^2\right)$$

and

$$\sigma_t^2 = \gamma_0 + \gamma_1 \cdot \sigma_{t-1}^2 + \gamma_2 \cdot e_{t-1}^2 \tag{3.17}$$

where e_{t-1}^2 is the squared error at time t, and ϵ_t is a random error term. The first of these equations is termed a random walk model of inflation as the change in the rate of inflation between any two periods is simply a random variable (ϵ_t). The second equation allows the conditional variance of the process to change over time in relation to lagged conditional variances, and is termed a generalized ARCH (or GARCH) process (see Mills, 1990, chapter 15). Given an initial value for σ_t^2 at time $t = 0$, these equations can be estimated to provide the parameter estimates of the γ_i coefficients. The conditional variance can then be obtained period-by-period by recursion. The assumption is that inflation uncertainty is correlated with this conditional variance. This measure was then used along with a time trend and a measure of the expected rate of inflation in a long-run model for real money balances. No other opportunity cost variables or income were used in this equation, primarily because of the distortion likely to be present in such variables during hyperinflationary episodes. A short-run error-correction model using the lagged residuals from the long-run model as an error-correction term was then estimated.

Both the first differences of expected inflation and the inflation uncertainty variable, along with the error-correction term, were statistically significant. The error-correction model was also estimated by a procedure that allowed the parameters of the model to alter over the sample. This model indicated that the reaction to monetary disequilibria was much more rapid during the hyperinflationary period. Error-correction models thus seem a resilient method of enquiry for money demand studies, even when used in situations of extreme monetary conditions.

It is clear that Domowitz and Elbadawi (1987, p. 273) provided an accurate prediction when they concluded that 'The error correction framework is a likely replacement for the partial-adjustment specification which has dominated the money demand literature, regardless of the country-specific application, in that it is both more general and nests the partial-adjustment process.' From the empirical results already generated from a wide range of countries and differing monetary conditions, error-correction models have confirmed the importance of variables thought to be significant in conventional studies. Error-correction models capture both the static long-run theory of money demand, and permit a more flexible approach to the modelling of the short-run dynamic adjustment of money balances than is implied by a simple partial adjustment assumption. Error-correction modelling techniques can also allow for the investigation of temporal causality patterns between variables (for example, see Miller, 1991).

The quality and range of data for LDCs is generally acknowledged to be inferior to that available for DCs, so that results need to be interpreted with some caution. In particular, the complete absence of quarterly data for many countries has meant that the effects of seasonality on money demand functions in economies dominated by large agrarian sectors has received little attention. Another relatively unresearched area is that of the effect on money demand of financial innovation, including the emergence of rural banking.

4. Monetary institutions in LDCs

The growth of the monetary institutions has played a very useful role in promoting the economic development of the LDCs. These monetary institutions usually include the central banks, the commercial banks, the currency boards, the co-operative banks, development banks and the hire-purchase finance companies. These institutions are generally organised and can be regarded as 'dealers of debt'. The central bank performs a variety of important functions in the LDCs as the principal pillar of a country's financial stability. The commercial banks usually accept deposits and lend money to credit-worthy borrowers, mainly to finance trade, commerce, industry and transport. In this way the commercial banks mobilise financial surpluses and allocate them to different sectors of the economy for real capital formation. The co-operative banks usually operate in the agricultural sector. Their major aim is to meet the credit needs of the agriculturists and bring the unorganised rural sector into the fold of the organised money market. The rural money market usually consists of a large number of heterogeneous agencies like indigenous bankers, landlords, merchants, traders, village moneylenders, pawnbrokers, shop-keepers, etc. Sometimes the lack of specialisation in different activities can lead to the growth of 'monopoly' institutions where landlords may be moneylenders as well as traders. The non-banking financial institutions usually consist of those financial agencies which promote economic development without being engaged in the traditional banking practices. The workings of these institutions will now be discussed.

4.1 The central bank: its functions in the LDCs

The central banks in the LDCs perform both traditional and non-traditional functions. The traditional functions of the central banks can be listed as follows:

Banker to the government The central bank in any LDC is a banker to the government. It advances money to the government and maintains the cash balances of the government. It also receives and makes payments for the government. It enables the government to issue public debt. The central bank carries out transactions in foreign receipts and payments on behalf of the government. It also acts as a financial and economic adviser to the government.

Monopoly of note issue Like the central banks of the DCs, the central banks in the LDCs also have the monopoly of note issue. The monopoly power of issuing notes by the central bank is important to maintain confidence in the value of the legal currency and to promote is acceptability among the members of the public.

The lender of the last resort The central bank is traditionally the 'lender of the last resort'. This means that the central bank will provide liquidity to the banks and other financial agents when other sources dry up. The central bank usually provides such liquidity by discounting bills of exchange.

The controller of credit The central bank usually regulates the amount and the availability of credit in the economy. This task is important to promote internal price stability. In the LDCs, it has been frequently pointed out that the economy behaves in a classical rather than a Keynesian way. This implies that the amount and the rate of growth of the money and credit supply could exert significant effect on prices. If one of the objectives of the central banks is to promote price stability, then clearly they have to act as careful controllers of money and credit.

The central bank as a bankers' bank The central bank acts as the commercial bankers' bank. It means that the relationship between the central bank and the commercial banks is similar to that between the commercial banks and members of the public. The central bank accepts deposits from the commercial banks and lends to them at times of need. It is obligatory for the commercial banks to maintain a certain proportion of their demand and time liabilities as cash balances. The central bank can regulate the credit supply to the economy by altering the cash reserve ratios.

Promotion of external stability External stability means stability in the rate of exchange of the domestic currency *vis-à-vis* the foreign currencies in the international market. It is the task of the central bank to maintain orderly exchange rates and avoid sharp fluctuations in these rates. For example, in an era of flexible exchange rates, if the value of the national currency continues to fall sharply, the central bank may raise the bank rate (i.e. the rate it charges for lending) to prevent such decline, since an increase in the bank rate is likely to increase the inflow of foreign currencies.

The role of central banks in the economic development of the LDCs

It has been acknowledged generally that the central banks in the LDCs have important roles to play in promoting economic development. Hence the central banks of many LDCs (for example India, Pakistan, Nigeria, Ghana, Tunisia, Malaya) have been given wide powers to promote the growth of the economy. Thus the Reserve Bank of India has followed a policy designed to help the agricultural sector of providing credit to the co-operative banks at a rate of interest lower than the bank rate. Sometimes the central banks in the LDCs have set out the guidelines to follow for some definite pattern of economic policies. In many cases the central banks have also taken steps to promote the integration of the dual money markets. Many central banks in the LDCs have taken active steps in publishing information regarding the state of the economy and in promoting research in money and banking.

It has been observed that despite the limitations of monetary policy, it has a major role to play 'in the process of economic growth and stability' (Iengar, 1962). Some writers argue that the central banks should not only try to expand the productive capacity of the economy but also try to ensure the full employment of such capacity. Whittlesay contends: 'Ideal output under the full employment objective is the country's economic potential at the prevailing level of technology; under the economic growth objective, it is the country's economic potential at a progressive level of technology, and specifically at a level which progresses in an ideal manner' (Whittlesay, 1956). Sayers also points out that where the growth of commercial banking is not quick enough to make adequate provision for the country's economic potentialities, 'the central bank should be ready to step in to fill the gaps' (Sayers, 1957).

The use of monetary and credit mechanisms by the central bank is regarded as and important way to achieve economic growth. However it is useful to remember that in achieving the objective of economic growth the central bank should not deviate from one of its major aims-that of promoting *internal* (that is price) stability. Many commodities in LDCs generally suffer from the short-term supply inelasticties and there is a danger unless monetary policies are manipulated with due caution, the economy might experience serious inflation.

4.2 The commercial banks: the creation of bank deposits

The commercial banks in the LDCs perform a variety of what are their traditional functions in DCs. These banks accept deposits and lend to credit-worthy borrowers against suitable collateral. They offer interest on the deposits. They also charge interest on loans advanced; these rates are known as the borrowing rates. The difference between the borrowing rates and the deposit rates is revenue for the banks.

The demand for bank credit very much depends upon the level of economic activity, the cost of credit and the rate of return on the use of bank credit. Similarly, the supply of bank credit also depends upon the level of income, the confidence in the banks and the interest rates paid by the banks *vis-à-vis* the rates which could be earned from other types of investment. Note also that the ability to create 'bank money' or credit gives the banks considerable power to satisfy the demand for bank credit. However the limit of credit creation is usually set by the rate of profit on assets held by the banks. Given the narrow size of the bill market and the limited stock of financial assets in the LDCs, the commercial banks are likely to reach their limits sooner in the LDCs than the banks in DCs.

The other important factor which sets a limit on the capacity of the banks to create additional deposits is the unwillingness of the members of the public to hold additional bank deposits. In most LDCs, it has been observed that a high proportion of money is held in currency and a low proportion in bank deposits (Furness, 1975). Such a situation implies that a majority of loans have to be made in currency which hinders deposit creation. Also, the lack of an array of domestic financial assets induces many to hold foreign securities. Such action will again lead to a reduction of bank deposits.

The third factor which restricts the deposit creation by the commercial banks is the statutory obligation under which the commercial banks are required to maintain a minimum ratio of reserve assets to deposits. The central banks are usually given the power to change these reserve ratios. Thus if the central bank wants to enforce a tight money policy it can raise the minimum reserve ratios and curtail the power of the banks to create deposits and credit. The banks have only limited power to replenish the reserves by selling securities to the government since the monetary authorities ultimately decide whether or not to buy such securities. The other way in which the banks can replenish their reserves is to borrow from the central bank. But since such borrowing will increase the power of the commercial banks to create more credit, it is very unlikely that at a time when the authorities have decided to 'squeeze' the credit market, the central bank will be willing to buy securities from the banks. Even when the central bank may decide to lend to the banks, such loans carry a high rate of interest (that is, the 'penal' rate).

The bank deposit multiplier

The process of deposit creation by the commercial banks to a certain multiple of the cash ratio has been called the deposit multiplier. This process of expansion can be stated easily. Let there be two banks, B_1 and B_2. It is assumed that these banks are required by law to maintain a cash–deposit ratio of 10 per cent. Suppose an individual (X) deposits Rs. 100.00 in his bank, B_1. Given the cash-deposit ratio of 10 per cent, the bank B_1 has now an excess cash of Rs. 90.00 which it lends to another person (Y) to earn profit. If Y decides to pay Rs. 90 to any person (Z) who is a client of B_2, then the bank deposit of B_2 will rise by Rs. 90.00 when B_2 receives Rs. 90.00 in cash. Given the 10 per cent cash-deposit ratio, the bank now has an excess cash of Rs. 81.00 which it is in a position to lend to credit-worthy borrowers. If these loans are paid to the clients of B_1, then the deposit of B_1 will rise by Rs. 81.00. After the cash transfer of Rs. 81.00 to B_1, this bank will now be holding Rs. 72.90 paisa (i.e. 90 per cent of 81.00) as excess cash which could be lent again and the whole process will be repeated. The total deposit creation will be given by the initial deposit of cash i.e. Rs. 100.00 × 10 = Rs. 1000.00.

This process of deposit creation can be algebraically presented. Let D be equal to deposits, C_b Cash of banks, b the cash ratio (see e.g. Newlyn, 1967; Newlyn and Bootle, 1978). Then

$$\Delta D = \Delta C_b + (1-b)\Delta C_b + (1-b)^2 \Delta C_b + (1-b)^3 \Delta C_b + \ldots + (1-b)^n \Delta C_b \qquad (4.1)$$

The sum of such an infinite series

$$\Delta D = \frac{1}{b}\Delta C_b \tag{4.2}$$

According to the minimum cash ratio rule, we have

$$D \leq \frac{1}{b} C_b \tag{4.3}$$

It implies that whenever a bank receives a cash deposit it can raise deposits by an amount which would be equal to the rise in cash times the reciprocal of the bank's cash ratio. Hence,

$$\Delta D = \frac{1}{b}\Delta C_b \tag{4.3a}$$

The above theory of 'bank deposit multiplier' rests on the assumption of a constant marginal propensity to hold cash. Clearly, this is an unrealistic assumption and bank's holding of currency is actually given by the choice of the public regarding currency holdings either in bank deposits or in cash. If C is total currency and C_p is the currency held by the public, then we have:

$$D = \frac{1}{b}(C - C_p) \tag{4.4}$$

However, if it is assumed that people's holding of currency ratio, a, is fixed, then the bank deposit multiplier is given by

$$D = \frac{1}{a+b} C \tag{4.5}$$

If money supply (M) is given by

$$M = D + C_p \tag{4.6}$$

then

$$M = \frac{C}{a+b} + a\frac{C}{a+b} \tag{4.7}$$

or

$$M = \frac{1+a}{a+b} C \tag{4.8}$$

or

$$\Delta M = \frac{(1+a)}{a+b}\Delta C \tag{4.9}$$

It must be pointed out that the above equation simply states a process of adjustment between cash and deposits and it says nothing about causality.

Criticisms of the bank deposit multiplier theory

Several criticisms of the bank deposit multiplier (BDM) theory have been suggested.

First, it is assumed in the BDM theory that the banks cannot raise their cash reserves by their own effort. But if banks can raise their cash holdings, then obviously their lending ability would not be restricted by their reserves. Since the commercial banks can borrow from the central bank (which acts as the lender of the last resort) to replenish their cash-holdings, the fixed relationship between changes in money supply and changes in the cash-holdings may not always be valid. Also, as Furness observes, given the high priority assigned to the maintenance of stable employment or of interest rates in many countries, the central bank may adjust the bank reserves to changes in credit demand. Here 'the cash-base plays a passive rather than a causal role' (Furness, 1975).

Secondly, many LDCs experience as *shortage* of demand for credit either because of a lack of investment opportunities or because of the absence of credit-worthy securities. Also, since the economies of the LDCs usually exhibit seasonal fluctuations due to the production cycles in agriculture, it is possible to observe a clear division between the 'slack' and 'busy' periods during a year (see, for example, *Reserve Bank of India Bulletin*, monthly publication). In such cases, an increase in the cash base may not lead to an automatic rise in bank lending.

Thirdly, it is assumed in the BDM theory that the cash-holdings of the banks remain fairly stable. But such an assumption is not very realistic since the cash-base is generally exposed to the effects of changes in the balance or payments as well as to the oscillations in the public debt.

Fourthly, the BDM theory assumes a stable demand for currency by the members of the public. This may be true in the DCs where banking habits are well-developed. However in the LDCs banking habits are less stable. The ratio of currency to bank deposits is usually high (see in particular the cases of Ethiopia, Ghana, Malawi, Nigeria, Sierra Leone, Sudan, Tanzania, as reported by Furness, 1975, p. 104). The system of payment by cheques is rather restricted and people's demand for cash is high. Under such conditions the relationship between currency holdings and holdings of bank deposits by the public may not remain stable.

It is necessary to point out that the budgetary policies of the government has an important influence on changes in money supply. Similarly, exports and imports affect money supply significantly. In brief, changes in money supply (that is, bank deposits plus currency) will be equal to bank loans to the government *and* the private sector plus changes in the net foreign assets of banks; this in turn will be equal to public expenditure *minus* revenue (that is, tax) minus public borrowing from the private sector and from abroad plus the private sector deficit expenditure minus borrowing from the non-banking private sector and from abroad plus exports and borrowings from abroad minus imports (for details, see

Furness, 1975). It is, however, clear that the public sector borrowing requirement (PSBR) is one of the crucial factors which will influence money supply. Clearly, it is necessary to know the factors which govern the PSBR. The most important elements in determining the PSBR are public expenditure and taxation. The greater the amount of deficit finance, the greater will be the demand for credit and the higher will be interest rates. High rates of interest could reduce the demand for investment in the private sector. This is the 'crowding out' phenomenon since the demand for resources by the public sector 'may crowd' out the availability of resources for the private sector from the market.

Lending by the private sector also depends on the rate of interest. But other factors, like per capita income and social habits (for example, thriftiness), the existence of an array of financial assets and the degree of confidence in the finance institutions, also play a major role. Bank lending depends crucially upon rates of return on such lending, the degree of credit-worthiness and the degree of risk. Foreign private lending depends on the rate of profit, confidence in the stability of political institutions, the system of taxation and the foreign-exchange controls and regulations of the recipient countries. The demand for exports largely depends upon the ratio of domestic prices to foreign prices and the rate of exchange. Frequently, the currencies of LDCs are highly overvalued. In such cases, exports will be discouraged while imports will be encouraged. Imports are usually determined by the level of income and terms of trade. However, distortions like tariffs, quotas and exchange controls also play an important part in influencing imports by the LDCs. Since the capital market in LDCs is narrow, while the financial assets are limited and interest rate changes are unlikely to have a major impact on the economy, the volume of money in most LDCs would, therefore, be influenced mainly by the PSBR as well as credit demand by the private sector, the difference between exports and imports and the inflow of foreign funds.

4.3 The changing pattern of commercial banking in the LDCs

The pattern of commercial banking has undergone considerable changes in the LDCs in the past four decades. In the past, many commercial banks in the newly-independent LDCs used to emulate the orthodox British principles of commercial banking. They followed 'sound' banking principles and as such adhered to the 'self-financing' rules. Many commercial banks were owned by the ex-imperial countries. They used to be run by expatriates under the general supervision of their parent banks in the metropolis (London, Paris, and so on). Little attempt was made to distinguish between deposits obtained in the colonies and deposits obtained in the metropolis. The system led to the belief that funds were diverted from the colonies at the periphery to the imperial nations at the centre. It is also believed that the 'foreign' banks made no efforts to evaluate the credit-worthiness of indigenous investors in the light of the general economic backwardness of their economies and the principles guiding lending to customers were not very different in the centre and the periphery. It is also contended that these banks used to lend in order to promote the trading and commercial interests of the metropolis without much regard to the colonies' need for economic development. Accordingly, commercial bank loans were advanced only for the short-term. These loans used to be risk-free as they were generally self-liquidating. The commercial bank loans were secured by physical goods. Sometimes bank loans facilitated movements of goods from one place to another and since repayments were fairly automatic after the sale of such goods, the nature of the self-liquidating principle is easy to understand. This principle is also known as the 'real bills doctrine'.

The commercial banks did not always adhere to the 'real bills' doctrine, since it was particularly difficult to apply in time of depression when debtors failed to repay their debts. Gradually it was acknowledged that the liquidity of the banks really depended upon the holding of assets which could be sold or 'shifted' irrespective of the dates of their maturity. According to the 'shiftability theory', as long as the assets of the commercial banks can be 'shifted' for necessary liquidity, the banks can extend the period of lending. Clearly, the application of this principle would enable the commercial banks to engage in 'medium-term' lending.

'Term lending' by the commercial banks has witnessed a rapid expansion in the USA. The maturity of these types of loans varies between one to five years. Such loans are usually advanced against such collateral as stock and bonds, real estate, machinery and equipment. Loans are given in anticipation of future income from assets and hence 'term lending' is actually based on an anticipated income theory of liquidity.

The commercial banks in many LDCs at present engage in 'term lending'. In some Latin-American countries (for example, Guatemala), the commercial banks are allowed to grant loans for a period that varies between one to three years. In Korea, the commercial banks are allowed to undertake both traditional commercial banking and long-term financing operations.

The commercial banks in India have shown considerable interest in the provision of hire-purchase finance (Basu and Ghosh, 1974). Some banks in India have granted hire-purchase finance of small companies. Others have granted personal loans to their customers so that they can acquire consumer durables.

With the growth of the LDCs it has been observed that the structure of commercial bank lending has changed in favour of industry and at the expense of commerce (for example, Ghana, India, Libya; see Basu and Ghosh, 1974). Usually the commercial banks have paid very little attention to the huge agricultural sector in the LDCs. It is true that the commercial banks in the LDCs provided loans to traders in agricultural goods and contributed to the debentures of the central land development banks. But the beneficiaries of the lending by the commercial banks were mostly the plantation estates and large commercial farmers. Direct financing of agriculture by commercial banks posed numerous problems because of the long gestation period in the return on agricultural investment, the large fluctuations in agricultural prices and income, the absence of proper records of land ownership and of other 'credit-worthy' collateral.

In India, the major commercial banks were nationalised in 1969. One of the main arguments in favour of such nationalisation was that the commercial banks had neglected the agricultural sector in the past. It is true that in India the commercial banks' lending to agriculture did not exceed 2 per cent of their total volume of lending at any time before 1969. After the nationalisation of the fourteen major commercial banks, direct financing to agriculture by such banks went up considerably. Between 1969 and 1990, the proportion of bank lending to agriculture went up from about 2 per cent to about 10 per cent (see Reserve Bank of India Bulletin, 1991). Also, the commercial banks in India are now required to assist the Agricultural Refinance Corporation of India as well as the Industrial Development Banks. Such measures are supposed to aid the balanced growth of agriculture and industry.

The above discussion makes it clear that the commercial banks in the LDCs have undergone a period of remarkable change and they are now playing a major role in promoting economic growth.

4.4 Rural money markets in LDCs

The rural money market in most LDCs is distinguished by its duality. Such a market may be divided into two broad sectors: organised and unorganised. The organised sector consists of the commercial banks, the rural banks, the co-operative banks, credit societies, government and semi-government agencies. The unorganised sector mainly consists of indigenous bankers, money lenders of various types, landlords, merchants and traders. Although specialisation has developed in the organised sector, such specialisation and division of labour is usually absent in the unorganised sector. Also, while the organised sector maintains accounts which are open to scrutiny, the accounts of the unorganised sector are not generally open to such inspection (for details see Ghatak, 1976).

The major characteristics of the unorganised money market may be briefly summarised as follows:

(a) secrecy about financial dealings;
(b) blending of money-lending with different types of economic activities, e.g., trading;
(c) flexibility of loan operations;
(d) personal and informal dealings with customers; and
(e) simple or crude system of maintaining accounts.

The existence of such financial dualism in the money market of the LDCs has had the following effects:

(i) It has reduced the size of monetary transactions and perpetuated non-monetary transactions.
(ii) It has restricted the growth of banks in the rural areas. This in its turn has diminished the use of bank credit.
(iii) The existence of the unorganised sector has deprived the economy of an array of financial assets with which savings could have been more effectively directed towards investment for realising a higher rate of economic growth.
(iv) The presence of financial dualism has perpetuated some ancient customs like gold hoarding which have prevented the use of available resources for productive investment. It may be pointed out that whether or not gold hoarding prevents productive investment depends upon the end use of the money so spent. It seems likely, however, that those who sell gold will not engage in 'productive' investment. However, if the gold is imported (legally or illegally) there is a definite *negative* effect on productive investment.
(v) The impact of monetary policy has been considerably weakened by the presence of the dichotomy in the rural money market.

The evidence suggests that the links between the organised and unorganised sectors are rather weak in most LDCs. The size of the unorganised market is probably declining very slowly in most LDCs. The flow of funds between the two sectors is still not great (Ghatak, 1976).

The empirical tests of links between the organised and unorganised sectors in the LDCs are imperfect. It is difficult to obtain reliable data on the assets and liabilities of the unorganised financial sector. Attempts have been made, however, to measure the growth of the organised money market by either the 'liquidity preference; or the 'loanable fund' method. Under the 'liquidity preference' method it is necessary to measure deposits as a proportion of the money supply. According to the 'loanable fund' method, claims are measured as a proportion of the national income. The former approach considers the matter from the liability side of the balance sheet of the banks and as such it really shows the growth of the banking sector. The latter approach treats the problem from the asset side where the ratio of the banking system's claims (that is , loans and advances plus bills discounted) on the private sector to national income is estimated (Wai, 1957; 1972). Further theoretical and empirical research in this area is badly needed in order to draw firm conclusions.

The task of promoting integration between the organised and unorganised money markets remains urgent for strengthening the efficacy of monetary policy in the LDCs. One of the important steps that could be taken to promote such integration would be to encourage the commercial banks to expand banking facilities in the rural areas. Another step would be to enable the co-operative banks to compete more effectively with money lenders and indigenous bankers. A third method would be to try to induce the indigenous financial agencies to operate within the organised market. The central banks in the LDCs could play a more effective role in realising these objectives. It is true that in the past the co-operatives in many LDCs have failed to weaken substantially the hold of the indigenous financial agencies on the rural money market. Nevertheless, a multi-agency approach seems to be a more appropriate way to promote linkages between the organised and unorganised money markets. It is well known that the instruments of intermediation used by the indigenous money lenders are such that they enable them to operate not only in finance but also in labour, land and product markets (Bardhan and Rudra, 1978). Naturally, the rural product and factor markets become interdependent rather than independent. Hence the multi-agency approach should not only consist of extending credit to the farmers but also include the promotion of trading and marketing operations to weaken the grip of the unorganised agencies on the rural money markets (see chapter 10).

4.5 Currency boards in Africa

The growth of banking and the currency system in Africa at the turn of the twentieth century can be traced back to the establishment of the African Currency Boards by the British government. For the West Africa colonies such as Gambia, the Gold Coast (now Ghana), Nigeria and Sierra Leone, the West African Currency Board was set up in 1912. Similarly, for the East African countries such as Kenya, Tanganyika (now Tanzania), Uganda and Zanzibar (now part of Tanzania), an East African Currency Board was set up in 1919; and a Central African Currency Board was set up to serve Rhodesia (now Zimbabwe and Zambia) and Nyasaland (Malawi).

These currency boards issued local currency at a given parity against sterling acquisitions from foreign trade. At the outset these local currencies were *fully* supported by sterling assets, though changes were introduced in subsequent years. The currency boards were also responsible for redeeming local currency in sterling on demand (Newlyn, 1967).

The major advantages of the currency boards can be stated briefly:

(i) They issued a medium of exchange to facilitate trade and transactions.
(ii) The local currency issued by the currency boards provided a satisfactory unit of account.
(iii) The currency issued by the boards promoted the financial confidence which is necessary for the growth of the economy.

The chief criticisms of the currency boards can be summarised as follows:

(i) Since the volume of currency was linked to the state of the balance of payments, the supply of money was reduced whenever the balance of payments was in the red. In other words, the economy had to deflated at a time of a deficit in the balance of payments. Similarly, with a surplus in the balance of payments, money supply was expanded. The major problem was that the supply of money became virtually exogenously determined and the authorities were unable to control it and thereby avoid some undesirable consequences.

(ii) Domestic finance was really governed by the vagaries of foreign trade and such a situation was considered unacceptable.

(iii) The financial system failed to promote the growth of the poor regions since it did not pay any attention to the allocation of funds for the backward regions.

(iv) The existence of currency boards deprived the different countries of 'monetary sovereignty', which they needed to pursue independent economic policies.

(v) The currency boards were also criticised because of the cost of the sterling reserves which had to be kept as currency backing. It has been contended that the LDCs of Africa could 'ill afford to hoard idle foreign exchange' (Newlyn, 1967, p. 33). Given the cost of the sterling reserves, this criticism has considerable validity.

With the independence of the African countries, the currency boards began to disappear. On balance, the currency boards had their demerits but they also performed some useful tasks in difficult conditions. Most African countries set up independent central banks to discharge the functions of the currency boards. These central banks were nationalized and they began to perform the traditional tasks of any other central bank. The establishment of these central banks in Africa (and Asia) symbolised national monetary sovereignty and economic as well as financial independence. They began to organise the domestic financial system and act as advisers to their governments. They now pursue independent monetary policies. they interesting point to stress is that they have shown concern for promoting economic growth and development of their countries and have taken active steps in such promotional activities.

5. Theories of money and economic growth

In Chapter 2 we saw that in the classical theory money does not play an important role in economic growth. The main function of the money supply is to determine the price level at which exchange will take place. The role of money is regarded as passive; it is simply to finance a certain level of transactions of goods and services. The improvement in the *financial system* is, however, regarded as a necessary condition for achieving a higher rate of growth, since a well-developed financial system plays a major role in mobilising saving and investment as well as allocating resources more efficiently.

Attempts have been made to introduce money into the neo-classical growth models. Money is usually defined here as 'outside' money which consists of currency, coins, that is 'fiat' money and bank money supported by government securities. The additional real balances, that is, M/P, are regarded as cash transfers to individuals. In a pioneering work, Tobin (1965) has examined the role of money in a neo-classical growth model. It was then developed and extended by Johnson (1967) and Levhari and Patinkin (1968). We shall examine the basic properties of the Tobin model. Next we will examine its implications for the LDCs. But, first, the Harrod–Domar growth model will be presented in a simple way to understand more clearly the monetary growth models.

5.1 A simple Harrod–Domar growth model

Following the analysis of Harrod and Domar, the actual growth rate of output of an economy (g) could be defined as

$$g = s/v \tag{5.1}$$

where s = S/Y
S = savings
Y = income
v = capital – output ratio or $\Delta K/\Delta Y$ or $I/\Delta Y$.
K = capital
I = investment
g = $\dot{Y}/Y$

The model can easily be stated. Let us assume a proportional saving function, i.e.

$$S = sY \tag{5.2}$$

Ignoring depreciation, let us assume that $\dot{K}$ or the rate of change in capital stock is equal to the flow of total investment (I) that is

$$\dot{K} = I \tag{5.3}$$

Now, given an accelerator type of relationship between capital and output and a fixed v, we can write

$$K = vY \tag{5.4}$$

$$\text{or} \quad \dot{K} = v\dot{Y} \tag{5.5}$$

By substitution, we have,

$$I = v\dot{Y} \tag{5.6}$$

Since equilibrium condition is $S = I$, therefore we have

$$sY = v\dot{Y} \tag{5.7}$$

$$\text{or} \quad \dot{Y}/Y = s/v \tag{5.8}$$

$$\text{since} \quad g = \dot{Y}/Y$$

$$\therefore \quad g = s/v \tag{5.9}$$

In a way, the above equation is a tautology since actual g will always be given by s/v. But to maintain the equilibrium between supply and demand, we need to look at the rate of labour or population growth, i.e., n or the natural growth rate. Hence, we must have, $g = s/v = n$ to maintain full employment equilibrium growth rate. But since s, v and n are determined independently of one another, it is only by chance that the above equation will be satisfied. This is the 'knife-edge' or the instability problem in the H–D analysis. It is generally known that to overcome the problem of instability, the neo-classical economists assumed that the capital–output ratio or v is flexible. Kaldor, on the other hand, tried to solve the problem of instability by assuming a flexible saving ratio. We shall confine our attention here to the neo-classical growth model and the effects of the introduction of money within such a model.

5.2 The neo-classical growth model

The neo-classical theory of growth is based upon the following assumptions (see, for example, Solow, 1956): (a) only one output (Y) is produced, which can either be consumed (C) or invested (I). This assumption clearly avoids problems of aggregation and the difference between savings and investment. Thus, $Y = C + I$.

(b) The stock of capital (K) does not depreciate and investment (I) is given by the incremental capital stock. Thus

$$I = \dot{K} \tag{5.10}$$

$$\therefore \quad S = \dot{K} \tag{5.11}$$

(c) It is assumed that the savings function is proportional, that is,

$$S = sY \tag{5.12}$$

By substitution, we then have

$$\dot{K} = sY \tag{5.13}$$

$$\text{since} \quad I = S$$

(d) The growth of labour force ($\dot{L}/L$) is given by exogenous forces. Thus,

$$\dot{L}/L = n \tag{5.14}$$

(e) Aggregate production (Y) is given by capital (K) and labour (L), that is

$$Y = f(L, K) \tag{5.15}$$

This production function is continuous and subject to the operation of constant returns to scale. Notice that it could also be written as

$$y = f(k) \tag{5.16}$$

where $y = Y/L$ and $k = K/L$. In other words, output per head is a function of capital per head. It is also assumed that $f'(k) > 0$, $f''(k) < 0$, $f(0) = 0$ and $f(\infty) = \infty$ (that is the marginal product of capital, $f'(k)$, is positive but diminishes as k rises; and no output could be produced without capital). These properties of the production function make it well-behaved.

Steady-state growth in the neo-classical model is attained by satisfying the following equation (see Jones, 1975; and Ghatak, 1995):

$$\dot{k} = sf(k) - nk \tag{5.17}$$

The first term on the LHS measures the rate of change of K/L or capital–labour ratio – which is given by the difference between savings or investment per head, that is, $sf(k)$, and the amount necessary to keep K/L fixed as the labour force increases. Clearly, the steady-state equilibrium will be obtained where $sf(k)$ is equal to nk. This is shown in figure 5.1. On the vertical axis, output per head (Y/L) is measured and on the horizontal axis, capital per head (K/L) is shown. The curve 0–$f(k)$ shows output per head as a function of capital per head. This production function is well-behaved. The curve 0–$sf(k)$ shows the relationship between savings per head and capital per head. The line 0–nk describes the *given* rate of growth of the labour force. The neo-

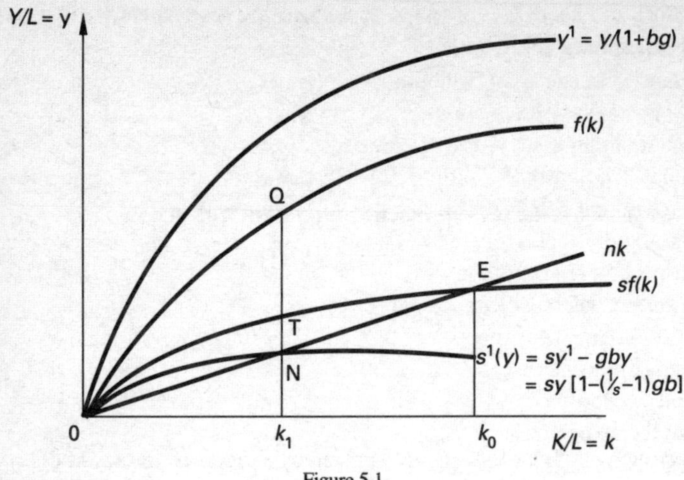

Figure 5.1

classicial condition for a steady-state growth rate is given by equation 5.17, $k = sf(k) - nk$, which implies that k should be equal to zero. This would happen when savings per head are equal to the amount necessary to maintain the increasing labour equipped with capital stock to leave $k = 0$. A fixed *K/L* will also imply a fixed *Y/L*. On the balanced growth path, therefore, the output growth rate is given by n, if *Y/L* is to remain fixed in the face of a growth of labour at the rate n. The existence of such a stable point is given at E in figure 5.1. To examine the stability at E, notice that at k_1 (which is less than k_0), output per head is k_1Q and savings per head is k_1T of which k_1N would be enough to equip new entrants in the labour market with the same capital per head as existing labourers. Hence *TN* would be available to raise capital per head. The *K/L* will eventually move to k_0. On the other hand, if the actual k is greater than k_0, savings will be inadequate to equip the extra workers with the same capital per worker as existing workers have and this will lead to a fall in *K/L* until k_0 is attained.

5.3 Money in a neo-classical growth model: the Tobin model

The effects of money on the economic activities within a neo-classical growth model was first shown by Tobin (1965). The work was then extended by Johnson (1967) and Levhari and Patinkin (1968). Here we shall discuss the Tobin model as formulated by Levhari and Patinkin.

Tobin argues that money affects the real disposal income (Y_D) which determines the level of consumption or saving. Let M be the quantity of money supplied, P the price level, μ the rate of change of money supply or $\dot{M}/M$, and $\pi = \dot{P}/P$, the rate of change in price level.

Then Y_D is given by

$$Y_D = Y + \frac{d(M/P)}{dt} = Y + \frac{M}{P}(\mu - \pi) \qquad (5.18)$$

Hence Y_D is given by real income (Y) plus the real value of the rise in the nominal quantity of money, that is, $\mu M/P$ minus the fall in the real value of the cash balances because of inflation, that is, $\pi(M/P)$. Tobin assumes that the government injects 'fiat' money by transfer payments. It is a debt to the government but an asset to the private sector. Hence we are concerned with 'outside' money. The costs of holding money are assumed to be small. The effect of an increase in real balance is shown by y^l in figure 5.1.

Let us assume that a given proportion(s) of disposal income is saved and a given proportion (λ) of income (Y) is held by individuals as real money balances. It is contended that λ is negatively related to the 'difference between what could have been earned from the holding of a unit of physical capital and what will be earned from the holding of real money balances', that is, the expected opportunity cost of holding these balances. If the expected and the actual rates of return are the same, this opportunity cost is given by $r + \pi$ where r is the real rate of interest. Note that $r + \pi$ is equivalent to Fisher's money rate of interest. It is assumed that

$$\lambda = \lambda(r + \pi) \tag{5.19}$$

$$\text{and} \quad \lambda'(\ ) < 0 \tag{5.20}$$

In equilibrium, the money rate of interest must be positive, that is, $-\pi < r$. The rate of capital accumulation in the Tobin model is given by the following:

$$\dot{K} = F(K, L) - (1 - s)\left[F(K, L) + \frac{M}{P}(\mu - \pi)\right] \tag{5.21}$$

Clearly, the second term on the RHS of the equation shows consumption. The demand for real money balances is given by

$$\frac{M^d}{P} = \lambda F(K, L) \tag{5.22}$$

which is equal to the supply of real balances, M/P, via rapid adjustment of the price level.

According to Tobin, the steady-state value of K/L, that is, k, is given by

$$\left[s - (1 - s)\lambda n\right] f(k) = nk \tag{5.23}$$

This could be illustrated in figure 5.1. $0y^l$ is the per capita disposable income which is given by the sum of output per head and the rise in real balances, the latter being given by output, the ratio of real balances to output, b, and the present growth rate, g. The amount of total savings available for physical investment is

$$s^l y = sy^l\left[1 - \left(\frac{1}{s} - 1\right)gb\right] \tag{5.24}$$

The proof is simple. Let $y = f(k)$ and disposable income y^1

$$y^1 = y(1+bg) \tag{5.25}$$

Savings will be sy^1. From this we must subtract savings devoted to raise real balances bgy, leaving real savings $s^1(y)$, that is,

$$s^1(y) = sy^1 \left[1 - bg\left(\frac{1}{s} - 1\right)\right] \tag{5.26}$$

This is shown in figure 5.1 by the line s^1y. The equilibrium is attained at a point where the line intersects kn. Notice that this point, N, shows lower capital intensity and lower level of output per head. The size of b, the planned ratio of real balances to income, will be larger the smaller the desired rate of price rise, or larger the desired rate of price fall, maintained by the government. Money is no longer neutral since the equilibrium growth rate is not independent of monetary policy. 'If the economy's saving behaviour causes it to overshoot the golden rule ratio of real investment (accumulation of material capital) to output, this can be counteracted by contraction of the money supply to generate a deflationary price trend.' (Johnson, 1977) There are, of course, limits to such deflationary policies. Similarly, it can be argued that *inflation* could be used to *raise* physical savings. Since real balances and physical capital are substitutes and since inflation reduces real balances, therefore, a rise in price level will raise capital and output per head.

Since the social cost of producing money is small, people could be induced to enlarge the holdings of M/P to the point where the marginal productivity of money is zero. As money competes with physical capital in the portfolios of the individuals, it is necessary to alter the money supply (M) in such a way that the rate of deflation is equal to the marginal product of capital. This can easily be illustrated. Let the production function be as follows:

$$Y = f(K, L, M/P) \tag{5.27}$$

Let the disposable income (Y_D) be the sum of real income (Y) plus the real balances (M/P). Therefore,

$$Y_D = Y + d(M/P)dt = Y + \left(\dot{M} - \dot{P}\right)M/P \tag{5.28}$$

Recall that savings (S) are a fraction (s) of Y, and $0 < s < 1$. Also, in the equilibrium, investment (I) would be equal to S. The change in capital stock (dK/dt) is equal to I. Hence,

$$dK/dt = f(K, L, M/P) - (1-s)Y_D \tag{5.29}$$

Substituting for Y_D,

$$dK/dt = sY + (s-1)\left(\dot{M} - \dot{P}\right)M/P \tag{5.30}$$

If $\dot{M} - \dot{P} > 0$ and $s - 1 < 0$, we obtain the curious solution that a rise in real balances *M/P* may reduce capital intensity or the real rate of investment as shown in figure 5.1, since s is given and savings can consist of *either* physical assets *or* real balances. In other words, real balances and physical capital are substitues and as such, a rise in real balances reduces equilibrium capital per head as well as output per head.

5.4 Problems in the application of neo-classical monetary growth theory to LDCs

It is difficult to apply the neo-classical growth theory to LDCs because of its ommisions of a number of major issues which are important in LDCs. These issues can be summarised as follows (see, in particular, McKinnon, 1973):

(a) the need for improving the quality of capital by lowering dispersion in rates of return (notice that these rates tend to vary significantly in the LDCs given their fragmented financial markets);
(b) the type of fiscal restraints on the authorities in manipulating the rate of capital accumulation;
(c) 'the extent to which real resources should be committed to the monetary system'.

Because of these omissions, McKinnon believes that the neo-classical theory, if applied to the LDCs, would yield misleading predictions regarding

(a) the substitution effect between real capital accumulation and *M/P*;
(b) the manipulation of inflationary tax to raise social savings (this point is pursued further in chapter 6);
(c) the independence of the rate of savings from monetary policy;
(d) the importance of the law of diminishing returns in the process of accumulation of capital;
(e) the generation of a determinate demand for money in imperfect financial markets where there are risks of default and the rates of return on financial and physical capital differ.

McKinnon points out that in the LDCs, people face upward-sloping and different supply curves for finance with constraints on borrowing. Under such circumstances, cash balances are required 'to intermediate between income and expenditure' and the demand for money is a rising function of $d - \dot{P}^*$, where d = nominal desposit rate and $\dot{P}^*$ = the expected rate of inflation (that is, real rates).

The economic policy derived from neo-classical theory could be biased in favour of inflation. Assume that the LDCs suffer from a scarcity of capital and their governments are too weak to manipulate tax policies to mobilise 'surplus' but they can generate inflation by increasing money supply. Clearly, inflation will lower the real rate of return on money balances. However since 'inflation is a taxation without representation', the government can utilise revenues from the inflationary tax to accumulate real capital in the public sector. Also, a fall in the real rate of return on money balances because of inflation may induce people to accumulate more *physical* rather than *financial* assets.

As against the above mentioned benefits, the *cost* of inflation is the fall in productivity because of a fall in the input of *M/P*. But given the degree of capital scarcity in the LDCs, 'the loss of transaction efficiency seems like a social cost well worth bearing as long as the inflation stops short of driving the economy to barter' (McKinnon, 1973, p.52). In fact, some writers exclude *M/P* as an input in the production function (Mundell, 1963; Tobin, 1965; Foley *et al.*, 1969), which suggests that there would be no reduction in productivity because of the use of an inflation tax to increase physical capital accumulation. In the light of such a model, the use of the inflation tax in Latin-American countries is not difficult to understand.

In the case of the Latin-American countries, a study by Harberger suggests that a ratio of 5:3 between the percentage rise in the supply of money and the rate of growth of output could be non-inflationary (Harberger, 1964). In other words, money supply could rise by 10 per cent annually when the real output grows by 6 per cent annually without generating any inflation, as the demand for money seems to rise per unit of output. In the case of Nigeria, it has been observed that given a certain rate of growth of output, a 5 per cent rise in the demand for money per unit of income would be consistent with the financing of a proportion of investment without engendering inflation (Bhambri, 1968). Empirically, it has been observed that the income elasticity of the demand for money in the LDCs is greater than that in the DCs. In addition, the ratio of money to income increases with a rise in income per head. The decline in velocity is statistically significant in most cases as long as the definition of money includes at least demand deposits (Ezekiel and Adekunle, 1969).

Inflation, then, has a dual effect on savings. It may *increase* the savings ratio via the real balance effect. But if the planned money–income ratio falls because of inflation, the ratio of savings would fall should a proportion of the additional money balances be spent.

Leaving aside the case of hyperinflation, some evidence suggests that the velocity is not significantly affected by inflation (Cagan, 1956; Melitz and Correa, 1970). It has been shown that between 1950 and 1969 for some Latin-American countries the elasticities of income velocity with regard to inflation varied between 0.07 and 0.12 (Hanson and Vogel, 1973). Since these elasticities are rather low, it has been suggested that the inflation tax can be used effectively since 'it seems unlikely that the decline in saving from a reduction in money-income ratio would more than offset the receipts from the inflation tax' (Thirlwall, 1974). On the other hand, Newlyn's study suggests that velocity in LDCs *is* usually responsive to inflation (Newlyn, 1977).

There is some evidence to suggest a positive relationship between growth in the rate of output and the rate of increase in money supply in some countries of Asia. The 'optimum rate of growth of the money supply' is regarded as 17 per cent annually for the Asian countries. Any attempt to expand money supply beyond 17 per cent annually could lead to inflation. For the Latin-American countries, the linear relationship between the output growth rate (y) and the rate of money supply growth (m), that is $y = a + bm$, shows a negative (but statistically insignificant) relation. When a quadratic function was used to estimate the relationship ($y = a + bm - cm^2$) the 'optimum rate of growth of the money supply' was found to be 16.5 per cent annually (Fan, 1970). However, the proportion of explained variation in y was only 26 per cent ($r^2 = 0.26$) and as such, the predictive power of the model must be regarded as poor. It can also be pointed out that it was assumed in Fan's study that the money supply is an independent variable and y is the dependent variable. Such a specification would be unacceptable to those who believe that the line of argument should be exactly opposite – that money supply adjusts to changes in output and m should therefore be the dependent rather than the explanatory variable. Hence, it is necessary to exercise caution in accepting the conclusions of Fan's study. In a similar study of forty-three countries between 1956 and 1965, Wallich found a peaked relationship between y and m and the 'optimum' rate of money supply was found to be 28 per cent (Wallich, 1969)! Clearly, the policy implication of this finding could be called into question.

When M/P was included as a separate variable in a production function study to explain the output growth rate in the USA, for a period between 1929 and 1967, the effect of real balances on growth was found to be positive and statistically significant (Sinai and Stokes, 1972). Similar studies for the Latin-American countries also suggest that inflation reduces the real level of demand, time, and savings deposits, which in its turn adversely affects capital formation and growth (Vogel and Buser, 1976; see also chapter 6).

As regards to the neo-classical prediction that an increase in the money–income ratio will reduce capital-intensity and output growth rate, it can be mentioned that the empirical evidence suggests the opposite; the relationship between the savings ratio and the money–income ratio in the long run is found to be *positive*. The contradiction arises partly because of the neo-classical assumption of a fixed propensity to save and partly due to the omission of the fact that money is both a consumption and producers' good. A fixed propensity to save follows from the assumption that there are two assets and it implies that physical assets and M/P must be substitutes. Hence whenever there is a rise in the holdings of money balances, investment and capital intensity declines. An increase in the real rate of return on physical assets (r) relative to the real rate of return on money-holdings (that is, $d - \dot{P}^*$ or the deposit rate minus the expected rate of inflation) will reduce the demand for money. Similarly the demand for money will rise if $d - \dot{P}^*$ rises. The substitution between physical and financial assets thus plays a crucial role in the prediction of neo-classical theory.

It has been argued by McKinnon (1973) that the demand for real and financial capital could be *complementary* rather than substitutes to one another in the LDCs. Such a line of argument would lead to conclusions which are different to those drawn in the neo-classical theory. Later we will discuss the McKinnon model.

5.5 Economic growth and the role of financial intermediaries

Financial intermediaries (FIs) generally consist of commercial banks, co-operative credit societies, building societies and housing loan associations, insurance companies, merchant banks, etc. They act as halfway-houses between the primary lender and the final borrowers. They accept deposits from the public and pay deposit rates. Thus the FIs issue their own liabilities to obtain funds from the public (for example, savings deposits, and so on). The FIs then lend these funds to investors. The difference between the lending and the borrowing rates are the profits of the FIs. The FIs cal also buy bonds and stocks with the acquired funds.

One of the important consequences of the growth of the FIs is that it reduces hoarding. Secondly, the FIs promote savings and investment habits among ordinary members of the public who lack adequate knowledge and information about investment behaviour. It may be pointed out that if the primary savers decide to lend to the final borrowers directly, then the opposite of financial intermediation will take place. It will mean *dis-intermediation* or a reduction of indirect finance.

Reflection suggests that the FIs are in a better position than ordinary people to incur the risks associated with the ownership of primary securities. The FIs can diversify their asset structure to minimise the risk in portfolio-holdings. They can appoint experts to undertake rational holding of such portfolios. They can also enjoy economies of scale by reducing the administrative costs through bulk buying and selling of bonds and shares. In bearing the risks for the individuals, the FIs render valuable service to the community. In short, the activities of the FIs open up safe channels of saving and investment which are vital for promoting economic growth. Economic growth needs more investment. Investment depends, among other things, upon the cost of borrowing or interest rates. To the extent that the growth of the FIs reduces risks and diminishes the rate of interest (or prevents its substantial rise), investment is expected to rise. Growth in developed countries has been significantly associated with the growth of the FIs. The role of the FIs has been particularly emphasised in the Gurley–Shaw thesis (1960). We shall now discuss the basic characteristics of this thesis.

5.6 The Gurley–Shaw model

It has been argued by Gurely and Shaw (1960) that the savings deposits of the different types of FIs are more or less the same as the demand deposits of the commercial banks because it is not really difficult to convert the savings deposits of the FIs into cash or demand deposits. In other words the savings deposits held by the FIs are *liquid* and they may be classified as *near-monies*.

Since near-monies are not conrolled by the central bank, it therefore follows the presence of these near-monies will frustrate a successful operation of the monetary policy. If the central bank wants to follow a tight money policy and reduces money supply, it will not automatically reduce liquidity since *near-*

monies could be converted into cash to replenish the depleted stock of liquidity. In other words, a reduction in money supply will not by itself be adequate to reduce the amount of liquidity in the economy. Clearly, this will be aggravated during an inflationary situation.

Figure 5.2 illustrates the problem. The demand for (M_d) and the supply of money (M_s) are measured on the horizontal axis and the rate of interest (r) is measured on the vertical axis. The initial equilibrium r is r_0 where $M_d = M_s$. Let the central bank cut M_s by a certain amount. This action will shift the M_s curve to the left to M_{s1} and at the new point of equilibrium , E_1, r will rise to r_1. Such a rise in r enables the FIs to raise their deposit rates which leads to a reduction in M_d by the public. The M_d curve will then shift to the left, to M_{d1} from M_d. The new equilibrium r will now be r_2 which is less than r_1. Thus the stringent effect of a rise in r has been diminished because of the activities of the FIs.

The weakness of the operation of monetary policy because of the growth of the FIs received considerable attention during the late 1950s and early 1960s in the USA. The Radcliffe Committee in the UK also held the view that the centre-piece of monetary mechanism was not the supply of money but the structure of liquidity (see chapter 1). There was some discussion regarding the measures that the Central Bank should adopt to deal with the FIs.

Events during the 1960s and the 1970s in the USA, however, took a different turn. Instead of a growth of financial intermediation, financial dis-intermediation occurred. Many members of the public withdrew funds from their deposit accounts and began to lend *directly* to investors by buying primary securities. The FIs found that their deposit rates were no longer competitive enough to

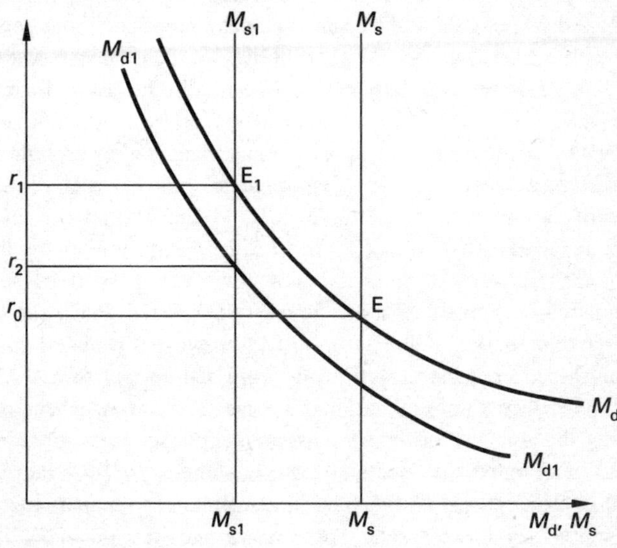

Figure 5.2

attract funds. The FIs could have raised the deposit rates as well as the lending rates, but in the USA they did not, primarily because they could not afford to raise rates.

The second reason was that the Federal Reserve System (FRS) imposed ceilings on deposit rates (Regulation Q). The rationale behind Regulation Q is simple. To enforce a tight monetary policy, a ceiling on the deposit rates of the FIs will induce individuals to withdraw their funds from the FIs and invest directly in primary securities. Banks, after being starved of funds, would be required to reduce their expansion of credit. Such a reduction will render monetary policy more effective.

The above experience of the DCs suggests that the Gurley–Shaw thesis may have more interesting implications for analysing the process of economic development rather than the formulation of stabilisation policies.

5.7 Economic development and 'financial accumulation'

Gurley and Shaw contend that in the course of economic growth, as per capita income rises, countries generally witness a rate of growth of financial assets which exceeds the rate of growth of output or real income. These financial assets generally include all intangible assets – claims against both non-financial spending units (primary securities) and financial institutions (indirect securities). In the USA the ratio of financial assets to GNP stood at unity at the end of the last century; by the end of the 1960s it was about 4.5. In Japan, it rose from 10 per cent in 1885 to over 150 per cent in 1966. By contrast this ratio is very low in low-income countries; for example, 10–15 per cent for Afghanistan and Ethiopia by 1966–7. For some middle-income countries such as Argentina, Brazil, Mexico, Venezuela, Korea (South), the ratio varied between 30 and 60 per cent. India seems to be an exception among the low-income countries with a ratio of around 35 per cent by 1966–7. It appears as though difference in per capita income is strongly correlated with differences in the ratio of financial assets to GNP.

The reasons for this secular rise in financial accumulation with growth could be explained in different ways. For one thing, financial growth crucially hinges upon a division of labour that is possible only in the framework of real development. The way specialisation, or division of labour, promotes the development of the size and form of financial assets via the growth of saving, investment and financial intermediation has already been stated. For another, the growth of the financial market depends upon the growth of demand for and supply of financial assets; but the growth of demand and supply forces significantly depend upon the growth of real national income. This is partly because the savings elasticity of the demand for financial assets is supposed to be greater than one. Though the real interest rate declines with economic growth and rise in savings, the trend rates of returns on financial assets remains so high as to generate significant *demand* for these assets. These trend rates are generally determined by economies of scale, technical progress and so on. The growth of the financial sector, in its turn, stimulates savings, bringing about a more rational allocation of resources and economising on the transfer of savings to investment.

It is necessary to point out that the differences in the ratios of financial assets to income in different countries depend on both the *levels* of real income and their *rates of growth*. Sometimes, instability in real income growth rate could be an important factor in accounting for differential finance/income ratios (*F/Y*). A high rate of inflation could also adversely affect the growth of *F/Y*. Historical forces, convention and the legal system can also influence the growth of *F/Y*[1] (see note at the end of this chapter).

Differences in the financial structures can be observed among countries with similar levels of income. This could be explained mainly by the differences in the effectiveness of alternative techniques for mobilising financial surplus. The main financial instrument for mobilising such surplus is the debt–asset system.

Two major instruments of finance could be mentioned here: (a) internal finance, that is when the investor uses his own savings; (b) external finance, that is when the investor uses the savings of others. Internal finance usually consists of self-finance and taxation. 'In self-finance, savings are put at the investors' disposal by adjustment in relative prices on commodity and factor markets and on markets for foreign exchange. The taxation technique employs taxes and other non-market alternatives to channel savings to the state for either governmental or private investment' (Gurley and Shaw, 1967).

The principal instrument of *external* finance is the debt–asset system, which mobilises domestic savings into investment. Foreign loans, aid and gifts could also be classified as external finance. The rate of interest plays an important role in external finance as it influences the rate and direction of investment.

In socialist countries, relative prices or terms of trade play a significant role in internal finance. Indeed, some countries have used a deliberate change in terms of trade to enforce involuntary savings upon target sectors (for example, upon agriculture as opposed to industry in the USSR after the revolution of 1917). In this context, inflation could also be regarded as an instrument of self-finance. The 'structuralists' or the supporters of the 'cost-push' theory of inflation argue that since the 'first-best' theory fails in the LDCs because relative price changes tend to move perversely for purposes of development, inflation should be deliberately used as a 'second-best' policy to prevent a reduction of savings through consumption or unemployment. The role of inflation in promoting savings and growth will be discussed in chapter 6.

5.8 Financial repression and economic growth: the McKinnon and Shaw model

The basic features of the McKinnon and Shaw model (1973) can be illustrated with the help of figure 5.3. Let the *real* rate of interest be measured on the vertical axis and the investment and saving be measured on the horizontal axis. Let saving (*S*), at different income levels (Y_0, Y_1, Y_2...), be a function of the real rate of interest. Let investment (I) be an inverse function of the real interest rate. In a free market without any financial constraint (C), r_e will be the equilibrium real interest rate where $S_e = I_e$. But because of a financial constraint or 'repression', the institutional interest rate is given by r' which is less than the free market equilibrium real rate, r_e. The amount of actual investment is constrained to I_a because of the limited saving that is available at r'.

If the monetary authorities decide to ease the financial repression and raise the real rate from r' to r'', both saving and investment will rise. The low yielding investment activities, as indicated by the shaded area in the diagram will be eliminated and the overall efficiency of investment will increase. This will lead to a rise in income and savings and hence the saving curve will shift to the right to SY_1. Actual investment will rise I'_a. If the monetary authorities are bold enough to abolish financial repression altogether and decide to dispense with the ceilings on the interest rate, then the level of actual saving and investment will rise further leading to a further expansion of income. The model thus implies that an increase in the real rate of interest will induce the savers in the LDCs to save more, which will enable more investment to take place. This will raise the rate of growth of the economy. It is in this context that Shaw contends that saving, investment and financial intermediation would be suboptimal when the real rate of interest is arbitrarily fixed at a point which is much lower than its equilibrium level. Financial intermediaries, in this context, render a valuable service in raising the real rate of return to savers and in lowering the real costs to investors by providing liquidity and information. They also reduce the risks by diversifying the asset structure.

The McKinnon model rests on the following assumptions: (a) all economic agents are restricted to self-finance; (b) there are important indivisibilities in invest-

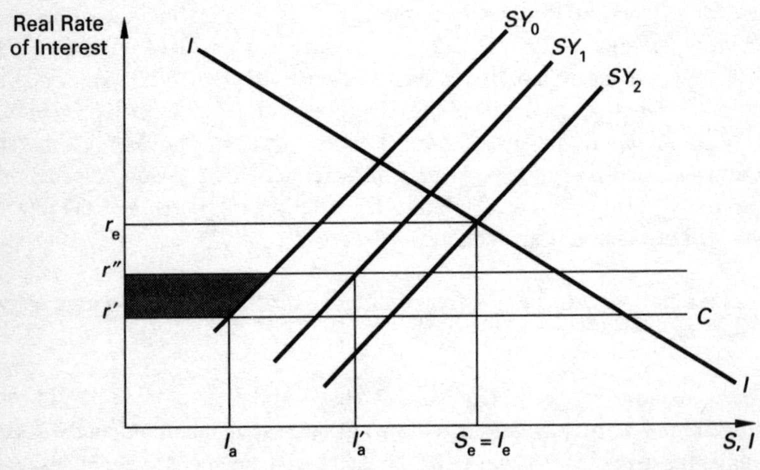

Figure 5.3

ment activities. Before undertaking actual investment, the potential investors must accumulate money balances. The higher the real interest rate, the greater will be the accumulation of money balances and the larger will be the inducement to invest. The indivisibility in investment means that the aggregate demand for money will be larger, the greater the ratio of investment to total expenditure. Hence McKinnon puts forward a hypothesis related to the basic complementarity between money and physical capital 'in contrast to the traditional theory where a substitution relationship is assumed' (McKinnon, 1973, p. 59). This complementarity is given in the following demand-for-money function:

$$\left(\frac{M}{P}\right)^d = f\left(\frac{I}{Y}, \frac{Y}{P}, d - \dot{P}*\right) \tag{5.31}$$

where

	M/P	=	the real money stock
	I/Y	=	the ratio of investment to output
	$d - \dot{P}*$	=	the real deposit rate of interest
since	d	=	the nominal interest rate on deposits
and	$\dot{P}*$	=	the expected future rate of inflation
	P	=	the price level.

McKinnon argues that 'conditions that make *M/P* attractive to holdings are normally the result of the monetary system's maintaining a high and stable real return to the holders of money. This complementarity leads to policy conclusions about inflationary finance, and about deposit rates of interest for accelerating development, that are quite different from the corpus of accepted monetary theory' (McKinnon, 1973, p. 40).

McKinnon's complementarity hypothesis could also be stated in the following investment function (see, for example, Fry, 1988),

$$I/Y = f\left(r,\ d - \dot{P}*\right) \tag{5.32}$$

where r = average rate of return to physical capital.

To show the complementarity, we have

$$\frac{\partial (M/P)}{\partial (I/Y)} > 0 \quad \text{and} \quad \frac{\partial (I/Y)}{\partial \left(d - \dot{P}*\right)} > 0 \tag{5.33}$$

If domestic saving is equal to investment, we have

$$(M/P)^d = f\left(Y/P,\ S_d/Y,\ d - \dot{P}*\right) \tag{5.34}$$

It has been pointed out by Shaw (1973) that the removal of financial repression via an increase in the real interest rate will provide greater incentives to save and invest and lead to a more efficient allocation of resources. Thus the demand-for-money function in Shaw's analysis, as shown below, is similar to that of McKinnon:

$$(M/P)^d = f\left(Y/P,\ c,\ d - \dot{P}^*\right) \tag{5.35}$$

where c = the opportunity cost of money holding.

In practice, the difference between real yield on government bonds (b) and $\dot{P}^*$, $b - \dot{P}^*$, is used as an estimate of c. Notice carefully that Shaw does not assume any complementarity between money and physical capital since investors do not simply depend upon own-finance.

A statistical estimate of McKinnon's demand function for money in terms of a two-stage least square with dummy variables for ten Asian countries has yielded the following result (Fry, 1978):

$$m = -2.129 - 0.752(S_d/Y) + 0.664(y^*) + 1.883\left(d - \dot{P}^*\right) + 0.726m - 1$$

$$t = (-4.93) \quad (-2.11) \qquad (5.33) \qquad (8.82) \qquad (14.23)$$

(5.36)

$$R^2 = 0.995, \qquad F = 1461, \qquad n = 123$$

where y^* = real per capita permanent income in natural logarithms (which was found to be a better explanatory variable than actual income)
$\dot{P}^*$ = expected inflation
d = nominal deposit rate of interest
m = demand for per capita real money balances shown in natural logarithms.

Since the coefficient of the saving ratio is negative, it can be said that the complementarity hypothesis of McKinnon has been refuted on the basis of Fry's statistical estimation. 'Instead of higher average money balances held for domestically financed investment than for consumption, the reverse result is found.' Investment in 'semi-industrial LDCs' has not been regarded as self-financed and it is argued that money is not the only financial repository of domestic savings because enterprises accumulate non-monetary assets. The substitution between money and other financial assets has been shown in the negative co-efficient of $b - \dot{P}^*$ in the OLS estimate of Fry.

However, the complementarity hypothesis in the demand for money has been strongly supported in other empirical studies conducted so far. Vogel and Buser (1976) have shown that for Latin-American countries 'the negative impact of inflation on the ratio of time and savings deposits to gross domestic product is not only highly significant but also approximately unit elastic' (Vogel and Buser, 1976, p. 53). Since the ratio of savings to gross domestic product and capital formation has been found to be directly and significantly correlated, the above study by Vogel and Buser would strongly uphold the complementarity hypothesis. Clearly, further research is necessary to deduce firm conclusions.

As argued by McKinnon and Shaw, the real rate of interest ($d - \dot{P}^*$) exerted a positive and significant effect on domestic saving and economic growth in some Asian LDCs. This result would support the emphasis given by McKinnon and Shaw on the importance of improving financial conditions by ending 'financial repression' (see Fry, M., 1988).

Note

For the application of the Gurley–Shaw model to the Puerto Rican economy, see Rita Maldonada (1970–1). The results of the econometric model of the writer seems to have confirmed the hypothesis that the supply of funds by the financial sector has significantly influenced the level of investment in Peurto Rico. The estimated coefficient of the entire financial sector's supply of long-term funds is 2.4 in the non-housing investment function and 1.1 in the investment-in-housing function. These estimated co-efficients are significant at the 0.01 per cent level. The tests of author also confirm that the public financial sector has had most influence on non-housing investment and that the private financial sector had most significant influence on housing investment. Clearly, the results suggest that public financial activities have played a more important role in the economic growth of Peurto Rico than have the activities of the private financial sector. For the exploration of a cause-and-effect relationship see Bennett (1965).

Appendix to Chapter 5

A neo-structuralist view of monetary growth and development – Van Wijnbergen–Taylor model (1982–3)

Neo-structuralists' models are based on the following premises that differ fundamentally from the basic assumption of the McKinnon–Shaw type of analysis:

(i) Wages are determined institutionally or exogenously.
(ii) Inflation is determined by the relative strengths of capitalists and workers.
(iii) Saving takes place only out of profits; wage-earners do not save.
(iv) The price level is determined by a fixed mark-up, the cost of labour, import costs and the cost of working capital (that is, the interest rate).
(v) LDCs have a critical need for imports of raw materials, capital equipment and intermediate goods.
(vi) 'Curb' markets, in which money lenders and indigenous banks intermediate between savers and investors, play a crucial role in the neo-structuralist models of developing economics. Because of reserve requirements, neo-structuralists claim that banks cannot intermediate as efficiently as 'curb' markets between savers and investors.

(vii) Neo-structuralists assume that funds flow freely between the organised banking system and the 'curb' markets; savers and investors can generally use both markets. Hence, the relevant interest rate in the neo-structuralists' models is the curb market rate because it represents the marginal cost of borrowing and enters the money demand function.

Any increase in the curb market rate raises the price level because a rise in the curb market rate increases the cost of working capital and reduces output by reducing investment. An increase in the deposit rate of interest may raise the curb market rates and so depress the rate of economic growth if it reduces the total supply of working capital supplied by both the banking system and the curb market.

Van Wijnbergen–Taylor model: 1983

This model stresses the importance of incorporating the 'curb' rate of unorganised money markets in monetary models of developing countries and analyses the effects of financial liberalisation.

Households allocate their real wealth, *W* between currency *CC*, time deposits *TD* and direct loans to the business sector through the curb market *LS*, all expressed in real terms:

$$CC = ft(\pi, i, rtd, Y)W$$

$$TD = ftd(\pi, i, rtd, Y)W$$

$$L_h^s = fL(\pi, i, rtd, Y)W$$

where π = inflation rate
i = nominal curb market rate of interest
rtd = real time deposit rate of interest
Y = real income
L_h^s = supply of loans by households in real terms.

Demand for *CC* and *TD* are positively related to *Y*; households' supply of funds to curb market is negatively related to *Y*, given level of *W*.

Cash base is created through transfer payments. Banks supply loans in real terms (L_b^s) to the business sector depending on their demand for excess reserves, the level of deposits and the required reserve ratio.

$$L_b^s = b(\pi, rL)q.TD$$

where rL = banking lending rate in real terms; q = required reserve ratio.

The normal lending rate is fixed by the government below equilibrium level. The firm's demand for loans (*Ld*) is determined by real product wage *W* and output.

$$Ld = L(W, Y)$$

Loan demand is completely inelastic with respect to the curb market interest rate. Equilibrium in the curb market is given by:

$$fL(\pi, i, \ rtd, \ Y)W = L(W, Y) - [b(\pi, rL)q \ TD + ftd(\pi, i, \ rtd, \ Y)W]$$

Differentiation of the above expression will give the *LM* curve. Output is given by the Keynesian output equation:

$$Y = A(i, \ \pi, Y) \quad Ai < 0, \quad 0 < AY < 1$$

Differentiation of the above equation will give the *IS* curve. Any change in *TD* has no effect on the *IS* curve (goods market). However, it has two effects on the *LM* curve (money market): (i) A higher *TD* rate increases money demand and shifts the *LM* upwards; (ii) Agents substitute out of *CC* into *TD*; money supply changes and the *LM* shifts to the left.

The net shift in the *LM* curve depends on the required reserve ratio and the relative elasticities of demand for currencies and curb market rates with respect to the *TD* rate (see figure 5.A1). From his model, Wijnbergen shows that a tight monetary policy reduces output growth rate by squeezing total credit availability.

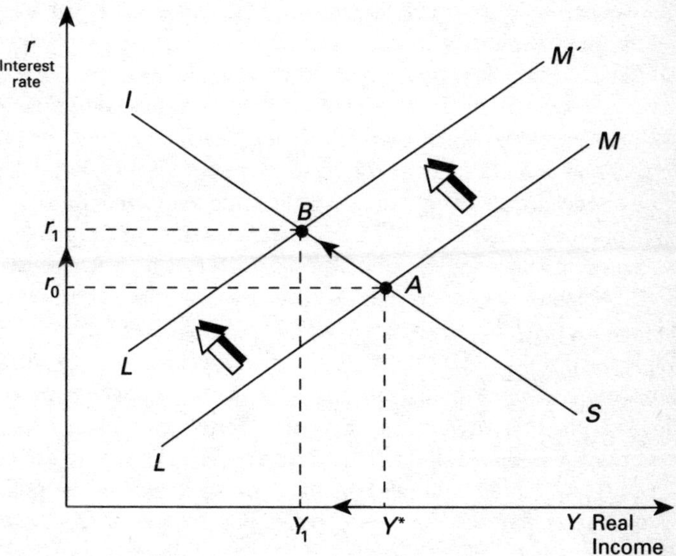

Figure 5.A1 The structuralist view of the impact of interest rate liberalisation in LDCs. The economy moves from $A \rightarrow B$ as $r_0 \rightarrow r_1$. Real income falls from $Y^* \rightarrow Y_1$.

6. Money, inflation and growth

In chapter 4 it was shown that it is possible that changes in the equilibrium rates of growth of the money supply may influence real variables in the economy, specifically the capital–labour ratio. However, the analysis involved a high level of abstraction and it is the purpose of this chapter to examine the causes and effects of inflation in developing countries in a more realistic context. The first section presents some evidence regarding the characteristics of inflation in developing countries, the second section examines causes of inflation and the third and fourth sections consider some of the possible consequences for growth.

6.1 Characteristics of inflation in developing countries

It is often claimed that developing countries are particularly prone to inflation and that they experience noticeably higher rates than do developed countries. In fact, there are great variations in the mean rates in inflation in the developing world, and outside Latin America very high rates of inflation are the exception rather than the rule. Even in Latin America, there are countries such as Guatamala and Venezuela which have experienced extremely low rates of inflation in the post-war period. Vogel (1974, p. 103) presents data showing that in the period 1950–69 mean rates of inflation in Latin America varied between 0.3 per cent per annum in El Salvador and 43.0 per cent per annum in Uruguay.

Table 6.1 presents data for the period 1972–6 from which it is clear that if Argentina, Chile and Uruguay are ignored that average inflation rates, although higher than in industrial countries, have not been of such magnitude as to justify the belief that the developing world is characterised by very high inflation rates.

The same source from which table 6.1 is drawn also presents data for the period 1967–72, and in a sample of seventy-eight developing countries, fifty-one had inflation rates over this period of 5 per cent or less and a further nineteen had rates between 5 and 10 per cent per annum. However, it should be pointed out that in 1976–7, forty-five developing countries in a sample of 86 had inflation rates of over 10 per cent. Cole (1976, pp. 146–7) in a study of the period 1960–72 presents data on trend rates of inflation for a large number of countries. In a group of ten developed countries, the rate varied from 2.90 per cent in Germany to 5.87 per cent for Denmark. Thirty-four less-developed countries had rates varying from 0.74 per cent for Guatamala to 4.57 per cent for Ecuador. A group of six countries categorised as having very high rates of inflation showed rates ranging from 21.28 per cent for Argentina to 77.67 per cent for Indonesia (the latter rate applying to the period 1963–72).

Table 6.1 Non-oil developing countries: inflation rates, 1972–76

	1972	*1973*	*1974*	*1975*	*1976*
1. Average rate of inflation (per cent)[1]					
a) Overall	13.5	22.1	33.0	32.9	32.3
b) Adjusted to exclude three countries with exceptionally high rates[2]	7.9	13.1	24.6	17.2	15.7
2. Number of countries included					
a) Total	87	87	87	87	88
b) With inflation (by comparison with preceding year)					
accelerating	41	68	71	23	17
decelerating	13	11	9	47	62
remaining unchanged	33	8	7	17	9
3. a) Number of countries with inflation rates of 10 per cent or more	17	50	78	63	42
b) Number with inflation rates below 10 per cent	70	37	9	24	46
4. Reference items:					
a) Average rate of inflation[1] in the industrial countries (per cent)	4.5	7.5	12.7	10.7	7.7
b) Difference between adjusted average rate of inflation in non-oil developing countries (line 1b) and average rate in the industrial countries (line 4a)	3.4	5.6	11.9	6.5	8.0

[1] As represented by weighted geometric means of consumer price indexes expressed in terms of national currency. Weights are proportional to gross domestic product (GDP) or gross national product (GNP) in US dollars, in the preceding year.
[2] Argentina, Chile and Uruguay.
Source: Lin and Siddique (1978)

To return to table 6.1, we can also note another important feature of developing-country experience. Not only are average rates of inflation different between countries, but the rate of inflation tends to vary from one year to another. Steady rates of inflation are the exception rather than the rule and this should caution us against drawing too many unqualified conclusions from models predicated upon a comparison of steady inflation rates.

It turns out that there is a statistically significant relation between the year-to-year variability of inflation rates (measured by their standard deviation) and their average level (Logue and Willett, 1976; Cole, 1976, p. 153). This feature of inflationary experience will be of some importance when we turn to consider the consequences of inflation in section 6.3; since it means that expectations about the future course of inflation are rarely, if ever, held with anything like certainty and that expectations are frequently not realised.

6.2 The causes of inflation

When one turns to a discussion of the causes of inflation in developing countries one finds that the literature contains two major competing hypotheses (or groups of hypotheses) which attempt to explain the phenomenon. First, there is the monetarist model which sees inflation as essentially a monetary phenomenon the control of which requires as a necessary and sufficient condition control of the money supply in such a way that it grows at a rate consistent with the growth of demand for money at stable prices. The structuralist model, by contrast, argues that the causes of inflation must be sought in certain structural characteristics of developing economies which make them particularly inflation-prone and that elimination of inflation, except at the cost of widespread recession, requires that policy be directed toward removing the various structural bottlenecks which are said to initiate and perpetuate inflation. These models will now be examined in turn and some attempt made to evaluate attempts to test them.

The monetarist model is predicated upon the existence of a stable demand function for *real* money balances. These balances are demanded for transactions and precautionary purposes and their level is postulated to be a function of the level of real income in the economy and of the opportunity-cost of holding money instead of alternative assets which could satisfy the precautionary and, perhaps also, the transactions motives. In addition, monetarists postulate that the money supply is exogenous and can be controlled by the monetary authorities.

The main opportunity-costs of holding money are the rates of interest available on other assets such as bonds and the rate of inflation (strictly speaking, the expected rate of inflation). Inflation acts as a tax on the holding of money and encourages people to find ways of economising on their money holdings. Another way of expressing this would be to say that the rate of inflation measures the rate of return derived from holding goods rather than money. This view emphasises the idea that holding goods (for example, inventories of raw materials, land) is an alternative to holding money in wealth portfolios, and alternative which becomes more attractive the higher the rate of inflation. The demand relationship implied can be represented by a diagram such as figure 6.1. In this diagram the level of real money balances (M/P) is measured along the horizontal axis. It is assumed that money bears no interest (not necessarily true of bank deposits) so that the opportunity-cost of holding money when the rate of inflation is zero is equal to the real rate of interest, r. This can be assumed equal to the nominal rate of interest on bonds when the expected rate of inflation is zero. Positive rates of inflation ($\pi > 0$) lead to a reduction in real balances demanded. For example, if inflation is proceeding at the rate π_1, the level of real balances held will fall from $0(M/P)_1$ to $0(M/P)_2$.

Inflation in this model is a consequence of money supply expanding more rapidly than money demand. Money demand in real terms will grow as a consequence of rises in income for a given level of the real rate of interest. If money supply rises by more than demand, then expenditure on goods and

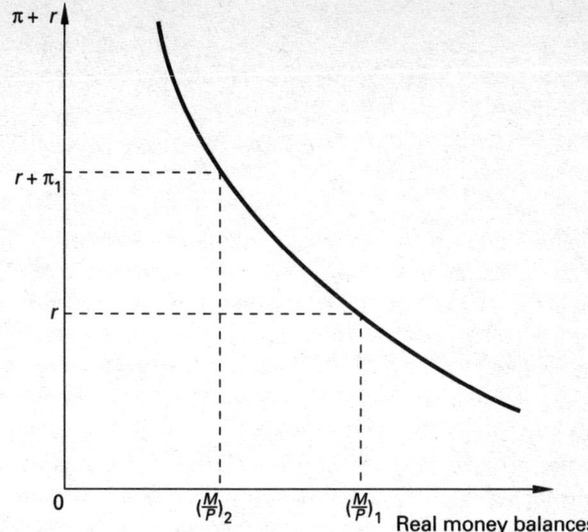

Figure 6.1

services will rise with a consequent rise in either output or prices. With the additional assumption that output is at or near to full capacity level, we get the direct relationship between money-supply changes and price-level changes as postulated in the famous quantity equation, $MV = PY$, where M is nominal money supply; V is the income velocity of circulation; P is an index of the general price level; and Y is real income. Velocity in this model is a function of per capita real income, the rate of inflation and possibly other variables.

A typical simple test of such a model is that carried out by Meiselman (1975, p. 82) on pooled data for sixteen Latin American countries in the period 1950–69. He estimates the following equation:

$$P' = a + bM' + cY'$$

where P' is the mean annual rate of inflation
M' is the mean annual money supply growth
Y' is the mean annual real income growth
He obtains the following results:

$$P' = 1.35 + 1.05M' - 1.38Y'$$
$$(0.57)\ (22.31)\quad (3.55)$$

$$R^2 = 0.98 \ (t \text{ values given in brackets})$$

This result suggests that for a given growth rate of real income price changes are the consequence of changes in the money stock. The result is consistent with there being a stable demand function for money of the type postulated above.

This study uses data drawn from a larger-scale study by Vogel (1974) which attempts to see if a functional from originally used by Harberger (1963) in a study of Chilean inflation fits the experience of other Latin American countries. The equation used is:

$$P_t' = k + dM_t' + eM_{t-1}' - (1+a)Y_t' + b\left(P_{t-1}' - P_{t-2}'\right)$$

A number of points may be noted about Vogel's study. First, whereas Meiselman simply regressed mean values of the sample countries, Vogel's study pooled times series data for the countries. Secondly, the presence of M_t' and M_{t-1}' signifies the hypothesis that there may be a lagged response of prices in money supply changes. Finally, and of considerable importance the final term is introduced as one possible measure of the effect of expectations on the outcome. Before discussing Vogel's results it will be useful to examine the problem of expectations briefly.

From the point of view of decision-makers in the economy the opportunity cost of holding money will be determined by the rate of inflation which they expect. There are a number of possible hypotheses about how these expectations are formed, but all give emphasis to recent experience. The final term in the equation suggests that *ceteris paribus* if the inflation rate increased in the recent past that this will tend to produce a higher rate of inflation in the current period. The assumed mechanism is that a higher rate of inflation in the recent past leads to a higher expected rate of inflation in the current period, and that this leads to a reduction in the demand for real balances and a movement up the curve in figure 6.1. It means that a given change in nominal money (M) will be relatively more inflationary than it would be if recent inflation had been proceeding at a lower rate (expectations and their formation will be further considered below).

Vogel presents a number of results for the pooled data and also for the individual countries. While the pooled data produced R^2s of over 0.8, the individual country results are more mixed. In particular, the equation does not produce satisfactory results for El Salvador, Mexico or Chile. The latter is particularly puzzling, since Harberger's own results for Chile for the period 1939–58 produced an R^2 of 0.87. This suggests that the model may apply to some periods, but not to others.

Despite these somewhat mixed results, Vogel is able to conclude (p. 113) that 'the most important result of the present study is that a purely monetarist model, with no structuralist variables, reveals little heterogeneity among Latin American countries, in spite of their extreme diversity'. (For comments on Vogel's results and Vogel's reply see Betancourt, 1976; Sheehey, 1976; and Vogel, 1976.)

This is perhaps a convenient point to outline the structuralist view of the causes of inflation. (For a useful survey of this area see Kirkpatrick and Nixson, 1976; Kirkpatrick, 1987; Thirlwall, 1974, pp. 220–31; Sunkel, 1960. It must be emphasised at the outset that there is no single model of structuralism in the sense that there is a monetarist model which is clearly recognised as a derivation from the postulate of a stable demand function for real balances. Rather, structuralist models present a variety of approaches which develop in different ways the idea that certain structural characteristics of developing countries can be considered either as initiating causes of inflation, or as providing propagating mechanisms by which inflation, once started in motion by some autonomous event, becomes built into the economy. It may be noted that the distinction between autonomous and propagating mechanisms plays an important role in a number of structuralist analyses.

A further important characteristic of the approach is the emphasis placed on the relationship between inflation and growth, with the argument often being put that inflation is necessary for growth, or at least that it is an unavoidable concomitant of investment programmes and that it can only be cured by long-run growth which removes the various structural rigidities seen as being of importance.

What are these structural characteristics? One of the most frequently mentioned is the relative inelasticity of the supply of food in developing countries. It is argued that there is a tendency for food supply to lag behind the demand generated by the expansion of income in the non-agricultural sector, which is a concomitant of economic development and that this causes food prices to rise. Now, it might be argued that this is simply a change in relative prices, and that there is no reason why this should result in the *continuously* rising prices which characterise inflations. It might also be argued that if domestic food supply is inelastic that imports of food could prevent any continuous rise in the relative price of food (this seems to have been the case in Central American: see Bulmer-Thomas, 1977). At this point, however, other structural features believed to characterise developing countries can be introduced to produce an inflationary process. To begin with, it may be that there is a foreign-exchange constraint which makes it impossible to import enough food to prevent a rise in its relative price. Where this is the case, urban wage earners are likely to press for wage rises to compensate for their fall in real incomes. If granted, these will result in a further increase in demand and a further rise in food prices. The foreign exchange constraint can also be argued to have been the cause of the introduction of industrialisation policies based on import substitution. Such policies, associated as they are with protective measures, tend to raise the price of industrial goods and also incomes in the non-agricultural sector. The extent of the relative price change, together with any induced rise in food prices due to the increase in demand for food, is such that the price level could probably only be kept stable by a monetary policy which would restrict the growth in real demand so much that unused capacity would emerge.

Chakrabarti (1978) argues that the rate of inflation can be expected to be a function of the behaviour of the relative prices of agricultural and non-agricultural goods – this, in turn, being related to the relative rates of growth of the two sectors. The model used postulates flexible prices, competitive behaviour in the agricultural sector and administered prices in the manufacturing sector.

Testing the model on Indian data for the period 1950–76, Chakrabarti (1978, p. 83) obtains the following equation:

$$P'_t = 4.74 - 0.57R'_{t-1} - 0.48Y'_{2,t-1} + 1.02M'_{t-1}$$
$$(3.68)\ (-3.83)\quad (-2.82)\ (16.33)$$

$$\overline{R}^2 = 0.995 \qquad \text{D.W.} = 2.58$$

where P'_t is the rate of increase of price in period t
R'_{t-1} is the rate of change of agricultural output relative to non-agricultural output (lagged one period)
$Y'_{2,t-1}$ is the rate of change of non agricultural output lagged on period
M'_{t-1} is the lagged rate of change in the money supply
(t ratios appear in parentheses)

As Chakrabarti points out, the high t ratio of the estimated coefficient of M suggests that money growth is the major determinant of price level behaviour. Nevertheless, 'the simple correlation between P'_t and P'_{t-1} is – 0.9592'. It must be pointed out, however, that the a *priori* expectation for the sign on Y'_2 is positive rather than negative.

It is extremely important to realise that structuralists do not deny that an inflationary process will require an expansion of the money supply. In the above example failure to expand the money supply will result in either a rise in unemployment and a fall in output in the industrial sector when wages rise, or possibly to political strife if wages do not rise. Structuralists would argue that in the circumstances it is preferable to allow the money supply to rise and that this is, in fact, what governments usually do. What they are saying is that monetary growth is in large part *endogenous* and a response to more fundamental underlying causes of inflation.

From such a vantage point evidence that there is a stable demand function for real balances is neither here nor there. It is clear, for example, from Meiselman's equation that a fall in the output growth rate will produce a rise in the inflation rate for a given rate of monetary expansion. This initial, autonomous rise in inflation may be propagated via its effect on real wages, and a feedback to money wage increases leading to a difficult policy choice in future periods between reducing the rate of inflation and maintaining output growth at the maximum level possible.

A further very important structural characteristic of developing countries relates to the nature of their tax systems and budgetary processes which means that they may be particularly prone to a perpetuation of inflation once it gets set in motion. Specifically, their tax systems tend to be characterised by low inflation elasticities in the sense that when the general price level rises, the real value of taxes often falls. This is because many taxes are fixed in money terms, or only adjust slowly to inflation. In addition, collection lags are often long, so that by the time taxes are collected they are worth less in real terms than when assessed (for a discussion of these points see Tanzi, 1977; 1978).

The expenditure side of the budget is rather different. Here there is evidence that expenditures tend to be fixed in real terms, and when prices rise the money value of expenditures is raised proportionately. The crucial consequence of these two budgetary features is that once prices begin to rise for whatever initial reason, the fiscal deficit tends to widen in real terms. Since the only way that such deficits can usually be financed is by means of borrowing from the central bank with consequent monetary expansion (capital markets are usually very limited in their ability to support large volumes of government borrowing – another 'structural' characteristic) and a further rise in the rate of inflation. Good examples of models which contain this feature as an integral element are Dutton (1971) and Aghevli and Khan (1977).

The initial price rise which sets this process in motion could be caused by a variety of circumstances. Three possible causes given emphasis by structuralist theorists are:

(a) a rise in the demand for food as a consequence of increases in non-agricultural incomes;
(b) a fall in the supply of food and other agricultural products following a bad harvest (note again how this would produce inflation in the standard monetarist model for a given growth rate of the nominal money supply); and
(c) a fall in export earnings with a resulting fall in imports due to a foreign exchange constraint, thus reducing domestic availability of importable goods. This fall in export earnings might be a temporary phenomenon or might reflect more deep-seated characteristics of the demand for exports.

In all these cases we may observe a close relation between money and prices, and produce statistical results supporting the view that there is a stable demand function for real balances. The crucial point is that the money supply process is no longer exogenous. Money supply is determined by a two-way process and is at least in part endogenous.

The following chart (figure 6.2) may help to clarify the structure of the alternative models.

This chart shows in the upper part the standard monetarist model with the rate of growth of the money stock assumed exogenous. The resulting rate of inflation follows from the rate of growth of real income, together with the income elasticity of demand for real balances, the impact of inflationary expectations and any lagged adjustment to changes to the money stock.

In the lower half a possible framework for a structuralist model is shown. It is to be noted that this model contains two important feedback effects in the form of an impact on money growth from an inflationary-induced rise in the real budget deficit, and a feedback from the realised inflation rate to the budget deficit and the wage determination process. Note that the lower part of the model is identical to the pure monetarist model.

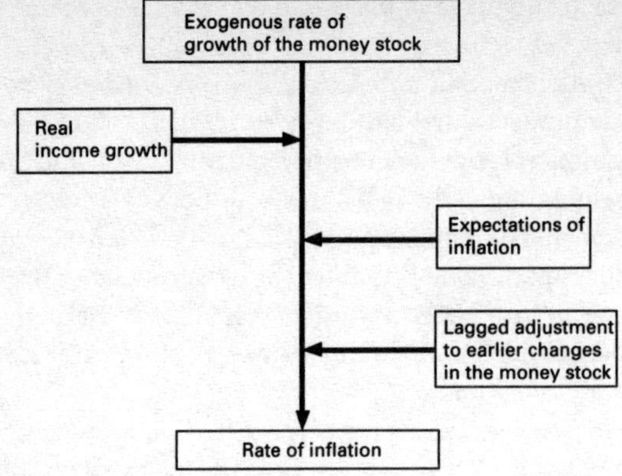

(a) A monetarist model

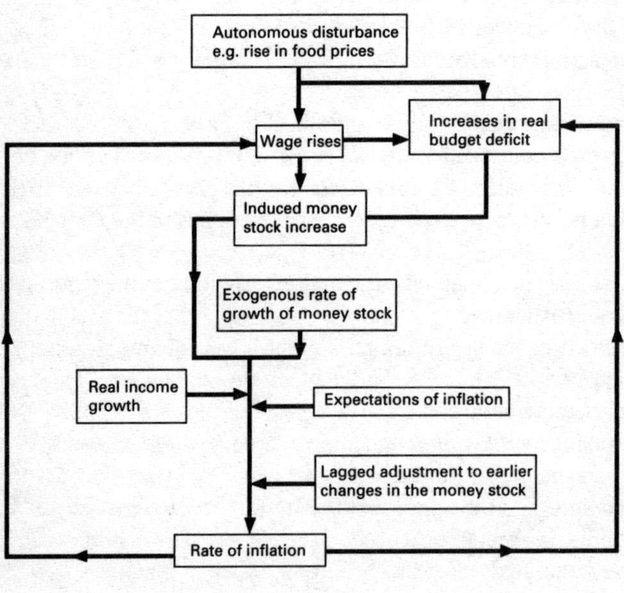

(b) A structuralist model

Figure 6.2

Attempts to test the structuralist group of models have not been noticeably successful in that when various indicators of structural bottlenecks are constructed and inflation rates regressed on them, the coefficients rarely turn out to be significant. One example of such a test is Argy's (1970). Argy uses data for twenty-two developing countries for the period 1958–65.

The indices which he uses are:

(a) an index of demand shifts based on changes in the weights of eight sectors in total production over the period studied. It can be argued that large demand shifts produce large changes in relative prices, and if prices in lagging sectors are inflexible downwards, that this produces an overall upward bias in the price level;
(b) an index of export instability;
(c) an index of the gap between the growth of food supply and the growth of food demand; and
(d) two alternative indices of the foreign exchange constraint.

In most of the equations the structural variables are not significant, whereas the addition of monetary variables improves the statistical fits, and the monetary variables are themselves significant. For example, one equation producing an R^2 of 0.52 with the index of the agricultural bottleneck (point c above) significant at the 5 per cent level is not such a good fit as the same equation with the addition of the standard monetarist variables which produces an R^2 of 0.92, and renders the agricultural bottleneck index insignificant.

Nevertheless, an Argy recognises, these results may not be an adequate test of the structuralist model due to the fact that the time period studied is short, whereas structuralist theorists tend to emphasise long-run considerations and, in addition, the indices used may not be adequate representations of the relevant phenomena. It is worth noting that in a detailed study of Latin America, Edel (1969) finds that inelasticity of food supply is a significant variable helping to account for differences in inflation rates between countries. To these points needs to be added the crucial question of how far differences in the rate of growth of the money supply between countries is a reflection of different structural characteristics. If this is the case, then good results for monetarist models can be interpreted as indirect tests of the structural models.

As a final comment on this section, it should be pointed out that monetarists often argue that the structural problems are a consequence of inflation rather than its cause. For example, it might be argued that the foreign exchange bottleneck reflects the failure to adjust the exchange rate to compensate for inflation with a consequent adverse effect on exports. The food supply bottleneck might in part be explained by price and import policies directed at maintaining a low price of food in the face of inflation.

6.3 The effects of inflation on growth

We turn now to an examination of the relationship between inflation and growth and of the more general consequences of inflation. Inflation can influence growth by changing the distribution of income in such a way as to raise the rate of savings and investment in the economy. There are two main ways in which this can occur:

(i) As a consequence of unanticipated inflation (or of anticipated inflation to which some groups are unable to adjust by raising their money incomes to maintain real incomes) there may be a shift of income between wage earners and profit earners.
(ii) Even if inflation is fully anticipated, there may well be a shift in the distribution of income towards the government, and perhaps to banks and their borrowers, as a consequences of the operation of the so-called inflation tax.

The first route has a long history and is predicated upon the possibility that when demand increases and prices rise, not all prices rise at the same rate. In particular, it is likely that wages will lag behind the rise in prices for some time, with a consequent rise in profits. Only when wage earners are able to adjust to the new situation by taking measures to restore their real wages, will this distributional change be reversed. In the meanwhile, if it is the case that profit receivers have higher propensities to save and invest than do wage earners, the overall savings and investment ratio in the economy will rise and growth will be favourably affected. It must be stressed that this mechanism rests on the inflation not being fully anticipated by some groups in the economy or, if anticipated, the failure of these groups to obtain an upward adjustment in their money incomes to compensate for the inflation. While possibly of some importance in the short run, it is arguable that in the long run more and more people will come to anticipate the inflation, and take measures to restore their real income.

The inflation-tax model has received considerable attention in the literature since it was first discussed by Cagan (1956) and Bailey (1956). This model is based on the fact that inflation acts as a tax on money holding. While the model as developed by Cagan and Bailey emerged from the monetarist tradition, the application to developing countries can take a structuralist slant, since it can be argued that if it is difficult to increase yields from other forms of taxation due to structural phenomena, the inflation tax can serve as a means of raising the share of government in domestic product and, as a consequence, the government will be able to expand its growth-promoting expenditures. This is the basis of Mundell's well-known application of the model (Mundell, 1965).

The model begins by postulating that there is a stable demand function for real balances of the type already discussed in section 6.2. The demand for real balances is seen to be a function of the expected rate of inflation and of the level of real income. The model can be discussed with the use of a diagram like figure 6.3, which is reproduced below for convenience:

The demand curve in this diagram shows the quantity of real balances demanded as a function of the opportunity-cost of holding money for a given level of population and real income. If inflation were proceeding at a steady rate of π_1, then real money balances would be at the level $0(M/P)_2$ compared to a level $0(M/P)_1$ if the inflation rate were zero. If it is the case that neither real income nor population are growing, then it can be argued, following the quantity theory, that the rate of inflation will be equal to the rate of growth of the money supply. The issuers of money obtain resources equal to the shaded area in the diagram. The reason for this is that the public want to hold $0(M/P)_2$ in *real* balances at the inflation rate π_1, which we are assuming for the moment is fully anticipated, so that this represents an equilibrium demand for real balances, and since inflation continuously erodes the real value of a given quantity of *nominal* money balances it will be necessary for the public to save (that is, give up resources) out of their incomes to obtain nominal balances sufficient to keep their real balances constant. One can then say that the level of real balances held represents the tax base and the rate of monetary expansion (in this case of zero growth also equal to the rate of inflation) is the tax rate.

Figure 6.3 can also be used to show the welfare costs involved in transferring resources to the issuers of money in this manner by using standard consumer surplus analysis, and one can compare, as Bailey (1956) did, the 'revenue' raised with the welfare costs involved and, further, compare these costs with those of obtaining resources by alternative means. The losses from raising the inflation rate from zero to π_1 are equal to $(M/P)_1\ EC(M/P)_2$, that is the loss of the area under the demand curve. (It may be noted that it is sometimes argued that the loss is only CDE, the consumer surplus triangle. But as Tower (1971) has shown, the area $(M/P)_1\ ED(M/P)_2$ is also a loss. It reflects the fact that people previously held $(M/P)_2\ (M/P)_1$ of real balances even though there was an opportunity-cost in terms of the foregone rate of interest, *r*. Hence these balances at the margin had a value to the consumer of *r*, and the fact that inflation leads to a reduced demand for real balances means that there is a loss of r on each unit given up in addition to the consumer surplus triangle CDE.)

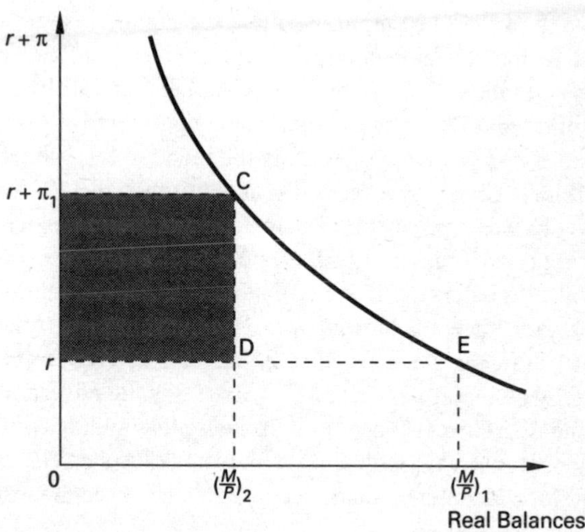

Figure 6.3

The precise relationship between inflation and growth which emerges from this model depends on the amount of real resources transferred to the issuers of money and what they do with them. Unless all money is issued by the government, its share of the resource transfer will not be 100 per cent. Specifically, in a fractional reserve banking system it will be the case that the government, or central bank, will control the issue of high-powered or base money, while the total money supply will be determined according to the relationship.

$$M = \frac{1+c}{b+c} \cdot H$$

where H is high-powered money (equal to currency plus bankers' deposits with the central bank), b is the banks' cash reserve ratio (assumed in this example to be the same for all types of deposits), c is the ratio of currency to bank deposits held by the public, and M is the sum of bank deposits and the public's holdings of currency.

It is therefore the case that since inflation transfers resources to the issuers of money (unless they pay a rate of interest equal to the rate of inflation) when private banks are in operation they share in this resource transfer as do borrowers from the banks if they pay nominal interest rates producing a real rate below r, which is a commonly observed phenomenon. (That the share of banks and their borrowers in the resource transfer can be significant is shown by the fact that in Chile between 1929 and 1955, an average of 72 per cent of the revenue raised as a tax on cash balances accrued to them: Deaver, 1970, p. 45.) The share of the government depends on the size of the bank credit multiplier (M/H) and on the share of government securities in the incremental assets of the banking system. If bank share holders, borrowers from banks and the government carry out productive investments with the resources transferred, this will be growth promoting. It must, however, be emphasised that the net increase in investment will only be equal to the resource transfer if the incidence of the inflation tax is entirely on consumption. This is by no means necessarily the case, especially when various indirect effects of inflation to be considered below are taken into account. (For a formal growth model using the inflation tax, the reader is referred to Mundell, 1965; Mundell's model is discussed by Ghatak, 1995).

It should be obvious from Figure 6.3 that the amount of resources transferred by the inflation tax is a function of the rate of inflation and of the elasticity of demand for real cash balances. There will be some rate of inflation (or, more generally, rate of monetary expansion) which maximises the revenue from the inflation tax. To show this we can utilise Friedman's derivation (Friedman, 1971) and for simplicity assume that all money is issued by the government.

Assuming that there is equilibrium in the sense that money demand is equal to money supply, and that we are dealing with alternative steady rates of inflation, let the demand for real money balances be written in per capita form:

$$m^{D} = f(y,\pi) \tag{6.1}$$

where m^D = real balances demanded per capita
y = real income per capita
π = the rate of inflation

Alternatively, on the assumption that the demand for money is homogeneous of the first degree with respect to prices and population, this equation can be written as:

$$M = NP.f(y,\pi) \tag{6.1a}$$

where N is the population and M is the nominal quantity of money. We can then write:

$$g_M = g_N + \pi + \eta_{my} g_y \tag{6.2}$$

where g_M is the rate of growth of the nominal money supply
g_N is the rate of population growth
η_{my} is the real per capita income elasticity of demand for money
g_y is the rate of growth of real income per capita

The revenue raised from money issue is:

$$R = \frac{M}{P}\left(g_N + \pi + \eta_{my} g_y\right) \tag{6.3}$$

(that is, all the terms in the brackets, if positive, contribute to the incremental growth in money demand, and so to the revenue of the money issuing authorities).

It may be noted that if the economy is not growing ($g_N = g_y = 0$), then we have:

$$R = \frac{M}{P}\pi \text{ (which is the formulation implicit in figure 5.3)} \tag{6.4}$$

If we differentiate R in equation 6.3 with respect to the inflation rate, we obtain:

$$\frac{dR}{d\pi} = \frac{M}{P}\left[1 + g_y \frac{d\eta_{my}}{d\pi} + \left(g_N + \pi + \eta_{my} g_y\right)\frac{d \log m^D}{d\pi}\right] = 0 \tag{6.5}$$

giving a revenue maximum rate of inflation of:

$$\left(g_N + \pi + \eta_{my} g_y\right)\frac{d \log m^D}{d\pi} + g_y \frac{d\eta_{my}}{d\pi} = -1 \tag{6.6}$$

which *in the case of an economy which is not growing*, becomes:

$$\pi . \frac{d \log m^D}{d\pi} = -1 \tag{6.7}$$

that is, the revenue is maximised when the elasticity of demand for real balances with respect to the rate of inflation is unity.

Friedman next proceeds to solve equation 6.6 for g_N and substitute the result into equation 6.2 to obtain:

$$g_M = \frac{-1 - g_y \dfrac{d\eta_{my}}{d\pi}}{\dfrac{d \log m^D}{d\pi}} \tag{6.8}$$

The resulting revenue-maximising rate of inflation can be derived from equation 6.2.

In order to give this formulation practical application, one must introduce an explicit demand function for money. Friedman uses a functional form originally used by Cagan (1956) in his seminal study of hyperinflation, and subsequently used by many studies of inflation (see, for example, Deaver, 1970).

$$m^D = l(y)e^{-b\pi} \tag{6.9}$$

$$\frac{d \log m^D}{d\pi} = -b \tag{6.10}$$

Since $\frac{d\eta_{my}}{d\pi}$ in this function, we can solve equation 6.6 for π:

$$= \frac{1}{b} - g_N - \eta_{my} g_y \tag{6.11}$$

and equation 6.8 can be solved to give:

$$g_M = \frac{1}{b} \tag{6.12}$$

This result is very important. It means that if we fit an equation of the form given by equation 6.9 of parentheses and estimate the value of the parameter b, we can immediately derive the revenue maximising rate of monetary growth and hence of inflation.

It must be stressed, a point emphasised by Friedman, that in a growing economy the revenue maximising rate of inflation will not be that rate at which the elasticity of demand for real cash balances is unity. This rate maximises revenue from a given demand curve for real balances, but in a growing economy there is another source of revenue to the issuers of money emanating from increases in demand due to g_N and/or g_y. These increments will be smaller the higher is the rate of inflation, and so the optimal rate of inflation is lower in a growing economy than in a stationary economy in this model. This point is clearly implied by equations 6.2 and 6.12. The latter equation shows that the revenue maximising rate of monetary growth is determined by b, whereas equation 6.2 makes it clear that the presence of growth in the economy results in a lower rate of inflation for any given rate of monetary growth.

As an illustration of the calculations which can be done within this framework, we can take Aghevli and Khan's results for Indonesia (Aghevli and Khan, 1977).

For the period 1950–72 they obtain a value of b equal to 0.55 which yields a revenue-maximising rate of monetary expansion of 182 per cent per annum. (Even if generous allowance for real income growth and for the income elasticity of demand for real balances is made this would produce a rate of inflation of at least 150 per cent per annum.) In the Indonesian case this produces revenue for the government from deficit financing equivalent to 6 per cent of national income. However, it is to be noted that the authors obtain a welfare cost equivalent to 14 per cent of national income, suggesting that this may be a very burdensome means of raising government revenue. This will be seen to be even more the case when the relation of other tax revenues to inflation is considered below.

Other studies have produced values of b substantially different from the value obtained for Indonesia. For example, Deaver (1970, p. 34) obtains values of various periods between 1932 and 1955 for Argentina varying between 1.1 and 7.4. The value for the period taken as a whole is 4.9, which produces a revenue-maximising rate of monetary growth according to equation 6.12 of 20.4 per cent per annum, and hence a revenue-maximising rate of inflation of between 10 per cent and 15 per cent per annum depending on the assumptions make about real income growth and income elasticity. Clearly this is of a very different order of magnitude to the result derived for Indonesia.

Obviously b is a crucially important parameter, and the two examples cited suggest that it can take on a wide range of values. Are there any generalisations we can make about the likely magnitude of its value in a particular country? One point which has emerged from recent discussions is that b is unlikely to be independent of the rate of inflation itself. It may be noted that Indonesia experienced very high rates of inflation in the 1960s and that Cagan in his study of hyperinflations obtained values by b suggesting revenue-maximising rates of inflation of between 12 per cent and 54 per cent *per month*. It has been noted by Friedman (1971) and Newlyn (1977) among others, that if the value of π is set equal to zero, using equation 6.9 one should obtain the value of velocity (that is, PY/M) at zero inflation. Typically, the value predicted by using equations like 6.9, which have been fitted to data for countries with relatively high inflation rates, is much greater than the values observed during more stable periods or for countries with lower rates of inflation at similar stages of development. Newlyn's results are broadly consistent with the behaviour of velocity shown in figure 6.4.

In this diagram the inflation rate is measured along the horizontal axis and velocity on the vertical. V_2 represents the predicted velocity at zero inflation derived from estimates of equation 6.9 using data from relatively high inflationary situations whereas V_1 represents the lower level of velocity observed for countries which have actually experienced very low rates of inflation.

A consideration of the functions of money suggests why such a relation is plausible. Money serves as a transactions medium and as a store of value, the latter having particular potential importance in developing countries where other stores of value are unlikely to be widely available, expecially to low income

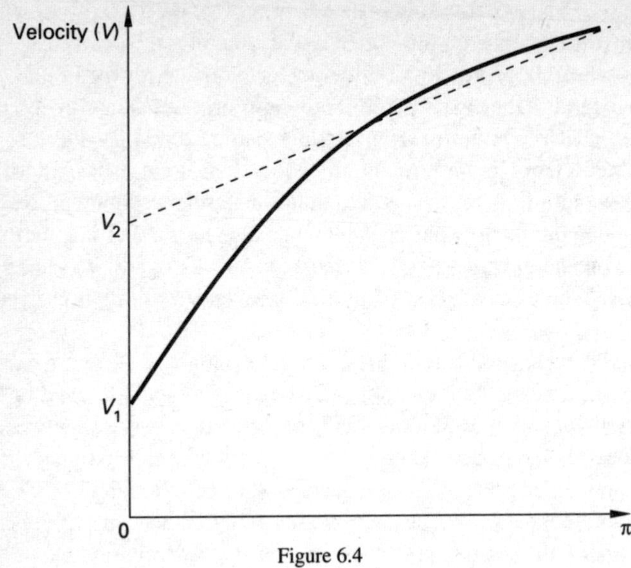

Figure 6.4

groups. As the rate of inflation rises, money becomes less and less desirable as a store of value to be held over any length of time, a point which has some important implications to be discussed below. On the other hand, its transactions function is less easily replaced by other assets, and so at relatively high rates of inflation money is held almost entirely for transactions purposes and the response of money-demand to inflation may be much smaller than at lower rates. Newlyn (1977, p. 55) finds that there is very little relationship between velocity and inflation for high inflation countries; 'on the other hand it is clear that a subatantial proportion of countries having very low rates of inflation show some evidence of sensitivity' of velocity to inflation. One may tentatively conclude that the value of *b* at low rates of inflation may differ significantly from its value at high rates so that the rate of inflation that maximises revenue to the issuers of money is probably not much greater than 10 per cent in most cases. (It must be noted, however, that Newlyn argues on the basis of his results that in most cases revenue would be increased by raising the rate of inflation to 30 per cent.)

In considering the efficacy of using a tax on cash balances as a means of increasing the level of investment in the economy, it is essential that the relationship between inflation and the revenue from other taxes, already referred to above, is not ignored. In developing countries the tax structure and administrative mechanism are likely to mean that quite mild inflation will reduce real tax revenues. (In addition, real expenditure may rise as a consequence of public utility rates remaining fixed in the face of inflation, leading to increasing deficits which must be financed by the government.) This is a consequence of the much lower degree of progressiveness in the tax structure, as compared to developed countries, a high degree of reliance on specific taxes and, most important of all, often significant lags in tax collection. The full implications of these features of developing-country tax structures with illustrative calculations have been thoroughly discussed by Tanzi (1977, 1978, 1992; and Ahmad and Stern, 1987). Two examples from Indonesia will help to show the importance of this consideration.

Aghevli and Khan (1977) in the study already quoted, show that the share of tax revenue to national income when prices are stable is 10.1 per cent. At the rate of inflation which maximises inflation tax revenue (6.0 per cent of national income) other taxes fall to 5.0 per cent of national income. Hence, the *net* effect of inflation at a rate of over 150 per cent per annum is to produce a net rise in revenue to the government of less than 1.0 per cent of national income. We have already noted that the same study gives welfare costs equivalent to 14.0 per cent of national income. Even if all the revenue were productively invested as well as any gains accruing to bankers and their borrowers, it is highly likely that this would be more than negated by other adverse effects on growth flowing from inflation, which will be examined below.

For a five-year period in the early 1960s when inflation in Indonesia reached very high levels, Hicks (1967) has presented the following data:

Table 6.2 Indonesia: government expenditure and revenue at 1960 prices (in billions of rupiahs)

	Expenditure	*Revenue*	*Deficit*	*Rate of Inflation*
1960	58.3	50.3	8.0	15.1
1961	64.0	45.0	19.0	39.3
1962	32.2	19.4	12.8	80.1
1963	38.4	18.9	19.5	88.9
1964	18.1	8.5	9.6	57.7

Source: Hicks (1967); rate of inflation from Aghevli and Khan (1977).

It can be seen from this table that there was a clear tendency for real revenue to decline as the rate of inflation increased. In Indonesia during this period it was not possible to keep the real level of government expenditure constant, but overall there is some tendency for the real deficit to rise with the rate of inflation.

To conclude this discussion of the inflation tax, some further problems relating to the instability of observed inflation rates will be discussed. It will be remembered that Willett and Logue (1976) found a statistically significant relationship between the level of inflation and its variability as measured by its standard deviation: high inflations are relatively unstable inflations. An important implication of this is that expectations regarding the inflation rate will frequently not be realised. This increases uncertainty and will tend to reduce the willingness of people to engage in long-term contracts. The pattern of investment may therefore be distorted towards short-term projects, which may well yield lower social returns than long-term projects. It is a great mistake when analysing the effects of inflation to concentrate on possible effects on the level of investment to the exclusion of its composition. (See, for example, Shaalan, 1962; Dorrance, 1963; Shaw, 1973; and McKinnon, 1973 for discussion of this point.)

A further point is that at high and unstable rates of inflation the efficiency of the price system as an indicator of desirable resource allocation is hindered. Not all prices adjust instantaneously to excess demand (this will be especially so in the case of public utilities whose rates are often fixed for long periods of time, as well as the foreign exchange rate), and therefore at any given time relative prices will be distorted by lags in adjustment in some sectors relative to others. This can be expected to produce adverse effects on the pattern of investment and resource allocation, so reducing the overall efficiency of the economy. It is a powerful argument against any but the most moderate rates of inflation.

Sjaastad (1976) has recently suggested that the fact that inflations typically are not steady is not an accident, but is the consequence of the lagged adjustment of expectations and the implications of this for the revenue which the government can raise from the inflation tax. Before examining his argument it is necessary to be more explicit about the formulation of expectations that heretofore.

Let us define the expected rate of inflation in period t as π^*. The adaptive expectations model which has been much used in empirical work (see Cagan, 1956) postulates that the expected rate is a geometrically weighted average of past observed values and may be expressed as follows:

$$\pi_t^* = \lambda_{t-1} + \lambda(1-\lambda)\pi_{t-2} + \ldots + \lambda(1-\lambda)^{n-1}\pi_{t-n}$$

with the weights summing to unity. This may also be written as:

$$\pi_t^* = \lambda\pi_{t-1} + (1-\lambda)\pi_{t-1}^*$$

or as

$$\pi_t^* - \pi_{t-1}^* = \lambda(\pi_{t-1} - \pi_{t-1}^*)$$

This last equation states that expectations are revised (adapted) each period by a constant fraction ($0 < \lambda < 1$) of the difference between the last observed inflation rate (i.e. π_{t-1}) and the rate that was expected for that period (i.e. π_{t-1}^*). The value of π_{t-1}^*, in turn, is determined by actual price behaviour in period $t-2$ together with expected behaviour for that period and so on back in time for as long as people have relevant memory. The parameter λ reflects the speed of adjustment of expectations on the assumption that money balances held are always fully adjusted to desired money balances (as determined by expectations). If this is not the case, then the parameter will also reflect lags in this latter adjustment. (For attempts to distinguish these two lags, see White, 1978; and Wong, 1977.)

The idea which is behind this model is that people make predictions about the behaviour of future prices from their observations of past price movements and that their behaviour (for example, in relation to money holding) is determined by the rate of inflation which they expect to occur. The hypothesis is that errors (that is, discrepancies between expected and actual rates of inflation) are corrected by a step-by-step process of adjustment. It is an implication of the model that the longer a given rate of inflation persists the more closely will people come to expect that rate of inflation. As already pointed out, the greater the weight which people give to recent events in the determination of expectations the higher will be the value of λ. (For a more complex but probably more realistic model of expectations formation see Flemming 1976, chapter 7.)

Sjaastad's application of this model of expectation formation can now be examined. Suppose that people expect, on the basis of past experience, that the rate of inflation will be π_1^* in figure 6.5(a). If the rate of inflation unexpectedly rises to π_2 the government will collect additional tax revenues equal to the shaded area in the figure. This exceeds the tax revenue from a fully-anticipated inflation π_2^* by the amount ABCD. The longer it takes for expectations to adapt, that is the smaller λ is, the better it is for the issuers of money. A small λ will mean that a rise in the rate of inflation will take a long time to significantly affect expectations so that the demand for money balances will adjust only slowly towards its new equilibrium level. As expectations adapt to the new rate of inflation and ABCD is being eliminated, the government may well be tempted to raise the rate of inflation to a higher level where revenue will be temporarily greater than at the steady rate of inflation of π_2 (which increasingly becomes the expected rate of inflation, π_2^*).

It should be pointed out that it is by no means impossible that the tax revenue collected at the fully-anticipated rate of inflation π_2^* is less that at π_1^*. This will occur if the elasticity of demand for real cash balances exceeds unity over the relevant range. This point is illustrated in figure 6.5(b) where it is also clear that there will be a period, the length depending on the magnitude of λ, during which a rise in the rate of inflation to π_2 will raise revenue. Raising the rate of inflation from π_1^* (= *rA) to* π_2 (= *rH*) initially increases revenue by BLHA. As expectations adjust (and holdings of real balances fall towards $(M/P)_2$) that revenue is gradually reduced and when the rate of inflation is fully anticipated (so that $\pi_2^* = (\pi_2)$ total revenue is equal to *r*EGH, which is less than the original revenue of *r*ABC (since AHGF < EFBC).

In addition, it should be noted that there is evidence that the coefficient of expectaction is not constant, but rather varies with the rate of inflation (Khan, 1977a, 1977b). This is not unreasonable since the higher the rate of inflation, the greater the costs of failing to anticipate it correctly and of adjusting slowly to changes in expectations. Because of this, continuously raising the rate of inflation will run into diminishing returns. (If the elasticity of demand for real cash balances at alternative, fully-anticipated rates of inflation rises with inflation, this effect will be further strengthened.)

Sjaastad suggests that this leads the government to try to induce people to change their expectations so as to expect a much lower rate of inflation. A stabilisation programme may be announced, for example, often following a

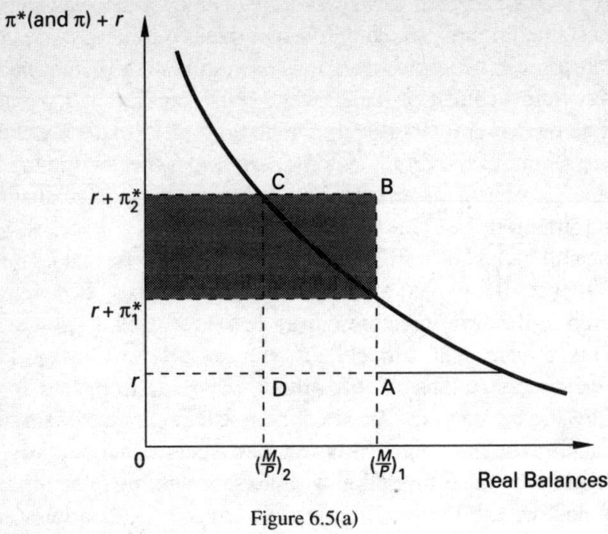

Figure 6.5(a)

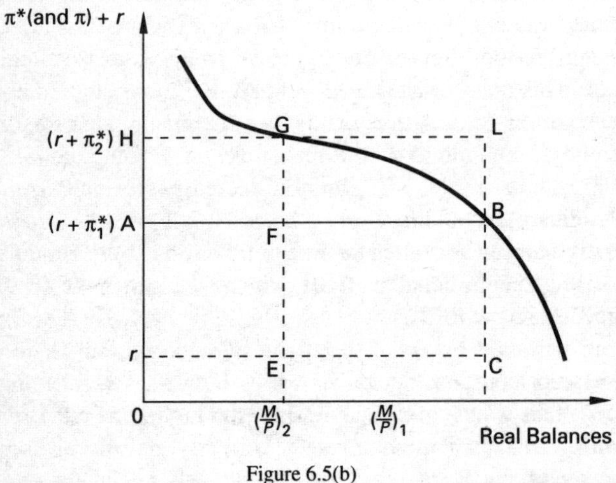

Figure 6.5(b)

change of administration, a situation which probably encourages people to be more flexible in their expectations. If successful, this will produce a sharp rise in the demand for real balances. However, this is a once and-for-all increase in demand, and in future years the government may well be tempted to raise the rate of inflation again so as to obtain the gains resulting from the lagged adjustment of expectations. Overall, there is a predicted tendency for governments to pursue policies of unstable inflation if they are using it as a means of raising their share of domestic resources. The fact that unstable inflation produces more adverse effects on economic efficiency than stable inflation means that the case against the inflation tax is to that extent further weakened. (Note, however, that the possible favourable effects on investment following from an inflation-induced shift of income distribution from wages to profits depends in part on the inflation being unanticipated!)

6.4 Financial repression and the case against inflation

It has been indicated in chapter 5 that the work by McKinnon (1973) and Shaw (1973) has drawn attention to ways in which inflation can have an adverse effect on the level and quality of capital formation. Two particular aspects of the points made by McKinnon and Shaw deserve emphasis. They relate to the effect of inflation on the intermediation activities of the banking system and on the willingness of people to accumulate money holdings prior to buying capital goods.

The banking system performs important intermediary functions by collecting deposits from individuals and making loans for productive investment. This is especially the case in developing countries where banks are usually the most important financial institutions and play a central part in bringing together flows of savings and channeling them into investment. In these circumstances, anything which reduces the volume of real bank deposits will tend to reduce those types of investment which are too large to be financed by individuals from their own resources. These investments may be just the ones which have a relatively high productivity due to the advantages of scale in the presence of indivisibilities.

Even if an entrepreneur does not, or is unable to, borrow from the banking system, he may be able to undertake investment in large-scale facilities if he is first able to save and accumulate over time the purchase price of the capital assets involved. The most obvious form in which these savings will be held in a developing country is either in currency or bank deposits, the latter having the attraction of safety and possibly a small interest return. Money is seen in this context as fulfilling a 'conduit' function by bridging the time gap between the accumulation of small amounts of saving and the ultimate purchase of a real capital asset (see McKinnon, 1973, chapter 6).

We know that inflation acts as a deterrent to holding money, particularly for long periods of time. It may therefore produce a tendency for investment, especially by small-scale entrepreneurs, to take the form of capital assets which can be purchased in small doses more or less continuously. These may have a much smaller return than more indivisible items of capital equipment. It may well turn out that the total level of investment would also be adversely affected.

The important point follows that in such circumstances, money holdings and physical capital accumulation are complementary and not, as some growth models imply, competitive. Complementarity also emerges if inflation reduces the real value of bank deposits and the extent of intermediation, so producing the characteristic 'shallow finance' noted by Shaw.

Study by Vogel and Buser (1976) shows clearly that in Latin America inflation has had an adverse effect on the real level of demand, time and savings deposits. The currency ratio rises from low to high inflation countries and rates of growth of deposits are slowest in high inflation countries (Vogel and Buser, 1973, p. 50). These authors conclude 'the negative impact of inflation on the ratio of time and savings deposits to gross domestic product is not only highly significant but also approximately unit elastic' (p. 53). This study also finds that the ratio of time and savings deposits to gross domestic product has a positive impact on capital formation, thus giving strong support to the complementarity hypothesis.

These are important findings since they suggest that any investment by the government or by those who benefit from being able to borrow from the banks at low or negative real rates of interest associated with the inflation tax, may well be more than offset by a decline in other types of investment and by adverse effects on the quality of investment.

Even if total investment rises, this may reflect the consequences of people shifting their assets from money balances to hedges against inflation which are recorded in the national accounts as investment. Examples would be houses, factory buildings and machinery (often operated at well below full capacity suggesting that they may partly serve a store-of-value rather than a productive function) and holdings of inventories larger than required by the needs of production. Such 'investments' have a very low social productivity, but are increasingly attractive to wealth holders in the face of rising rates of inflation.

Because high rates of inflation also tend to be unstable, we can expect a tendency for entrepreneurs to opt for projects of a short-term nature rather than projects which yield returns over a long period which are particularly vulnerable to the unforeseen and erratic effects on real cash flows of changes in the rate of inflation and the associated changes in credit availability.

McKinnon and Shaw have also stressed that in practice inflation does not affect all prices equally. In particular, exchange rates, interest rates and public utility prices are often fixed for considerable periods of time producing substantial distortions of relative prices. Real interest rates on time and savings deposits are frequently negative with effects already noted. Low or negative real rates on loans tend to encourage relatively capital intensive investments and may be associated with high levels of surplus capacity. Fixed exchange rates, by artificially cheapening foreign exchange, produce similar results, especially if imports of consumer goods are controlled more tightly than capital goods.

Nicholls (1974) has recently suggested that controls and restrictions are an integral part of the inflationary process in that they can be seen as attempts to limit the extent to which people are able to switch out of real balances, by limiting the availability of substitutes. Hence there may be restrictions on the interest rates which can be paid by non-bank financial institutions, and foreign exchange controls can be seen as an attempt to limit the availability of a potentially very close substitute for domestic money in the form of foreign currency and bank deposits held in foreign countries.

Attention has been drawn above to the intermediary and conduit functions of the monetary system, and the adverse effects which inflation has on these. A further dimension which deserves mention is the impact of inflation on the degree of monetisation of the economy. It is not always realised how important non-monetary transactions and subsistence production are in developing countries. Chandavarkar (1977) has shown that the non-monetised sector may be as large as one-third of gross domestic product in these countries, and that even in relatively developed Malaysia it is about one-fifth. Monetisation of transactions makes possible a higher degree of specialisation, and hence a higher level of productivity than is possible in subsistence and barter systems. If inflation increases the risks and costs of using money, it can be expected to have an adverse effect on the growth and efficiency of the economy by slowing up, or even reversing, the trend towards monetisation. It should be emphasised that the scope for producers to revert to subsistence and to engage in barter transactions is very much greater in developing countries than in developed countries. This provides a further reason for expecting that the coefficient b may have a much higher value in the long run than that derived from studies of relatively short periods, especially of hyperinflationary periods in relatively developed countries, as in Cagan's study.

We have tried to suggest in this chapter that the relationship between inflation and growth is likely to be both complex and varied. We might, however, ask what evidence there is on the net outcome of all these considerations.

A number of studies have been well surveyed by Thirlwall (1974; and Fry, 1988), and the broad conclusion emerging is that for developing countries a moderate rate of inflation (up to, perhaps, 10 per cent per annum) may promote growth. Thirlwall and Benton (1971), for example, in a cross section study, found that for inflation rates over 10 per cent there was a negative impact on growth. U Tun Wai (1959) obtains a positive relation up to a rate of inflation of about 13 per cent, while Dorrance (1966) finds that mild inflation seems to be associated with growth. Thirlwall (1974) also presents some further results of his own, and finds that when the relation between inflation and growth is examined, the coefficient is either positive, but not significant, or negative, according to the sample.

A brief mention may be made of the experience of Brazil, a country which has had high and variable inflation and on which there are a number of excellent studies (Langoni and Kogut, 1977; Kahil, 1973; Lemgruber, 1977, for example). The inflation rate in the period 1948 to 1975 varied between a minimum of 7 per cent in 1957 and a maximum of 92 per cent in 1964. Langoni and Kogut show that three basic sub-periods emerge:

(a) a period of acceleration of both growth and inflation from 1957 to 1961;
(b) a period of deceleration of growth and acceleration of growth and acceleration of inflation from 1962 to 1965; and
(c) a period of acceleration of growth and reduction of inflation from 1966 to 1975.

Overall, there does not appear to be any consistent relation between inflation and growth, but it is to be noted that the period 1966 to 1975 was accompanied by considerable development of the financial system, with an expansion of real credit to the private sector and a decline in the public sector deficit, a combination of events which is consistent with the view that low rates of inflation are more favourable to financial and general development, as stressed in work in this field (McKinnon, 1973).

The overall conclusion which might be suggested is that there are a number of reasons for expecting that inflation much in excess of 10 per cent per annum is likely to have an adverse effect on the long-run development of a country, since any positive impact on total investment can easily be outweighed by adverse effects on the composition of investment, the degree of monetisation and the efficiency of the financial system. In the long run, growth and development may be best promoted by having a target rate of inflation of zero, while erring on the side of inflation rather than deflation.

6.5 Major problems and policies for stabilisation in LDCs

Three major reasons for discussing stabilisation policies in LDCs are usually stated (see, for example, Jansen and Vos, 1985, for a good summary; see also Kapur, 1977; and Wijenbergen, 1982, 1983):

(i) the substantial fall in terms of trade of non-oil LDCs during the 1970s due a massive rise in oil price;
(ii) the impacts on inflation of the big oil price shocks in 1973–4 and 1978–9; and
(iii) the rise in fiscal deficits usually financed by a rise in money supply.

Thus three different kinds of instability can arise: first, balance of payments instability can occur because of a sharp fall in terms of trade; secondly, there may be price instability due to a rise in the rate of inflation; and lastly, there could be budgetary or fiscal instability because of a rise in government deficit. Obviously, these instabilities are not always mutually exclusive. The stabilisation or 'adjustment' policies usually advocated by the IMF for LDCs can be summarised as follows (for example, Aghevli *et al.*, 1979):

(a) Devaluation and trade liberalisation to cure the balance of payments deficit. Such a policy also implies removal of exchange controls, quotas, and reduction of tariffs.

(b) Allow the market to work freely and 'get prices right' to remove the excess demand and inflation. The usual instruments of control comprise a rise in interest rates and removal of fiscal controls and subsidies.
(c) A substantial reduction in public-sector deficit by cutting government expenditure and raising government revenue by improving the performance of the public enterprises. Here the control of money supply is regarded as a key instrument to control public expenditure.

The nature of these 'adjustment' policies clearly shows the strong emphasis on the use of monetary policy with target growth rate of money supply and domestic credit creation and high interest rates to reduce excess demand, the rate of inflation and the balance of payments deficit. However, the following major problems could arise if LDCs follow the IMF prescribed standard 'adjustment' policies (see, for example, Jansen and Vos, 1985).

'Adjustment' policies and problems in LDCs

(i) The usual models formalised by the IMF emphasise the need for demand restrictions in LDCs (see, for example, Polak, 1957; Aghevli *et al*., 1979) presumably because it is assumed implicitly that the supply side will be taken care of by the free market forces. As most LDCs are supply rather than demand constrained, the standard prescription of 'demand management' is open to question.
(ii) It is well acknowledged that the 'Paretian efficiency' of an economy is ensured when markets are perfect. But in LDCs, markets are usually imperfect. In the light of the theory of the second best, it can be argued that when some markets are imperfect, it is inefficient to liberalise some markets but not others. Thus, the liberalisation of trade by itself is unlikely to achieve optimal solutions when the financial sector is imperfect.
(iii) The 'adjustment policies' of the IMF are supposed to be uniformly applicable to all LDCs. It is well known, though, that LDCs are not really a homogeneous group. Whether inflation is caused by monetary or structural factors in LDCs is very much an open issue (see Saini, 1982; Kirkpatrick *et al*., 1983; Kirkpatrick and Nixon, 1987). For example, an increase in agricultural production in India has consistently led to a fall in the rate of inflation (see Chakrabarty, 1977).
(iv) The price rather than output effect of a budgetary deficit in LDCs is supposed to be very strong. However, such a 'transmission mechanism' which comprises the core of the monetarist argument has seldom been tested in LDCs. The precise nature of price and output effect of a change in budgetary deficit financed by money supply should therefore be tested carefully, particularly when the IMF is prone to preach the 'virtues' of a cut in government expenditure almost as a matter of faith. Later, we will try to test the 'causality' between money and prices for a number of LDCs (see the Appendix).

(v) The gradual integration of LDCs with the international capital market, coupled with the policy of trade liberalisation which engenders rapid short-term capital flows, could easily have destabilising effects. In a regime of flexible exchange rates, movements of short-term capital could increase the degree of instability and here the manipulation of domestic macro-economic policies could fail to stabilise the domestic economy.

(vi) An analysis of the major IMF models seems to suggest that savings and investment decisions are independent of one another. But in most LDCs, such as assumption is open to serious doubts, as savings and investment units could be identical. In fact, savings could be regarded as a residual and/or given by the willingness to invest. If this is true, then the policy of interest rate liberalisation is unlikely to be a very efficient tool for allocating resources.

Case studies

In view of these qualitative criticisms, it is necessary to look further into the nature and causes of imbalances in some LDCs. A number of case studies available show different scenarios of country imbalances (see Brown, 1984; Fitzgerald, 1984; Jansen, 1984; Nicholas, 1984; Parikh, 1984; van Themat, 1984; Vos, 1984; Wutys, 1984; and Parikh *et al.*, 1985). A major reason for imbalance between aggregate demand and aggregate supply, according to the IMF is the excess of government expenditure over revenue, financed mainly by an increase in money supply and domestic credit creation and reflected in accelerating inflation and/or a rise in a balance of payments deficit and consequent devaluation.

Given this type of analysis, stabilisation can be approached in a framework where aggregated demand has to be dampened to the level of aggregate supply. This view can be questioned, and has been questioned by the structuralists because rigidities in production and demand prevent monetary restraint from being reflected in a moderation of inflationary pressures and a redirection of resources towards the external sector. Also, experience in LDCs shows extreme rigidity in cutting government expenditure (Jansen, 1984). Indeed, demand restrictions via rises in interest rates may lead, and have lead, to a fall in output and investment in the long run (Wijnbergen, 1983; see also pp. 91–3). Thus, the long-run capacity of earning foreign exchange to restore the external balance is considerably reduced. If this line of argument is followed then stabilisation policy should try to eradicate structural rigidities so that the overall production capacity is increased. Such an increase will reduce excess demand and release resources for stabilising the balance of payments (Jansen, 1985).

The case studies show clearly that in many cases it is difficult to take a monetarist or structuralist view of the world. For one thing, the underlying reasons for instability are very complex and difficult to separate. It seems, that the phenomena of excess demand, fiscal imbalance, foreign trade deficit and monetary growth are fairly interrelated. The case studies, however, do confirm a significant expansion of the public sector and an increase in the public-sector deficit, which is the main villain of the drama narrated by the IMF. This deficit has partly been financed by an increase in money supply in most cases. But beyond this immediate reason, there are other factors which have caused an expansion of the deficit. Such factors are:

(a) Terms of trade losses after the oil-price shocks in 1973–4 and 1978–9 also implied a fall in the share of import duties and export tax revenues of LDCs. To absorb these exogenous shocks, public sector deficits were expanded. The problem became acute when it was difficult to raise taxes or introduce new ones.
(b) In a number of countries, the public-sector deficits were expanded considerably to finance military expenditure for defence and internal security (for example, Nicaragua, Sri Lanka, Sudan, India, Pakistan, Thailand and Somalia). Indeed, given the massive growth of defence expenditure in these countries it is possible to speak of a structural factor and hypothesise a correlation between political security and economic instability.
(c) It has been argued that foreign borrowing has invited budgetary imbalances because the availability of foreign financing allowed public-sector expenditure to rise without 'crowding out' private resources.

However, the impact of a budgetary deficit is not always the same for all LDCs. In a number of cases, such deficits have led to balance of payments problems, and foreign debt had to be accumulated to finance such deficits. In the case of least developed countries such as Tanzania, imports are under state control and the possibility of foreign borrowing is not great. The main effect of a rise in aggregate demand, due to fiscal imbalance, has been on the home market. Inability to meet the excess demand has led to the development of parallel markets for goods and foreign exchange. In some other cases, for example, Sudan, a budgetary imbalance might have stimulated inappropriate imports and reduced resources for raising exports and domestic production.

When the LDCs faced recession in world trade during 1981–3, an increasing proportion of available foreign exchange was obtained from capital flows, that is, aid and loans. This implied a flow of foreign exchange to the public sector. In order to adjust for these inflows, public expenditure becomes very difficult to cut.

Thus fiscal expansion and balance of payments problems can influence the financial system as both types of imbalances lead to increase in money stock.

The scope for stabilisation policy

The scope for stabilisation policy can be analysed in the framework of the Keynesian-monetarist controversy (though we believe that the nature of disagreement has sometimes been exaggerated: see, for example Aghevli *et al.*, 1979, for a good analysis: see also Mathieson, 1979). According to the Keynesians and neo-Keynesians, the major cause of instability is the change in aggregate demand which causes changes in interest rates. If the demand for money is interest-elastic, there could be either an excess supply or an excess demand for money. An increase in aggregate demand results in higher prices (through an excess supply of money). Similarly, a decrease in aggregate demand results in excess liquidity. If we now assume downwards rigidity of wages and prices, then a decrease in output and employment will occur. So, demand shocks lead to the classic trade-off between inflation and unemployment. The nature of the oscillation of the economy due to demand shocks depends on the following (see Chapter 2):

(a) The nature of the marginal propensity to save (MPS). The lower the MPS, the larger will be the impact of the initial demand shock via the operation of the multiplier, and the greater the degree of instability.
(b) The value of the interest elasticity of investment. The lower this value (that is, the compensating change in investment because of a fall in interest rate), the larger the instability.
(c) The size of the interest elasticity of the money demand functions, that is, the higher the rise in excess liquidity due to an initial change in the interest rate, the larger the degree of instability. It is noteworthy that these factors which aggravate the effect of demand shocks also magnify the superiority of fiscal over monetary policy.

In other words, the Keynesians argue that given a low marginal propensity to save, a low interest elasticity of investment and a high interest elasticity of the money demand function, it is possible to demonstrate the relative effectiveness of fiscal policy in stabilising the economy. However, Keynesians do not rule out the use of monetary policy. They point out that variations in aggregate expenditure can alter output and employment in the short run and, notwithstanding the adjustment lags, short-run stabilisation policy can be effective.

The limited evidence available so far enables us to draw the following conclusions:

(a) In most LDCs the MPS is quite low and hence the value of the multiplier should be high. *A priori*, this implies that demand shocks can cause instabilities, and fiscal policy can be used as an important instrument of stabilisation. If, however, supply factors account for instability in production, then of course demand management policies will be ineffective.
(b) Very little is known about the interest elasticity of investment functions in LDCs. The type of financial dualism that prevails in LDCs hardly helps us to get a clear idea about the flow of funds and its elasticity due to variations in interest rates. Rural money markets are quite large while the money market is subject to control. In a controlled financial market, the availability of credit becomes a more important determinant of investment than its cost (Ghatak, 1976).

(c) The econometric estimates of the elasticity coefficients of the interest rates in money demand function are usually small. Such a conclusion strengthens the argument of the monetarist school when the estimated money demand functions are generally found to be stable (see Deadman and Ghatak, 1981).
(d) Furthermore, we find, on the basis of preliminary estimates, that the effects of a rise in interest rates on savings (the ratio of fixed deposits to GDP) in some LDCs (for example, Sri Lanka) is positive, but not always significant for all countries. Hence, it is difficult to say anything conclusive about the policy of raising interest rates (see table A6.1 in the appendix).

Although the two schools cite empirical studies to support their views, such empirical studies are rather inadequate. Also, results of such studies are hardly conclusive. Indeed, the *practical effectiveness* of alternative stabilisation policies in LDCs has been one of the under-researched areas of investigation.

Case study: Bangladesh

Two empirical studies on money supply and prices in Bangladesh could be mentioned. In the first study, Parikh and Starmer (1988) presented a framework for investigating bivariate causal relations using Granger's notion of causality. This framework is employed to test the relationship between the money supply and prices in Bangladesh using monthly data for the period 1973 to 1986. The results indicate evidence of significant unidirectional feedback running from prices to money. The analysis is extended to investigate the relationship between rates of change in money and prices and once again there is evidence of feedback from prices to money. The main conclusion is that strict exogeneity of the money supply is rejected. These results are consistent with a 'structuralist' view of the Bangladesh economy. Policy implications are briefly discussed by the authors.

In the second study, Parikh and Starmer (1993) formulated and estimated an econometric model of the monetary sector of Bangladesh using annual date for the period 1974–87. The model is evaluated using a range of diagnostic tests and the results from dynamic simulations. The simulations indicate that, historically, inflation, real output growth and monetary growth are all consistent with a structuralist framework in which exogenous shocks, such as harvest failures, play a leading role in monetary expansions via their effects on food prices. Accommodationist monetary policies may generate further inflationary pressures, through there may be short periods during which monetary expansions increase real output. Excess supplies of real money balances do not appear to have any significant impact on real expenditures.

Case study: Indonesia

The relationship between money supply and prices in Indonesia during 1969 and 1980 has been investigated by Parikh (1990). He tried to integrate the influence on prices which flow not only from monetary changes but also from other exogenous shocks (harvest failures, devaluations, or changes in world market prices on key export commodities) with the influences of money supply caused not only by government policy changes but also from previous or expected price changes. The findings suggest that although monetary authorities have some control over the money supply they are also subject to powerful forces in the economy which limit the extent to which money supply changes can be exogenously determined. By contrast, it is also found that the rate of inflation (proxy for the interest rate in a developing economy), which is generally considered to be an important element in the money demand function, does not turn out to be a significant factor in recent Indonesian experience. The formulated model in this chapter is simulated dynamically and seems to possess desirable properties, namely, positive prices and stable solutions.

Case study: Pakistan

The relationship between money and inflation in Pakistan has been tested by Siddiqui (1990). By using Granger–Sims causality tests, and different proxies for money and inflation, both of which have direct bearing on the causal inferences, the author found that both narrow and broad money are endogenous with respect to the consumer price index (CPI); however, apparent independence was observed with WPI. The estimated money–inflation feedbacks were interpreted to be 'caused' by the link of money and inflation with government budget deficits and balance of payment adjustment.

Other countries

After analysing a large number of country studies, Taylor notes that countries in which IMF-sponsored 'old-fashioned monetarism' had some success in the 1980s were marked by the dominance of 'flex-price' markets (the Philippines and African countries) and/or repressive regimes (for example, Chile in Latin America, where it took five years of unemployment rates well over 20 per cent to drive down inflation from 600 per cent to 300 per cent).In the case of African countries such as Tanzania and Ghana, inflation abatement was helped by good weather – validating the structuralist line of argument – and capital inflows at the crucial time. Excess demand for goods that was initially caused by poor weather and fed into forced savings was reduced (Taylor, 1991). 'New' monetarism in Latin America took the guise of exchange rate 'liberalisation' targeted at getting rid of inflation by lowering expectations and applying the 'law of one price'. Many such attempts failed in the 'Southern Cone' economies, leaving behind enough evidence of severe financial dislocation in such countries. Evidence of financial instability in Latin-American countries during the 1980s showed up clearly in huge movements of short-term capital (that is, the so-called problem of 'capital flights'). Apart from the problem of bearing the cost of financial dislocation because of liberalisation programmes of the IMF, some economies in the 'Southern Cone' had to bear the very high cost of large-scale unemployment and loss of output. Indeed, the Latin-American experience with the IMF-sponsored programmes suggest that the road to liberalisation could be a rocky one and it is important to proceed with such programmes with due caution. The *timing, sequence* and *extent* of liberalisation programmes are also quite important in most LDCs, given their market imperfections, high inflation, chronic balance of payment problems, composition of output, and structural rigidities.

Appendix to Chapter 6

A model of inflation generation and stabilisation

To understand the price output effects of an expansion in money supply, we adopt a model originally developed by Vanderkamp with the following ingredients (see Vanderkamp, 1975, for a useful analysis):

(a) a simple money demand function; and
(b) a Phillips curve incorporating price change expectations. In the short run these expectations are constant and in the long run they fully reflect the reality of inflation;
(c) a mechanism which equilibrates the system with real output acting as the equilibrator through its effect on the unemployment rate:

$$M = kPy \tag{A6.1}$$

where M is money demand as well as supply (there is continuous market clearing), P is the price level, y is the real output and k is the reciprocal of velocity of money and is constant.

We are interested in the rate of inflation. We differentiate equation A6.1 logarithmically to get

$$\dot{M} = \dot{P} + \dot{y} \tag{A6.2}$$

where the dot on a variable shows percentage change in the variable.

Equation A6.2 states that changes in money supply determine changes in nominal income levels. Note that we do not know how much of this money supply change will go into prices and how much into output.

To determine the split between price and output change we use the Phillips curve relation:

$$\dot{P} = a_0 + a_1 U^{-1} + \dot{P}* \tag{A6.3}$$

$$a_0 < 0, a_1 > 0,$$

where U is the unemployment rate and appears in inverse form to reflect the non-linearity of the Phillips curve, $\dot{P}*$ is expected rate of inflation which has a coefficient of unity reflecting the presumption that price change expectations are fully absorbed in wage (and thus price) changes. The expected rate of inflation is influenced by past rates of inflation. In the short run, inflation expectation can be assumed to be zero, and in the long run, inflation expectation fully catches up with actual inflation experience.

Next we have the equilibrating mechanism which works by adjustment of the rate of change in output and the unemployment rate. Let $\dot{y}*$ be the fixed growth of real output consistent with the long-run growth rate of the labour force productivity. When actual output growth exceeds $\dot{y}*$ unemployment falls. When $\dot{y} < \dot{y}*$ unemployment rate rises. Hence, we have:

$$\dot{U} = b(\dot{y} - \dot{y}*), \quad b < 0 \tag{A6.4}$$

where $\dot{U}$ is rate of change in unemployment.

The model

In the following model we present a diagrammatic representation (figure A6.1) of the Phillips curve, showing the interrelationships between money, output and inflation.

The diagram is drawn from the above equations. From equation A6.2, $\dot{M}$ lines are 45° angles to the axis, showing that a rise in money supply can all be used for inflation or all for real output rises, or linear combinations of the two.

The past rate of inflation (which determines $\dot{P}*$) is a predetermined variable. $\dot{M}$ is exogenous in this system. Equation A6.2 to A6.4 are shown in figure A6.1. The vertical axis measures P and the horizontal axis in the right quadrant measures unemployment, U. Equation A6.3 – the Phillips curve – is presented in $\dot{P}U$-space where $D\dot{P}_0$ shows the trade-off and the expected rate of inflation $\dot{P}*$ is a horizontal line. The left quadrant shows y, with output growth increasing further towards the left. $\dot{y}*$ is the fixed long-run rate of growth of real output. Two different rates of money supply rise are shown by the lines $\dot{M}_0$ and $\dot{M}_1$.

The initial equilibrium positions of the variables are $\dot{M} = \dot{M}_0$, $\dot{y} = \dot{y}*$ $\dot{P} = 0$ and $U = U*$.

A rise in $\dot{M}$ to $\dot{M}_1$ changes the equilibrium positions as follows: $\dot{y} = \dot{y}_1$ and $\dot{P} = \dot{P}_1$ and $U = U_1$ (assuming that initial $\dot{P}* = 0$ and does not change). To see this happening, we go back to the initial period (0). When the rate of growth of money is increased from $\dot{M}_0$ to $\dot{M}_1$, the rate of output will initially go to $\dot{y}_1$ since for the moment unemployment is given by $U = U*$. Note that $\dot{y}_1 > \dot{y}*$. The rate of

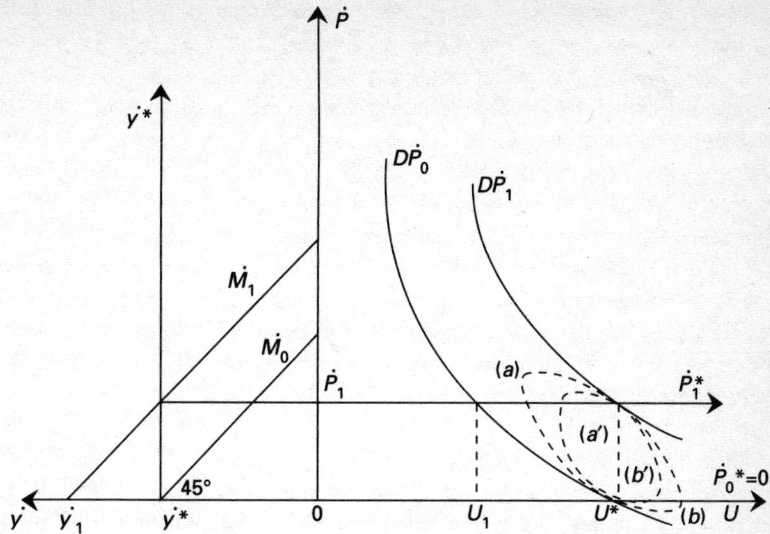

Figure A6.1

unemployment falls. As U falls we travel up the Phillips curve, which implies that $\dot{P} > 0$. At $\dot{P}_1 - U_1$, the process stops and equilibrium is restored with $\dot{y} = \dot{y}^*$, $P = \dot{P}_1$ and $U = U_1$. It is interesting to notice that while the RHS of the diagram gives us a Phillips curve explanation of inflation, the LHS of the same figure gives us a quantity theory explanation of inflation.

The position with $\dot{P} = \dot{P}_1$ and $\dot{P}^* = 0$ cannot be sustained for long. To evaluate the long-run shifts, it is assumed that $\dot{P}^*$ catches up with actual $\dot{P}$. The long-run equilibrium is restored at $\dot{y}^*$, and $\dot{P}_1$ and U^* with $\dot{P}^*$ shifting up to $\dot{P}_1$. Thus, in the long run, quantity theory holds as $D\dot{P}_0$ shifts to $D\dot{P}_1$ and the price equation stands as

$$\dot{P} = \dot{M} - \dot{y} \tag{5}$$

In the long run, rate of growth of output and unemployment are equal to their respective natural growth rates. The effect of increase in money supply is wholly reflected in increase in the rate of inflation and inflation expectation.

However, the Phillips curve is important in determining the adjustment path traced out between long-run equilibrium and the short-run, and the Phillips curve determines U^*, the natural rate of unemployment. The role is more important the less rapidly inflationary expectations adjust to actual experience. If $\dot{P}^*$ is constant, then monetary policy can be used to move along to the most desired $\dot{P} - U$ combination. Only a reliable estimate of the Phillips curve can give us a measure of trade-off costs between $\dot{P}$ and U. Such an estimate will give us the size of the natural unemployment rate which will not only reflect structural imbalances and downward rigidities but also cost-push type of inflation pressure.

Second, the Phillips curve is an important factor in determining the adjustment path between long-run equilibria (Vanderkamp, 1975).

From the diagram, if expectation adjusts slowly (for example, in LDCs because of structural rigidities), (*a*) will be a more probable path of adjustment, while rapid expectation adjustment will produce a path like (*a*′) (for example, in DCs because of less imperfections in the markets). On the other side of the coin, a period of monetary contraction can produce an adjustment path like (*b*) or (*b*′). Path (*a*) shows slow adjustment of inflationary expectation. Adjustment will be painful given the non-linear shape of the Phillips curve, as large doses of unemployment are needed to reduce inflation by a substantial amount. If $\dot{P}^*$ reacts slowly, then monetary policy can be used effectively to reduce unemployment for a while. If incomes policy is used along with a restrictive monetary policy, then *DP* shifts to the left and further employment gains are possible.

Causality between money and prices

The model above shows how an increase in money supply can increase the rate of inflation without altering output and the rate of unemployment in the long run. Whether in practice this is, in fact, the outcome of a monetary expansion in less-developed countries needs empirical investigation. Clearly, if there is no consistent pattern in the relationship between money and prices in the LDCs, 'global' policy rules of the sort outlined above may be inappropriate.

Since the pioneering work of Granger (1969) and Sims (1972) there has been a substantial amount of work done on the theory of testing for the direction and pattern of causality between economic variables. As has been pointed out, however (for example, Greenberg and Webster, 1983, or Jacobs *et al.*, 1979) there are several problems shared by all methods rooted in the 'Granger–Sims' causality framework with respect to how causality should be defined, and to whether such definitions correspond to what economists generally understand causality to mean. Despite these reservations, these methods do constitute the best available techniques to investigate the relationship between money and prices in different countries.

The particular method adopted in this paper is that detailed in Vandaele (1983) and used by Schofiled *et al.* (1986, chapter 6). The significant step in this approach compared with some other methods is the pre-whitening of the output series (prices) by the use of the univariate autoregressive integrated moving average model (ARIMA model) estimated for the input series (money). This follows the original suggestion by Box and Jenkins (1970) and which it is now argued (see, for example, Vandaele, 1983, p. 291) provides the appropriate methodology for a leading indicator (unidirectional) model which has no feedback. This seems to best capture the idea under discussion of global restrictive monetary prescriptions for LDCs based on a presumed relationship of monetary expansions leading to inflation. Before the filter for the input series is used for the output series, both series must be tested for stationarity, and if necessary, transformed to achieve this. Causality is inferred from inspection of the cross-correlation function (CCF) between the filtered or pre-whitened output and input series. Evidence that 'money leads prices – that is current and lagged values of the money supply series determine the current level of prices – would be provided by significant spikes or pulses for positive lags in the CCF. 'Prices leading money' might be inferred by significant spikes at negative lags (leads) in the CCf, but, as noted above, the method is specifically set up to investigate a leading indicator model. Hence, such results (which do occur in some of the empirical work reported below) may indicate some causal feedback which would call for more complicated analysis than is pursued here.

The data used in each case below was post-war annual data, obtained from *International Financial Statistics* (IFS). Hence the number of observations used for any country is only around 35, which is less than generally advocated in time-series analysis. If these techniques are to be useful for economists, however, some experience of their practical application for annual data series of lengths typically available is desirable. The preferred option of moving to quarterly data (which in any case is not available for most of the countries considered below) to increase the data set is also likely to introduce more parameters to be estimated (for example, seasonal effects estimated comprehensively for Indonesia by Parikh, 1984). What is required is the determination of a general rather than precise relationship or pattern between the input and output series, in a situation where it is expected on theoretical grounds that the maximum lag of interest in the CCF would be of the order 3 only. 'Significant' pulses outside of this range can probably be ascribed to sampling error given the shortage of data.

India (1950–1985)

Narrow money The time series plot of the data suggested more variability in the series than that for broad money (see below), but is still subject to a relatively smooth and increasing trend. The plots suggest 'off-trend' values between 1974 and 1976 for the price deflator (perhaps reflecting the OPEC price increases) and between 1976 and 1978 for the money data. A model in which prices lead money rather than the reverse might be suspected for this case, a result previously suggested by Chakrabarty (1977). A more detailed analysis of the data confirms this suspicion. For both the narrow money and price deflator, first differences of the logarithms generated stationary series. An autoregressive filter for narrow money seemed indicated, and an ARIMA (1, 1, 0) model produced a filter with white noise residuals (as judged by the Ljung–Box statistic) and a CCF with significant spikes at lags (–3) and (–1). An ARIMA (1, 1, 1) filter produced this same pattern of significant leads for prices over money, but with the autoregressive parameter marginally breaking the stationarity condition. The possibility of a unit root problem was not evident in the ARIMA (1, 1, 0) model. The only significant spike for an ARIMA (0, 1, 0) filter was at (–1), so that low-order ARIMA models for this case were *consistent in indicating prices leading money.*

Broad money The form of the data for broad money in India mitigates against the finding of any causal links between it and the price deflator. The time-series plot of the broad-money series (annual 1950–85) indicates a remarkable long smooth and increasing trend rate of growth. This resulted in the need to take second rather than first differences of the logarithm of the money supply to achieve a stationary series. The ACF of the transformed series suggested no particular filter outside of white noise. As Box and Jenkins (1970, p. 377) indicate, the CCF between a white noise variable and an autocorrelated variable will have a CCF of the same form as the ACF for the autocorrelated variable. It is not surprising then, to find that the CCF's for the transformed money supply series and the first differenced logarithms of the price deflator when both were being filtered by low-order processes gave consistent *but probably unconvincing significant positive spikes at lag* (+1) and a general pattern of CCF coefficients corresponding with those of the ACF for the transformed price deflator series.

Turkey (1950–1986)

Narrow money Both the narrow money series and the consumer price index data exhibited a marked change in their growth around 1975, possibly associated with the oil price shock. Second-order differencing of the logarithmic data was required to achieve stationarity in both series. The best determined ARIMA models were (1, 2, 0) and (0, 2, 1), that is, autoregressive or moving average models of order 1. There was little to choose between them in terms of fit, the diagnostic checks on the residuals, or the Ljung–Box statistic. A mixed model (1, 2, 1) had neither the AR nor MA coefficient significant in the estimated model. In every case, however, the plot of the CCF *had no significant spikes or pulses at any lead or lag.*

Broad money As for the narrow series, second-order differencing was required to achieve stationarity for a series exhibiting a very rapid rate of growth from the middle of the 1970s. The preferred model for the filter for the broad money series was an ARIMA (0, 2, 1) model. For this definition of money, there was a *marked pulse or spike at lag zero in the CCF, indicating either instantaneous causality, or perhaps a very short lead/lag relationship between money and prices* which is masked by the use of annual data.

Philippines (1950–86)

Narrow money The time series of the annual data for both narrow money and the price deflator needed transforming by the use of first differences of the logarithms to produce stationary series. The ACF and PACF of the transformed money series indicated that a third-order autoregressive model might be appropriate. The residuals from this fitted model were acceptable as white noise (when judged by the Ljung–Box statistic), and the associated CCF with the pre-whitened price *deflator indicated money leading prices with a one year lead.* A lower (second) order autoregressive process replicated this lead of money over prices, but with less satisfactory residuals for the pre-whitened money data

Broad money The growth in broad money of the period 1950–86 has been substantially greater than that for narrow money, particularly towards the end of the period. The first differences of the logarithms of this series produced a series in which the ACF coefficients failed to die down quickly, although not individually statistically significant. The best-determined model from this series (an ARIMA 1, 1, 1) produced white-noise residuals as judged by the Ljung–Box statistic, and when used as a filter for the price deflator, failed to indicate any significant lead/lag or coincident pattern between broad money and prices. As there was some question as to whether first-differencing of the log of the broad money series was sufficient to achieve a stationary series, the analysis above was repeated using the second difference of the log of broad money. The ACF of the second-differenced series was clearly stationary. When modelled by low-order ARIMA processes (of which a first-order moving average was the preferred model) to provide the filter for the price series, the associated *cross-correlation functions* did not give us *any significant lead/lag or coincident relationships between money and prices*, thus duplicating the results of the first-differenced data.

South Korea (1951–1986)

Narrow money Stationary series for both the narrow money series and the consumer price index were obtained by use of the first differences of the logarithms. An ARIMA (1, 1, 1) model for the money series was chosen on the basis of evidence from the associated ACF and PACE, and when used as a filter for the transformed price series, yielded a CCF indicating *no significant lead/lag concurrent* relationship between narrow money and prices. This conclusion was not altered by the choice of other low-order ARIMA models for the money supply series.

Broad money Annual data was available for a slightly shorter time span than for the narrow money series (1953–86). As for narrow money, first differences of the logarithms produced a stationary series for money. An ARIMA (1, 1, 0) model was the preferred model for this series, and as for narrow money, produced *no significant spikes in the CCF with the filtered price series*. An ARIMA (1, 1, 1) did produce a marginally significant spike at lag (–2), but as part of a generally unconvincing and probably spurious pattern of CCF values. The moving average term in this formulation was not statistically significant so that little confidence can be expressed in this finding.

Malaysia (1951–86)

Narrow money The narrow money data exhibited a marked trend such that second-order differencing of the logarithms was required to achieve stationarity. First-order differencing of the log of the price deflator series was sufficient to achieve stationarity of this series. The preferred model for the money series was an ARIMA (2, 1, 1), which yielded white-noise residuals as judged by the ACF, and implied a *one-year lead of money over prices* when used as a filter for the price series.

Broad money There was some evidence of non-stationarity in the first differences of the logs of money, with the ACF failing to die down quickly. As for the narrow money series, second-order differencing of the logs of money achieved stationarity. A variety of low-order ARIMA models for the transformed data when used a filters for the first-differenced logs of the price series consistently indicated a *one year lead of money over prices*, though whether or not there was also a significant spike in the CCF at a lead of three years was sensitive to the precise ARIMA model used.

Conclusions

In this chapter, we have argued that a restrictive monetary policy could bring down the rate of inflation in the long run, but the short-run costs (for example, fall in output and employment) can perhaps be avoided. In the case of Thailand, it has been shown elsewhere that the main cause of inflation was the oil price increase, and not a rise in government expenditure (Jansen, 1984). Indeed, the Thais have been credited by the IMF with careful management of budgetary expenditure. In many other cases, the scope for reducing government expenditure is limited. If the reduction of budgetary deficit is regarded as an important target, then it may be useful to raise import levies or taxes.

If the reasons for an increase in the rate of inflation have been the result of oil-price shocks reflected in import price indices rather than a rise in money supply and public expenditure deficit, then the traditional prescription of some international agencies to control the money supply is questionable. Even if there is a close relationship between prices and money supply, we have shown that ARIMA causality tests for a number of LDCs suggest a 'feedback' between money and prices. This means that increase in money supply may passively respond to price increases. Indeed, the 'dose' and 'response' relationship between money and price could also depend significantly on the choice of the definition of money ('narrow' or 'broad'). Furthermore we find that the effects of a rise in interest rates on savings (the ratio of fixed deposits to GDP) in some LDCs is positive, but not always significant. Hence, it is difficult to say anything conclusive about the policy of raising interest rates. Finally, information available on interest elasticity of investment function is rather poor, and hardly any conclusion can be drawn about it.

Table A6.1 Estimates of savings function in some LDCs: log linear estimates

Country	*Dependent variables* Δ *R DEP*	Δ *RPY*	*Independent variables* Δ *RR*	$\bar{R}^2$	*DW*	See
MALAYA	Δ *R DEP*	0.719**	0.0519	0.996	1.70	0.718
		(29.62)	(0.698)			
INDIA	Δ *R DEP*	0.0974**	0.374	0.91	1.71	0.091
		(4.52)	(1.79)			
SRI LANKA	Δ *R DEP*	0.573**	0.354*	0.98	1.97	0.106
		(17.98)	(2.80)			

Δ *R DEP* = change in real deposit rate
Δ *RPY* = change in real per capital income
Δ *RR* = change in real interest rate
D*W* = Durbin-Watson statistic
$\bar{R}^2$ = adjusted coefficient of multiple determination
Annual data: 1957-81 in each case.
'*t*' values in parentheses.

7. The Polak model: its application to the LDCs

The discussion of the relationship between money and economic growth in Chapter 5 has largely taken place in the context of a closed economy. However, in 'open' economies, the impact of foreign trade or money supply and domestic economic activities could be important.

One main reason for the lack of consideration of the role of trade in the economic development of the LDCs is that trade does not form a large part of the total income of these countries. On the other hand, there are quite a few exceptions. Further, it is at present difficult to see how the LDCs in general could be wholly immune to the ebb and flow of world trade. A general recession in the DCs is likely to affect most LDCs adversely because a fall in the level of income and aggregate demand in the DCs could also reduce the exports, output and employment in many LDCs. It is, however, true that LDCs which rely more on trade than others (more 'open' or 'dependent') are likely to be harder hit by a general recession in the DCs than others which are less 'open'. In any case, it is interesting to analyse the interrelationships between output, income, exports, imports and prices in the 'open' LDCs and try to quantify the effects as far as possible. One attempt has been made by Polak (1957, 1971) and Polak and Boissonneult (1959) to which we now turn.

7.1 The Polak–Boissonneult (PB) model

The PB model is a simple way to analyse the effects of imports, exports and money supply within the circular flow model. Once the imports, previous exports and credit creation of a country are known, the PB model can be used to find out the specific values of such imports, exports and credit creation that would be needed to reach target levels of income and reserves. The basic PB macro-model can be set out as follows:

$$Y_t = Y_{t-1} + \Delta MS_t \qquad (7.1)$$

where Y = nominal national income
MS = quantity of money
t = income period in which money supply turns over once in income-generating transactions.

Thus t could be regarded as a fraction of a period given by the ratio of money to national income which would indicate the reciprocal of the average velocity of income. Thus the equation states that, given a stable income velocity, next year's income will be given by the sum of the present year's income and the change in the quantity of money. Alternatively, with a given income velocity, the quantity of money will change from one year to the other by an amount equal to the change in income. Now, the ΔMS_t is divided as follows:

$$\Delta MS_t = \Delta R_t + \Delta D_t \tag{7.2}$$

where R_t = net foreign assets
D_t = net domestic assets

Next we have a balance of payment equation:

$$\Delta R_t = X_t - M_t + C_t \tag{7.3}$$

where X = exports
M = imports
C = net capital inflows

The change in MS and thus in Y can now be defined as

$$\Delta MS_t = X_t + C_t + \Delta D_t - M_t \tag{7.4}$$

Let the exogenous variables be classified as Q_t, so that we have

$$Q_t = X_t + C_t + \Delta D_t \tag{7.5}$$

The equation for imports is given as

$$M_t + mY_t \tag{7.6}$$

By substituting the last three equations into (7.1) we have

$$(1+m)Y_t = Q_t + Y_{t-1} \tag{7.7}$$

Dividing equation (7.7) by (1 + m) and eliminating the terms with Y in the right hand side (RHS) of equation (6.7) yields

$$Y_t = \frac{Q_t}{1+m} + \frac{Q_{t-1}}{(1+m)^2} + \frac{Q_{t-2}}{(1+m)^3} \tag{7.8}$$

and the corresponding equation for imports is given by

$$M_t = \frac{mQ_t}{1+m} + \frac{mQ_{t-1}}{(1+m)^2} + \frac{mQ_{t-2}}{(1+m)^3} \tag{7.9}$$

The last two equations give income and imports in terms of Q_t i.e. the exogenous variables.

For the sake of easy computation and to determine Y and M without first obtaining the value for exports, Q_t could also be defined as

$$Q_t = \Delta MS_t + M_t \quad (7.10)$$

It is generally argued from the above presentation that since PB have tried to determine income via changes in the quantity of money, their approach is monetarist (Schotta, 1966; Baker and Falero, 1971). Notice that in the PB model, income is sought to be determined by both money supply *and* the foreign-exchange reserves, so that such a model could provide simple policy guidelines to a LDC experiencing a foreign-exchange bottleneck. The model is also useful for analysing the relationships between goods and financial flows. The advantage of the PB model is that it is simple and does not require too much information about a large number of variables and hence becomes suitable for application to the LDCs.

7.2 The application of the PB model

The general case

In order to facilitate the application of the PB model to any developing country it is important to find out the velocity (v) and the import–income ratio (m). The former could be estimated by dividing the gross national product or national income (Y) by money (MS). Thus, v is given by Y/MS. Similarly, m is given by M/Y. Notice that the PB model assumes a proportional relationship between (a) imports and income and (b) income and money. It has a practical advantage in the sense that one is not required to know the *separate* estimates of m and v because the product of m and v would always be the same. For the derivation of $m.v$ it is only necessary to know the ratio of imports to money supply because

$$m.v = \frac{M}{Y} \cdot \frac{Y}{MS} = \frac{M}{MS} \quad (7.11)$$

Thus the estimations of m and v separately from the national income statistics of the LDCs (which are not always very reliable or accurate) are no longer necessary.

The statistical form of the PB model

The statistical form of the PB model to estimate the various coefficients and to predict the changes in income can now be illustrated. The model contains seven stochastic equations and it was originally used for the Mexican economy (Schotta, 1966),

$$\Delta M_d = a_1 + k\Delta Y + u_t \quad (7.12)$$

where ΔM_d = the change in demand for money
k = the fraction of income held as cash.

The equation (7.12) simply states that change in money demand is related to change in income (ΔY) and a constant (Cambridge k) and the only motive for holding money is the transaction demand for cash balances. This is a fairly classical interpretation. Next, we have

$$\Delta MS = a_0 + b_1 B + b_2 \Delta L + b_3 D + u_2 \tag{7.13}$$

where $B = X - M$ (or exports–imports) or balance in current account
L = long term capital liabilities to foreigners
D = government taxes net of spending

Following Prais (1961) it is assumed that domestic expenditure (E) is equal to income (Y) and a parameter, b_4, which takes into account the difference between planned (M_d) and actual (MS) liquidity. Thus,

$$E = Y + b_4 \left(MS - M_d\right) \tag{7.14}$$

The import equation is written as:

$$M = a_4 + mY + u_3 \tag{7.15}$$

The export, and ΔL equations are given exogenously, that is,

$$X = x\left(t\right) \tag{7.16}$$

$$\Delta L = l\left(t\right) \tag{7.17}$$

Finally, we have the identity:

$$Y \equiv E + X - M + \Delta L \tag{7.18}$$

The central argument discussed above can be stated as follows. Any exogenous change in exports or ΔL will lead to a disequilibrium between planned and actual holding of liquidity, which in its turn will alter prices; such changes in prices will lead to changes in money income and imports. The model implicitly assumes unit elasticity of prices for exports and imports as well as unit elasticity of import demand. Note that it also assumes away any changes in domestic credit creation (Schotta, 1966).

7.3 The PB model within the Keynesian income analysis

The PB model could now be presented within the Keynesian framework. Thus we have,

$$Y = C + I + G + X - M \tag{7.19}$$

where C = total consumption
I = total investment (domestic)
G = government expenditure.

In the previous section the argument was that the changes in money supply would lead to changes in money national income. But within the Keynesian framework it may be argued that the changes in autonomous expenditure will lead to changes in national income. In the statistical form of the model, we have five definitional and three structural equations. Next we have

$$C = cY_d \tag{7.20}$$

$$Y_d = Y - T \tag{7.21}$$

$$T = gY \tag{7.22}$$

$$M = mY \tag{7.23}$$

$$I = I(t) \tag{7.24}$$

$$G = G(t) \tag{7.25}$$

$$X = X(t) \tag{7.26}$$

where

Y_d = disposable income
C = consumption
T = total taxes

The change in income (ΔY) via the multiplier is then given

$$\Delta Y = \frac{1}{1 - c(1-g) + m} \cdot \Delta I + \Delta X + \Delta G \tag{7.27}$$

Thus, given the estimated coefficients of c (the marginal propensity to consume), m (the marginal propensity to import), and, g (the marginal propensity to tax), and the values of ΔI, ΔX and ΔG (given exogenously), changes in national income (ΔY) could be predicted.

7.4 The empirical results

The empirical results which are obtained through the application of the PB model to the LDCs have lent support to both the monetarist and the Keynesian views. However, in the case of Mexico, the monetary model is supposed to give better prediction of the changes in money national income (ΔY) than the Keynesian income model since the Keynesian model explained about 50 per cent of the changes in money national income, while the monetary model explained about 70 per cent of such variations. The value of the Keynesian multiplier has been found by estimating the consumption, import and tax coefficients in the following way:

$$\Delta Y = \frac{1}{1-.87(1-.07)+.19} \cdot \Delta I + \Delta G + \Delta X \tag{7.28}$$

$$\text{or} \quad \Delta Y = 2.63 \cdot \Delta I + \Delta G + \Delta X \tag{7.29}$$

The use of the ordinary least square (OLS) regression has yielded the following result:

$$\Delta Y = 2.55 + .72\,\Delta I + 3.37\,\Delta G + .96\,\Delta X \tag{7.30}$$

$$(1.55) \qquad (2.48) \qquad (.97)$$

$$R^2 = .50 \qquad \text{D.W.} = 2.09$$

(figures in parentheses are the relevant t – values).

The above result shows that about 50 per cent of the variations in income are explained by changes in investment (ΔI), changes in government expenditure (ΔG) and changes in exports (ΔX). The D.W. statistic does not show any specification error. But two problems remain. First, the explained variation is not high; second, strong inter-relationships between ΔI and ΔG (multicollinearity) could substantially vitiate the estimates obtained.

The use of the monetary model to predict the changes in ΔY has yielded the following equation:

$$\Delta Y = 3.32 + 2.45B + 4.96\,\Delta L \tag{7.31}$$

$$(.77) \qquad (.81)$$

$$R^2 = .70 \qquad \text{D.W.} = 1.72$$

(figures in parentheses are the relevant standard errors).

The result shows that both the balance of payments (B) and changes in long-term capital inflows (ΔL) exert significant effect on ΔY and the explained variation in ΔY by B and ΔL is about 70 per cent, and the D.W. statistic shows the absence of auto-correlation. It should, however, be pointed out that the above results are derived on the basis of a reduced form of the structural equation shown previously in the statistical form of the model. Since the explained variation in ΔY is said to be higher in the monetary model in comparison with the income model, the monetary model is preferred to an income model for Mexico.

It may be interesting to know the derivation of the money and the trade balance multipliers. Such derivations are easy when the reduced form of the equations are obtained from the structural equations. Recall the structural equations for demand for and supply of money (equations 7.12 and 7.13) which together state the equilibrium conditions for the money market. Thus for Mexico, we have:

$$\Delta M_d = .40 + .08\,\Delta Y \qquad (7.32)$$

$$(.003)$$

$$R^2 = .31 \qquad D.W. = 1.37$$

$$\Delta MS = .50 + .32B + .47\,\Delta L - .82D \qquad (7.33)$$

$$(.13) \quad (.12) \quad (.32)$$

$$R^2 = .60 \qquad D.W. = 1.65$$

The money market equilibrium is thus given by:

$$.40 + .08\,\Delta Y = .50 + .32B + .47\,\Delta L \qquad (7.34)$$

ignoring the effect of any change in government revenue (D). The trade balance and the capital inflow multipliers are then given by Scotta as:

$$\Delta Y = 1.3 + 4.0B + 5.9\,\Delta L + u \qquad (7.35)$$

It must, however, be mentioned that in actual practice, care should be taken to analyse the precise relationship between money inflows and the reserve base of the money supply. In particular it is necessary to examine the impact of changes in currency to money and high-powered money on money stock and the effects of changes in money stock on output, prices, imports and exports in a well-developed model.

The case of Peru

The PB model has been applied to the Peruvian economy by Baker and Falero (1971) and the direct estimation of the monetary model for Peru has yielded the following result:

$$\Delta Y = -202.17 + 2.08D + 1.44B + 46.54\,\Delta L \qquad (7.36)$$

$$(784.69) \quad (0.28) \quad (0.53) \quad (14.85)$$

$$\overline{R}^2 = 0.879 \qquad D.W. = 0.0829$$

(figures in parentheses are the relevant standard errors).

Thus, the monetary model explains about 88 per cent of the variation in national income of Peru. The effects of trade balance, change in capital inflows and government expenditure are all positive and significant. But the low value of the D.W. statistic shows the specification error and the presence of the significant influence of the omitted variables. The same problem arises when the income model has been tested which also explains about the same proportion of the variation in national income (about 89 per cent) as equation (7.37) illustrates:

$$\Delta Y = \underset{(620.14)}{777.98} + \underset{(0.28)}{.4709}\,\Delta I + \underset{(0.65)}{4.61}\,\Delta G + \underset{(0.35)}{0.54}\,\Delta X \tag{7.37}$$

$$\bar{R}^2 = .893 \qquad \text{D.W.} = 0.1778$$

It seems that both the monetary and the Keynesian models operate in the case of the Peruvian economy. The explanatory power of the two models is almost the same. In both, the effect of government expenditure is positive and more significant than is usually believed. However, both the models are affected by specification errors, as revealed by the very low values of the D.W. statistic and this reflects the complex nature of inter-relationships among major economic variables in the LDCs which may not be fully captured in simple economic models.

The Ugandan and Nigerian case studies

The PB model has also been applied to the Ugandan (Newlyn, 1968) and the Nigerian (Gray, 1963) economies. In both cases, the monetary version of the PB model has been applied and separate estimation of the income model is not available. Hence no conclusion can be drawn about the relative merits of the monetary or the income approach of the PB model. In the case of Nigeria, it has been argued that changes in money supply have led to changes in expenditure which, in their turn, have led to changes in income and imports (Gray, 1963). It is also estimated for Nigeria that the value of credit creation has tended to match the level of imports within three years (Gray, 1963).

For Uganda, Newlyn has found that imports tend to increase by about 90 per cent of the initial investment credit (Newlyn, 1968). However, Newlyn argues that Polak's definition of money would only include currency and current account in banks whereas in the context of the East African monetary system, the definition of money should also include savings and deposits accounts.

7.5 Policy implications of the PB model

The major policy implications of the PB model can now be summarised. It should, however, be remembered that these conclusions are based upon the assumption of a constant velocity and other simple assumptions (e.g. that the average and the marginal propensities to import are the same and constant.

I. A permanent rise in exports will, by itself, (that is, without expansion of credit or relaxation of import controls), gradually lead to:

(1) the same percentage rise in the level of nominal national income;
(2) a rise in the rate of imports equal to the rise in the level of exports;
(3) a rise in the quantity of money and in foreign assets of the order of 50 to 300 per cent of the rise in the annual exports rate.

II. A permanent rise in the rate of credit creation will, by itself, lead to:
(1) the same rise in the rate of nominal income and of the quantity of money as would be created by a lasting rise in exports of the same order;
(2) a rise in the rate of imports equal to the rise in the rate of credit creation;
(3) a rate of loss in reserves that will approach the rate of credit creation;
(4) a total loss of reserves which will be given by the cumulative credit expansion *net* of the rise in the quantity of money shown in I(3).

III. A transitory rise in exports will, by itself, result in:
(1) a transitory rise in nominal income which will be (aggregated over periods) the same proportion as the rise in exports;
(2) a transitory rise in imports which will be of the same size as the rise in exports;
(3) a transitory rise in money and reserves.

IV. A transitory enlargement of credit will, by itself, lead to:
(1) a transitory rise in nominal income and the quantity of money;
(2) a transitory rise in imports and a lasting reduction of reserves equal to the amount of credit enlargement.

As regards the assumption of constant velocity, it has been stated that temporary oscillations in velocity due to a sudden capital inflow or outflow need not alter the conclusions. But they would be vitiated if velocity changes, say, due to changes in interest rates. But it is argued that such a response is more likely to be observed in the economically advanced countries. 'The variability of money holdings in these countries in response to changes in the interest rate implies the necessity of greater intensity of credit policy than would be needed in most of the less developed countries in order to obtain a given change in money income' (Polak, 1957).

7.6 Limitations of the PB model

Several limitations of the PB model can be pointed out.

(i) The assumption of constant velocity in the PB model has been called into question (Newlyn, 1969). 'The constant velocity postulate is not a reflection of a propensity to hold money in relation to the level of income like that in the "Cambridge *k*". It is simply a reflection of structural factors' (Newlyn, 1969, p. 6). However, since the basic equation stated at the outset of the PB model is that all income should be spent, it is important to retain the assumption of constant income velocity (Ghatak, 1995). Nevertheless, the PB model need not necessarily imply that a change in the equilibrium in cash balances would lead to income changes. Indeed, it may be argued that if the first three equations are regarded as basic to the PB model, they could easily be given a Keynesian interpretation, while ΔD, X and C could be regarded as injections to the income flows. To maintain a constant velocity, it is conceivable that a change in income which leads to a change in the demand for money will have to be adjusted by changing the money supply (Bolnick, 1975). As Polak himself says in his original article, an increase in the quantity of money 'is determined by the increase in income … and the assumed ratio of money to income' (Polak, 1957, p. 23). Thus, the PB model could be give both a monetary and a Keynesian interpretation.

(ii) It has already been noted that Polak defines money in a narrow sense to include only currency and current account with the banks, whereas it may be argued that a broader definition of money should also include, time and savings deposits apart from currency and current accounts (Newlyn, 1968).

(iii) In the PB model, the marginal and average propensities to import are regarded as the same and constant. But this can be argued to be a dubious assumption and in some LDCs the marginal propensity differed significantly from the average propensity. It is contended that a more realistic approach would be to consider marginal rather than average propensity (Newlyn, 1968). The same argument is levelled at the assumption of constant velocity on the ground that the average velocity could be different from the marginal one. In practice, both the import and the velocity functions may not always remain stable for the LDCs particularly when structural changes occur (for example, transformation of a subsistence economy into a monetised economy) and foreign trade is subject to government intervention via exchange and import controls.

(iv) In the PB model, domestic credit expansion and capital inflows have been regarded as exogenous variables. This need not be the case.

Conclusion

The PB model has its merits and demerits. It has the advantage of being simple, intuitive and straightforward in its application. It provides a useful analytical framework of analysis of changes in income with regard to the changes in money supply, changes in exports, imports and capital inflows. It is, however, based on a few simplifying assumptions but this happens to be the case with most models. However, it boldly assumes constancy of velocity and import functions. As long as the demand function for money is stable, the PB model would be a useful framework of analysis. As has been pointed out, the model could be given both a monetary and a Keynesian interpretation.

8. Monetary policies in developing countries

8.1 Objectives of monetary policies in the LDCs

The objectives of monetary policies in the LDCs are usually related to money and credit control, price stabilisation and economic growth. Many consider price stability as the most important objective of monetary policies in the LDCs since they are supposed to suffer more from inflation than the DCs, and monetary policies are considered to be more effective than the fiscal policies in dealing with inflation. A modest rise in prices (say between 5 per cent and 10 per cent: see Chapter 6) is not regarded as harmful to the economy. Indeed, in a growing economy, the rate of growth of money supply should keep pace with the rate of growth of output to avoid deflationary pressure, and a rate of price rise between 5 and 10 per cent could boost the level of profit, investment and rate of economic growth. In this way, some argue that monetary policy could enable the economy to achieve a higher rate of economic growth. The contribution of monetary policy in achieving a higher rate of economic growth could enable the authorities to attain another objective, full employment. In many LDCs, the existence of unemployment and underemployment, particularly in the agricultural sector, has emerged as a major problem. A better utilisation of resources is regarded as imperative to promote a more decent standard of living and a greater equality of income distribution in the LDCs.

It has been pointed out by Friedman (1968) that the use of monetary policy to choose a certain rate of unemployment contrary to the rate which is *natural* for the economy (given the free market operations of the supply of and demand for labour) could eventually destabilise the economy. The argument runs as follows: in the face of a rise in unemployment, the monetary authorities could decide to increase money supply which would lead to a rate of unemployment below its natural rate and close to the target set by the authorities. But prices would rise in the short run and real wages would fall; money wages would tend to rise and supply of labour will rise too (given the money illusion). On the other hand, a fall in real wages will increase the demand for labour. But as inflation gets under way in the long-run, unemployment will appear again. If the authorities increase the rate of growth of money supply to control the situation, further unemployment would result in the long-run as the rate of inflation accelerates. As a result the economy would be destabilised. It, however, important to point out that the concept of a natural rate of unemployment is neither fixed nor easy to measure (Fisher, 1976).

Monetary policies are also regarded as useful for achieving equilibrium in the balance of payments and stabilise the exchange rates in the LDCs. A country with a balance of payment surplus would reduce interest rates whereas the LDCs which suffer from balance of payment deficits would raise the interest rates to encourage the inflow of foreign funds. Such capital movement into the economy is supposed to bridge the balance of payments gap. It is generally acknowledged that monetary policy could be used to promote external balance whereas fiscal policy should be used to promote internal balance and full employment (see for example Mundell, 1960; Sodersten, 1971; Chacholiades, 1978).

8.2 The theory of monetary policy

In macro-economics, it is well known that the classical theory assumes a vertical aggregate supply curve. A change in monetary and fiscal policy can alter the price level and the distribution of goods and services. But a change in demand could not change the level of output since the latter is given by the supply side (that is the equilibrium level of employment). In contrast to the classical model, the supply curve slopes upwards within the Keynesian model. Here a change in both monetary and fiscal policy (for example, changes in interest or tax rates) can change the aggregate demand curve and output (y) and prices (P) could be changed.

The recent controversy regarding the effectiveness of monetary and fiscal policies centres around the problem of changing the aggregate demand curve by monetary of fiscal instruments. The monetarists seem to argue that only monetary policy can change the aggregate demand curve and thereby change GNP. On the other hand, the 'fiscalists' argue that only fiscal policy can alter the aggregate demand curve and thus change the level of GNP. Sometimes the 'fiscalists' are also regarded as Keynesian though it is questionable whether Keynes actually held such a simple view about the effects of fiscal policy.

To demonstrate the relative effectiveness of the monetary and fiscal policy, it is very useful to show the general equilibrium of the economy by using the Hicksian *IS–LM* schedules. The Hicksian synthesis between the *classical* and the Keynesian theory can be summarised by using the following notations (for details, see Hicks, 1937).

classical	*simple Keynesian*	*Hicksian*	
$MV = PT$	$M_d = f(r)$	$M_d = f(r, y)$	(8.1)
$S = S(r)$	$I = I(r)$		
$I = I(r)$	$S = S(y)$	$S = S(r, y)$	(8.2)
$S = I$	$S = I$	$I = I(r, y)$	(8.3)

where S = savings,
I = investment,
r = rate of interest,
y = real income or output,
M_d = demand for money.

The geometric exposition of the general equilibrium in the money and product market is well known in terms of the *IS–LM* curves (for the derivation of the *IS–LM* curves, see any good textbook in macro-economics, such as Branson and Litvack, 1976; Dernburg and McDougall, 1976; Perlman, 1974). Let the interest rate (r) be measured along the vertical axis and the level of income (y) be measured along the horizontal axis. The *LM* curve slopes upwards because as y rises, r rises as the demand for money (M_d) rises. If the M_d is written as a demand curve for real balances, we have

$$\frac{M_d}{P} = m(r, y) \text{ that is, } M_d = P \cdot m(r, y) \tag{8.4}$$

With a given preference of the people for money and currency and fixed amount of unborrowed reserves supplied by the central bank, the money supply function is $M = M(r)$, $M' > 0$. In equilibrium,

$$M_d = \mathrm{M} \tag{8.5}$$

so that

$$M(r) = P \cdot m(r, y) \tag{8.6}$$

or

$$\frac{M(r)}{P} = m(r, y) \tag{8.7}$$

If M/P is given by

$$m(r, y) \simeq h(r) + k(y);\ h' < 0 \text{ and } k' > 0 \tag{8.8}$$

then the *LM* curve could be derived. Clearly $h' < 0$, since it shows the inverse relation of both transaction and speculative demand for money to changes in r. The demand for real balances, $k(y)$, is positively related to y and as such $k' > 0$. Each point on the *LM* curve is a point of equilibrium between the demand for money and the supply of money. Similarly, each point on the *IS* schedule is a point of equilibrium between S and I which keeps the product market in equilibrium. The *IS* curve slopes downwards since as y rises, S rises and r falls. The intersection between the *IS* and *LM* curves determines the equilibrium y and r (see figure 8.1).

A rise in price will increase the demand for nominal balances and reduce the supply of real balances and this will shift the *LM* curve to the left. The price rise could occur due to an excess of demand over supply. The rise in interest rate will

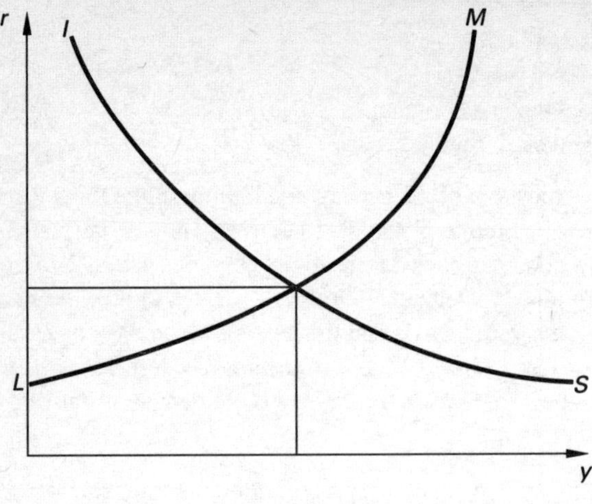

Figure 8.1

remove the disequilibrium as the demand for money will fall and supply of money will rise.

The 'fiscalist' model could be presented within the Keynesian framework:

$$y = c + i + g \tag{8.9}$$

If

$$c = c\left(y - t(y), a\right) \tag{8.10}$$

where i = investment,
g = government expenditure,
t = tax rates,
a = the real value of assets (A/P),

then we have

$$y = c\left(y - t(y), a\right) + i + g. \tag{8.11}$$

Note that the investment demand is exogenous in the equilibrium for the goods market. If i, g, t, a are given, the above equation will determine y independent of the factors in the money market. In the fiscalist model a change in M will change only the *LM* schedule. The r will be changed, but given the interest inelasticity of the investment function (that is, a vertical or near-vertical *IS* schedule), P or y would remain unaffected. However, a change in g or t will shift the *IS* curve. Now the aggregate demand curve will shift and both y and P could change. In the extreme 'fiscalist' model the *LM* curve slopes normally upwards but the *IS* curve is vertical or very inelastic. The movements of the M and *LM* curves therefore change only r, not y. In the extreme monetarist model, the *IS* schedule slopes

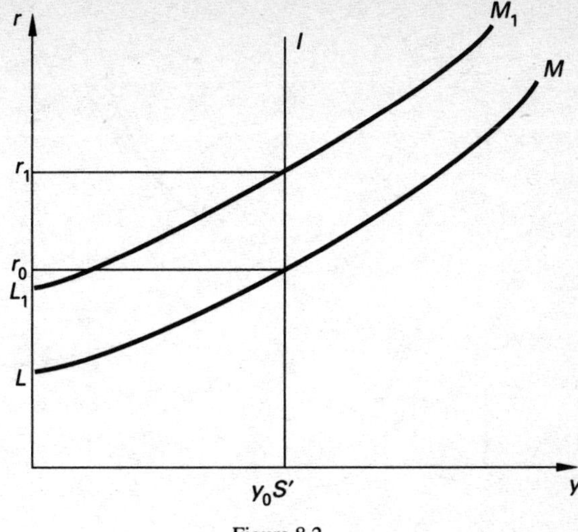

Figure 8.2

normally downwards, but the *LM* curve is vertical so that only changes in the *LM* curve could change *y*, not the changes in *IS* curve (see figures 8.2 and 8.3).

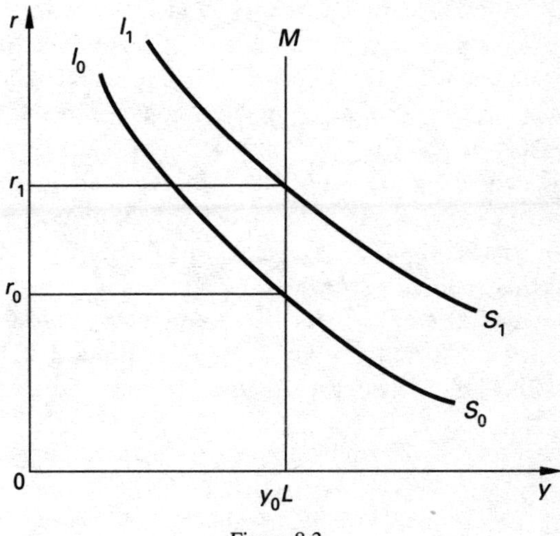

Figure 8.3

These two extreme cases are shown in figure 8.4.

The monetarist model works when the *LM* curve is near-vertical with y_0 income and r_0 interest rate. The fiscalist model operates with income at y_1 and *r* at r_1. In the monetarist case (recall the quantity theory in chapter 2):

$$P_y = Y = V\bar{M}$$

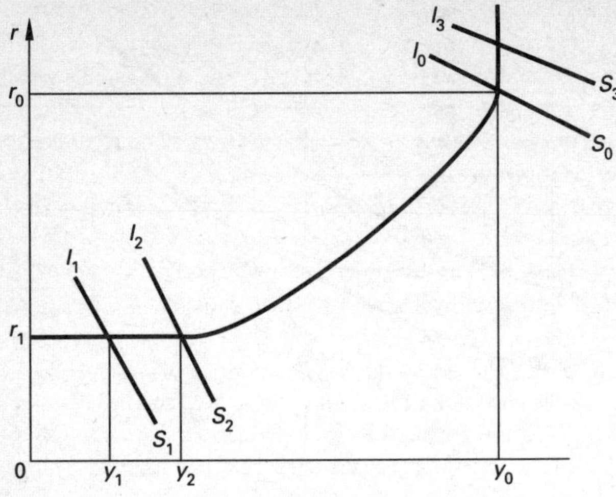

Figure 8.4

Here the limit to nominal GNP is $\bar{M}$ (given money supply). Since r is very high, speculative M_d is at a minimum and V should be at its highest level. Any change in GNP must stem from changes in $\bar{M}$.

In the fiscalist case, r is very low and a rise in M is unlikely to reduce r any more as LM is almost perfectly elastic. Even if we assume a further reduction in r, investment may not increase because of a depression and fall in business expectation. Only a change in g or t or both could shift the IS curve to the right and raise y ($y_1 \rightarrow y_2$). Thus the utility of the fiscalist model lies in forecasting changes in y when the economy is in depression. But at a near full employment situation, the monetarist model will be more useful to forecast changes in GNP as M is the limiting factor to a rise in GNP. It has been correctly observed that 'neither model will be applicable in general in an economy operating near full employment. Both key interest elasticities will then be non-zero, money will matter, and so will fiscal policy. How much each will matter will depend on the exact situation' (Branson and Litvack, 1976, p. 310).

8.3 The instruments of monetary policy

The types of monetary policy which are generally used in the LDCs are similar to those in the DCs. We shall first discuss the types of monetary instruments usually used in the LDCs. Then we will demonstrate the theory of the use of monetary policy. Next we will indicate the limitations of the use of monetary policies in the LDCs.

Bank rate policy

The bank rate is generally the rate at which the central bank of any country discounts first class bills. The term 'bank rate' is English in origin. It used to mean the rate which the Bank of England charged for discounting bills or for stabilising the balance of payments. In England this rate is now regarded as the minimum lending rate (MLR), whereas in other countries, the same rate may have different names. The MLR in the UK is a *penal* rate since it is always above the market rate. When the London discount market fails to obtain call-loans from the commercial banks, the market goes to the Bank of England and obtains funds which the Bank rediscounts at a rate higher than the market rate earned in the discount market by holding the bills. In this way the Bank of England acts as 'the lender of the last resort'. In the USA, however, the bank rate (Fed rate) is *lower* than the market rate and therefore the Federal Reserve Bank acts as the lender of the *first* resort.

Most central banks in the LDCs have used the bank rate as a *penal* rate. The *modus operandi* of the bank rate is simple. A rise in the bank rate pushes up the cost of borrowing and since the commercial banks in the UK remain 'loaned up to the hilt', a rise in the bank rate almost automatically raises the market rate of interest. If the objective of the authorities is to reduce aggregate demand, then such a rise in market rate would be useful to control expenditure as borrowings would be more expensive. Investors will also face a higher cost of borrowing. The economy eventually will be deflated. Similarly a fall in the bank rate is supposed to have a stimulating effect on the economy because a fall in the market rate of interest is likely to boost consumption and investment expenditure.

The effectiveness of bank rate policy in the LDCs has been called into question for several reasons. First, it may be pointed out that rediscounting is not a normal and regular feature of the central banks in the LDCs. The indigenous banks in India do not always discount their bills with the central bank (the Reserve Bank of India).

Secondly, the bills which are presented for discounting in the DCs are usually drawn against production or sale. Hence these short-term bills are generally self-liquidating. But in many LDCs, the orthodox borrowing methods do not help the issue of such bills. Sometimes confusion arises between genuine trade and accommodation bills. Note that an accommodation bill does not represent a specific business transaction.

Thirdly, the excess liquidity that many commercial banks experience in the LDCs hinders the growth of rediscounting of bills. Under such circumstances, even if the bank rate is raised to squeeze the credit market, the commercial banks may not be obliged to raise their interest rates and neither the cost nor the availability of credit will be affected.

Fourthly, the narrow size of the bill market and the presence of barter transactions can render bank rate policy rather ineffective. If a developing country has a substantial non-monetised sector where barter transactions take place, then clearly changes in the bank rate will have very little effect.

The empirical evidence available so far suggests that investment expenditure in the LDCs is generally interest-inelastic. Sometimes the value of the elasticity coefficient is extremely low (Basu and Ghosh, 1974). This could be explained by the fact that interest cost forms a very low proportion of total cost of investment in the LDCs.

Open market operations (OMO)

Open market operations (or OMO) generally mean the act of buying or selling government securities by the central bank. Thus at times of inflation, a *sale* of government securities to the commercial banks, insurance companies, business houses and individuals will lead to a fall in money supply and contraction. What happens is a transfer of cash from the institutions and public to the government. Similarly if the authorities decide to stimulate the economy at a time of recession, they may decide to *buy* securities from the institutions and individuals and inject more money into the circulation. Such an injection is supposed to add to the circular flow of income.

The central bank can engage in OMO for a variety of reasons. It may wish to maintain order in the market for government securities. Such order could be maintained by stabilising the rate of interest. Since bond prices and interest rates are inversely related, therefore by buying or selling securities the authorities can push bond prices up or down; this, in turn, will imply a decrease or increase in interest rates. Sayers observes that OMO was used in England during the inter-war period to insulate the domestic credit and currency supply from the ebb and flow of speculative funds (Sayers, 1957, pp. 51–2).

Sometimes the central bank may undertake OMO as a supplementary device to strengthen the effects of changes in discount rates. If the central bank is sceptical about the effectiveness of, say, a rise in discount rate in reducing aggregate demand at a time of inflation, it can first try to absorb excess liquidity by selling government securities. The central bank may also be engaged in OMO for floatation and redemption of government debt. For example, an adequate sale of government securities via OMO by the central bank is necessary at the time of redemption of public debt.

It should be observed that the real strength of OMO by the central bank lies in its capacity to alter the structure of interest rates and liquidity. Its effects are direct and immediate, and, as such, it has been regarded as an important and useful tool of monetary policy.

OMO in LDCs

The success of OMO by the central banks in LDCs depends upon a number of conditions. First, the market for government securities should be sufficiently large, active and diversified; otherwise even a small sale of securities will lead to a significant fall in their prices. This could destabilise the gilt-edged market. Secondly, some central banks in LDCs may not have adequate gilt-edged securities. In such cases the impact of OMO will be very limited. Thirdly, the existence of a developed call-loan market in the DCs allows the commercial banks to lend their surplus funds and the commercial banks in the DCs generally maintain a reasonably stable cash–deposit ratio. It follows that in the DCs, the selling or buying of gilt-edged securities by the central bank will at once reduce or increase the cash–deposit ratio of the commercial banks. But in the LDCs many commercial banks maintain a fluctuating cash–deposit ratio. Sometimes these ratios are substantially higher than the minimum legal requirements. Under such circumstances, the use of OMO may not be effective. However, in recent times, the cash–deposit ratio of the commercial banks in many LDCs has edged towards the minimum legal limit. It should be borne in mind that, to make OMO really effective, the discount rate must be penal. In other words, the discount rate charged by the central bank should be higher than the interest rates on gilt-edged securities; otherwise the commercial banks could neutralise the effect of a sale of gilt-edged securities by borrowing money to replenish their reserves by rediscounting their bills at a concessional rate with the central bank.

Variable reserve ratios (VRR)

The VRR was first introduced by the Federal Reserve Bank (the Fed) in the USA in 1935 when the Fed was empowered to prescribe the minimum reserve requirements for commercial banks to counteract the impact of a large inflow of gold and foreign exchange within the economy. Given the amount of excess liquidity, the Fed regarded the manipulation of discount rate policy and OMO as inadequate and a new policy had to be invented to mop up the excess liquidity.

It is interesting to observe that many central banks of the LDCs decided to adopt VRR as an instrument of credit control. Thus the central banks of Costa Rica, Mexico, Ecuador and Venezuela were empowered to vary the reserve ratios of the commercial banks before the end of the 1930s. Similarly, many central banks in Asia and Africa were given similar power during the 1950s and 1960s.

The use of VRR by the central banks of the LDCs became very popular. The reasons for such popularity are simple. First, the narrow market for gilt-edged securities usually limits the effectiveness of OMO. As has been pointed out before, in a narrow gilt-market even a small sale of government securities could lead to a sharp change in their prices. But the effects of VRR are more drastic and immediate *without* any adverse repercussion on the prices of government securities. Here the central bank simply raises the reserve ratios of the commercial banks to enforce a tight money policy. Secondly, given the fact that many commercial banks in the LDCs enjoy an excess liquidity, a rise in bank rate or an increase in the sale of gilts may not be enough to mop up excess liquidity. Here it is necessary to use a more direct weapon like VRR to siphon off the surplus liquidity.

It is obvious that in some LDCs the bank rate policy cannot be very effective because of the existence of a large unorganised money market. But the VRR has a greater chance of success than either OMO or the changes of bank rate even when it operates in an underdeveloped money market.

It has been suggested that the effects of VRR are discriminatory since a change in the reserve ratios by the central bank will influence the credit-creating capacity of the commercial banks but the non-banking financial intermediaries (NFI) will not be affected at all. Recall that the NFI do not maintain any deposits with the central bank. Also, while some commercial banks in the LDCs may enjoy excess liquidity, others may not. Clearly, those banks which do not maintain excess liquidity will be more affected than those who do.

To avoid the discriminatory effect of the use of VRR, some central banks in the LDCs (for example, Guatemala, India and the Philippines) have now decided to enforce *additional* reserve requirements against any *future* increase in deposits. For commercial banks which maintain an excess liquidity, the additional reserve requirements could be raised to 100 per cent, which would effectively limit their credit creating capacity. The commercial banks which do not maintain any excess liquidity will not be affected by the additional reserve requirement schemes against future deposits.

Some consider the impact of VRR as too drastic. But this argument is not very compelling if the reserve requirements are varied (to quote Keynes) 'with due notice and by small degrees'.

The use of VRR has been regarded as 'clumsy' in its effect and rigid in its operation. Its effects are regarded as 'clumsy' because when the reserve ratios are changed there is no way to tell *how much* of *active* or *potential* reserve base has been affected. The VRR has been regarded as rigid in its operation because it could affect equally both the 'desired' and the 'undesired' credit flows. Also the use of VRR is not considered as helpful for 'fine tuning' of the money and credit system by making marginal changes.

As against these criticisms regarding the use of VRR, it should be mentioned that bank lending is generally directly related to the liquidity ratio of the commercial banks and a change in the VRR is most likely to affect significantly the liquidity ratios of the banks. If this is true, then the use of VRR as a stabilisation device is much more a question of degree rather than the method.

However, the point has been made that the use of VRR may be counter-productive under certain circumstances (Aschheim, 1961) Assume that the central bank has raised the reserve requirements. This will reduce the volume of earning assets of the commercial banks and increase the marginal utility of income of such assets. In short, a rise in the VRR generates an 'income effect', particularly when the commercial banks do not have any excess reserves. The banks may then decide to provide *more* loans to the private sector and earn more income. Indeed, there could be a 'liquidity effect' if the commercial banks sell their low interest-earning gilt-edged securities. Notice that an *increase* in the VRR also increases the ratio of reserves to assets of the banks and as such they may consider themselves to be *more* liquid. Such a 'liquidity effect' will induce the banks to sell more gilt-edged securities and provide more loans to the private sector. This is exactly the opposite of what is intended by a rise in the VRR. Aschheim argues that to avoid such 'income' and 'liquidity' effects of VRR, OMO should be undertaken, since when the commercial banks buy government securities, they earn income (interest on gilts). Hence the holding of gilts in the portfolios of the banks will keep their income unchanged and there will be no 'income effect' to induce the banks to provide more loans to the private sector. Also, when the commercial banks buy gilts, there will be a simple substitution between private and gilt-edged securities without any 'liquidity effect'. Therefore the banks will not be obliged to provide loans to the private sector because of the 'liquidity effect'. Aschheim also argues that in the face of the growth of the NFI (whose reserve ratios cannot be varied by the central bank), OMO should be regarded as a more useful technique than VRR. It can be added that OMO do not have discriminatory effects on the use of VRR. They are also more useful in achieving marginal changes without producing drastic effects. Such effects, however, could be moderated if the rise in the VRR is accompanied by a *purchase* of the gilt-edged securities in target areas to ease bottlenecks in credit flows in a desired direction (say in the export sector). It is then possible to imagine the integrated use of both OMO and VRR.

A variant of VRR is the 'special deposit system' under which the commercial banks may be required to maintain a certain percentage of their assets as deposits with the central bank. In fact, the Bank of England in the UK issued treasury deposit receipts (TDR) in the past to change the reserve of the banks. At present the Bank of England is empowered to call for a special deposit from the banks to enforce credit control policies. Special deposits are generally excluded from the liquidity ratios of the banks. Since interest is paid to the banks on these deposits, the 'income effect' tends to be weak.

Selective credit controls (SCC)

Selective credit controls have been used in the USA in the past to prevent borrowing by the commercial banks for speculation in securities. During the 1930s the speculative purchase of securities in the USA was mainly funded by bank credit and prices of securities soared to a record level. The speculative boom fed upon itself as the dealers could obtain credit against the collateral of these securities. To prevent the speculative boom, the Fed was empowered by the Securities Exchange Act of 1934 to fix 'margins' which were equivalent to that fraction of security price which the buyer was required to provide in cash. Once prices of securities were in excess of certain limits, the authorities had the power to impose minimum margins of own funds that the buyers of securities had to provide. The instrument was selective as the Fed aimed to reduce the flow of commercial bank credit to the stock exchange. Notice that the margin is variable as the central bank had the power to increase or decrease the margin with the increase or decrease in security prices. The margin could go up to 100 per cent.

However, the movement in stock prices is not the only criterion in fixing margin requirements. The main criterion is the general credit situation. Thus SCC could also be used to control consumer instalment credit (Regulation W in the USA). To reduce the rate of inflation, the central bank can increase the level of down-payments and reduce the period of repayments. Likewise, to stimulate the level of demand during a recession, the central bank can increase periods of repayments and reduce the level of down-payments.

Many LDCs have found SCC very useful credit control devices, given their under-developed money and capital markets. Also, unlike the DCs, the LDCs are more likely to suffer from bottlenecks and inflation due to uneven growth and structural rigidities. SCC could be very effective in dealing with such bottlenecks in the LDCs.

SCC in the LDCs could take many forms. In many Latin-American and Asian countries, differential discount rate has been used in a selective way. Thus, the central bank in the LDCs could charge a rate lower than the bank rate to encourage movements of foodgrains within the country to reduce inflation in food prices. A common feature of many LDCs is the hoarding of certain essential goods to create a scarcity and reap large profits. To avoid such a phenomenon, the central bank could charge a rate higher than the standard rate for rediscounting bills created against bank loans for inventory holdings. Similarly, the central bank could apply different types of eligibility rules for discounting different types of bills. For example, the central bank may wish to favour the growth of exports and therefore it may apply lenient eligibility criteria for rediscounting the bills which would make credit available to the export sector.

Import predeposit requirement (IPR) is another type of SCC which has been used in many LDCs. Under IPR, importers who need foreign exchange are required to deposit in advance a specific fraction of the total value of commodities to be imported. Such an import deposit does not earn any interest and as the real cost of imports goes up, home production and import substitution would be encouraged. Also, IPR could be used so selectively as to discriminate against the imports of luxuries rather than necessities.

The central banks in the LDCs may use the quantitative credit instruments like changes in the reserve requirements of the commercial banks in a selective way. Thus the central bank may raise the minimum reserve requirement against certain types of assets held by the commercial banks if they are regarded as speculative. Differential reserve requirements against commercial bank deposits have been regarded as a useful SCC device.

Another type of SCC instrument is to set limits selectively for certain types of loans and advances by the commercial banks. This instrument is called *fixation of portfolio ceilings*.

In some LDCs, such as India, the central bank has frequently used the technique of margin requirements to loans and advances by the commercial banks against essential agricultural goods (for example, wheat, paddy, jute, sugar, and so on). The basic objective has been to achieve price stability. In India, the use of the SCC has been very flexible and discriminatory to bring about the necessary adjustments between demand and supply in different regions.

The fixation of differential capital-assets ratios for commercial banks is another type of SCC that has been used in some LDCs. Here the central bank is empowered to prescribe a higher proportion of capital against certain types of assets to prevent an undesirable flow of credit.

It must, however, be maintained that SCC could only be fully successful if it is used as an integral part of a 'package deal' programme by the central bank. The experience of SCC in many LDCs has so far suggested that its isolated use is unlikely to achieve much. But as a mechanism to allocate credit to the priority sectors, the use of SCC has gained some success.

Moral suasion

Another instrument of monetary policy is generally known as moral suasion. Moral suasion has no legal backing. It is really a method to persuade bankers and businessmen to follow policies which the central bank believes are in the interest of the whole country. The central bank of some LDCs (for example, the Reserve Bank of India) has sometimes issued directives to the commercial banks to change their credit policies. The governors of the central banks may sometimes address the commercial banks informally and such exhortations are really the expressions of the wishes of the central bank regarding the desirability of following some guidelines to achieve a certain objective. The evidence, however, suggests that moral suasion or 'jawboning' is effective only when it is supported by the threat that more positive action will be taken if the central bank's advice is not heeded. 'Moral suasion at its best is only a temporary device to influence economic decisions until more fundamental policy actions can be taken (Thorn, 1976, p. 353).

8.4 The role of monetary policy in LDCs

It has been generally acknowledged that monetary policy can play only a limited role in the LDCs. Several reasons are advanced to explain such a restrictive role. First, the existence of a large, non-monetised sector would clearly act as an impediment to the success of monetary policy. Secondly, the narrow size of the money and capital market and the presence of a limited array of financial stocks and assets would also hinder the effectiveness of monetary policy. Thirdly, in most LDCs, currencies comprises a major proportion of total money supply, which implies the relative insignificance of bank money in the aggregate supply of money. As has been indicated earlier, the ratio of currency to money supply is significantly influenced by the demand for money by the public, whereas, the effects of the changes in the central bank's monetary policies will mostly be on bank credit. In such situation, the scope of monetary policy will be severely limited. Fourthly, the rise of the NFIs in LDCs also poses a serious challenge to the effective manipulation of monetary policies so long as the NFIs are excluded from the purview of controls by the central bank. Fifthly, many commercial banks in the LDCs enjoy a high level of liquidity (for example, in Libya) and, as such, changes in monetary policy could not possibly significantly affect the credit policies of such banks. Finally, foreign-owned commercial banks can easily neutralise the restrictive effects of a strict monetary policy, as they can replenish their reserves by selling foreign assets, and can also draw on the international capital market.

However, since it has been shown before that the economies of the LDCs are likely to behave in a classical rather than a Keynesian way, it may be argued that monetary policy can play a useful role in demand management in the LDCs, particularly at times of inflation. Also, the interest rate device could be used to stabilise the external balance. For example, a high rate of interest could raise the inflow of foreign funds to narrow the balance-of-payments deficit. There is another strong case in favour of raising the domestic interest rate in the LDCs. In view of the capital scarcity that is generally experienced by most LDCs, the interest rate that usually prevails hardly reflect the opportunity-cost of capital. Given such a situation, a high interest rate could promote a more rational allocation of resources. It might also be beneficial for increasing the size of the organised money market. Paradoxically, despite the low interest rate charged by the organised financial institutions, the moneylenders and other non-institutional agencies (such as retail shops, landlords, merchants who supply credit at a high interest rate) still remain a major source of credit in many LDCs. Clearly, the dual rural money market could be more integrated by following a more sensible monetary policy which would involve a rise in interest rate charged by the organised financial agencies. This would reduce the 'attrition' of organised finance, promote savings and investments, develop banking habits and a greater monetisation of the economy. Such a process of financial development would contribute enormously to the efficacy of monetary policy. The other important point which should be borne in mind is that in LDCs, conflicting instruments are found in operation to achieve a certain target (for example, to increase the rate of growth). An expansionary fiscal policy, say, deficit financing, may be adopted alongside the operation of a stringent monetary policy. Clearly, such conflicts in the use of instruments must be reduced to the minimum to achieve a given objective.

9. International liquidity, LDCs and Special Drawing Rights

9.1 The need for international monetary reserves

Because countries engage in trade with each other they need to hold balances of an internationally acceptable money in just the same way that an individual who buys and sells goods and services needs to do so. Indeed, it may be said that in principle balances of international money might be entirely held by private traders but, in practice, central banks usually also hold balances of international money. As with the case of domestic money, it is possible to analyse the reasons why individuals and central banks hold international monies in terms of transactions, precautionary and speculative motives.

A country's holdings of internationally acceptable media of exchange are normally referred to as its reserves, a distinction being made between officially-held reserves and those held by private banks and individuals (in some countries there are controls on the amounts which may be held by private institutions and individuals). Reserves consist of gold, convertible foreign exchange (of which the US dollar is by far the most important currency involved) and, since 1970, certain liabilities of the International Monetary Fund (IMF) called Special Drawing Rights (SDRs). To these may be added the amounts which countries can borrow unconditionally from the IMF under general account arrangements.

A country which maintains a fixed exchange rate between its domestic money and foreign currencies and which in a given period makes import payments and capital transfers in excess of its export receipts and receipts from capital inflows will have to use reserves of foreign exchange to finance the deficit. (Similarly, a country which has an overall surplus on international transactions will experience an inflow of reserves.) This suggest that, other things being equal, the need for reserves will be greater the larger the expected deficits and the longer they persist. It is reasonable to argue that the more difficult it is for a country to eliminate a deficit by deflating domestic income or by using exchange controls or other devices, the greater will be the need for reserves. A country which frequently experiences large fluctuations in export receipts, as is the case with many LDCs, will require larger reserves than one which experiences little fluctuation in these receipts, though account needs to be taken of the possibilities for a country to borrow either from official institutions or from foreign capital markets. Less developed countries usually find it more difficult and costly to borrow from private sources than do developed ones.

9.2 The exchange rate and the need for reserves

It is important to emphasise that the requirement for reserves is not independent of the exchange rate regime which a country operates. At one extreme, in the case of a fully flexible exchange rate we have a situation where the monetary authorities of the country do not buy or sell foreign exchange and hence where receipts and payments are brought into balance at all times by changes in the price of the foreign currency in terms of domestic currency. Any tendency for payments to exceed receipts means there will be an excess demand for foreign currency and the price of foreign currency will tend to rise, so reducing demand for it by persuading people to import less and to purchase fewer foreign assets. In addition, it will become more profitable to export relative to producing for the home market so that the supply of foreign currency will tend to rise. In this way the foreign exchange market maintains equilibrium between the supply and demand for foreign currency. Under this arrangement every unit of domestic money offered in exchange for foreign money (needed to pay for imports, etc.) must find someone with foreign money willing to make the exchange. In these circumstances the central bank will not need to hold any reserves (though private individuals may wish to hold balances of foreign currencies) except perhaps a precautionary balance or 'war chest'.

At the other extreme, a completely fixed exchange rate system will require the monetary authorities to hold reserves sufficient to support the exchange rate (by selling foreign currency in exchange for domestic money when there is a payments deficit) pending the introduction of policies to bring about adjustment by reducing imports and/or expanding exports. Of course, it is quite possible that in due course the policies involved could include a change in the exchange rate itself.

It may be noted that under a fixed exchange rate regime there is an automatic tendency for deficits to be corrected by means of domestic deflation. This follows from the fact that the counterpart of a fall in international reserves is a fall in the domestic money stock because when domestic residents are buying more foreign money than they are receiving from abroad the difference is made up by the central bank exchanging some of its foreign currency reserves for domestic currency. This fall in the domestic money supply will tend to depress domestic expenditure and reduce the level of imports. It must be noted, however, that this 'automatic' mechanism is often frustrated by central banks so as to avoid the adverse consequences of deflation on the domestic economy. The central bank is able to prevent the money stock from falling by purchasing domestic assets (for example, government securities) so as to compensate for the drain on the domestic money stock from the foreign sector. It is in this sense that it can be said that a persistent balance of payments deficit is a monetary phenomenon – it is the consequence of not allowing the deficit to bring about a decline in the domestic money stock.

9.3 The Bretton Woods system and the dollar standard

From 1944 to the end of the 1960s the international monetary system was based on fixed exchange rates between currencies with occasional changes in parity values in the face of 'fundamental disequilibrium'. The system came to be known as the Bretton Woods system as it was based on agreements reached there in 1944 which set up the IMF and its sister institution, the International Bank for Reconstruction and Development (IBRD). The system is also often referred to as the gold exchange standard since countries held their reserves in the form of gold and foreign currency balances, with the US dollar being by far the most important foreign currency involved, though the pound sterling continued in this period to serve as a reserve asset for some countries.

During the 1960s the arrangements making up the Bretton Woods system came under increasing pressure and eventually broke down. Triffin (1960) in a classic work drew attention to one of the major problems surrounding its operation. He pointed out that the main source of growth in world reserves was, in fact, an increase in US dollar holdings. This was because gold, the price of which had remained fixed at $35.00 per ounce since the 1930s, was becoming increasingly costly to produce and so supply was declining. (Until 1968 the price was held at that level by sales from the United States' very large – but declining – stock of gold.) Of the amount being produced, virtually all was flowing into non-monetary use. In these circumstances the only way that countries could maintain a balance in the composition of their reserves between gold and dollars was to exchange dollars for gold held by the United States. This, however, introduced the potentiality for a loss of confidence in the dollar since the stock of gold held by the USA was continually declining in relation to US dollar liabilities. The USA was like a bank whose cash reserve was continuously falling. It became apparent that some changes would be needed which might have involved an increase in the price of gold, an acceptance on the part of the rest of the world of the US dollar as the key reserve asset without requiring it to be convertible into gold, or the introduction of some acceptable reserve asset other than gold or dollars. In addition, as we have already noted, more flexibility of exchange rates would reduce the need for reserves. In the event, a combination of all these changes occurred. (The reader is referred to Tew, 1977; Williamson, 1977; and Crocket, 1977, for details.)

9.4 Problems of international liquidity

One of the main worries in the 1960s was that the supply of world liquidity might not grow fast enough to permit a smooth expansion of trade between countries. It was felt that with the incremental supply of monetary gold becoming negligible, supply of US dollars to the rest of the world (related to the state of the US balance of payments) might be inadequate in relation to the felt needs of countries to add to their reserves, with the consequence that countries might well introduce trade barriers and deflate to try to generate payments surpluses so as to build up reserves. This would introduce a strong contractionary force into world trade and could, it was argued, precipitate a world recession.

A further problem which was becoming increasingly apparent in the 1960s was that of potential instability of the international monetary system resulting from the coexistence of a number of reserve assets – gold, the dollar and the pound being the main ones. Any reduction in the confidence which holders had in the relative value of these different assets could produce massive shifts from one to the other with potentially very disruptive effects on trade and other transactions. Although co-operation between central banks prevented a disastrous crisis from occurring it was nevertheless an ever-present threat and was made more likely by the much greater degree of international financial-capital mobility which developed in this period.

While it may be generally agreed that the LDCs, like the developed countries, have an overwhelming interest in ensuring that international monetary arrangements are such that world trade and payments function smoothly and are not restricted by a perceived shortage of liquidity leading to trade restrictions or to crises which threaten to plunge the world economy into deep depression, they are not indifferent regarding the various possible arrangements which might be established.

In the following discussion we will concern ourselves mainly with the role of SDRs in relation to the interests of LDCs. However, the issues will become clearer if we first consider a system in which international money consists only of gold. This is a form of commodity money and the key point is that its supply depends on costs of production and increases in supply involve the use of scarce resources. The overall rate of growth of international reserve money in these circumstances is determined by the relative costs of production of gold in relation to other goods and by the demand for gold for industrial and other non-monetary uses. Changes in costs of production (for example, the discovery of a new goldfield or method of extraction) will change the flow of monetary gold. On the other hand, those who favour a system based on gold would stress that the supply of gold cannot be manipulated by institutions in the same way that domestic fiat money can be increased at will by central banks.

Why is this important? The reason is that changes in international reserves typically lead to changes in domestic money stocks and so influence the rate of inflation in the country experiencing these changes. Gold-producing countries would use their gold to buy goods and services from other countries and this would raise reserves in the rest of the world (note the counterpart of this process is that the rest of the world has to export goods and services in excess of imports in order to obtain gold – a point with important implications to be discussed below). If traders who receive gold exchange it with commercial banks or the central bank for domestic currency (which then forms the base for further monetary expansion), it is easy to see how increases in monetary gold holdings will lead to an increase in the supply of domestic monies. This general point applies to all forms of international reserves and raises the important question of what is the best rate of growth of international reserves and, by implication, of domestic monies – though the exact relation between increases in a country's reserves and its domestic money stock will depend on reserve ratios and public preferences as between currency and deposits. It is by no means obvious that the technology of gold-mining will produce an optimal increment of international reserves over time.

Let us next consider a system where reserves take the form of holdings of the currency of a single country and gold plays no part. The use of a currency such as the US dollar instead of gold leads to a *social saving* from the world point of view. It involves the substitution of a virtually costless fiat money for a commodity money which requires resources for mining, transport and storage. Since these resources have alternative uses, and since in principle the dollar can serve the monetary role which gold would serve in a pure gold standard, world real income will be higher if a fiat money such as the dollar is used in place of gold.

It needs to be emphasised that under a system where countries rely on holdings of dollars or some other currency for purposes of their reserve holdings, they must still earn increments in reserves, in this case by having surpluses with the reserve-centre country. It immediately follows that if other countries are accumulating reserves that the reserve-centre country will have a 'deficit' of an equal amount, the deficit being financed by an increase in liabilities reflected in the increased holdings of the reserve currency by foreign countries. So if the world were to operate on a pure dollar standard (where all international reserves consisted of dollar balances) resources would be being continually transferred from the rest of the world to the USA, so that the richest country would appear to gain all the social savings flowing from the substitution of a fiat money for gold. This gain to the issuer of money is usually referred to as seigniorage.

It is, however, by no means necessarily the case that a reserve currency country will earn seigniorage equivalent to the above mentioned social saving. It is even possible that a country whose currency serves as a reserve currency might not earn any seigniorage at all. This limiting case would occur if the holders of the reserve currency earn interest on their holdings equivalent to the return which they could get by investing the resources used to earn the reserves in productive uses. To the extent that the rate of interest paid by the reserve-currency country to holders of its currency is less than this opportunity cost some seigniorage is carried. It is, of course, because of these interest payments that many countries in practice choose to hold a substantial proportion of their reserves in the form of foreign currency rather than in the form of gold when both assets are available.

To the extent that dollars replace gold as reserve assets the supply of world reserves becomes a function of the US balance of payments and this may give rise to changes in world liquidity which other countries consider to be non-optimal (the large US deficits and associated large increases in US dollar holdings in the rest of the world in the early 1970s is a case in point). To have the world supply of reserves largely determined by the policies of one or a few countries may be considered by some to be worse than having it determined by the technology of gold production, especially if the reserve-centre country or (countries) earn significant seigniorage. It is because of these considerations that the idea of an internationally-controlled fiat money appears attractive to many people. Indeed, the notion that an internationally-controlled reserve currency should be introduced was put forward by Keynes at the discussions which led to the Bretton Woods Agreement. However, his advocacy of 'Bancor' was too revolutionary to be accepted by the United States and the world had to wait until 1970 before an international reserve money appeared on the scene in the form of SDRs.

Before discussing SDRs, it may be useful to set out rather more rigorously the determinants of seigniorage, using the following simple formula (see Gruble, 1977 p. 169), which assumes the life of the fiat money to approach infinity:

$$S = \frac{R - r - c}{d} \cdot D \tag{9.1}$$

where S is the present value of seigniorage gained by the issuer of D units of fiat money, R is the marginal productivity of resources which would have been needed to produce D units of commodity money, r is the rate of interest paid to holders of the money, c represents the costs of servicing the fiat money, and d is the social rate of discount. It can be seen that if we assumed $R = d$ and that no interest is paid to holders of money and that c is negligible, then seigniorage will equal the social savings of resources no longer needed to produce commodity money. On the other hand, as r approaches equality with $(R - c)$ seigniorage earned by the issuer of money approaches zero. Nevertheless, it is still true that there has been a saving of resources from the point of view of the world as a whole following the substitution of fiat money for a commodity money such as gold.

9.5 The nature and role of SDRs

These points will be useful to bear in mind in considering the nature and possible role of SDRs, which were introduced in 1970 and are a form of international fiat money, being book entries at the IMF. They are a form of international money because they are acceptable for the settlement of international transactions between countries – though they can only be transferred between governments. Their acceptability simply rests on an international agreement which specified certain rules concerning minimum and maximum holdings.

It is important to be clear that SDRs introduce a new element into the international monetary scene. Previously the IMF had made loans from its holdings of currencies (which were subscribed by members) to countries to help them with financing balance of payments deficits pending the introduction of corrective policies. These loans eventually had to be repaid and so did not constitute a permanent addition to world reserves. Furthermore, as the size of the loan grew, increasingly stringent conditions were applied so that the temporary addition to a country's reserves was said to be through *conditional* liquidity. By contrast, SDRs represent a permanent addition to world reserves and their use is *unconditional* (subject only to the rules regarding maximum and minimum holdings).

Over a three-year period beginning in 1970 $9.5 billion-worth of SDRs were used. These were distributed to countries in proportion to the IMF quotas, which had the very important consequence that about three-quarters of the issue went to the developed countries. Initially SDRs were valued in terms of gold, but since 1974 they have had their value specified in terms of a weighted average of currencies – a change which reflects both the ending of the link between gold and the dollar and the objective of phasing out gold as an international reserve asset. SDRs were seen as a supplement to gold, though the possibility that they might eventually replace the dollar and the pound as reserve assets was not ignored.

Countries can use SDRs to settle deficits but until December 1978 they had to hold on average 30 per cent of their allocations over a five-year period (they also need not accept more than three times their allocation). Net users of SDRs pay a rate of interest which was initially 3 per cent, became 3.5 per cent in 1974 and has subsequently been raised to 3.75 per cent. These rules have been liberalised since 1980.

Since the allocation of SDRs, along with access to the conditional borrowing facilities mentioned above, is directly related to the quota of a country, it is important to point out the determinants of quotas. These include (a) the voting rights of a member of the Fund; (b) the degree of a member's access to special facilities in the IMF; (c) the size of a member's ordinary drawing rights with the IMF; (d) the amount of the subscription of a member to the IMF. These quotas were not firmly based on any fixed set of rules. Quotas are subject to a five-yearly review. Also any individual country could request a review of its quota at any time. In 1976 the quota was raised to SDR 39 billion under the Sixth General Review. For the oil-exporting countries, the quota share was doubled from 5 per cent to 10 per cent. But the total share of the other LDCs remained stable at 20.85 per cent. It was also decided in 1976 that 25 per cent of a member's subscription which previously had had to be contributed in gold, should in future be paid either in SDRs or in currencies of some other members of the IMF subject to their consent or in the member country's own currency *without any obligation to repurchase*. This was an important change for the LDCs. As Bird observes: 'This change in the mode of payment is quite significant for LDC members whose currency is held by the Fund in excess of 100 per cent of the relevant quota, since previously the only way in which they had been able to derive the extra conditional liquidity associated with a quota increase was to sacrifice a measure of unconditional liquidity, by paying out gold' (Bird, 1978, p. 183).

Some criticisms of the quota system

(a) It has been argued that the quota system is based on principles which do not take into account some important problems faced by most LDCs, for example, commodity concentration in trade and instability in export earnings. If the quota system could be based on a general principle which would pay due attention to the above problems, then the LDCs could be allocated larger quotas. This would confer substantial benefits on the LDCs without imposing too much cost (such as inflation) on the DCs.

(b) It has been observed that during the first half of the 1970s the ratio of quotas to imports declined by about 50 per cent for the LDCs. The real value of quotas must have been reduced still further because of the rate of inflation during this period. The rise in exports has only partly offset the loss but it was inadequate to cover the large deficits that the LDCs experience today. A rise in quotas would have been very beneficial for the LDCs in helping to mitigate the incidence of deficits.

(c) The system of quotas has failed to protect most LDCs from the severe effects of some exogenous shocks that they experienced during the mid-1970s because of a quadrupling of oil prices. Note that the system of repayment of credit to the IMF is strictly related to the short-run objective of stabilising the balance of payments rather than the long-run aim of achieving growth and development.

(d) To the extent that the balance-of-payments difficulties experienced by the LDCs are the result of domestic policies (such as demand (mis)management), the IMF's policies for internal adjustments could be appropriate. But in many cases the LDCs suffer from external disturbances like a fall in external demand or a sudden fall in supply of major exports. Under such conditions, deflation in the LDCs would increase costs substantially. In such cases, an appropriate revision of quotas may help many LDCs to reduce the short- and long-run costs of deflation in the face of balance-of-payments deficits by providing them with a longer period in which to bring about needed adjustments.

(e) Ideally, quotas should reflect the *economic* need for reserves by the member countries. In practice, it reflects to a large degree the relative political bargaining power of the members of the Fund. Also, quotas are very much biased towards the DCs since they have larger reserves and more convertible currencies. Hence, the existing system of distribution of SDRs according to quotas aggravates the present global inequalities.

Some implications of the main features of SDRs

First, it is to be noted that the method of distribution used did not involve the recipients earning the reserves as they would have had to do if they had accumulated either gold or dollars. Furthermore, to the extent that IMF quotas (based on a country's income, importance in world trade and other considerations) reflect the demand for reserves to hold on average as part of permanent reserves, the method of distribution can be said to be distributionally neutral in that no transfer of resources takes place between countries as a result of reserve creation (Johnson, 1972 p. 268). As it happens, LDCs have been net users of SDRs so that there has been some transfer of resources to them from developed countries, that is, less developed countries have used some of their allocations to finance payments deficits.

Secondly, it is necessary to distinguish the case where SDRs substitute for gold from the case where they substitute for dollars or some other reserve currency. In the former case, as we have already seen in relation to the substitution of dollars for gold, there is a resource saving. In the first instance this saving of resources accrues to the countries in proportion to their receipt of SDRs – their reserves rise without them having to use resources to obtain gold from gold-producing countries. If, however, the SDRs substitute for dollars or other reserve currencies there is no additional resource saving. What happens is that the reserve currency country ceases to earn seigniorage and there is merely a redistribution involved to nonreserve currency countries.

The above points need to be qualified to the extent that interest payments are made on reserve-currency holdings and are made on the net use of SDRs. We have already seen that if the interest rate paid on dollar liabilities reflects the opportunity cost of capital no seigniorage accrues to the USA. Similarly, if net users of SDRs pay interest and this interest is paid to countries whose holdings exceed their allocations, the transfer of resources to net users will to that extent be reduced and, in the limit, no transfer will take place. Since interest on SDRs is, in fact, less than commercial rates of interest there is a transfer of resources to those countries (basically LDCs) which are, on average, net users.

The use of SDRs by the LDCs

The transfer of resources involved under the present arrangements for distributing SDRs, when allowance is made for interest payments, is not very large. The determinants of the resource transfers can be clarified by considering the use made of SDRs by the LDCs.

It is possible to explain the use of SDRs by both demand and supply forces. Attempts have been made to explain the use of SDRs from the demand side (see Leipziger, 1975). For the moment we will assume that the supply of SDRs is given. The use of SDRs(S) can now be written in terms of the following equation:

$$S = S(A, B_{t-1}, R, G) \tag{9.2}$$

where A = the allocation of SDR to any country

B_{t-1} = The balance of payment deficit (net) with a lag of one year given the delay between trade flows and actual payments

R = The reserve shown as a change in non-SDR reserves over the last year

G = The ratio of foreign exchange to gold

It has been hypothesised that

$$S = S(A, B_{t-1}, R, G) \tag{9.2}$$

(to know whether the SDRs are substitute for either foreign exchange or gold).

The ordinary least squares regression for forty-three LDCs in 1971 has produced the following result

$$S = 4.57 + 0.44A + 0.05B_{t-1} - 0.06R + 0.002G$$

$$(1.65)\quad(7.97)\quad(3.24)\quad(-3.91)\quad(0.004) \tag{9.3}$$

$$\overline{R}^2 = 0.63 \qquad n = 43$$

(The figures in brackets show the relevant t-values.) (Source: Leipziger, 1975)

The above equation shows that the independent variables together account for 63 per cent of the variation of SDR use. Leaving aside G, all the explanatory variables are highly significant, given the t-values and have the right signs. Since LDCs are not a homogeneous group, two other equations for Latin America and for other LDCs were separately tested and the following results have been obtained.

Latin America

$$S = 0.58 + 0.06B_{t-1} - 0.10R + 0.11G$$

$$(11.64)^{**}\quad(4.63)^{**}\quad(-8.71)^{**}\quad(2.45)^{**} \tag{9.4}$$

$$\overline{R}^2 = 0.89 \qquad n = 19$$

Other LDCs

$$S = 4.74 + 0.308A + 0.04B_{t-1} + 0.02R - 0.09G$$

$$(1.54)\quad(6.76)^{**}\quad(1.73)^{**}\quad(1.01)\quad(-1.33) \tag{9.5}$$

$$\overline{R}^2 = 0.70 \qquad n = 24$$

** significant at 95 per cent confidence level or better

n = number of observations

(Source: Leipziger, 1975)

When the Chow test was applied (Chow, 1960), it has been demonstrated that the determinants of the use of SDRs by the Latin-American and other LDCs differ substantially (since $F = 9.12$). It can be pointed out that the above model does not explain very satisfactorily the use of SDRs by the 'other' LDCs. Nor is it clear why the independent variable A has been dropped from the equation for

Latin American countries. Given the diversity of LDCs, a more disaggregated model could be useful method of further research.

The allocation of SDRs and the transfer of resources

On the basis of the data on net use of SDRs by the LDCs and net acquisition of SDRs by the DCs, it has been claimed that between 1970 and 1973 the real resource transfer from the DCs to the LDCs has been considerable. By July 1973 all the LDCs have used US $835 million out of the total allocation of US $ 2348 million. During the same period the net use of SDRs of the DCs was US $308 million out of an allocation of US $6967 million (Helleiner, 1974).

However, the data on net acquisition of SDRs by the LDCs over-estimates the degree of real resource transfer from the DCs to the LDCs. It has been pointed out that the permanent potential real resource gain (R_p) would be equal to 70 per cent of the initial allocation of SDRs(A) – because of the obligation to maintain a minimum average balance of 30 per cent of SDRs (the Reconstitution provision) – *net* of interest charges(I) for full potential net use of SDRs. Symbolically, if Q denotes quota, then

$$R_p = \frac{70}{100} Q(A) - I \qquad (9.6)$$

Here R_p varies inversely with I and positively with Q and A. Let R_a denote the *actual* gain in real resources. This would be given by the following equation:

$$R_a = Q(A) - G_t - RS \qquad (9.7)$$

where G_t = the transfer to the general account of the IMF to pay some charges or for repurchases

RS = the part of the SDR allocation which is added to reserves

A transfer to the general account (G_t) could reflect repayment of debt owed to the IMF. It is also clear that receivers of SDRs are not obliged to spend them as they could merely be held as a permanent portion of reserves. Indeed, $R_a < R_p$ if the SDR recipient is not using all its potential access to real resources (Bird, 1978). Thus Helleiner seems to have over-estimated the extent of real resource transfer, since he has assumed rather unrealistically that either G_t or RS or both are equal to zero. Recalculation of Helleiner's data shows that, R_a = $303.7 million which is much less than the original estimates of resource transfer (Bird, 1976).

The SDRs and aid: the 'link'

Throughout the discussions on reforming the international monetary system which have taken place since 1960 there has been suggestions put forward for linking the creation of international fiat money to the provision of aid to developing countries. It is argued that in the absence of SDRs all countries other than reserve-centre countries have to earn their reserves by exporting more than they import. If the whole or part of any issues of SDRs were channelled in the first instance to less-developed countries (or to the International Bank for Reconstruction and Development and its agencies so that they could make soft loans or grants to less developed countries) the developed countries, other than reserve-centre countries, would not lose relative to a situation where SDRs did not exist. The less-developed countries, on the other hand, would benefit by being able to use SDRs to obtain resources from developed countries. To the extent that SDRs replaced gold this would simply mean that some or all of the social savings involved in replacing a commodity money with a fiat money would accrue to the relatively poorer members of the world community of nations. To the extent that SDRs acted as a replacement for dollars and other reserve currencies there would be, as we have seen no additional resource saving, but there would be a redistribution of seigniorage from countries like the USA to poorer countries, which would seem to be attractive on equity grounds.

What are the objections to changing the distribution arrangements relating to any future creation of SDRs so that their creation in linked to the provision of development finance? First, it can be argued that international liquidity needs and development finance needs are separate objectives and it is not wise to link the two together. However, so long as it is clearly realised that the total amount of SDRs to be issued in any period must be determined by an estimate of world liquidity needs there does not seem to be any necessary reason why the opportunity should not be taken to transfer resources to less-developed countries. Nevertheless, it must be emphasised that any tendency for the issue of SDRs to be related to development needs rather than to international liquidity needs would very seriously jeopardise the chances of moving towards a system where world financial arrangements are based on the issue of a single reserve asset.

Secondly, it may be asked how far other resource transfers would remain constant if an SDR–aid link were to be established? It is possible that countries would reduce other aid transfers and this may be especially likely in the case of reserve currency countries who most obviously lose from such an arrangement. However, this outcome is by no means certain, and it is perhaps being too pessimistic to think that there would a dollar-for-dollar cut in other forms of aid. It may also be pointed out that under most proposals for an SDR–aid link the spending of SDRs would be completely untied so that the real value of any SDRs spent by less-developed countries would be greater than the same nominal amount of tied aid.

Thirdly, a more serious potential criticism is that an aid link would be inflationary. This follows from the fact that the spending of SDRs by less-developed countries would increase demand for goods and services in the rest of the world. The likely empirical magnitudes are, however, such that this is unlikely to be a significant problem and, in any event, could be taken into account in deciding on the appropriate total to be issued in any given period (Cline, 1976, pp. 118–22).

Fourthly, an important point arises in relation to interest payments on SDRs. There is a real conflict here between the objective of promoting the use of SDRs and the eventual substitution of them for outstanding reserve-currency balances and the use of SDR issues to provide development aid. This follows from the fact that, as the formula on page 162 makes clear, the aid element is greatest the lower the rate of interest which must be paid on net use, yet the chances of SDRs replacing dollars and other reserve currencies in portfolios depends on them earning a rate of interest comparable to that on reserve currencies. However, the conflict is not total since the notion of a comparable interest rate is a slippery one. To the extent that SDRs, now valued in terms of a basket of currencies, have a more stable value in terms of goods and services than any one currency, they are likely to be competitive reserve assets even if their interest rate is lower than the commercial rate obtainable by holding reserve currency balances. In addition, there is a grant element involved in their use by LDCs to the extent that the interest rate payable on their use is lower than the rate which LDCs would have to pay for untied loans – which will almost certainly be the case.

Further changes in allocation of SDRs and quotas

In a meeting of the Interim Committee (IC) of the IMF on 24 September 1978, the following recommendations were made regarding the allocation of SDRs and changes in interest rates and quotas. First, it was recommended that the Fund should make an allocation of 4 billion SDRs in each of the next three years, 1979 to 1981. The Board of Governors were accordingly instructed to act upon the resolution by 31 December 1978. It was also decided that the interest rate should be increased from 60 per cent of the weighted average of short-term interest rates in the five member countries with the largest quotas to 80 per cent of this figure, and the rate of remuneration should be fixed at 90 per cent of the interest rate on the SDR, that is, 72 per cent of the weighted average interest rates. The Executive Board is also expected to consider the financial position of the Fund shortly before the end of each financial year and decide whether it would justify a rate of remuneration of up to 100 per cent of the rate of interest on the SDR.

As regards the reconstitution obligation, the IC decided that the requirement of reconstitution of SDRs (the obligation to maintain a minimum average balance of SDRs over specified periods) should be brought down gradually from 30 per cent to 15 per cent of net cumulative allocations, and this requirement should be discussed further in the light of experience.

Regarding the general quota increases, the IC recommended that the overall size of quotas should be raised by 50 per cent, increasing the total member quotas from about SDR 39 billion to about SDR 58 billion. The IC also decided that there should be selective quota increases for eleven LDCs whose current quotas are regarded as most out of line with their calculated quotas. These proposals regarding quota changes were acted upon by the Board of Governors by December 1978. Further revisions were made by 1992–3.

As regards the method of payment, the IC decided that 25 per cent of the quota increase is to be paid in SDRs by participants in the SDR department and in foreign exchange by members which are not participants in the SDR department. It was also decided that the remaining 75 per cent is to be paid in the member's currency.

It has been mentioned already that the value of the SDR has now been fixed in terms of a 'basket' of currencies rather than in terms of either gold or dollar. On 1 July 1978 the Fund made an important change in the calculation of the amounts of each of the sixteen currencies which determine the value of the SDR. The present value of the SDR is given by the sum of the following values of the various currencies:

US dollar	0.40
West German mark	0.32
Japanese yen	21.00
French franc	0.42
UK pound	0.05
Italian lira	52.00
Dutch guilder	0.14
Canadian dollar	0.07
Belgian franc	1.60
Saudi Arabian riyal	0.13
Swedish krona	0.11
Iranian rial	1.70
Australian dollar	0.017
Spanish peseta	1.50
Norwegian krone	0.10
Austrian schilling	0.28

(Source: *Finance and Development*, vol. 5, no. 3, September 1978, p. 4.)

In March, 1978, the Fund decided to adapt the composition of the basket of sixteen currencies which determines the value of the SDR on the basis of data for the period 1972-6 and to change the percentage weights given to each currency in the basket. On 30 June 1978, the Fund made the calculations required to change these weights into units of each of the sixteen currencies, as stated above, so that the value of the SDR in terms of any currency was exactly the same on that day under the revised valuation basket as under the previous valuation basket (see *Finance and Development*, September–December 1978).

9.6 The Extended Fund Facility

In response to some of the criticisms which have been made concerning the amount of assistance provided by the IMF to LDCs, the IMF introduced the Extended Fund Facility (EFF) in 1974. Under the EFF, the need for long-term finance, the structural problems of the LDCs and the consequent balance of payment difficulties have been acknowledged. The EFF allows for larger drawings than those permitted by some other credit tranche drawings over longer periods (three years as against one). Also, the length of time over which repurchases are carried out has been raised from four to eight years under the EFF as against three to five years. It should, however, be borne in mind that the EFF is conditional upon the acceptance of domestic economic policies as prescribed by the IMF.

In order to help the LDCs to tide over the balance-of-payments difficulties caused by the sharp rise in oil prices, the Fund has introduced the Oil Facility. For helping the least-developed countries, (those with a per capita income of less than $200 per annum), a Subsidy Account has been designed to enable the poorest countries to draw at a concessionary rate of interest. The designing of the Oil Facility is laudable. Unfortunately, it is a temporary measure. Moreover, the drawing facilities do not fully compensate for the extent of the rise in oil prices.

9.7 The Trust Fund

The Trust Fund was set up by the IMF in May 1976 to render balance-of-payments assistance to eligible members of the Trust (those whose per capita incomes in 1973 did not exceed SDR 300) mainly from the profits derived from the sale of gold. The assistance is generally rendered to the least-developed countries in the form of loans which are additions to normal drawings at a concessionary rate of interest. These loans are to be repaid over a long period. In other words, the IMF has now set up an agency to provide long-term finance to the least-developed countries, which must be regarded as a part of international monetary reform to promote development.

The resources of the Fund are obtained mainly from the sale in public auction of 25 million ounces of gold, after subtraction of the proportion of profit or surplus value of gold that corresponds to the share of LDCs in Fund quotas on 31 August 1975. The amount subtracted is then transferred to each LDC in proportion to its quota.

The surplus from the sale of gold (12.5 million ounces) between June 1976 and May 1978 was SDR 1.1 billion, of which SDR 841 million was lent by the Trust at a concessionary interest rate to forty-three LDCs that had qualified for balance-of-payments assistance. The balance of SDR 259 million as distributed directly to the other LDCs.

Some members of OPEC – Iraq, Qatar, Kuwait, Saudi Arabia, the United Arab Emirates and Venezuela – have made irrevocable transfers to the Trust Fund of their shares of the direct profit in order to raise resources. The total of such transfers reached US $33.85 million in July 1978.

It is interesting to point out that the total of Trust assistance for the two years up to June 1978 was greater than the size of the balance-of-payments financing received from the Fund itself. Also, the two sources together amounted to about 20 per cent of the qualified members' inflow of official balance-of-payments and other financing during the period. Clearly, the size of the financing has been substantial for the poor countries (see Gupta, 1978). Table 9.1 provides details of the Trust Fund's activities in this period.

Table 9.1 Trust Fund loans and related data 1 July 1976–30 June 1978 (in millions of SDRs)

Member[1]	*Quota as of 31 December 1975*	*Projected balance of payments deficit plus repurchases*[2]	*Total loan assistance*[3]	*Total purchases during 12-month programme period*	*Reserve tranche*	*Credit branches First credit tranche*	*Higher credit tranche*	*Com-pensatory financing*	*Oil facility*	*Extended facility*
Bangladesh (March 1978)	125	71.5	51.8	–	–	–	–	–	–	–
Benin (November 1978)	13	5.6	5.4	–	–	–	–	–	–	–
Bolivia (April 1979)	37	31.0	15.3	–	–	–	–	–	–	–
Burma (March 1978)	60	49.2	24.9	35.00	–	4.98	30.11	–	–	–
Burundi (December 1976)	19	12.1	7.9	–	–	–	–	–	–	–
Cameroon (December 1978)	35	25.5	14.5	–	–	–	–	–	–	–
Cent. Afr. Emp. (December 1978)	13	8.7	5.4	–	–	–	–	–	–	–
Chad (December 1978)	13	9.6	5.4	–	–	–	–	–	–	–
Congo, P.R. (December 1977)	13	10.2	5.4	13.23	2.03	4.70	–	6.50	–	–
Egypt (March 1978)	188	1,228.0	77.9	105.00	–	63.00	–	–	–	–
Ethiopia (May 1979)	27	79.0	11.2	–	–	–	42.00	–	–	–
Gambia, The (May 1978)	7	3.0	2.9	2.53	–	1.72	–	–	–	–
Grenada (December 1977)	2	low reserves	0.8	0.41	–	0.23	0.81	–	0.18	–
Guinea (June 1978)	24	12.4	9.9	8.70	–	8.70	–	–	–	–
Haiti (June 1977)	19	low reserves	7.9	3.00	–	3.00	–	–	–	–
Ivory Coast (March 1979)	52	55.9	21.6	–	–	–	–	–	–	–
Kenya (June 1977)	48	82.4	19.9	24.00	–	–	–	24.00	–	–
Lao P.D.R. (May 1979)	13	13.25	5.4	–	–	–	–	–	–	–
Lesotho (March 1978)	5	low reserves	2.1	–	–	–	–	–	–	–
Liberia (January 1977)	29	low reserves	12.0	4.56	4.56	–	–	–	–	–
Madagascar (December 1978)	26	16.5	10.8	9.43[6]	–	9.43[6]	–	–	–	–
Malawi (March 1978)	15	9.5	6.2	5.43	–	5.43	–	–	–	–
Mali (September 1978)	22	n.a.	9.1	–	–	–	–	–	–	–

Table 9.1 *continued*

Member[1]	*Quota as of 31 December 1975*	*Projected balance of payments deficit plus repurchases*[2]	*Total loan assistance*[3]	*Total purchases during 12-month programme period*	*Reserve tranche*	*Credit branches First credit tranche*	*Higher credit tranche*	*Com-pensatory financing*	*Oil facility*	*Extended facility*
Mauritania (December 1977)	13	20.0	5.4	4.71	–	4.71	–	–	–	–
Mauritius (December 1978)	22	10.8	9.1	16.49	5.49	–	–		11.0	–
Morocco (December 1976)	113	115.0	46.8	143.70	28.24	40.96		56.50	18.00	–
Nepal (January 1977)	14[4]	12.0	5.8	7.61	3.11	4.50	–	–	–	–
Niger (March 1979)	13	5.9	5.4	–	–	–	–	–	–	–
Pakistan (March 1978)	235	146.0	97.4	107.00	–	–	80.00	27.00	–	–
Papua New Guinea (April 1979)	20	25.0	8.3	–	–	–	–	–	–	–
Philippines (December 1976)	155	268.7	64.2	222.66	–	–	–	77.50	55.16	90.00
Senegal (September 1978)	34	17.0	14.1	–	–	–	–	–	–	–
Sierra Leone (June 1978)	25	14.0	10.4	7.00	–	7.00	–	–	–	–
Sri Lanka (November 1978)	98	134.6	40.6	55.00	–	21.93	33.07	–	–	–
Sudan (May 1979)	72	197.5	29.8	4.70						
Tanzania (December 1977)	42	n.a.	17.4	–	–	4.70	–	–	–	–
Thailand (June 1978)	134	160.0	55.5	–	–	–	–	–	–	–
Togo (November 1978)	15	15.5	6.2	–	–	–	–	–	–	–
Upper Volta (November 1978)	13	7.0	5.4	–	–	–	–	–	–	–
Viet Nam (May 1979)	62	8.3	25.7	–	–	–	–	–	–	–
Western Samoa (December 1977)	2	1.4	0.8	0.50	–	–	–	0.50	–	–

Table 9.1 *continued*

Member[1]	*Quota as of 31 December 1975*	*Projected balance of payments deficit plus repurchases*[2]	*Total loan assistance*[3]	*Total purchases during 12-month programme period*	*Reserve tranche*	*Credit branches First credit tranche*	*Credit branches Higher credit tranche*	*Com-pensatory financing*	*Oil facility*	*Extended facility*
Yemen, P.D.R. (March 1977)	29	32.5	12.1	13.18	–	5.76	–	–	7.42	–
Zaire (December 1976)	113	107.9	46.8[5]	129.49	–	40.96	–	56.00	32.53	–
Total	2029		841.0[5]	923.33	43.43	231.62	185.99	259.00	113.29	90.00

n.a. denotes data not available.
[1] Dates in parentheses signify end of the 12-month programme period.
[2] Projected balance of payments deficit when programme presented to Fund excluding possible financing by the Fund plus repurchases due in programme period as provided in Section II, paragraph 3 (f) of Trust Instrument. 'Low reserves' means that member has very low level of reserves and was deemed to have unlimited need.
[3] The loans were in proportion to members' quotas at 31 December 1975.
[4] Amount to which Nepal has consented as at 31 December 1975.
[5] Total resources available for loan assistance in the first period.
[6] Just prior to beginning of programme period.
Source: IMF, *Finance and Development*, July 1979.

10. Rural financial institutions in LDCs

The major aim of this chapter is to discuss the nature and working of rural financial institutions. The network of rural financial agencies may be illustrated with a chart (see figure 10.1). It can be seen from the chart that the unorganised sector comprises different types of moneylenders and indigenous banks. The organised sector usually consists of commercial banks, development banks (for example, co-operative banks) and different types of credit societies. The organised sector is generally financed by the central bank of the country. These institutions provide short-term funds.

On the other hand, a capital market generally provides long-run funds for economic growth and development. A capital market comprises long-term

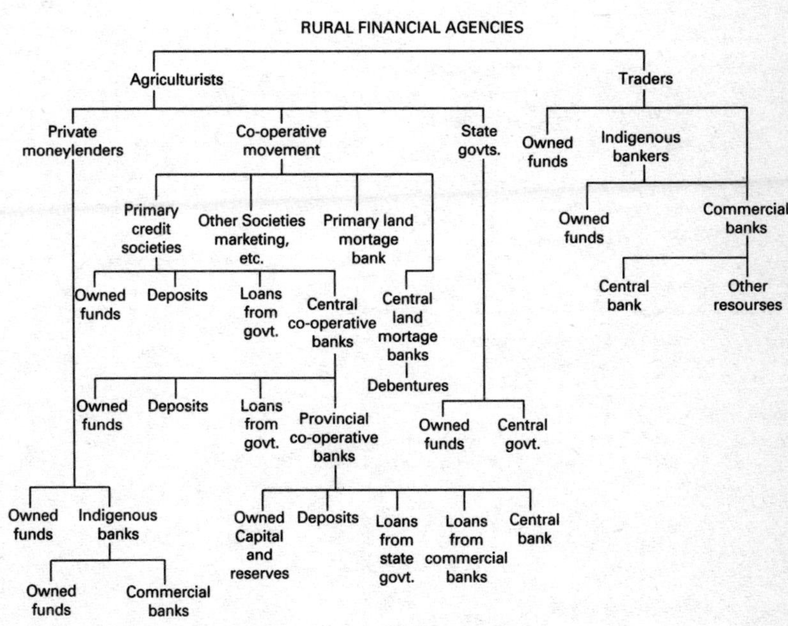

Source: S. Ghatak, *Rural Money Markets in India*, Macmillan, India, 1976.

Figure 10.1 Rural financial agencies

finance corporations, agricultural credit associations – mainly the land mortgage banks, insurance companies, investment trusts and stock exchanges. In some cases, the commercial banks in many less developed countries (LDCs) try to provide funds for the capital market, though such funding is usually very selective and indirect.

10.1 Unorganised money markets in LDCs and some consequences

The unorganised money markets in LDCs deserve some elaboration as they are quite complex and heterogeneous. A typical picture of the unorganised money market is shown in figure 10.2. Moneylenders and indigenous bankers are the two major sources of credit but there is a variety of other sources which can be quite important in some LDCs. There is a large number of non-professional groups of people who provide credit to the rural sector. Landlords, pawnbrokers, merchants, traders, commission agents, even friends and relatives – all act as sources of credit in varying degrees of importance.

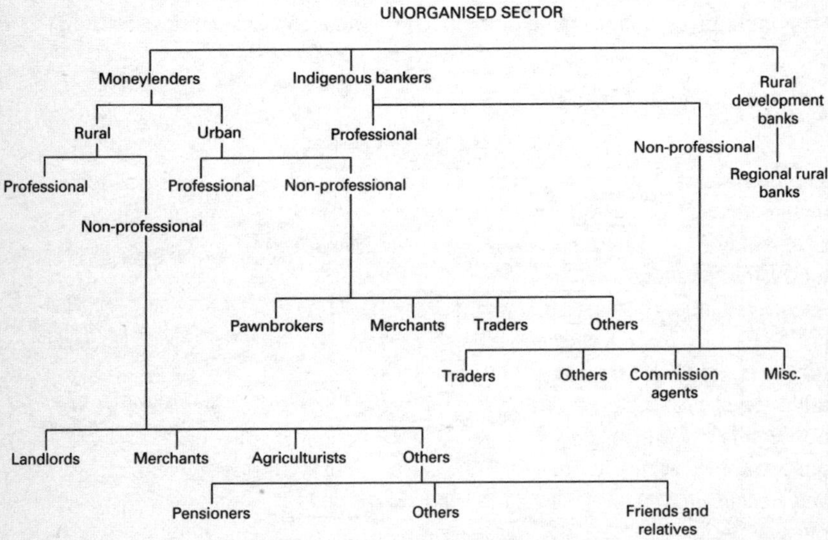

Sources: (i) Ghatak, *Rural Money Markets in India*, Macmillan, 1976.
(ii) Karkal, *Unorganised Money Markets in India*, Lalvani Publishing House, Bombay, 1967, pp. 21 and 45.

Figure 10.2 Unorganised financial markets in LDCs

The moneylenders in LDCs

One of the chief sources of credit in the rural economies of LDCs is the moneylender, and hence the nature of his activities deserves special consideration. The primary business of the moneylender in LDCs is moneylending and not banking.

A typical moneylender in a LDC does not accept deposits. Their activities are not usually open to public examination. They sometimes mix moneylending with other types of economic activities and hence lack of specialisation is the hallmark of their operation. In many LDCs, landlords, merchants and traders also act as moneylenders and they provide a significant proportion of the total supply of credit to the rural economy even today.

In may be useful at this stage to indicate the reasons for the stronghold of the moneylenders on the rural economy. First, the moneylender has a very good idea of the nature and repaying capacity of the borrower. Moneylenders generally know the borrowers personally and the borrowers can approach the lenders easily.

Secondly, in many cases, credit is granted by moneylenders for the borrower's family expenditure. Such consumption loans are not available from the commercial or co-operative banks operating in the rural sector of the LDCs.

Thirdly, the moneylender can be elastic in his operations. Indeed, one of the major reasons for the survival of moneylenders in LDCs is the extreme flexibility of their operation.

Finally, the moneylender has different types and extents of control over the borrowers. It should be noted that such forces are mainly socio-economic in character. The social force can take the form of loss of face or local prestige. The economic power lies in the possible drying up of the credit source.

Some undesirable consequences of imperfect rural credit markets in LDCs

The combination of a backward and sometimes quasi-feudal structure of land-ownership and an absence of specialisation in moneylending activities in many LDCs may have a number of undesirable consequences. Consider, for instance, the system of *share-cropping* which is prevalent in many parts of Asia and South America. Under this system, the landowner leases out his land for at least one full production cycle and the net harvest (= gross total harvest minus seed required for the next harvest) is shared between the landlord and the tenant on some mutually agreed basis. Unfortunately, in a large number of cases, tenancy rights are not legally well protected. Further, terms of contract under share-cropping are quite complex. It is a common practice for the landlords to act as moneylenders, and tenants may sometimes remain heavily indebted to their landlords. Interest rates are generally high, particularly on consumption loans. Payments of interest as well as the principal can take place in cash or kind, or both. Tenants usually borrow partly because of loan repayments with interest which reduce the size of the available harvest and partly in order to survive during the 'lean' months when the level of their own foodstock is very low. Notice that the tenant leases his land from the same person to whom he is perpetually indebted. As such, he is reduced to the miserable status of a traditional 'serf'. In other words, in a 'semi-feudal' agrarian economy, a landlord can 'exploit' the tenant both through usury and through his property rights on land. If we assume that the tenant has no access to the credit market, then the landlord can easily act as a pure monopolist. The price for credit or the rate of interest can be very high; the supply of credit will be very low; and the tenant is a price taker. If it is further assumed that the tenant has very little access to the commodity markes and fails to sell his harvest at the highest price, then his economic plight is readily seen. He has to sell at a very low price just after the harvest. If he repays his principal plus interest to the landlord in grain units, then it will be 'underpriced'. Note that his borrowing from the landlord is probably 'overpriced' as the interest rate charged by a 'monopolist' moneylender/landlord is very likely to be higher than the competitive rate. As the unholy 'trinity' of moneylender–landlord–trader takes a firm grip over the agrarian economy, the tenant is driven into a state of perpetual poverty, if not near-slavery (for details, see Bhaduri, 1973, 1977; also Ghatak and Ingersent, 1984). As Wolff observed (Wolff, 1919):

> It is usury – the rankest, most extortionate, most merciless usury – which eats the marrow out of the bones of *raiyat* (*raiyat* means tenant) and condemns him to a life of penury and slavery in which not only is economic production hopeless, but in which also energy and will become paralysed and man sinks down beaten into a state of resigned fatalism from which hope is shut out and in which life drags on wearily and unprofitably as if with no object in view.

The existence of 'monopoly' profit or 'usurious' interest rate can be illustrated with the help of a simple diagram (see figure 10.3). Let the interest rate be measured along the vertical axis and the amount of loanable fund along the horizontal axis. Let DD' be the demand curve for loan in the underdeveloped rural areas. Let there be constant returns to scale so that average cost (AC) is equal to marginal cost (MC). Given the principle of profit maximisation, the monopolist moneylender maximises 'profit' at a point where the marginal revenue (MR) is equal to the marginal cost of lending (that is, point E). The interest rate is r_m and the volume of lending is only OO_m.

The results will be different if the credit market is competitive. According to the standard economic theory, interest rate will be determined at E' in a competitive market since at that point price (= P as given by the demand curve) is equal to the MC (which in this case is equal to AC, given the assumption of constant returns to scale). The equilibrium 'price' of capital or interest rate is now r_c and the equilibrium supply of credit is now OO_c. The loss of welfare due to the presence of a monopolist moneylender is clearly shown by the shaded triangle (AEE').

Although the theory of 'usurious' interest rate is quite interesting, it is not always possible to accept such a theory on the basis of *current* empirical evidence. Looking at the 1950s and the 1960s, some evidence for the existence of 'monopoly profit' in the underdeveloped credit market does exist (see Gamba, 1958; Chandavarkar, 1965; Nisbet, 1987). On the other hand, the 'interlocking of factors' theory which suggests that the tenants have no other option but to sell to single landlord-cum-moneylender *has not* been substantiated on the basis of more recent information (see Bardhan and Rudra, 1978; Bardhan, 1980; Bliss and Stern, 1982). Nor is there much evidence to accept the assumption that

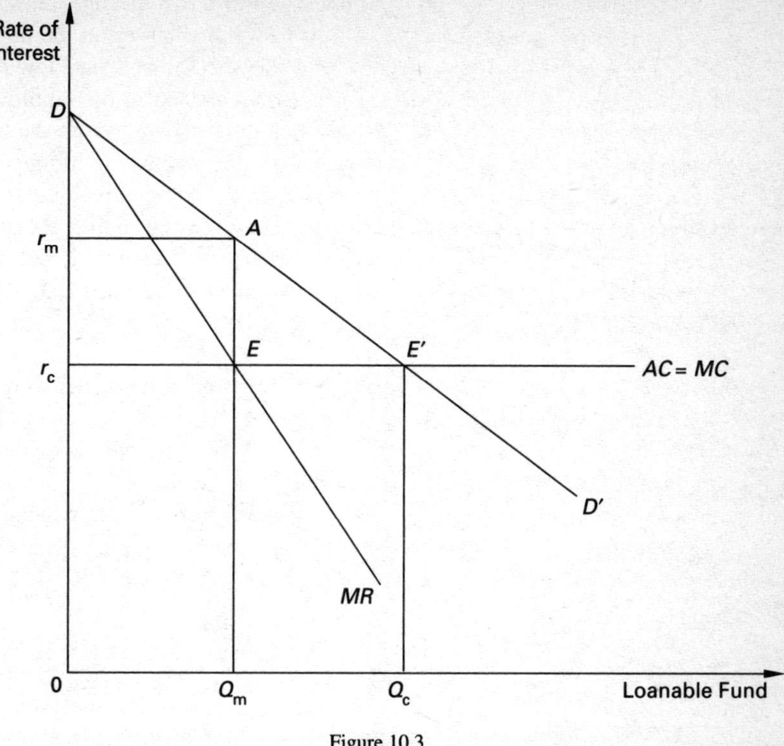

Figure 10.3

tenants have no other choice but to borrow from a single moneylender who is also the landlord. It is, however, possible to mention cases where rural interest rates are indeed very high, particularly in very backward regions. Such rates can easily be 'exploitative'. But the reasons for such high interest rates can be explained by a number of important economic and institutional factors. We discuss these reasons in the next section.

10.2 Determination of rural interest rates in LDCs

There are basically two different theories for determining rural interest rates in LDCs. One is economic, the other is institutional. First, we shall discuss the economic view.

The 'economic' view

According to the supporters of the economic school, rural interest rate will be determined by the intersection of the demand for and supply of loanable funds (see, r_o in figure 10.4).

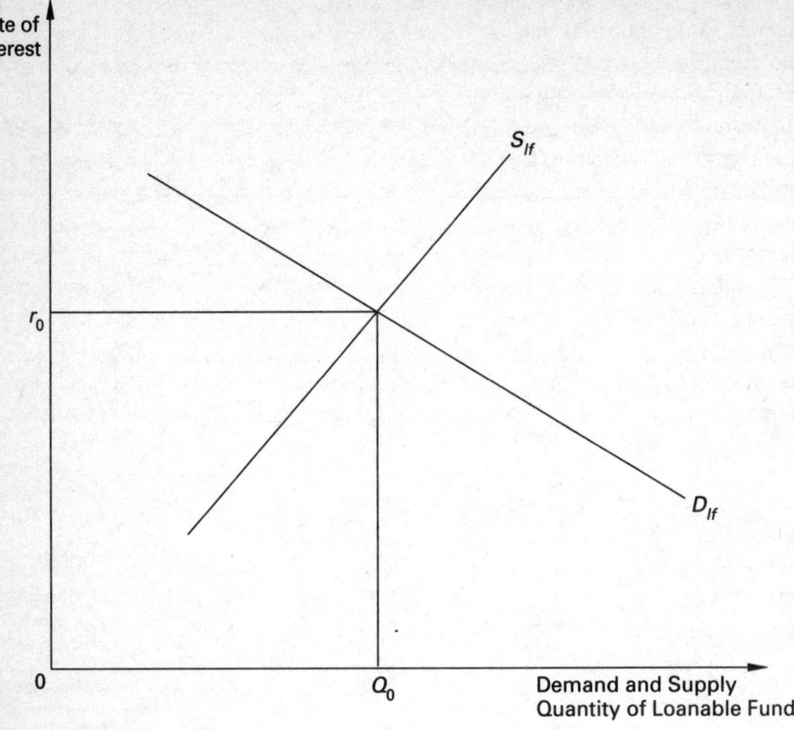

Figure 10.4

Since cultivators in LDCs do not usually make a clear-cut distinction between short- and long-run credit, most writers have tended to ignore the difference between short- and long-run interest rate. As many have found it difficult to estimate the demand side, attention has usually been paid to analysing rural interest rates from the supply or cost side. It is generally agreed that the demand curve for loans will be downward sloping.

From the supply side, the rural interest rate (= r) may be regarded as the sum of (a) administrative cost, (b) risk premium, (c) opportunity cost of lending and (d) the monopoly profit (see Bottomley, 1971; 1975). The empirical significance of some of these components is not always very well known.

Now, the economic view can be stated in a simple way: high r is the *effect* of high risk premium which the village moneylenders usually charge for lending to peasants, who are frequently without sound collateral. The lack of credit-worthiness is really a reflection of the poor income and saving of peasants. Hence, the introduction of modern technology, fetilisers, improved variety of seeds and better irrigation should raise the real income of the farmers, and their repayments. Consequently, the probability of default will fall, which will reduce the risk premium. As such, r will fall.

Figure 10.5 illustrates: in the first quadrant (I), the relationship between real income (= *Y*) and rural interest rate is shown. In quadrant IV, the 45° line shows the identity between real income and output. In quadrant III the positive relationship between output and repayment is shown. An increase in repayment is supposed to reduce the risk of default on the risk premium and hence we observe an inverse correlation between repayments *R* and *r* in quadrant II. When the level of real income is low, for example, OY_1, output is Oy_1, repayment is low at OR_1 and hence the rural rate is high at Or_1. However, when the real income is OY_2, output is Oy_2, repayment rises to OR_2 and the rural rate falls to OR_2

The negative correlation between the rural interest rate and a rise in farm real income can now be readily understood. The policy implication of this model is also quite clear. It is necessary for the authorities in LDCs to raise rural real income through rural innovation; price support or other fiscal and monetary policies should be used accordingly to achieve the objective of raising farm income.

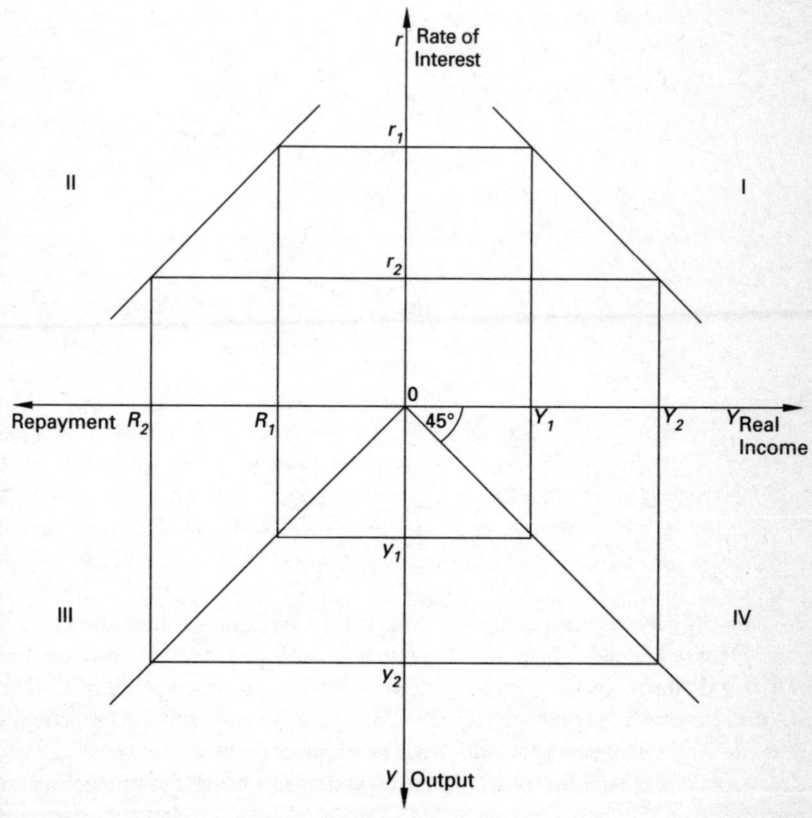

Figure 10.5

The same theory can be explained by using simple algebra. More formally, assume that p is the probability of loan recovery and β is the opportunity cost of loanable funds (which could be measured either by the bank rate or the post office savings rate in the LDCs). To show that the lower the probability of loan recovery, the greater the value of risk premium and the higher the r, we simply write:

$$r = \frac{1+\beta}{p} - 1 \tag{10.1}$$

or

$$\frac{\delta r}{\delta p} = -\frac{(1+\beta)}{p^2} \tag{10.2}$$

It is clear that p and r are inversely related so that $[(1-p) = q] > o$, given the value of β which is usually positive.

A positive risk premium exists whenever the second derivative of $[(1-p) = q] > o$.

From (10.1), we have

$$r = \frac{1+\beta}{p} - 1$$

or,

$$r = \frac{1-p}{p} + \frac{\beta}{p}$$

or,

$$r = \frac{q}{1-q} + \frac{\beta}{1-q} \tag{10.3}$$

Since

$$1 - p = q$$

or,

$$\frac{\delta r}{\delta q} = \frac{1+\beta}{(1-q)^2}$$

In support of the use of equation (10.3), it may be pointed out that evidence indicates that in countries such as India, two-thirds of the moneylenders said that many were doubtful about repayment (RBI, AIRCS, 1, pt. 2, pp. 476, 501). The logic of the use of the equation (10.1) is thus clear, since it shows that moneylenders in many villages in LDCs do make loans, parts of which are subject to the risk of default and therefore r would be inversely related to the probability of recovery.

$$\frac{\delta^2 r}{\delta q^2} = \frac{2(1+\beta)}{(1-q)^3} > 0 \tag{10.4}$$

whenever $1-q \geq 0$.

While some believe that the unit monopoly profit may be greater than the sum of the other three components in the rural interest rate, others argue that this may not be the case, for the following reasons:

(a) The moneylender's opportunity cost is equivalent to the return that he can get on alternative riskless investment as the reward for sacrificing liquidity. But since the village moneylender's opportunity cost also depends upon the duration of loans, and since for about six months in a year the funds of the moneylenders remain idle, if the interest rate on riskless alternative investment is 8 per cent per annum, the village moneylender will be justified in charging 16 per cent for six months to cover the opportunity cost of the seasonally idle funds. This will be true only if money is not loanable at 8 per cent in the slack months.
(b) The unit administration cost of a typical small and short-term loan advanced by the money lender is not negligible.
(c) The risk-premium for the village moneylender is treated as being high, since the farmers frequently fail to provide suitable collateral for getting credit.
(d) Even if monopoly profit is reaped by village moneylenders in certain villages, it will be difficult to sustain such monopoly profits in the face of increasing inter-village mobility of moneylenders, which will eventually reduce the rural rate of interest.

The risk-premium may be higher also because of the anticipation of a price rise and such risk is discussed next.

Inflation generally leads to a fall in the value of money and, as such, during inflation, creditors stand to lose in real terms when they get repayments. The loss of creditors largely depends upon the rate of price rise and the time lag between the advance and repayment of loans. The probability of charging higher interest rates to safeguard against the loss of repayment has been observed in South Korea (Campbell and Ahn, 1962). In the following section, we shall try to explain the moneylender's interest rate when he anticipates inflation.

Let us assume that R is the expected monetary returns over the monetary cost of moneylenders (that is net monetary income). Let R be a decreasing function of time (t). Implicit is the assumption that, as the moneylender advances more money, the rate of return will fall. This will be the case even when there is no inflation. The net return curve is thus (see figure 10.6)

$$R = f(t) \tag{10.5}$$

Now if we assume that money-lenders are anticipating inflation, that R will shift downwards to R' (Figure 10.6). Such a shift takes place mainly because of the state of imperfect knowledge and greater uncertainty in the face of the anticipated price rise. Assume now that α is the cost of capital in the absence of inflation. With no inflation, when a future payment is being converted to its present value equivalent, it is discounted at α. The present value of sum P in n years is given by $P/(1+\alpha)^n$. If money values are not stable, then discounting P at rate α may not show the present value equivalent of P received in n years. Let prices rise at the rate of g each year. Then the present value of a given sum of money, P, due in n years, when the cost of capital is α, is given by

$$\frac{P}{(1+\alpha)^n(1+g)^n} \quad \text{or} \quad \frac{P}{[(1+\alpha)(1+g)]^n}$$

The cost of capital in money terms, α^i, under inflation at rate g is

$$\alpha^i = (1+\alpha)(1+g) - 1 \qquad (10.6)$$

that is, the cost of capital is to be multiplied by the rate of inflation and their product used to discount future payments.
Let $g = 3$ per cent and $\alpha = 4$ per cent. Then the appropriate discount factor is:

$$(1.04 \times 1.03) - 1.0 = 7.12 \text{ per cent} \qquad (10.7)$$

If both g and α are low, then almost the same result would be obtained by adding r to g, and thus 4 per cent + 3 per cent = 7 per cent.

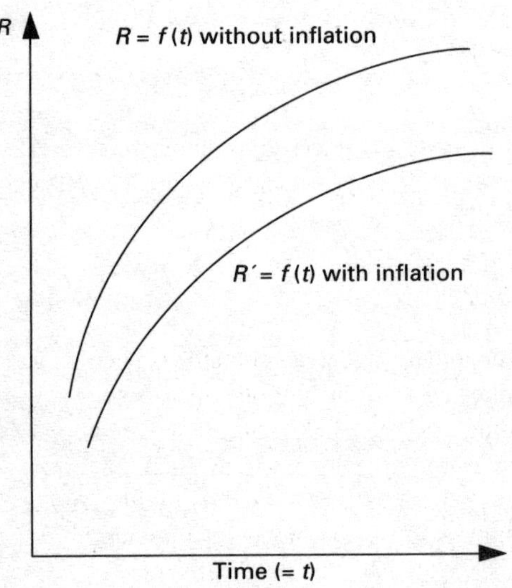

Figure 10.6

If we combine the risk of price rise with the risk of default in repaying loans, then for measuring the rural interest rate we can devise a different formula and by using it to the data we may try to show rural interest rates (ri) where different types of risks are involved. Thus we have

$$\text{ri} = \frac{1+\alpha}{P} - 1 + \left[(1+\alpha)(1+g) - 1\right] \tag{10.8}$$

or

$$\text{ri} = \frac{1+.04}{.90} - 1 + \left[(1.04)(1.03) - 1\right] \tag{10.9}$$

$$= .1555 + .0712 = .2267 \text{ or } 22.67 \text{ per cent}$$

where

$P = .90$ (proportion of loan repayment)

$g = .03$ (rate of inflation)

$\alpha = .04$ (bank rate)

It follows, therefore, that the provision for risk-premium for both inflation and default in loan repayment makes the rural interest rate higher than it would have been, with the risk of default but without inflation. The evidence from India shows the rationale of using the formula for deriving the rural interest since the village moneylenders do make loans in situations with little expectation of full recovery, and hence, the rate charged would rationally be dependent on the probability of recovery.

It may, however, be argued that although an anticipated price rise would surely raise the normal rate of interest, this may not have much to do with the risk premium except in so far as uncertainty about price anticipation is causing the money interest rates to exceed $k + g + kg$, where k is the real rate of interest and g is the rate of inflation.

The 'institutional' view

Contrary to the economic view, it has sometimes been argued that r could be determined by a complicated set of institutional factors such as systems of land–holding and tenancy, trading, and their links with moneylending activities. Within a semi-feudal, backward economy where the division of labour and specialisation is largely absent and certain activities such as trading and moneylending are combined by the landlords, there the moneylending activity could easily be 'exploitative' (Bhaduri, 1973; 1977). The argument runs as follows: consider a typical landlord who is engaged in both trading and moneylending activities. Since the peasants usually approach their landlords for credit first, partly due to custom, partly due to class relations, partly due to the flexibility and simplicity in their operations, these landlords/moneylenders usually find themselves in a monopolistic situation. Such a situation arises partly because of the absence of organised financial agencies (like commercial banks and co-operatives) and partly because of the habitual allegiance owed by the peasants to the landlords. Since in many cases landlords are the only effective agencies to grant credit, they tend frequently to expropriate 'monopoly gains' by 'over-pricing' loans (that is, by charging a very high interest rate, or at least a rate which is much higher than the competitive rate) and 'underpricing' repayments of the borrowers (that is, by enforcing repayments from the peasants *in kind* at a time when the agricultural prices are at their lowest). It is also contended that the local landlords/moneylenders derive further strength from the socio-political forces which frequently render the law against 'usury' in moneylending virtually ineffective. In extreme cases, it is believed that to perpetuate a semi-feudal agricultural system and to protect the interest of the landlords, tenants are prevented by the landlords from adopting modern farming methods which might increase their income.

Thus, even if it is economically profitable for the landlord to adopt new technology by raising crop yield and productivity, he will not be keen to adopt such techniques, as it will mean a decline in his usury income. A tenant whose real income has gone up will tend to borrow less as the gap between his consumption and income diminishes. Such a reduction means a fall in interest income of the landlord and the consequent decline of his economic *and* political control over his tenants. Clearly, a system of age-old indebtedness of the poor peasants will be perpetuated (Bhaduri, 1973; 1977).

10.3 An evaluation

It is important to emphasise that the economic and institutional factors are not always independent of one another. Indeed, both schools have overlooked the interdependence of the economic and institutional factors. It is possible to argue that institutional factors such as the dominance of moneylenders are influenced essentially by the state of economic factors such as the low income of the agriculturists.

The theoretical point that is raised about landlords preventing farmers using modern technology to perpetuate a system of age-old indebtedness is difficult to understand under a monopoly situation. Given the complete dominance of the landlords over the poor farmers and given the principle of profit/income maximisation, the landlord can always maximise his income by 'expropriating' the gains from productivity flowing from the adoption (*rather than non-adoption*) of new technology without taking resort to usury. Bhaduri argues that investment on land will be prevented by the landlords since gains through 'usury' are larger than those from increased gains in productivity. Such an argument is unsatisfactory, because if landlords have enough control to prevent innovation, they should also have sufficient power to obtain from the peasants additional gains from increasing productivity via technical progress. In any case, 'usury' as a mode of 'expropriating' the 'surplus' could be unnecessary in labour surplus economies where the bargaining strength of the poor peasants and tenants is very weak. Also, as Rahman argues, the two models of Bhaduri are not mutually consistent, since in the earlier (1973) model the rate of interest is treated as an 'exogenous' variable, whereas in the later (1977) version it is a control variable. If landlords as creditors can control this variable for usurious extraction, they need not fear that tenants would be made 'free' through innovation and investment (Rahman, 1979, p.179; see also Srinivasan, 1979). The landlords can regulate the rate of interest to keep the tenants always indebted. Finally, empirical evidence does not support the strong interlinkage between the product and the credit market, as suggested by Bhaduri (see, Rahman, 1979, Bliss and Stern, 1982).

10.4 Policies for an integrated development of rural financial markets in LDCs

A number of policies have been suggested to promote an integrated development of the rural financial markets in LDCs. We discuss the major ones below.

(a) One of the major steps taken by many governments in LDCs is the creation of public-sector credit institutions such as co-operative credit societies, agricultural credit corporations, regional rural banks and agricultural development corporations. In countries such as India, one of the major reasons for the nationalisation of commercial banks in 1969 was to promote commercial banking more extensively in the agrarian sector. The nationalised commercial banks in India have opened a large number of branches in rural areas since 1969 and have increased bank lending to the agrarian sector substantially, though at the time of writing agricultural borrowing from the banks is about 10–12 per cent of their total credit demand. The proportion of bank offices in rural areas to the total, which was 22.3 per cent at the time of nationalisation of fourteen major banks in 1969, increased to 42.1 per cent at the end of June 1978 (see Desai, 1981, for details). However, at the end of the 1970s, an impartial assessment of the policy of branch expansion by commercial banks showed that these banks were much more concerned with fulfilling physical targets assigned rather than achieve the 'social purpose' for which they were brought under public control (Shetty, 1978). These banks have also failed to achieve the aim of a wider geographical spread and balanced growth. The other important failure has been in the field of deposit mobilisation on a substantial scale. But this failure may be due partly to the low interest rate policy pursued by the government. It can be shown easily that a policy of offering a low interest rate on savings deposits will only discourage farmers from depositing money with commercial banks. Although in some cases the interest elasticity of savings in LDCs has been questioned, in India, such elasticity has been found to be positive and significant (see Williamson, 1968; Gupta, 1970). Hence, the policy of a rise in rural interest rates deserves serious consideration.

Government-controlled agricultural credit agencies in Jamaica, however, reflect the extremes of an output planner's approach to credit as contrasted with a banker's approach. Although output in the agricultural sector grew in the 1970s in a rather depressed economy, most, if not all, government credit programmes suffered serious 'delinquency problems' (that is, non-repayment of loans). Similarly, in India, despite a substantial improvement in the lending by cooperative credit societies and banks, most co-operatives suffer from a problem of loan-overdues. Hence the ideas of credit supervision and efficient loan administration deserve serious consideration in the rural money markets of LDCs (see Graham and Bourne, in Pischke *et al.*, 1983).

(b) Evidence from Brazil suggests that in the first twenty years of rural development programme starting in 1948, *extension education* has been much easier to expand than supervised credit (in terms of both the number of people reached and the number of services offered). It has, however, been reported that credit to early adopters of modern farming methods have shown 'excellent' results. The initial objective of intensifying agricultural production and improving the economic and social conditions of rural life seems to have been substantially accomplished, though there has been criticism about the high costs of such programmes (called ACAR). The policy of subsidising interest rates on loans (made worse by inflation in Brazil) also attracted considerable criticism (see Wharton in Pischke *et al.*, 1983). Evidence from Nicaragua tends to suggest that appropriate management systems can be crucial in deciding the success or failure of the operation of government credit agencies (Bathrick and Gomez-Casco, in Pischke *et al.*, 1983).

(c) It has been argued by some that instead of setting up a big, complex and centralised credit system to increase poor farmers' access to credit and to reduce lenders' administrative costs, it might be more useful to adopt a very decentralised and informal approach. Miracle (1983), for instance, argues that since public agricultural credit associations experience problems in dealing with poor and small peasants in LDCs, loans should be granted through local village agents closely acquainted with borrowers. These village agents should be paid fees based on their collection performance and on other functions specified by government policy.

(d) It is sometimes argued that the demand for financial services in the rural sector depends on the growth of output in the agricultural sector and the rate of growth of monetisation of the rural economy. The greater the growth rate of the rural sector, the larger will be the demand for external funds and thus also for financial intermediation. But this sort of 'supply response of the financial system' may not be automatic. For one thing, the supply of entrepreneurs in the financial sector is not elastic in LDCs; for another, a favourable legal, institutional and economic environment for the growth a modern rural money market is generally lacking in many LDCs. Demand-following approach usually means that finance is 'essentially passive'. As Patrick put it: 'Restrictive banking legislation, religious barriers against interest charges and imperfections in the operation of the market mechanism may dictate an inadequate demand-following response by the finance system' (Patrick, 1966).

Patrick thus proposes 'supply-leading finance'. This means the creation of financial institutions, assets and instruments in advance of demand for them to stimulate growth by transferring resources from the traditional to the modern sectors, apart from encouraging the supply of entrepreneurs. The policy is to make the allocation of capital more efficient. In this way, the rural financial system will provide necessary incentives for economic growth. It is acknowledged that at the outset a supply-leading financial institution may fail to operate profitably. But with government support (for example subsidies), public confidence and price stability (which effectively reduces the opportunity cost for holding money), supply-leading financial institutions should stand a good chance of being successful. As regards deposit mobilisation in the rural areas, the post office savings schemes should be given considerable support by the government as they are very cost effective. The problem here is that the post offices in most LDCs offer very low interest rates, even in nominal terms. This, again, makes the case for raising rural deposit rates (either by post offices or by regional rural banks) worthy of serious consideration, since it is known that even small farmers can save substantial amounts (see the case study on Taiwan by Ong *et al.*, 1976).

(e) It is necessary to evaluate the impact of agricultural credit programmes on farm output *and* rural welfare from time to time. However, regression analyses used so far have failed to isolate the exact nature of the impact of credit on farm output. It is very easy to overestimate the impact of the use of agricultural credit (AC) if a production function of the following form is used:

$$Q = f(K, L, AC) \tag{10.10}$$

where

$Q =$ farm output

$K =$ capital

$L =$ labour

The simple reason is that there are factors other than K, L and AC, for example, management and water availability, which have been ignored in the production function of the above form. Moreover, methodologically, specifying credit (AC) as a separate input poses problems, since loans are claims on resources and do not directly generate farm output (see David and Meyer, 1983, for a good discussion). Results of some econometric studies that (see Pischke *et al.*, 1983) show that the impact of credit is sometimes significant, sometimes not. Indeed, the relationship between loans and higher farm output may be simultaneous: sometimes, higher use of input can lead to higher output and income, which can raise the demand for loans; also availability of more loans can raise the level of output and income. It may thus be necessary to set up a simultaneous-equation model for a more realistic appraisal of agricultural credit policies. Sometimes, the demand for inputs (for example, fertiliser) studies can evade the problem of directly relating loans to farm production function. Schulter, for instance, has tried to analyse the effect of uncertainty on allocation of resources. In the estimated input demand function, factors such as credit availability, farm size and income enter as constraints. Access to credit and land planted with modern rice varieties turned out to be the most significant factors affecting fertiliser use. Access to loans seems to be less important in explaining demand for inputs other than rice and fertiliser. This conclusion is based on the entire study by Schulter (see Pischke *et al.*, 1983).

In mathematical programming studies of technical change, adoption of new seeds and cropping systems and income are usually found to be constrained by the lack of formal loans. On the whole, most econometric studies confirm that the effects of agricultural credit on farm production are positive and statistically significant, though more research needs to be carried out in this area, particularly about the sources, uses and impacts of *long-term* agricultural loans on farm production and investment.

(f) Some arguments have been made against the possibility of carrying out successful reforms of rural interest rate structure in LDCs. But such arguments are not always very convincing. Consider first the argument that a high interest rate will lead to financial bankruptcy. Here the usual policy is to offer government subsidies to rural credit agencies. Vogel argues that a better policy is to raise interest rates on outstanding loans (Vogel, 1981).

The second argument in favour of a low-interest-rate policy is stated in terms of compensation principle. Since the agricultural sector is at a disadvantage *vis-à-vis* the industrial sector because of adverse terms of trade (that is, ratio of agricultural to industrial price), it is argued that the agricultural sector can be compensated if it is charged a low rate of interest. Once again, this argument does not hold water, since a low rate of interest hardly affects relative input or output prices and farmers' net income, and hence the amount of compensation is very little, if any.

Thirdly, it is argued that a high-interest-rate policy is undesirable as it will reduce output and employment by reducing the supply of credit. This may result in inflation. But a high-interest-rate policy may work the other way round, as demand for goods will be curtailed and savings will rise, which can be channelled into more productive investment. In the long run, the efficiency of the economy could improve considerably.

Finally, because of problems of international capital flows that might be created due to financial reforms, it might be necessary to introduce international trade reforms along with monetary reforms. The gains arising from a higher flow of foreign exchange because of a higher-interest-rate policy need not be overlooked either (see Vogel, 1981, for details).

10.5 Rural money markets and implications for monetary policy

It is now widely acknowledged that the existence of two different types of money markets – one organised (OMM) and the other organised (UMM) – has important implications for the conduct of monetary policy in LDCs (see for example, Ghatak, 1976; Taylor, 1983; Van Wijnbergen, 1983(a), 1983(b)). A 'dual' money market could complicate the smooth operation of monetary policy as it implies the presence of two very different interest rates – one for the OMM and the other for the UMM. Such 'dual' rates are in fact observed in many LDCs (see, for example, Pischke *et al.*, 1983; Ghatak, 1976). The two segments of the money market are separated for a variety of reasons; for example:

(i) differences in transaction costs;
(iii) informal system of loan administration in the UMM;

(iii) pattern of flexibility of loan operation;
(iv) asymmetric flow of information; and
(v) problems of moral hazard and adverse selection, and so on (see, e.g., Stiglitz and Weiss, 1981).

The quantity of loans of a particular borrower is generally determined by his/her 'credit-worthiness' (for example, the 'asset' or land holding) and ability to repay; the 'status'; lenders' information about the borrower; and the nature of moral hazards perceived by lending agents. These 'dual' rates, if unconnected, could render the use of an official discount rate ineffective either as a weapon for controlling credit or as a device for raising savings and investment, and thereby the rate of economic growth (see, for example, Fry, 1988; 1989).

It has been argued by the 'structuralists' (for example, Taylor, 1983; Van Wijnbergen, 1983,) that the practical usefulness of financial liberalisation caused by a rise in interest rates could be limited in LDCs because such rises in rates in the OMM lead to outflow of funds from the UMM. Thus a credit shortage raises interest rates in the UMM and a consequent fall in the level of investment and output. Structuralists therefore argue that a positive interest rate policy could be counter-productive.

Clearly, the strength of the arguments stated by the 'structuralist' school depends on a number of assumptions: for example, it is assumed that funds flow freely between the UMM and OMM. The validity of such assumptions are empirical issues. The argument of the 'structuralists' would be validated if the UMM rates readily respond to changes in the bank rates in the OMM. A rigorous analysis of the relationship between the OMM and the UMM rates in LDCs is a matter of important research. Further, we need a measure of 'virtual' interest rates to indicate the extent of changes to be made in the dual money markets. Such estimates are useful as they approximate the 'equilibrium' interest rates in a LDC with segmented money markets (see, for example, Neary and Roberts, 1981; Charemza and Ghatak, 1994).

According to one study on South Korea, changes in the interest rates in the OMM can influence directly the rates in the UMM – confirming the structuralist line of argument. Such a rise in the UMM rates led to 'stagflation' in South Korea for a certain period in the 1970s (Van Wijnbergen, 1983). The use of co-integration analysis for the Indian bank rate (a proxy for the OMM rate) and the bazaar rate (a proxy for the rate in the UMM) also confirms a direct and significant relationship (Charemza and Ghatak, 1994). Such results show that in *some* newly industrialised countries (NICs) interest-rate policy can play an important role as an instrument of stabilisation. However, an isolated policy of raising the real interest rate without a sound macro-economic policy framework for generating sustained real income growth can be counter-productive. It is also important to ensure an improvement in the *quality* of investment (by observing the changes in the capital–output ratios) to improve the rate of economic growth.

The role of positive interest rates in organised credit is first, to encourage more savings in the rural sector and, second, to encourage commercial banks to shift

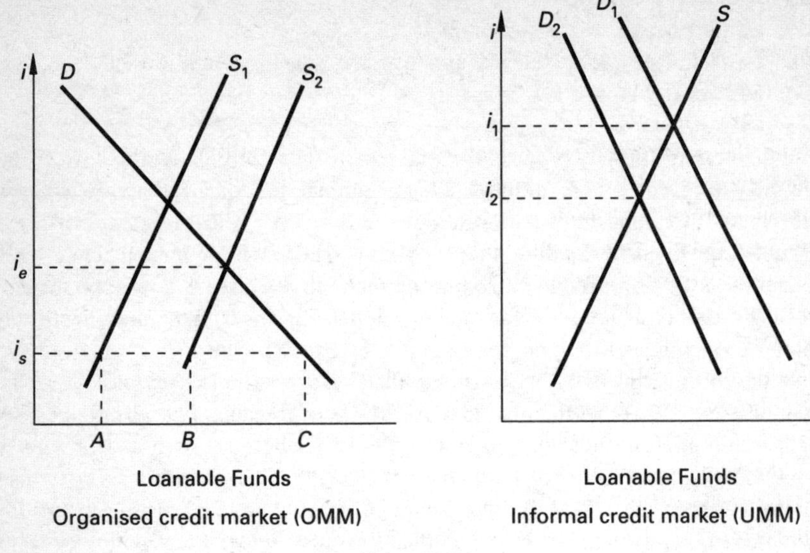

Figure 10.7

part of their lending activity from industry to agriculture. Also, additional credit could be supplied from government sources. The effect of these two measures would be to put pressure on the UMM to *reduce* interest rates paid by those who must have recourse to this source. Once the total supply of credit available to the agricultural sector has increased, the government should adopt policies whose purpose is to ensure that peasants have access to the organised market on terms which are not inferior (and perhaps even superior) to those enjoyed by landlords.

The argument can be illustrated diagrammatically (see figure 10.7). In the OMM we assume that interest rates are fixed at a level of i_s (as a result of laws against usury, the policies of state sponsored rural banks and so on) and that rationing is used to close the excess demand gap of *AC*. In the OMM, however, we assume supply and demand for credit are equated at a rate of interest of i_1. If, first, additional credit from government sources were channelled into the OMM this would (a) reduce the excess demand in that market to *BC*; and (b) lead to a shift to the left of the demand curve in the informal market, thereby lowering interest rates there. Second, if i_s were allowed to vary in accordance with market conditions, this would lead (c) to a rise in the rate of interest in the UMM to i_e and the elimination of rationing; plus (d) to a further shift of the demand curve and a decline in the rate of interest in the informal credit market to i_2.

In principal, similar policies should be adopted to ensure that small-scale owner-operators have equal or preferential access to irrigation water, technical assistance and all the other inputs that are vital to the success of the 'green revolution'. At present they are discriminated against in virtually all factor 'markets' – either in terms of price, or because of the way scarce resources are allocated by rationing, because of restricted access to the bureaucracy.

Appendix to Chapter 10

The Grameen Bank: an alternative approach to non-corporate finance in Bangladesh

While the government struggled to create a viable rural banking system in Bangladesh, a small private initiative was started in 1976 to help the landless without normal bank collateral to obtain credit. This program has become the Grameen (Rural) Bank. The unique operating procedures of the Grameen Bank grew out of several earlier attempts to reach the rural poor and were a sharp departure from traditional banking. The bank's customers, who are restricted to the very poor, are organized into five-person groups, and each group member must establish a regular pattern of weekly saving before seeking a loan. The first two borrowers in a group must make several regular weekly payments on their loans before other group members can borrow. Most loans are to finance trading and the purchase of livestock.

By February 1987, the Grameen Bank was operating 300 branches covering 5400 villages. Nearly 250 000 persons were participating, among them an increasing number of women, who accounted for about 75 per cent of the total. The membership included about 13 per cent of households with less than half an acre of land in the areas in which the bank was operating. Loans are small – on average, about 3000 taka ($100) in 1985. By the end of 1986 about Tk1.5 billion had been disbursed, of which almost Tk1.2 billion had been recovered. Outstanding loans were thus about Tk300 million, with almost 70 per cent held by women borrowers.

In sharp contrast to the Bangladesh commercial banking system, the Grameen Bank has experienced excellent loan recovery. As fo February 1987 about 97 per cent of loans had been recovered within one year after disbursement and almost 99 per cent within two years. This good performance is reportedly attributable to a combination of factors: close supervision of field operations, a system of peer monitoring, dedicated service by bank staff, borrowing for purposes that generate regular income, solidarity within groups, and repayment in weekly installments. Another factor which encourages repayment is the borrower's knowledge that the availability of future loans depends on the repayment of borrowed funds.

Bank staff meet weekly with groups to disburse loans, collect savings deposits and loan payments, and provide training in financial responsibility. This means high operating costs. The ratio of expenses to loans rose from 9 per cent in 1984 to 18 per cent in 1986. These high costs have been partially offset by low-cost funds from international agencies.

(Source: World Bank. *World Development Report*, 1989, Oxford University Press.)

11. The international debt crisis

A major economic issue in recent times has been the analysis of the impact of external debt on the economies of the less developed countries (LDCs). The main focus of attention has been the cost of servicing foreign debt and the potential benefits from default. It has been argued that if the cost of debt service is higher than the cost of default, then debt repayment by an LDC is not incentive-compatible. Others have discussed the relationship between external and internal public debt and concluded that a developing country should increase domestic taxes, curtail aggregate demand and attain a sustainable debt/export ratio.

The problem of debt repudiation by LDCs could be aggravated by an increase in real interest rates. The incentive to default depends upon the debt/income ratio, access to international capital markets, the monetary and fiscal policies of the donor countries, the nature and impact of the demand and supply shocks and the nature of domestic budget solvency constraints in the borrowing country. A highly indebted developing country may still have an incentive to repay, however, because of the fear of losing access to the international capital market. Imperfect information about the characteristics of borrowers can occasionally compound the problems for lenders. Thus, some argue that external lending to LDCs could be explained by a theory of repeated games with incomplete information. The major snag here is that games have multiple equilibria, and the precise nature of equilibrium is extremely sensitive to the specific assumption made about the information obtained by different players. Furthermore, these game-theoretic models are not easily testable.

To examine the welfare implications and incentive-compatibility of debt repayment, it is necessary to derive the national solvency condition facing a debtor country by delineating the balance-of-payments identity for the current-account surplus. Such a national solvency condition facing a debtor nation is easy to explain: the current external debt as a proportion of the gross domestic product (GDP) must be proportional to the present value of future primary surpluses discounted at a rate equal to the 'growth adjusted' real foreign interest rate (namely the steady-state real foreign interest rate minus the domestic real output growth rate).

The sign of the 'growth-adjusted' real foreign interest rate is crucial to the nature of the external constraint facing a debtor nation. Where the GDP growth rate exceeds the real interest rate, and the growth-adjusted real foreign interest rate is negative, a debtor country must only stabilise the trade balance/GDP ratio and need never run primary trade surpluses to stabilise the debt/GDP ratio. By contrast, if the growth-adjusted real foreign interest rate is positive, stabilising the debt/GDP ratio requires the debtor country to run surpluses, for at least some periods in the future, in order to service debt. These principles have been explained in Appendix to this chapter.

To understand the incentive-compatibility of debt repayment, we must examine two options facing the government and the private sector. First, debt can be repaid, which means that fiscal and exchange-rate policies are adjusted so that national and government solvency conditions are satisfied. Second, debt can be repudiated, which will cause a loss of foreign capital inflows and the consequent inability to run a trade deficit. Debt repayment is incentive-compatible if, on the basis of some welfare criterion (which has consumption, government spending and inflation as arguments), repayment and functioning within the national solvency condition is preferable to the consequences of immediately eliminating the trade deficit. It is also necessary to consider the possibility that financial autarky leads to lower long-run growth rates. The financial outcome depends on:

(i) the initial size of the debt/GDP ratio;
(ii) the initial trade balance ratio;
(iii) the drop in the long-run growth rate; and
(iv) the form of the required adjustment to solvency implied by the model.

11.1 LDC borrowing before 1973

The practice of borrowing from foreign countries as a method of promoting economic growth is not new. Historically, most DCs of today, including the USA, depended significantly on the imports of foreign capital to achieve a high standard of living. Besides the lessons of history, there are a number of sound reasons to explain the borrowing of LDCs from abroad, for example:

(a) Most LDCs have low per capita income and savings. The required rate of economic growth to attain a better standard of living may need a high level of investment which may not be financed by domestic savings. Thus, LDCs may wish to borrow foreign capital to eliminate the 'savings gap', that is, $(I - S > 0)$.

(b) Most LDCs suffer from serious shortages in their foreign exchange earnings as their imports (M) are generally much greater than their exports (X). Such an imbalance, that is, $(M - X) > 0$ is defined as a 'trade-gap', which could be a serious constraint on achieving a higher rate of economic growth and per capita consumption. Many LDCs depend substantially on the imports of capital and intermediate inputs to increase their production. Sometimes, food imports play a very crucial role in averting the threat of hunger and famine. Imports of foreign technology and skill can ease the trade gap and accelerate economic growth.

(c) Many LDCs suffer from capital scarcity relative to labour supply and they should enjoy higher returns at the margin on capital flows from DCs. Such returns are known as 'marginal efficiency of capital' (MEC). In capital-abundant countries, the MEC tends to be lower than in the LDCs. So, as long as capital is fully mobile across nations, on efficiency grounds, capital should flow from the rich to the poor countries to equalise the global MEC. However, such capital movements depend on the condition that funds are invested in sectors where the rate of return is higher than the interest rate charged on the use of foreign capital.

It is now easy to see why the LDCs depended on foreign borrowing and debt accumulation throughout the 1950s and 1960s. Foreign debt helped to supplement low domestic savings to finance the required investment rate to achieve high growth rate of real income and consumption. Besides, it was a vital ingredient in reducing the foreign exchange gap. However, foreign debt accumulation (as a percentage of the GDP or exports) becomes problematic when the trade or savings gaps persist over a long period, and returns from the foreign investment are less than the rate of interest. Many LDCs were tempted to maintain highly over-valued exchange rates (for example, India, Pakistan, Brazil, Mexico, Argentina, Turkey and so on, to keep down the import cost and save foreign exchange). They also adopted import–substitution–industrialisation (ISI) policies to save foreign exchange. Unfortunately, such highly over-valued exchange rates ('distortions' – see, for example, Agarwal, 1983), penalised exports and diminished the international competitiveness of their exportables substantially. Sometimes, LDCs borrowed from abroad to finance unproductive expenditures, for example, military expenditure and prestigious capital projects, which turned out to be 'white elephants' (Healey, 1990). The wide use of the ISI policies simply led to the mushrooming of 'directly unproductive activities' (Bhagawati, 1984) in a 'rent-seeking economy' (Krueger, 1978). Over-valuation of exchange rates also allowed the 'new-rich' in the LDCs to import luxury goods at a highly subsidised price, or to export their savings (that is, flight of capital) particularly in the Latin-American countries.

11.2 Debt problems after 1973

There are other external reasons for debt accumulation by LDCs after 1973. Such reasons can be summarised as follows:

(a) A huge rise in oil prices after 1973 and 1979 administered a great shock to the current-account balances of non-oil exporting LDCs (NOLDCs);
(b) A big fall in the terms of trade of NOLDCs;
(c) A rise in the global rate of inflation; and
(d) A consequent rise in the rate of interest which increased the debt-service burden significantly in the 1980s.

In the next section, we discuss a general theory of the costs and benefits of default and debt repayment to understand more clearly the incentive compatibility of debt repayments.

11.3 Benefits and costs of default theory

A developing country is likely to default if the benefit of default (*B*) is greater than the cost of such default (*C*), that is,

$$B - C > 0$$

If, however, the cost of default is greater than the cost of repayment, then an LDC will continue to repay and meet its debt-service burden, that is,

$$C - B \leq 0$$

The decision to default by an LDC can be analysed with a simple model originally developed by Krugman and Obstfeld (1988). Assume that D is the total amount of foreign debt, $\bar{D}$ is the principal due for repayment in the present period, and R is the interest rate the country pays to external lenders. The total debt-service is then equal to interest payments and principal due in the current period, that is,

$$\overline{D} + R \cdot D$$

Let L denote new loans to be given to the LDC currently in debt; then the net repayment by a non-defaulting LDC is:

$$\overline{D} + R \cdot D - L = RT$$

Where RT = resource transfer from the borrowing to the lending country. Thus, in case of default, RT denotes debtor country's savings by defaulting. Note that when $RT < 0$, resource is transferred from the creditor to the debtor country.

The benefit from default function (B) can then be written as follows:

$$B = B\left(Q, \overline{D} + R \cdot D - L\right)$$

where Q = aggregate output.
The expected signs of the partial derivatives are:

$$\frac{\partial Q}{\partial B} < 0;$$

$$\frac{\partial \overline{D}}{\partial B} > 0; \frac{\partial D}{\partial B} > 0; \frac{\partial L}{\partial B} < 0$$

For an LDC with any income Q, B is zero when RT is nil. Alternatively, an LDC gains nothing from reneging on debt when lenders are providing funds just enough to service the existing debts, that is,

$$B(Q,0) = 0 \text{ for any } Q$$

Figure 11.1 illustrates the options that LDCs face to repay or renege on debt. The choice of option depends on R (the lending rate), the flow of new loans (L), given Q, $\bar{D}$ and D. The line AB shows combinations of L and R where the cost of default is just equal to benefits, that is,

$$C = B\left(Q, \bar{D} + R \cdot D - L\right)$$

At any point above the line AB, an LDC will default as $B > C$, whereas at any point below AB, $B < C$ and hence an LDC will not be inclined to default. The AB slopes upwards because an increase in R increases the debt-service obligation, increasing the transfer of resources from an LDC, while an increase in L reduces such transfer 'back to its original level'. At a point such as V (which is above the line AB), an LDC is likely to default if it has to pay OR' rate of interest for OL_1 amount of loan. But at a point such as Z, the country will not default as $B < C$.

Let SS' be the supply of loan schedule by banks to LDCs. This line slopes upwards as banks charge high rates of interest as the supply of funds rise. The

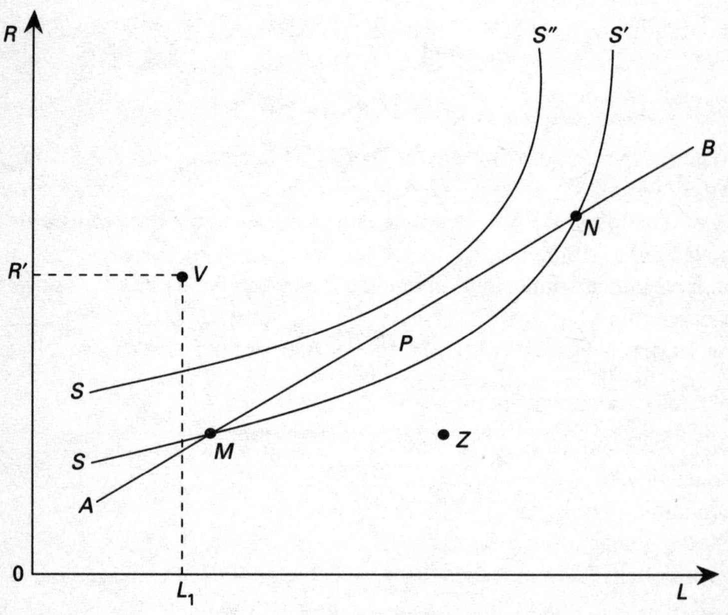

Figure 11.1

reason is, albeit strangely, the demand for higher rewards for the banks to offset the risk of default by the debtor country. A greater flow of new loans today will reduce the probability of default today; but it raises the probability of default in the next period by simply increasing the debt-service burden of the country. Thus, the greater the borrowing, the higher the interest payments.

It is now easy to show that where the line *AB* intersects the *SS* curve (*M* and *N*), an LDC will not default at that loan-interest rate combination. In fact, any loan-interest rate combination between *M* and *N* will be prefered by an LDC to default as $B < C$. If the *SS* line (for example, *S′S′*) lies above the *AB* line, then default is preferable to any package of loan-interest rate and the LDC reneges on its external debt.

11.4 Application of the model to the debt crisis of 1982

Krugman and Obstfeld (1988) show the application of this type of model to the international debt crisis of 1982, when Mexico defaulted on loan repayments, and several other LDCs, particularly in Latin America, were on the verge of reneging on foreign debt. The Western economies in general, and American banks in particular, faced a major financial crisis. The main reasons are as follows.

(i) The significant rise in the real rate of interest in the DCs after the second oil-price rise of 1979 (on top of the quadrupling of oil price in 1973) to control inflation made *domestic* lending in the DCs more appealing than lending to the LDCs, thus shifting the *SS′* curve to the left. It means that, for any lending rate, the volume of credit that banks were willing to offer to LDCs must have declined. This was the major factor that accounted for the 'liquidity crisis' in LDCs in the summer of 1982.

(ii) The massive rise in oil-price worsened the terms of trade on non-oil LDCs. It also led to a fall in their real income and repayment capacity. Bankers immediately regarded lending to such countries as highly risky and asked for a greater risk premium, shifting the *SS′* curve again to the left. As the *SS′* shifted to the left, for LDCs, especially those which were heavily indebted (for example, Mexico), default became incentive-compatible.

(iii) Apart from the exogenous factors which led to a debt crisis, sometimes domestic economic mismanagement, because of the inappropriate use of macroeconomic policies in the debtor countries, led to the perpetuation of persistent excess demand at home, fed by government budget deficits. Besides this when such deficits were monetised (given the small equity and bond markets in most LDCs as a result of the inadequate development of the financial sector), the consequences were highly inflationary, particularly in some Latin-American countries. Such conditions eroded the degree of competitiveness of the domestically produced goods in the international market, leading to a fall in exports and a rise in imports. Countries contracted debt on a larger scale to overcome such foreign exchange 'gaps', only to finance their fiscal imbalances. Thus, the economic situation (twin deficits on the external and internal fronts) became unsustainable when creditors, mainly from the USA and Western Europe decided to cut down on their lending programmes to LDCs.

(iv) Although the lending banks in North America and Western Europe recognised that it was in their interest to continue lending enough to them to avoid a potential default by LDCs, unfortunately it was not in the interest of a *single* bank to carry on lending to LDCs as the *perceived* risk in lending by such a bank could be deemed to be too high relative to returns. Some banks acted as single agents and tried to minimise lending to LDCs, assuming other banks would continue to lend. Unsurprisingly, if *all* the banks tend to be 'free-riders' and act as single agents, they could refuse to make any more new loans to LDCs and defaults would become inevitable. The 'free-rider' problem simply underlines the problem of macro-economic policy co-ordination failure.

(v) Historically, countries accumulated debt to finance a target rate of growth in the face of a 'savings gap', that is, the difference between required investment and actual domestic savings. Even countries such as the USA and Sweden financed a higher growth rate and better standard of living by borrowing from abroad. The repayment is generally financed by a higher growth rate. Unfortunately for some LDCs, the 'adjustment' programmes initiated by the IMF after the two oil-price rises led to substantial rise in costs of investment (mainly public) in LDCs, reducing the output growth and the ability to repay.

11.5 Managing the debt crisis

The main aim of debt strategy is generally described to be that of facilitating the return of debtor countries to normal access to international capital markets. Following the Mexican debt crisis of August 1982, financial management was mainly conducted by the IMF, and the progress since 1982 can be seen in stages.

(i) The first phase. This has been regarded as '*concerted lending*'. The role of the IMF in this management was to maintain a net flow of capital of LDCs, giving all concerned a breathing space. Policy-makers had therefore to generate enough new bank lending to deter immediate default. Concerted lending required that banks contribute new funds in proportion to their loan exposure at the beginning of the crisis. This occurred because the only other option was to become insolvent. However, the individual banks clearly wanted to reduce their exposure to developing country borrowers.

(ii) The second phase. This is characterised by an attempt to 'muddle through'. During this period the IMF has promoted structural adjustment to increase the debt-servicing capacity of LDCs in the long run. Concerted lending had succeeded in the sense that widespread defaults and consequent bank collapses were averted, but subsequently it ran counter to the wishes of banks to lower their exposure. Furthermore, in this phase, the burden of adjustment was imposed on the LDCs. Increasingly, the structural adjustment programmes combined with their debt payments undermined the economic development of LDCs. With debt creating debt, much of the debt stock comprised money from which no economic benefit had been received. Furthermore, the IMF had envisaged that banks would continue to supply LDCs with more capital, which would help them to grow out of their problems. This did not happen, as it was in the interests of each individual bank to lend only what was necessary to keep its assets performing. Thus the banks sought to take advantage of any new lending by other banks to reduce their own involuntary lending (that is, there was a serious 'free-rider' problem).

(iii) Many banks following Citicorp's dramatic decision in mid-1987 to make a special $3 billion provision against its claims on troubled debtor countries have been able to make loan loss provisions and retain solvency. The provision essentially makes new loans less easily available by 'taxing them', and tension between banks has developed over the use of what is considered to be an 'aggressive weapon of competition'. With the banks no longer constrained to protect the book value of their claims, they are less concerned to negotiate terms. Clearly, the major banks are in the position of being able to write off the debt but this option has been ignored in favour of the sale of debt at a discount (creating a secondary market for debt) and so long as this debt retains even a secondary market value there is no incentive for more loans.

For the debtor nations, 'muddling through' has meant falling living standards and rising debt (Healey, 1990). With 'debt slavery' existing since 1982 many LDCs are now experiencing debt fatigue. The interdependence of the world economy has meant that the Third World has seen diminishing market for its exports and has had to cut imports as they are too expensive. Structural adjustment programmes (SAPs) initiated under the guidance of the IMF have reduced public sector spending in LDCs (with obvious consequences for infrastructure and the well-being of the population) and have promoted the export of primary products for which supply is inelastic (hence reducing export revenues). Default therefore sometimes becomes an increasingly attractive alternative.

An indicator of the total debt burden of LDCs is the aggregate net transfer (ANT) which is given by the following equation:

$$ANT = L - S - O$$

where

L = New loans to debtors (including roll-overs of maturing debt)
S = Total debt service payments (with interest)
O = Other net capital flows from debtor to lender (for example capital flight).

Table 11.1 explains ANT to indebted LDCs.

Table 11.1 ANT to indicate developing countries, in billions of US$

Krugman and Obstfeld (1993).

1980	*1981*	*1982*	*1983*	*1984*	*1985*	*1986*	*1987*	*1988*	*1989*	*1992*
27.9	49.6	38.2	–8.5	–43.5	–39.2	–23.1	–50.9	–57.7	–66.9	–16.8

Sources: IMF, *World Economic Outlook* (1992), and Krugman and Obstfeld (1993).

A positive value of ANT means that, on balance, debtors are receiving resources from abroad. A negative ANT means that new loans are insufficient to cover debt service plus other capital outflows. It must be noted that any country taking on a debt must expect a negative net transfer at some time in the future, but Bird (1992) argues that 'the turn around in the case of the major borrowers has come too quickly for them to be able to cope with it and...has been achieved at the cost of domestic investment that holds the key to future growth'. It can be seen that with the onset of the debt crises, ANT became negative and has continued to grow even though the debt servicing capacity of LDCs has not improved. In this sense, the 1980s were a 'lost decade' for LDC growth, and debt has mounted.

The debt crisis of 1982 and the recession in the DCs during 1981–3 had three major effects in LDCs. First, the fall in aggregate demand in the DCs led to *a fall in the terms of trade* of LDCs *vis-à-vis* DCs as the demand for products exported by LDCs fell sharply. Secondly, a fall in the demand in DCs for exports from LDCs reduced the income and the real output of LDCs. Thirdly, the emergence of the protectionist policies pursued by many DCs during the recession resulted in further loss of exports for LDCs, worsening their terms of trade even more during 1981–5.

11.6 Policy responses to the debt crisis of 1982

Policy responses to the dramatic debt crisis of 1982 have followed the following major avenues:

(a) *Rescheduling* of debt and extension of new credits: After the debt crisis of August 1982, many small banks wanted to stop lending to LDCs, particularly to some Latin-American countries such as Mexico. However, the large American banks decided in favour of 'rolling over maturing debts'; that is, payments of principals were postponed and short-term debts were transformed into long-term debts However, payments of principals in rescheduled debt were charged extra interest rates. Besides, to cover primary-account deficits in LDCs, banks offered new credits.

(b) The IMF played a very significant role in averting the debt crisis of 1982. LDCs rescheduling debts also borrowed substantially from the IMF. The Fund imposed some conditions on the borrowing countries (the so-called 'conditionality clauses') to adjust their economies and the balance of payments. Typically, such conditions included:

(i) *devaluation of the domestic currencies*; and
(ii) a substantial cut in the fiscal deficit and government expenditure in heavily indebted countries to balance the books. Such measures of austerity became an important cornerstone of the 'structural adjustment lending (SAL)' programmes initiated by the IMF for the borrowing countries. The SAL policies also included removal of government subsidies, cuts in public-sector wages, and an increase in prices of public goods and services (the price liberalisation programme).
(iii) LDCs, under pressure from the IMF, took several steps to deflate their domestic economies which resulted in very low (and even negative) output growth rates, falling employment and real wages between 1982–5. Some LDCs devalued their currencies sharply; others deflated their economies and went into recession to restore some stability in the external account. In general, the NICs and the Asian countries performed better than the debt-ridden countries of Africa.
(iv) Recently, many banks in Western Europe and the USA have made efforts to reduce their lending for ill-conceived projects in LDCs. In the late 1980s, all such lending banks raised their loan-loss reserves drastically. Sometimes bad debts to some LDCs have been written off completely, as an example of 'debt forgiveness'; on other occasions, LDC debts have been disposed of at a discount–leading to the creation of a *secondary market for LDC debt*. With large secondary markets for such loans that are now trading below face value, it is suggested that this gives LDCs a chance to *buy back* debt. However, *debt buybacks* raise the value of outstanding debt, and valuable resources are simply transferred to creditors. Furthermore, a chance of repayment gives creditors an incentive to retain debt until its value rises. For instance, in 1988, Bolivia owed $53 million, which had been priced at 7 cents on the dollar, when some countries gave the government $34 million to buy back part of its commercial debt. After the buy-back, Bolivia's debt was valued at 12 cents on the dollar, raising the market value of the total debt to $43 million. Clearly, Bolivia's expected debt payments,

because of the buy-back provisions, reduced by about \$10 million (Krugman and Obstfeld, 1993).

(v) Dealing in the secondary market of LDC debt is a major reason for the reluctance of the lenders from DCs to forgive debt. Any 'debt forgiveness' (that is, funds for the debt buy-back are provided by the creditors themselves) by one creditor benefits remaining creditors (the 'free-rider' problem). Hence, there is a co-ordination problem requiring lenders to act as a group. According to the debt 'overhang theory', lenders would even gain by forgiving and increasing their expected payments. This latter idea can be shown in the Debt–Laffer Curve. It has been argued forcefully that the existence of an unmanageably large external debt can be a strong disincentive for debt repayments (Krugman, 1988). Krugman (1988) admirably argues as follows:

> When a country's obligations exceed the amount it is likely to be able to pay, these obligations act like a high marginal tax rate on the country: if it succeeds in doing better than expected, the main benefits will accrue, not to the country, but to its creditors. This fact discourages the country from doing well at two levels. First, the government of a country will be less likely to be willing to take painful or politically unpalatable measures to improve economic performance if the benefits are likely to go to foreign creditors in any case. Second, the burden of the national debt will fall on domestic residents through taxation, and importantly through taxation of capital; so the overhang of debt acts as a deterrent to investment.
>
> Over and above these costs to potential repayment is the fact that no clean Chapter XI proceeding exists for sovereign debtors, and a confrontational disorderly default may reduce the actual receipts to a creditor below what could have been obtained if debt had earlier been reduced to a level that could have been paid.
>
> The upshot of these negative effects is that the higher is the external debt of a country, the larger the probability of nonpayment: and thus the greater the subjective discount on the debt. If debt is high enough, further increases in the level of debt may actually lead to a *smaller* expected value of payments (Krugman, 1988, pp. 9–10).

The relationship between the level of debt and a creditor's expectations is shown in figure 11.2. The horizontal axis shows the level of debt and the vertical axis shows the expected present value of repayments. For low levels of debt from D to R, full repayment is expected, and so the outcome lies along the 45° line. At higher levels of debt, however, the possibilities of non-payment arises and grows, so that the expected payment line traces out a curve that falls increasingly below the 45° line. Beyond some point (L), the disincentive effects outlined above

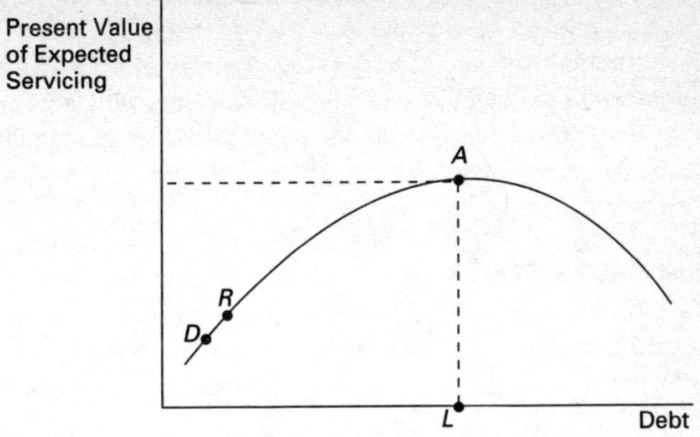

Figure 11.2 The Debt Laffer Curve

begin to outweigh the option value to the creditors of being able to share in the debtor's good fortune, should outcomes prove unexpectedly favourable. Krugman (1988) argues as follows:

> The curve DRLC should by now be a familiar sort of object. It is the *Debt Relief Laffer Curve*. That is, just as governments may sometimes actually increase tax revenue by reducing tax rates, creditors may sometimes increase expected payment by forgiving part of a country's debt. In both cases, the proposition that less is more depends on an initial extreme situation, whether of taxes that provide extreme disincentives or of a debt burden that is crippling in its effect on economic growth. Arguments that debt relief is in everyone's interest are, in effect, arguments that countries are on the wrong side of the debt relief Laffer curve. (Krugman, 1988, pp. 11–12)

Obviously, the existence of such a Debt Laffer curve would make the case of 'debt forgiveness' stronger.

11.7 The International Monetary Fund (IMF), adjustment policies and LDCs

In the original Bretton Woods Conference, the IMF was given the following major responsibilities:

(a) to control the volume of international liquidity;
(b) to ensure the stability of exchange rates;
(c) to promote free trade and capital flows across nations;
(d) to help members with persistent balance-of-payments (BoP) difficulties; and
(e) to co-ordinate the economic policies of member states.

When the Bretton Woods system broke down in the early 1970s, some of these aims became unattainable, leaving the IMF with the major duty of providing the BoP aid. The questions that are usually asked are: how effective has the IMF's assistance been, and how well did it adapt itself to dealing with these countries in the 1980s? In the next section, we analyse some of the major complaints about the IMF's activities in the past.

11.8 Criticism of the IMF action

Past criticisms of the IMF's activities in LDCs can be grouped as follows (see ODI, 1993):

1. That Fund programmes are inappropriate. Its approach to policy is pre-occupied with the control of demand, too little concerned with BoP weaknesses stemming from the productive system; and it imposes large costs on borrowing countries through losses of output and employment, by further impoverishing the poor, and through the politically destabilising effects of its policy stipulations.
2. *The Fund's modes of operation and inflexibility in negotiations.* These infringe the sovereignty of states and alienate governments from the measures they are supposed to implement; there is an increasing overlap with the World Bank; and between them they are likely to swamp governments with policy conditions.
3. That its credits and programmes are too small, expensive and too short-term. The programmes are criticised as being too short-term for economies whose BoP problems are rooted in structural weaknesses and who often face secular declines in their terms of trade. The credits are also criticised for their short maturity periods and the near-commercial rates of interest which they often bear, and as being too small relative to financing needs.
4. The Fund is dominated by a few major industrial countries. They pay little heed to developing countries views. The industrial countries, it is alleged, use their control to promote their own interests – for example, in using the Fund to impose a post-1982 approach to the debt problem which shifted a disproportionate burden on to debtor countries – and to reward 'favourites'.

11.9 Response of the International Monetary Fund

The core of the IMF approach to programme design is its 'financial programming' model. This takes a broadly monetarist view, with a BoP deficit seen as being caused by a surplus in the supply of money over the demand for it, emanating from excessive domestic credit expansion. Hence the essential task of an IMF team is to analyse the money supply-and-demand situation and to restrict credit, to restore BoP viability. As a consequence, programmes almost always try to reduce budget deficits to reduce governments' credit needs.

The IMF team does not confine itself to this task, however. For one thing, it regards the exchange rate as being an important influence on the BoP, so that (except in currency union countries such as the African member-states of the Franc Zone) almost all its programmes involve devaluation. In recent years the Fund has reduced its reliance on quantified indicators of demand control, such as ceilings on credit to the public and private sectors, observance of which determine continued access to the negotiated line of credit. While such 'performance criteria' remain central to the Fund's modalities, it now makes greater use of (usually half-yearly) Review Missions, to take an overall view of programme execution and adjust programme details in light of the most recent economic data.

The Fund is also moving away from concentration on simple budgetary aggregates, such as total spending or the budget balance, in favour of paying more attention to the 'quality' of fiscal adjustment. Since the economic impact of its fiscal provision will be much affected by which expenditures are trimmed and what is done with taxes, the Fund is becoming more insistent on knowing how a government proposes to implement a promised reduction in the budget deficit, increasingly urging governments to install social safety nets, and asking questions about military spending.

In other respects too it is paying more attention to achieving a better balance between demand-management and supply-side measures, even in its short-term (typically eighteen month) stand-by programmes, which now place greater weight on the goal of economic growth. In many cases, the privatisation or reform of public enterprises is stipulated – to reduce budgetary pressures but also to raise productive efficiency. Price and subsidy reforms are also common ingredients, for example, raising petroleum prices or cutting food subsidies. While stand-bys remain short-term there is now a greater willingness to countenance a succession of such programmes, so that some countries (Ivory Coast, Jamaica, Morocco, for example) have enjoyed the mixed pleasures of near-continuous support for a decade or more.

The extension of the Fund's conditionality into measures bearing directly on the productive structure is taken a good deal further in its Extended Fund Facility (Eff) – first introduced in 1974, kept in limbo during most of the 1980s but now reactivated as a major lending vehicle – and furthest of all in the Structural (and Extended Structural) Adjustment Facilities (SAF and ESAF) initiated in recent years. By the end of 1992, these three facilities accounted for nearly three-quarters of the total value of all lending. The EFF, SAF and ESAF have taken the Fund in the direction of medium-term lending, with the EFF providing 3–4-year support largely to middle-income and former Comecon countries, and SAF-ESAF offering a 3–5-year programmes to low-income countries, chiefly in Africa (see also table 11.2)

Table 11.2 Debt and growth in severely-indebted countries

	Outstanding Debt 1990 ($bn)	*Debt/GDP 1990 (%)*	*Interest/ Exports 1990 (%)*	*Average GDP Growth 1982–90 (%)*	*Average Import Growth 1982–90 (%)*	*Average Investment Growth, 1982–90 (%)*	*Average Growth of Per Capita Consumption 1982–90 (%)*
Algeria	26.8	52.9	15.1	1.9	–2.2	–1.2	–0.6
Argentina	61.1	61.7	18.4	–0.0	1.2	–8.3	–1.1
Bolivia	4.3	101.0	15.9	1.0	2.2	–10.5	–1.7
Brazil	116.2	22.8	8.6	2.5	–0.1	1.3	0.5
Bulgaria	10.9	56.9	6.4	1.0	–0.2	3.0	3.8
Congo	5.1	203.6	9.3	1.1	0.7	–18.9	–0.7
Cote d'Ivoire	18.0	203.9	13.3	–0.4	2.8	–12.4	–4.7
Ecuador	12.1	120.6	14.5	2.0	–1.5	–4.1	–0.5
Mexico	96.8	42.1	16.7	1.6	5.0	–2.6	–1.1
Morocco	23.5	97.1	11.7	4.0	5.4	1.4	0.9
Nicaragua	10.5	–	3.0	–3.8	–0.8	–7.5	–6.5
Peru	21.1	60.1	5.2	–1.4	–1.8	–9.3	–3.5
Syria	16.4	118.1	3.9	1.8	–2.6	–9.1	–1.7
Venezuela	33.3	71.0	15.6	1.1	–7.7	–10.7	–1.2
Nigeria	36.1	117.9	12.1	1.9	–8.4	–9.6	–2.3

Source: *World Bank, World Development Report*, Washington, DC, 1993.

Uniquely, SAF and ESAF programmes are based on a Policy Framework Paper (PFP) setting out a three-year adjustment programme, supposedly drafted jointly by borrowing governments, the IMF and the World Bank. In the early days of this innovation the involvement of governments in the drafting process was often minimal, but they have gradually acquired more influence.

The Fund has also changed its stance on the social effects of its programmes. It formerly insisted that it was for national governments to decide whether to protect the poor from hardships resulting from programmes. Now, its missions commonly discuss distributional aspects with governments when preparing programmes. PFPs are required to include measures to protect the well-being of vulnerable groups, and programmes increasingly contain safety-net provision.

The PFP has also provided a useful mechanism for co-ordination between the Fund and the World Bank. There is plenty of scope for disagreement between them, for example, about the desirable levels of government spending, bank credit, imports and the exchange rate, and these tensions were heightened when the World Bank increased its structural adjustment lending during the 1980s. There were some problems over such countries as Argentina, Nigeria and Zambia, but it appears that top-management agreements on the division of labour and staff co-operation have resolved these difficulties substantially. Borrowing governments are now less likely to be bewildered by conflicting 'advice' from the two institutions.

11.10 New critiques of the International Monetary Fund

First, critics point out that the Fund's use of more supply-side measures has been *additional* to its traditional demand-control policies, not in substitution of them. The Fund has thus widened the range of conditionality without diluting its monetarist hard core. There has been particular criticism of the ESAF credits, which frightened off potential borrowers, causing a slow take-up rate. The Fund's approach to the supply side is criticised as blinkered: largely addressed to the reduction of price distortions and privatisation, taking a negative view of the state and associated with sharp fall in government investment. Moreover, while the EFF and SAF–ESAF facilities and toleration of repeated stand-bys have taken the Fund into medium-term lending, these are no substitute for programmes conceived as long-term.

Doubts persist about the appropriateness of the financial programming model. Its strength is that it confronts governments with the BoP and inflationary consequences of their budget deficits, but the model remains open to a range of criticisms. First, it is seen as resting upon assumptions that may often not be valid for developing-country conditions. In particular, it assumes that the demand for money is known and stable – so that non-expansionary levels of money supply and domestic credit can be estimated – a condition which may not always hold. Secondly, it requires that governments are able to hold credit within agreed ceilings, whereas their control is often highly imperfect because of unreliable data, the difficulties of forecasting and regulating budgetary outcomes, vulnerability to 'shocks', and unpredictable responses by banks and other financial institutions to governments' policy signals.

The model is criticised as being too static, and not well designed to cope with time lags and uncertainties, or to trace the effects of the private sector's reactions to stabilisation measures. The static nature of the model has caused the Fund particular difficulties since it was pushed in the later 1980s towards more 'growth-orientated' programmes. The incorporation of a growth objective alongside BoP viability generates a host of complications and increases the difficulties of using the model for policy purposes.

Finally, the model is criticised for focusing on only a few economic aggregates, diverting attention from important qualitative aspects of policy. Programme negotiations are often preoccupied with fruitless disputes about the merits of rival statistics and the exact numbers that should be included as performance criteria.

However, there is now less controversy than formerly about the main thrust of the Fund's advice, about the importance of macro economic stability and of fiscal–monetary discipline to that end. Further criticisms have, however, arisen regarding the cost of IMF credit and its overall direction of flow.

11.11 How effective are IMF programmes?

Another approach to assessing the policies of the Fund in developing countries is to examine how programmes work in practice and what impact they have. There are major methodological problems here: the difficulties of disentangling programme effects from other influences on economic performance; of choosing adequate performance indicators and the best period for analysis. Above all, skill is required to construct a plausible assessment of what would have happened in the absence of a programme (see ODI, 1993, for a good summary).

Empirical research nevertheless makes it possible to offer some generalisations about programme effects.

(a) Fund programmes usually strengthen the BoP. Moreover, these results are not typically achieved by means of swinging import cuts; export performance is usually improved. It takes time for these improvements to show up but they are then usually sustained into the medium term.
(b) About half of the programmes break down before completion (two-thirds in recent years). This does not seen to make much difference to outcomes, however, which suggests that the BoP improvements are less attributable to the programmes than to a greater concern with macro economic management among governments which sign Fund agreements.

(c) Overall, programmes do not make much difference to the inflation rate. While demand – control measures may reduce inflationary pressures, this tends to be offset by the price-raising effects of devaluation and interest-rate liberalisation.
(d) Programmes have a muted impact on economic growth: neither the crippling deflation of which the Fund's critics complain, nor the revived expansion which the Fund seeks to achieve. Programmes often result in substantially reduced investment levels and sometimes in shortages of imported inputs.
(e) There is little evidence that programmes typically impose large social costs, although the urban labour force commonly suffers reduced real earnings, and cuts in budget subsidies can have serious effects. Programme effects on the distribution of income can be large but are usually complex, with the overall effect on poverty depending on country circumstances and policies.There is no systematic evidence of political destablisation, although there have been specific instances of this.
(f) Many of the programmes that break down do so because of adverse external developments. In the absence of adequate contingency financing, countries get into difficulties because world prices turn against them, and quite often because of natural disasters, such as droughts and hurricanes.
(g) Programmes may fail to trigger additional inflows of capital from the rest of the world, despite claims that the Fund's 'seal of approval' has a catalytic effect on capital inflows. While some countries have benefited, evidence shows that the BoP capital account does not typically improve, even though debt relief and development assistance are included. Indeed, a shortage of supporting finance is a common reason for programme breakdown.
(h) Programmes may not always have a *strong* influence on fiscal and monetary policies. This helps to explain the Fund's imperfect ability to achieve programme targets. However, the exchange rate is strongly influenced; programmes are associated with substantial currency depreciations, and these are sustained in real terms.
(i) There has been a good deal of political interference in Fund lending decisions. Successive US administrations have in particular used their weight to favour (or oppose) friendly (or hostile) LDCs. In some countries, this forced the Fund into providing effectively unconditional finance to governments with proven records of economic mismanagement (for example, in the Philippines under President Ferdinand Marcos, Sudan under President Gaafar al-Nimeri and Zaire under President Mabutu) swelling the number of ineffective programmes. However, the end of the Cold War may diminish such geo-politicking. (This section draws generously from the ODI, 1993.)

Appendix to Chapter 11

A small model of India (with Paul Levine)

The national solvency condition

In this section we derive the national solvency condition facing a debtor country. Let us begin by writing down the balance of payments identity at time t as

$$CA_t = TB_t + i_t^* E_t A_t / P_t = E_t (A_{t+1} - A_t) / P_t \tag{A11.1}$$

where CA is the current account surplus; TB is the trade balance (both measured in real terms using the GDP deflator); E is the nominal exchange rate; P is the domestic price level; i^* is the foreign interest rate, and A is the beginning-of-period nation's stock of net foreign assets, which are assumed to be denominated in terms of foreign currency. Current transfers such as foreign aid are ignored.

It is convenient to express both assets (A_t) and the trade balance (TB_t) as proportions of GDP. Thus we let $a_t = E_t A_t / P_{t-1} Y_{t-1}$ be the stock of net foreign assets measured as a proportion of the previous period's nominal GDP (where real GDP is denoted by Y). Similarly, define $tb_t = TB_t / Y_t$. Then taking first differences of a_t we have

$$a_{t+1} = \frac{(1 + \Delta e_t)(1 + i_t^*) a_t}{(1 + \pi_t)(1 + n_t)} + tb_t \tag{A11.2}$$

where $\Delta e_t = (E_t - E_{t-1})/E_{t-1}$, (The reason for this notation is that later we define $e_t = (E_t - \overline{E}_t)\overline{E}_t$ where $\overline{E}_t$ is the long-run trend and so $\Delta e_t = e_t - e_{t-1}$.) $\pi_t = (P_t - P_{t-1})/P_{t-1}$ and $n_t = (Yt - Y_{t-1})/Y_{t-1}$ are the rate of depreciation of the nominal exchange rate, the rate of inflation, and the rate of GDP growth respectively.

Now define competitiveness to be EP^*/P where P^* is the foreign price level. Then ignoring second order terms in Δe_t, π_t, n_t and i_t^* and linearising about a long run in which competitiveness, i_t^* and n_t are constant and a_t is small, we have that $\overline{\Delta e} = \overline{\pi} - \overline{\pi}^*$ (denoting long-run values by a bar). In other words, we assume relative purchasing power parity in the long run) and (A11.2) then becomes approximately

$$a_{t+1} = \left(1 + \overline{i}^* - \overline{\pi}^* - \overline{n}\right) a_t + tb_t \tag{A11.3}$$

Equation (A11.3) is now in deviation form about an equilibrium in which the nation's debt is zero. The approximation is accurate in the vicinity of such an equilibrium.

Let $\overline{r} = \overline{i}^* - \overline{\pi}^* - \overline{n}$ be the steady-state real foreign interest rate minus the domestic growth rate. If GDP growth exceeds the real interest rate in the steady state then $\overline{r} < 0$ and then any stable path for the trade balance/GDP rate is consistent with a stable asset to GDP ratio a_t. If, on the other hand, $\bar{r} > 0$, we can then solve (A11.3) forward in time to give

$$a_t = -\sum_{i=0}^{\infty} \frac{tb_{t+i}}{(1+\bar{r})^{i+1}} \quad \text{(A11.4)}$$

provided that $\lim_{i\to\infty} a_{t+i}/(1+\bar{r})^{i} = 0$. This is guaranteed if a_t itself is stable (though not necessarily asymptotically stable). Strictly speaking solvency does not require a stable debt–GDP ratio. We have chosen this strong solvency condition (referred to as a 'practical solvency criterion' by Buiter and Patel, 1990).

Equation (A11.4) expresses the national solvency condition facing a debtor nation. It says that the current external debt, a proportion of GDP, must be proportional to the present value of future primary surpluses (also as a proportion of GDP) discounted at a rate $\bar{r}$. A debtor country with $a_t < 0$ at time t must at some time in the future run primary surpluses. The contrast between the cases where $\bar{r} < 0$ and $\bar{r} > 0$ should be noted. In the former case (where the domestic GDP growth rate exceeds the real rate of interest), in order to stabilise the debt to GDP ratio, a debtor country need only stabilise the trade balance to GDP ratio and need never run primary trade surpluses. In the later case (where the real rate of interest exceeds the GDP growth rate), stabilising the debt to GDP ratio requires the debtor country to run surpluses, for at least some periods in the future, in order to service the debt.

In the 1980s and 1990s, India (along with other LDCs) faced high real foreign interest rates far in excess of its growth rate. In what follows we take the growth-adjusted real interest rate $\bar{r}$ to be positive.

An estimated trade sector

The aim of this section is to model the trade balance/GDP ratio, *tb*, for India in terms of policy instruments and exogenous variables. By definition we have that

$$tb_t = \frac{E_t\left(X_t^{\$} - M_t^{\$}\right)}{P_t Y_t} \quad \text{(A11.5)}$$

where $X_t^{\$}$ and $M_t^{\$}$ are total exports and imports in dollars and E_t, P_t and Y_t are defined as before. Now define export and import volumes $X_t = X_t^{\$}/P_t^{x}$ and $M_t = M_t^{\$}/P_t^{m}$ where P_t^{x} and P_t^{m} are import and export price indices respectively, in dollars. Then log-linearising about a long-run equilibrium or trend with a zero trade balance we have that

$$tb_t = \frac{E_t(P_t X_t - P_t M_t)}{P_{tY_t}} = \alpha^{x}\left(x_t + p_t^{x}\right) - \alpha^{m}\left(m_t + p_t^{m}\right) \quad \text{(A11.6)}$$

where $x_t = \log X_t/\bar{X}_t$; $m_t = \log M_t/\bar{M}_t$; $P_t^{x} = \log P_t^{x}/\bar{P}_t^{x}$; $P_t^{m} = \log P_t^{m}/\bar{P}_t^{m}$; $\alpha^{x} = \bar{E}\bar{P}\bar{X}/\bar{P}\bar{Y}$; $\alpha^{m} = \bar{E}\bar{P}\bar{X}/\bar{P}\bar{Y}$, where (dropping the subscript t), $\bar{X}$, $\bar{M}$ and so on denote long-run values or trends. The empirical strategy is now to calibrate α^{x} and α^{m}, the ratios of exports and imports to GDP respectively, and to estimate the trade volumes x_t and m_t using data for $M_t^{\$}$, $X_t^{\$}$, P_t^{x} and P_t^{m} and for the determinants of the trade volumes.

The general form of the estimated equations for x_t and m_t are

$$x_t = f\left(c_t^x, y_t^*\right) \tag{A11.7}$$

and

$$m_t = f\left(c_t^m, y_t\right) \tag{A11.8}$$

where c_t^x and c_t^m are measures of competitiveness for exports and imports respectively, y_t^* denotes world demand for exports, and y_t denotes domestic demand which we take simply as GDP. (All lower-case variables are in logarithms in terms of deviations about a long-run trend.)

Our measures of competitiveness are $c_t^x = \log E_t P_t^x / P_t$, $c_t^m = \log E_t P_t^m / P_t$ and for y_t^* we choose the logarithm of world industrial output. The domestic price level P_t is proxied by the consumer price index so that the choice of competitiveness of exports is from the supply-side view. The following error correction mechanisms were then estimated using annual data

$$\Delta x_{t=} = 0.23\, c_t^x - 0.069\, x_{t-1} \tag{A11.9}$$

$$(2.80) \qquad (2.12)$$

$$\Delta m_t = -0.51 \Delta c_t^m + 1.13 \Delta y_t - 0.59 m_{t-1} + 1.66 y_{t-1} \tag{A11.10}$$

$$(3.75) \qquad (2.67) \qquad (3.78) \qquad (3.44)$$

where Δ denotes the first difference, and the constants are omitted since variables are measured in deviation form about their long-run trends; *t*-ratios are in brackets.

Equation (A11.9) describes a sluggish adjustment of export volumes towards a long-run relation $x_t = 3.3\, c_t^x$ (relative to trend); that is, a 1 per cent real devaluation (an increase in c_t^x) brings about a 3 per cent increase in export volumes. Similarly (A11.10) describes adjustment towards a long run in which $m_t = 2.8 y_t$; that is, the import elasticity with respect to GDP in the steady-state is close to 3. More econometric details of the estimated equations are given in Ghatak and Levine (1994). It should be noted that we failed to find a significant effect of world demand on exports.

The government budget constraint

The government issues nominal debt D_t consisting of non-indexed one-period bonds. The debt is denominated in terms of foreign currency and delivers a nominal interest rate equal to the foreign interest rate i_t^*. The government budget identity corresponding to the national budget identity (A11.1) is then

$$\frac{\Delta MS_t}{P_t} + \frac{\Delta D_t}{P_t} = i_t^* \frac{E_t D_t}{P_t} + G_t - T_t \tag{A11.11}$$

where MS_t is the beginning-of-period money stock, $\Delta MS_t = MS_{t+1} - MS_t$; D_t is measured at the beginning of the period (that is, issued over the interval $[t-1, t]$); G_t is real government spending on goods and services; and T_t is real taxation (net of transfers).

Define $PD_t = G_t - T_t$, the government primary deficit. As before we express all variables as proportions of GDP. Let $d_t = E_t D_t / P_{t-1} Y_{t-1}$; $ms_t = MS_t / P_{t-1} Y_{t-1}$ and $pd_t = PD_t / Y_z$. Then (A11.7) d_{t+1} may be written as

$$d_{t+1} = \frac{(1+\Delta e_t)(1+i_t^*)d_t}{(1+\pi_t)(1+n_t)} + pd_t - ms_{t+1} + \frac{ms_t}{(1+\pi_t)(1+n_t)} \qquad \text{(A11.12)}$$

which is analogous to (A11.2) with added seigniorage terms. Linearising about a long-run in which competitiveness, i_t^* and n_t are constant, and d_t is small (A11.12) becomes approximately

$$d_{t+1} = \left(1+\bar{i}^* - \bar{\pi}^* - \bar{n}\right)d_t + pd_t - \left(\Delta ms_t + \overline{ms}(\pi_t + n_t) + (\bar{\pi} + \bar{n})ms_t\right) \text{(A11.13)}$$

Equation (A11.23) (which is analogous to (A11.3)) is now in deviation form about an equilibrium in which government debt is zero. A convenient assumption – for which there is some empirical support for India (see, for example, Ghatak. (1981), in which further references may be found) – is that of a constant velocity of circulation for money. Then $\Delta ms_t = ms_t = 0$ in (A11.13) (as ms_t is in deviation form) and the seigniorage form becomes $\overline{ms}\ (\pi_t + n_t)$. The government solvency condition can be expressed in a form analogous to the national solvency condition, (A11.4).

Aggregate demand

Write aggregate demand as

$$Y_t = C_t(YD_t, V_t) + I_t + TB_t + G_t \qquad \text{(A11.14)}$$

where C_t is real consumption; $YD_t = Y_t - T_t$ is real disposable income; $V_t = E_t\ (A_t + D_t)/P_t$ is real non-human wealth; and I_t is investment, considered to be exogenous in this model. The consumption function in (A11.14) can be justified by assuming that consumers are myopic (that is, not forward-looking) and some of them are liquidity-constrained.

Linearising (A11.14) about a long-run trend gives

$$Y_t = \alpha_1 c_t + \alpha_2 (g_t + tb_t) \qquad \text{(A11.15)}$$

where $y_t = (Y_t - \bar{Y}_t)/\bar{Y}_t$, $c_t = (C_t - \bar{C}_t)/\bar{C}_t$, $g_t = G_t/Y_t - \bar{G}_t/\bar{Y}_t$, $tb_t = \overline{TB}/Y_t - \overline{TB}_t/Y_t$, Y_t and so on, denoting the long-run trend. Parameters α_1 and α_2 are given by $\alpha_1 = \bar{C}/\bar{Y}$ and $\alpha_3 = (1 - \overline{TB}_t/\bar{Y}_t - \bar{G}_t/\bar{Y}_t)^{-1}$. Linearising the consumption function gives

$$c_t = y_t + \eta_{cv} Y_t / V_t v_t - \eta_{c_y}\left(1 - \bar{T}_t / \bar{Y}_t\right)_{\tau t}^{-1} \qquad \text{(A11.16)}$$

where $v_t = V_t/Y_t - \bar{V}_t/\bar{Y}_t$, $\tau_t = T_t/Y_t - \bar{T}_t/Y_t$ and η_{CV} and η_{CY} are elasticities of consumption with respect to wealth and disposable income respectively. In (A11.16) the assumption that $\eta_{CV} + \eta_{CY} = 1$ is used, which ensures that in the steady-state consumption, output wealth and taxes all grow at the same exogenously determined rate.

The supply side

Let PC be the consumer price index and define $pc_t = (PC_t - \overline{PC}_t)/\overline{PC}_t$. Similarly define all other variables on the supply side in terms of a proportional deviation about a long-run trend. Then the full supply side takes the form

$$p_{ct} = \theta p_t + (1-\theta)(e_t + p_t^m) \tag{A11.17}$$

$$p_t = \beta w_t + (1-\beta)(e_t + p_t^m) \tag{A11.18}$$

$$\Delta w_t = \alpha y_t + \Delta pc_t^e \tag{A11.19}$$

$$\Delta pc_t^e = \Delta pc_{t-1}^e + \lambda(\Delta pc_{t-1} - pc_{t-1}^e) \tag{A11.20}$$

Equation (A11.17) defines the consumer price index as a geometric average of the domestic price and the price of imported goods. Equation (A11.18) expresses the domestic price level as a mark-up on the wage rate w_t and the price of imported goods. Equation (A11.19)) is an expectations-augmented Phillips curve and (A11.20) describes an adaptive expectations scheme.

Defining the real exchange rate $er_t = e_t - p_t$ as before, (A11.17) to (A11.19) can be written as

$$\pi c_t = \Delta pc_t = \Delta p_t + (1-\theta)/\theta(\Delta er_t + \Delta p_t^m) \tag{A11.21}$$

$$\pi_t = \Delta p_t = \beta(\alpha y_t + \Delta p_t^e) + (1-\beta)(\Delta er_t + \Delta p_t + \Delta p_t^m) \tag{A11.22}$$

and the wage rate w_t has been eliminated.

The budget identities (A11.3) and (A11.13) (with $ms_t = 0$); the aggregate demand side, equations (A11.15) and (A11.16); the supply side (A11.21) and (A11.22); constitute our small macro-model of India expressed in linearised state-space form. We take government spending and taxation as a proportion of GDP (g_t and τ_t) and the real exchange rate er_t to be the instruments available to the government. The latter can be set by the government if it is assumed that the current price level is observed and the nominal exchange rate is directly controlled. (In India, the nominal exchange rate is, in fact, controlled by the government)

The policy choice: debt repayment or repudiation?

In order to examine the incentive compatibility of debt repayment, two options facing the government and the private sector are compared. (We assume that the government and private sector act as one; but the mechanism for achieving this co-ordination is not explored.) The first option is to repay the debt. This implies that fiscal and exchange-rate policy are adjusted so that the national and government solvency conditions are satisfied (for the case where the real interest rate exceeds the growth rate in the long run which, in view of the discussion in section 2 above, we assume to be so). The alternative facing the government is to repudiate the debt and face the consequences. We assume that the penalty for repudiation is that no further borrowing by the nation or inflows of foreign investment are possible. The nation must then 'balance its books' and cease to run a trade deficit.

Debt repayment is then incentive compatible if on the basis of some welfare criteria, repayment and functioning within the national solvency condition are superior to the consequences of immediately eliminating the trade deficit. The outcome will depend on a number of factors – the initial size of the debt to GDP ratios, the initial trade balance ratio, and the form of the required adjustment to solvency implied by the model.

In order to explore these issues we first define a welfare criteria for the government in terms of a welfare loss

$$W^1 = \sum_{t=0}^{\infty} \mu^t \left(a(c_t - \bar{c})^2 + b(\hat{g}_t - \bar{g})^2 + c(\pi c_t - \bar{\pi})^2 \right) \tag{A11.23}$$

where $0 < \mu < 1$ is a discount factor, $\hat{g} = (G_t - \bar{G}_t/\bar{G}_t \;-\; \bar{Y}/\bar{G}$ (recall that $g_t = G_t/Y_t - \bar{Y}_t/\bar{G}_t$ is the government spending/GDP ratio in deviation form), π_{ct} is consumer price inflation measured (as for c_t and $\bar{g}_t$) about the underlying long-term trend. According to (A11.23) the government penalises proportional deviations of consumption, government spending and inflation from bliss points $\bar{c}$, $\bar{g}$ and $\bar{\pi}$ respectively (all measured relative to a long-run trend in which consumption output and government spending are growing at the same rate). The first two terms in (A11.23) may be obtained as the first two terms of a Taylor-series expansion of $\log C_t/\bar{C}_t + b \log G_t/\bar{G}_t$ with $\bar{c} = \bar{g} = 1.0$. Consumption and government spending on goods and services enter the utility of consumers directly. The social costs of inflation have been widely discussed in the literature (see Driffill *et al.*, 1989 for a useful review).

Suppose that at the time $t = 0$ the initial conditions faced by the government consist of government and national debt and a trade deficit. Denote these by values for $d_0 > 0$, $a_0 < 0$, $x_0 < 0$ and $m_0 > 1$ measured about an equilibrium in which debt, the trade balance and the public deficit are zero. In order to satisfy the solvency conditions, some combination of demand reduction (reducing y_t) and real exchange rate devaluation (increasing er_t) is necessary. Both these effects are penalised indirectly in the welfare loss function. We assume that the government can control the real exchange rate by directly fixing the nominal exchange rate. Since $er_t = \log(E_t/P_t)$ and the price level P_t is given at time t, control over the nominal exchange rate implies control over the real exchange rate.

The optimisation problem is then to choose paths for g_t, τ_t and er_t to minimise W given by (A11.23), given the national and government solvency conditions and rest of the model. There is nothing in the model as it stands to enforce government solvency. A convenience way of proceeding is to assume that the tax rate τ_t is used to stabilise the government debt/GDP ratio d_t through a feedback rule $\tau_t = \gamma d_t$ where γ is chosen to be small, but greater than the growth-adjusted real interest rate $\bar{r} = \bar{i}^* - \bar{\pi}^* - \bar{n}$. Distortionary effects of varying the tax rate are ignored. But, of course, raising the tax rate reduces consumption (see (A11.16)) and lowers welfare. Then d_t is stabilised, which is a sufficient (but not necessary) condition for government solvency. Let us now return to the two options described at the beginning of this section – repayment of debt and repudiation.

Option 1 – Repayment of debt

The optimisation problem under option 1 is then to minimise W with respect to g_t and er_t given the model, given exogenous processes for p_t^x and p_t^m (about their long-term trend) and given initial states a_0, d_0, m_0 and x_0. It is possible to estimate or assume particular exogenous processes for p_t^x and p_t^m. In this study, however, we fix $p_t^x = p_t^m = 0$ (that is, these exogenous prices are fixed at their long-term trends).

Option 2 – Debt repudiation

The government and nation now repudiate all external debt but are constrained by having immediately to cease to run a trade deficit. Recalling that variables are measured in deviation form about a long run in which the trade balance is zero, the constraint then becomes $tb_t = 0$. The modified welfare loss function (A11.23) is now replaced with

$$W^2 = \sum_{t=0}^{\infty} \mu^t \left(a(c_t - \bar{c})^2 + b(\hat{g} - \bar{g})^2 + c(\pi c_t - \bar{\pi})^2 + dtb_t^2 \right) \quad \text{(A11.24)}$$

where the weight d is chosen to be very large. The optimisation problem is otherwise as before.

As it stands, the welfare loss function captures the cost of adjusting to a zero trade balance with all variables measured about a long-term trend, but fails to include costs associated with a *change* in that trend. One important cost is the loss of foreign inflows of capital, either in the form of direct investment or of lending to the domestic and private sectors. Suppose that the consequence of this financial autarchy is a reduction in the trend growth path. Then, measuring the welfare loss about the *original* output growth path, we need to add to (A11.24) a term W_n:

$$W_n = \sum_{t=0}^{\infty} \mu^t \left((1+n)^t - 1 \right)^2 (a+b) = (a+b)\left[\frac{1}{1-\mu(1+n)^2} - \frac{2}{1-\mu(1+n)} + \frac{1}{1-\mu} \right] \quad \text{(A11.25)}$$

when n is the drop in the trend growth of output. (In evaluating the geometric progressions in (A11.25) we assume that $\mu\,(1+n)^2 < 1$.)

The incentive compatibility of debt repayment is found by comparing the welfare loss under repayment W^1 (defined by (A11.23)) with that under debt repudiation $W^2 + W_n$. Debt repayment is optimal for the debtor nation only if the following condition is satisfied:

$$W^1 < W^2 + W_n \tag{A11.26}$$

Condition (A11.26) is expressed in terms of the initial welfare loss evaluated at time zero. But the condition must hold at subsequent times too; that is at *any* point along the trajectory of the Option 1 policy. Define the welfare loss at time (or the 'cost-to-go') as

$$W_t = \sum_{i=0}^{\infty} \mu^t \left(a(c_{t+i} - \bar{c})^2 + b(g_{t+i} - \bar{g})^2 + c(\pi c_{t+i} - \bar{\pi})^2 \right) \tag{A11.27}$$

Then the necessary and sufficient condition for debt repayment to be optimal is that along the trajectory corresponding to the repayment Option 1 we have

$$W_t^1 < W_t^2 + W_n \tag{A11.28}$$

Suppose that $W_t^2 < W_t^1$ or, in other words, there always exists a short-term stabilisation gain from debt repudiation. If we denote $W_t^1 - W_t^2$ as the *'temptation'* to renege, then condition (A11.28) says tht reneging will not occur if the temptation is less than the long-term *'penalty'* W_n which arises from the consequent drop in the trend growth. From (A11.25) we can see that the penalty depends on three factors: the weight attached to total private plus government consumption in the welfare loss function; the drop in trend gorwth; and the discount factor μ. In general the penalty will be high if $a + b$ and n are high and if the discount factor μ is close to unity. In fact, as $\mu (1 + n)^2$ approaches unity W_n tends to infinity. This means that for any a, b and n there always exist *some* discount factor sufficiently large for which the non-reneging condition (A11.28) holds. The actual configurations of a, b, n and μ which ensure repayment is optimal can only be assessed empirically. This we turn to in the next section.

Simulation results

The complexity of the model precludes an analytical solution, so we now turn to the results of numerical simulations. The trade sector has been estimated. The remainder of the model is calibrated, drawing upon a variety of empirical sources which are summarised in table A11.1.

The model has been linearised about a hypothetical long run in which the primary trade and government budget deficits are zero. Given the ambitious targets for consumption and government spending in the welfare loss function (A11.23), optimisation starting at the initial long run results in trajectories for instruments and variables which depart from this long run. This constitutes our baseline, about which all perturbed trajectories are measured. The perturbations we

Table A11.1 Calibration of model

Parameters	*Value*	*Source*
$\bar{C}/\bar{Y}^{***}$	0.80	GOI, CSO (1976, 1988).
$\bar{G}/\bar{Y}^{***} = \bar{T}/\bar{Y}^{***}$	0.15	GOI, CSO (1976, 1988).
$\overline{TB}/\bar{Y}^{***}$	0.0	Imposed
$\bar{V}/\bar{Y}^{***} = \bar{K}/\bar{Y}^{***}$	3.0	Ghosh (1989).
η_{CYD}	0.80	Sen (1991), Ghatak (1985).
η_{CV}	0.20	Sen (1991), Ghatak (1985).
$\theta = \beta$	0.15	Ram (1986), Samanta (1986).
λ	0.30	Ram (1986).
α	0.30	Ram (1986), Samanta (1986), Dholakia (1990).
d_0	0.52	Buiter and Patel (1990).
tb_0	–0.05	IMF (1980–91).
a_0	–0.20	Buiter and Patel (1990).

World Bank (1988–9).

examine are currently observed initial displacements (relative to the initial long run) of 52 per cent to the debt/GDP ratio of the government (d_0) – 20 per cent to the foreign assets/GDP ratio (a_0) and – 5 per cent to the trade balance/GDP ratio (tb_0).

The remaining parameters to choose relate to the welfare loss function (4.1). Normalising the weight on consumption to unity (that is, $a = 1$), a weight $b = \bar{G}/\bar{C}$ is chosen which would be consistent with the actual ratio $\bar{G}/\bar{C}$ in equilibrium being optimal. The other parameter values are imposed and taken to be $\bar{c} = \bar{g} = 100$ per cent; $\bar{\pi} = -10$ per cent; $c = 1$ (the weight on inflation) and $\mu = 0.95$ with an alternative $\mu = 0.90$.

Table A11.2 compares the repayment of debt, Option 1 with the repudiation Option 2. Figures A11.1 and A11.2 compare changes to consumption (*con*), the government spending ratio (*gr*) and output (*y*) for the two options following the perturbations above. Figures A11.3 and A11.4 compare inflation (*dp*), the real exchange rate (*er*) and the primary trade balance/GDP ratio (*tbr*). Both options require a substantial real-exchange-rate depreciation, an initial drop in output and

Table A11.2 Comparison of Option 1 (Repayment) and Option 2 (Repudiation): $\lambda = 0.95$

Options	*5-year average drop* in output (%)	*5-year average rise in inflation (%)*	*5-year average drop in gr (%)*	*5-year average drop in consumption (%)*	*Welfare loss*
1. Repayments	3.2	2.4	0.8	2.6	36
2. Repudiation	1.2	2.2	1.4	0.8	27

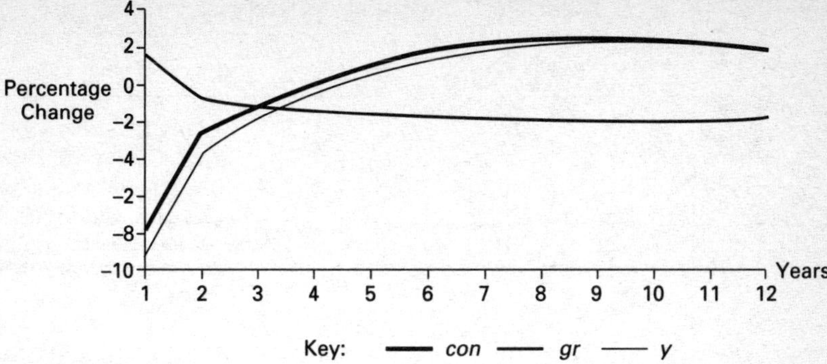

Figure A11.1 Option 1 (Repayment): graphs of consumption (*con*), government spending/GDP ratio (*gR*) and output (*y*)

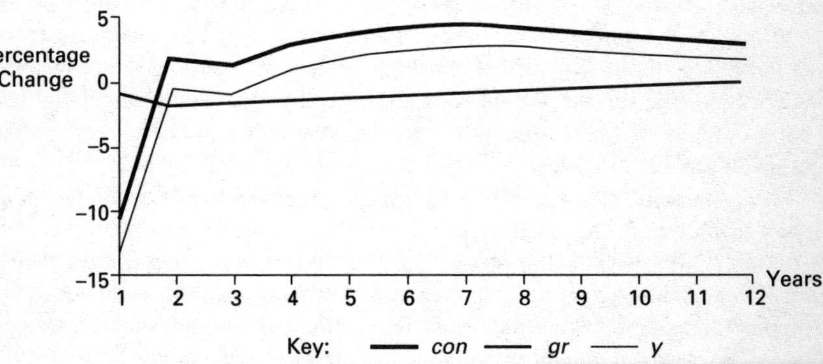

Figure A11.2 As figure A11.1 but for Option 3 (Repudiation)

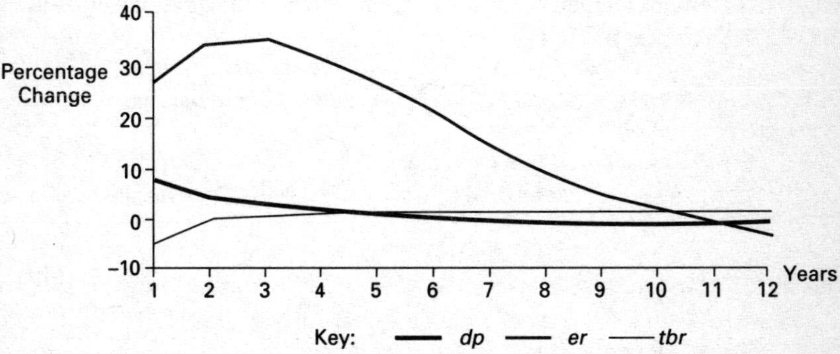

Figure A11.3 Option 1 (Repayment: graphs of inflation (*dP*), the real exhcange rate (*er*) and the trade balance/GDP ratio (*tbr*)

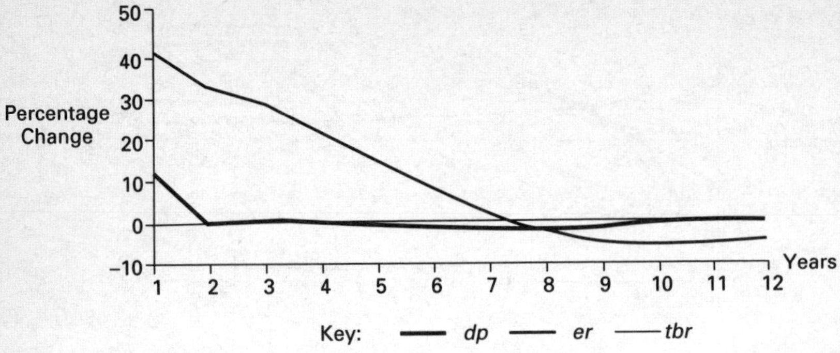

Figure A11.4 As figure A11.3 but for Option 3 (Repudiation)

a fall in government spending, at least (for Option 1) in the long run. As a consequence, consumption falls and inflation rises. What distinguishes the options is that – with repudiation – the initial changes are greater but the subsequent adjustments are less drawn-out when compared with repayment. The repayment option requires a more prolonged spell of consumption loss in order to generate an eventual primary trade surplus. Repudiation requires a sharper depreciation to achieve a zero trade deficit but relatively less pain thereafter. Consequently the welfare loss under repudiation is less than under the debt repayment option.

What to these results say about the incentive compatibility of debt repayment? Consider the welfare losses W_t^1 and W_t^2 at time t for repayment and repudiation respectively; W_t^2, it should be stressed, is the welfare loss along the repudiation path after switching from the repayment policy. Table A11.3 shows the maximum temptation along the path of the repayment option and compares it with the penalty for various assumptions of the fall in growth rates. Also shown in table A11.3 is the corresponding maximum temptation when debt repayment is made more attractive by writing off 50 per cent and 75 per cent of the initial foreign debt. Two sets of results are shown for discount factor values $\mu = 0.95$ and 0.90. Figure A11.5 graphs temptation $W_t^1 - W_t^2$ from which the maximum temptation is obtained, for the case $\mu = 0.95$.

Table A11.3 The incentive compatibility of debt repayment

μ	*Debt relief (%)*	*Maximum temptation* W^1–W^2	*Penalty* W_n $n = 0.01$,	$n = 0.02$,	$n = 0.03$	$n = 0.04$
	0	39				
0.95	50	22	38	67	89	106
	75	19				
	0	50				
0.90	50	38	10	18	26	32
	75	35				

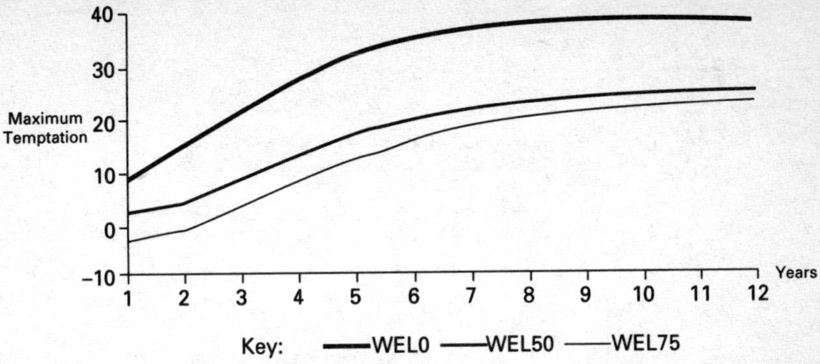

Figure A11.5 Maximum temptation for 0% debt relief (WEL0), 50% relief (WEL50) and 75% relief (WEL75); $\theta = 0$

For the higher discount factor $\mu = 0.95$ a drop in trend growth of only 1 per cent is sufficient to deter repudiation. With debt relief this required drop in trend growth becomes extremely small. For the lower discount factor even a drop in trend growth of 4 per cent plus debt relief of 75 per cent are together insufficient to make debt repayment incentive compatible.

Conclusions

This appendix sets out a partly estimated and partly calibrated macoreocnomic model of the Indian economy. The model is used to examine the cost of adjustment required by government and national solvency given currently observed levels of government debt, foreign debt and the trade deficit. This cost is compared with the corresponding cost if India were to repudiate its debts and experience financial autarky as a consequence.

Our empirical results suggests that without debt relief, a small drop in the trend growth rate, resulting from a loss of foreign investment and lending to the domestic sector, is sufficient to deter reneging; but only if the government is sufficiently far-sighted and chooses a discount rate of 5 per cent (or less) a year. If the Indian government were to discount at a 10 per cent rate per annum, then a drop in trend growth of as much as 4 per cent is insufficient to deter reneging. Debt relief makes repayment relatively more attractive and the necessary penalty in the form of a fall in the trend growth rate becomes less severe. With a 10 per cent discount rate, even writing off 75 per cent of India's debt fails to make repayment of the remaining debt incentive compatible.

12. Exchange rate policies in developing countries

Kate Phylaktis

In this chapter we will look at issues related to an open economy, that is an economy which trades in goods, services and assets with the rest of the world. For such international transactions, the monetary authorities have to decide on the important issue of what exchange rates to use between their country's currency and the currencies of other countries. There are various exchange rate arrangements that a country can adopt, and each one has different consequences for monetary and credit control and the insulation of the domestic economy from various exogenous shocks.

In general, developing countries have adopted one of two approaches to exchange-rate policy: the nominal anchor approach; and the real exchange rate target approach. In the first approach, a country's exchange rate is credibly fixed to the currency of a low-inflation country, so that low inflation is imported. The developing country obtains in this way restraint in its government budget, because the main source of prolonged inflation in such countries is usually the monetisation of the fiscal deficit.

In the second approach, the nominal exchange rate is a policy tool which is changed, frequently or occasionally, to attain real targets. Many developing countries switched to this more flexible exchange rate arrangement in the early 1980s, forced by the fluctuations in the exchange rates of major currencies, the increase in their inflation rates and adverse external shocks, such as changes in commodity prices.

Before tackling these different exchange rate policies, we will examine how exchange rates influence an economy, what the various exchange rate regimes that a country can adopt are, and how the exchange rate arrangements in developing countries have changed since the 1970s.

12.1 The role and influence of exchange rates in the economy

Exchange rates (domestic currency per unit of foreign currency, say, peso per dollar) are one of the key linkages between a small, open economy and the rest of the world. The exchange rate links a country's economy to the rest of the world through the goods market and the assets market.

In the goods market, the exchange rate establishes linkages between prices in the domestic country and given prices in the world market. For a given level of domestic costs and prices, a higher exchange rate makes foreign goods less competitive in the domestic economy and makes the domestic goods more competitive in the rest of the world. The linkage to the goods market can be formalised in terms of the real exchange rate, R. The real exchange rate is the ratio of domestic prices, say, in pesos, to foreign prices in pesos. In symbols, the real exchange rate is

$$R = P/eP^* \tag{12.1}$$

where P is the domestic price level in pesos; e is the exchange rate (pesos per dollar); and P^* is the foreign price level in dollars.

The real exchange rate measures competitiveness by showing the number of units of foreign goods required to buy one unit of domestic goods. An increase in the real exchange rate, or a real appreciation, means that it takes more units of foreign goods to buy one unit of domestic goods. Thus, real appreciation is synonymous with a loss of competitiveness. Conversely, if the real exchange rate declines, we speak of a real depreciation. The domestic economy becomes more competitive because it now takes fewer units of foreign goods to buy one unit of domestic goods.

This discussion highlights how the choice of the exchange rate regime can influence a country's competitiveness. For example, if domestic prices are rising and the exchange rate is fixed, then according to Equation (12.1) there will be a real appreciation. Inflation under fixed exchange rates causes competitiveness to decline and the balance of trade to deteriorate.

There is a separate economic concern with exchange rates. A depreciation of the exchange rate tends to raise the domestic level of prices and cause inflation. This happens because the prices of imported goods in domestic currency rise when the currency depreciates. In addition, workers may start asking for wage increases to make up for the higher cost of living. Thus, exchange-rate movements tie in very closely with inflation policy.

There is also an exchange rate linkage with the asset market. Residents in the domestic country must choose what type of assets to hold in their portfolio. They can hold real assets (houses and land) and domestic financial assets such as deposits at banks or government bonds; or they can hold a range of foreign assets, from deposits in banks in the UK, to US Treasury bills or Eurocurrency bonds. The investors' choice will depend on the relative rate of return and risks of these assets. In general, investors will prefer to hold foreign assets, if these yield a higher return than domestic assets and bear the same risk.

Investors, in comparing the rate of return of domestic and foreign assets, have to express them in the same currency. For example, an Argentinian investor considering buying a US Treasury bill will have to convert the dollar rate of return into pesos. This implies that the rate of return of the US asset will consist of two components: the dollar interest rate i^*, plus the expected percentage rate of peso depreciation, d. If i is the return of the peso assets, then foreign assets will be preferred if

$$i < i^* + d \tag{12.2}$$

When domestic residents buy foreign assets, capital moves out of the domestic country, causing the balance of payments to deteriorate. Thus what happens to the exchange rate is very important to the rate of return on foreign assets, and therefore also to the balance of payments.

12.2 Alternative exchange rate regimes

Exchange rate regimes can be classified into two main categories: fixed exchange rates and floating exchange rates. Under fixed exchange rates the monetary authorities fix the rate between the domestic currency and the foreign currency. If there are pressures on the rate to change, say to depreciate (one needs more pesos to buy one unit of foreign currency) because there is excess demand for foreign currency, then the monetary authorities of the domestic country will have to intervene in the foreign exchange market. They will provide the needed foreign currency in exchange for domestic currency to prevent the exchange rate from changing. In doing so, the monetary authorities run down their reserves of foreign currency and also reduce the amount of cash in the economy.[1]

Pegging the rate to a particular major currency entails movements in the exchange rate of the domestic country that are independent of factors affecting its own external sector. An alternative regime is to fix the rate of a basket of currencies of major trading partners. In following this arrangement, the authorities have to decide on the weights attached to each currency. They can use weights which reflect the share of each trading partner in total exports (export-weighted index); or they can use weights which reflect the share of each trading partner in total imports (import-weighted index). Finally, the authorities can use an arithmetical average of the export-weighted index and the import-weighted index, weighted by the share of exports and imports respectively, in the sum of total imports and exports (bilateral trade index). Bilateral trade weights are used most commonly.[2] These trade-related indices, however, do not take into account the effects of movements in the exchange rate on services, transfers and capital flows.

When a country adopts a floating exchange rate regime its exchange rate is determined by market forces, that is, the supply and demand for foreign currency. The monetary authorities will not intervene in the foreign exchange market, and as a result they will not have to hold foreign currency reserves.

Quite often, however, countries adopt a 'managed floating' exchange rate regime. Under such a regime, the exchange rate is floating, but at the same time there is occasional intervention by the authorities in the foreign exchange market. The intervention might be in order to slow down the movement of the exchange rate towards its equilibrium following a shock, or to affect the direction of the exchange rate movement. The latter, however, becomes difficult in the presence of substantial speculative flows. Most of the time the authorities do not disclose their exchange rate target which governs the intervention in the foreign exchange market.

There is yet another type of exchange rate regime which combines in a different way fixed and floating exchange rates. A country might have a fixed exchange rate for certain international transactions (for example, current account transactions) and a floating exchange rate for capital transactions. This regime is called *dual exchange rate system* and its objective is to insulate international transactions in goods from the fluctuations of the exchange rate when it is market-determined.

A variation of this is instead of having one exchange rate for current account transactions, a country administers specific exchange rates for different commercial transactions. Such a regime is known as a *multiple exchange rate regime.* Countries make use of this regime in order to reallocate resources and affect the real incomes of different sectors and the factors of production. The effect of special exchange rates for redirecting resources is similar to that of taxes, subsidies, tariffs and quotas. For example, if the authorities want to protect an industry against foreign competition and consequently give the owners of resources in the industry higher real incomes, they can either impose a tariff or they can have a special rate for this particular type of good.[3]

A dual exchange rate system might also arise when access to the official exchange market is restricted. For example, a government draws up a list of specified transactions (an import list, an authorised transfer list, and an authorised capital outflow list) for which foreign currency is supplied at a specified rate. Exporters have to surrender all foreign exchange they receive at the specified rate. For unauthorised transactions, no foreign exchange is available and a 'black market' for foreign currency develops.[4]

12.3 Exchange rate arrangements in developing countries

When the industrialised countries adopted floating exchange rate regimes in the early 1970s, developing countries did not follow suit, so as to increase nominal exchange rate flexibility. Their reluctance could have been based on their structural characteristics, which reduced the effectiveness of devaluation to improve the balance of payments position. For example, they tended to have large non-tradable sectors because the most tradable component of production (namely manufacturing), formed a small share of GDP. In addition, the lack of transport infrastructure made many agricultural activities non-tradable in developing countries, whereas they were tradable in developed countries. Secondly, since there was very little substitutability between locally produced goods and imported goods, the price elasticity of demand for imported goods was likely to be low. Thirdly, since primary products could not be differentiated and the export share of each LDC in the particular export good was in most cases small, most LDCs were price takers. This situation, together with the fact that commodity prices have always been denominated in US dollars, implied that a devaluation would not reduce the price of their exports in dollars and increase external demand for them.[5] The price elasticity of the supply of exports was also likely to be rather low in the short run since the production of primary goods had long gestation periods in addition to other possible production bottlenecks, such as shortage of capital and poor infrastructure.

During the 1980s the developing countries moved away from pegging to a single currency towards either pegging to a basket of currencies or adopting a more flexible arrangement under which the domestic currency is adjusted frequently. The switch to pegging to a basket of currencies became necessary because of the high volatility in the exchange rates of major industrial countries. These fluctuations created problems for the developing countries, they discouraged foreign inward investment and made more difficult the management of the external debt and that of foreign exchange reserves.

Many developing countries adopted more flexible exchange rate arrangements because their expansionary monetary policies, which led to high inflation, and the adverse external shocks produced great variations in real exchange rates and unfavourable effects on trade performance. In addition, by the 1980s, many developing countries had achieved substantial product diversification and had become less dependent on a few primary goods. That improved the price sensitivity of their exports and imports.

These trends are shown in tables 12.1 and 12.2. Table 12.1 gives the IMF's classification of exchange rate regimes in 1993. Table 12.2 presents the pattern of exchange rate arrangements of developing countries during the period 1973–93. The number of countries pegging to a single currency has declined steadily, from 83 to 50, and the number of countries that pegged their currency to the US dollar has been more than halved during this period, from 54 to 23. No country now pegs its exchange rate to the pound sterling, and the number of countries which peg to the French franc has marginally declined. As a result of the disintegration of the USSR, seven countries peg their exchange rate to the Russian rouble.

A number of countries have chosen to peg their currencies to the SDR as a convenient method of approximating the relative importance of the major currencies in international transactions. The number of countries has, however, declined, from 11 in 1976 to only 4 in 1993. In contrast, the number of countries opting to peg to a trade-weighted basket of currencies has risen sharply, from 14 to 26.

It should be kept in mind that the IMF's classification relates to exchange rate arrangements in the major currency market of each country. It is compatible with dual exchange markets, black exchange markets, and with trade and capital controls. In addition, the countries pegging their exchange rates quite often follow an adjustable peg regime.

Developing countries have increased their reliance on more flexible arrangements under which the exchange rate is adjusted frequently. These arrangements are often officially described as 'adjusting to indicators', 'managed floating', or 'independently floating'. If these arrangements are described as being 'flexible' for the purpose of the present discussion, then the number of countries in this category has increased from 11 in 1973 to 67 in 1993. That is, 46 per cent of the developing countries have a flexible arrangement.

Table 12.1 Exchange rate arrangements as of 31 March 1993

Pegged					
Single currency				*Currency composite*	
US dollar	*French franc*	*Russian rouble*	*Other*	*SDR*	*Other*
Angola	Benin	Amenia	Bhutan (Indian rupee)	Libyan Arab Jamahiriya	Algeria
Antigua and Barbuda	Burkina Faso	Azerbaijan	Estonia (Deutsche Mark)	Myanmar	Austria
Argentina	Cameroon	Belarus	Kiribati (Australian dollar)	Rwanda	Bangladesh
Bahamas, The	Central African Republic	Georgia	Lesotho (South African rand)	Seychelles	Botswana
Barbados	Chad	Kazakhstan	Namibia (South African rand)		Burundi
Belize	Comoros	Kyrgyzstan	Swaziland (South African rand)		Cape Verde
Djibouti	Congo	Moldova			Cyprus
Dominica	Ivory Coast				Fiji
Ethiopia	Equatorial Guinea				Hungary
Grenada	Gabon				Iceland
Iraq	Mali				Jordan
Liberia	Niger				Kenya
Marshall Islands	Senegal				Kuwait
Mongolia	Togo				Malaysia
Nicaragua					Malta
Oman					Mauritania
Panama					Mauritius
St Kitts and Nevis					Morocco
St Lucia					Papua New Guinea
St Vincent and the Grenadines					Solomon Islands
Suriname					Tanzania
Syrian Arab Repulic					Thailand
Yemen					Tonga
					Vanuatu
					Western Samoa
					Zimbabwe

Table 12.1 *cont.*

Flexibility limited against a single currency or group of currencies		*More flexible*			
Single currency	*Co-operative arrangements*	*Adjusted according to a set of indicators*	*Other managed floating*	*Independently floating*	
Bahrain	Belgium	Chile	China	Afghanistan Islamic State of	Romania
Qatar	Denmark	Colombia	Equador	Albania	Russia
Saudi Arabia	France	Madagascar	Egypt	Australia	Sierra Leone
United Arab Emirates	Germany		Greece	Bolivia	South Africa
	Ireland		Guinea	Brazil	Sudan
	Luxembourg		Guinea-Bissau	Bulgaria	Sweden
	Netherlands, The		Indonesia	Canada	Switzerland
	Portugal		Israel	Costa Rica	Trinidad and Tobago
	Spain		Korea	Dominican Republic	Uganda
			Lao People's Democratic Republic	El Salvador	Ukraine
			Maldives	Finland	United Kingdom
			Mexico	Gambia, The	United States of America
			Pakistan	Ghana	Venezuela
			Poland	Guatemala	Zaïre
			Sao Tome and Principe	Guyana	Zambia
			Singapore	Haiti	
			Somalia	Honduras	
			Sri Lanka	India	
			Tunisia	Iran, Islamic Republic of	
			Turkey	Italy	
			Uruguay	Jamaica	
			Vietnam	Japan	
				Latvia	
				Lebanon	
				Lithuania	
				Mozambique	
				New Zealand	
				Nepal	
				Nigeria	
				Norway	
				Paraguay	
				Peru	
				Philippines	

Table 12.2 Developing countries: exchange rate regimes in selected years, number of countries

	1973	*1976*	*1982*	*1987*	*1993*
Pegged to a single currency, of which:	86	67	56	52	50
US dollar	54	46	38	34	23
French franc	17	13	13	14	14
Pound sterling	11	3	1	–	–
Russian rouble	–	–	–	–	7
Other	4	5	4	4	6
Pegged to a composite of which:	–	25	34	36	30
SDR	–	11	15	10	4
Other	–	14	19	26	26
Flexible arrangements, of which:	11	15	35	42	67
Limited flexibility against single currency	–	2	10	4	4
Adjusted according to a set of indicators	8	6	4	4	3
Managed floating	–	4	16	22	21
Independent floating	3	3	5	12	39
Total	97	107	125	130	147

Source: IMF *Annual Reports*.

12.4 The choice of exchange rate regimes

There are some general considerations regarding the choice of the exchange rate regime which apply to both developed and developing countries. These considerations relate to the effectiveness of fixed and flexible exchange rates in insulating the economy from external and domestic shocks. Insulation in this discussion is taken to mean minimisation of the changes in domestic output. Thus, if the economic objective of the policy-makers is the stabilisation of real output, the source of shocks to the economy and the structural characteristics of the economy, such as the degree of openness of international trade and the degree of capital mobility, will be important considerations in choosing the degree of exchange rate flexibility.

The various shocks to an economy can be domestic (originating in the domestic economy) or external (originating abroad), and they can be real (originating in the goods market) or monetary (originating in the money market). If, for example, we take a monetary shock that originates in the domestic economy, such as an increase in the demand for money, fixed exchange rates would be more effective in stabilising output. For an explanation, see Box 12.1. If, on the other hand, we take an external real shock, such as an increase in the foreign price level, a flexible exchange rate regime has better insulating properties. This is explained

Box 12.1

Using the familiar *IS–LM* framework for an open economy, which is otherwise called the Mundell–Fleming model, we will show the effects of an increase in the demand for money on the level output. Figure 12.1 shows the equilibrium conditions for the three markets under fixed exchange rates. The *IS* schedule shows the combinations of the interest rate and the level of nominal output (and real output in the case of an underemployed economy) which maintain equilibrium in the goods market, that is, the aggregate demand for goods is equal to the supply for them. The *LM* schedule shows the combinations of the interest rate and the level of nominal output which maintain equilibrium in the money market, that is, the demand for real money balances is equal to the supply of money. Finally the *FF* schedule shows the combinations of the interest rate and the level of nominal output which maintain equilibrium in the balance of payments and the foreign exchange market, that is, current and capital account transactions equilibrate the demand and supply for foreign currency. If the current and capital account transactions give rise to a balance of payments disequilibrium, then the monetary authorities have to intervene in the foreign exchange market and sell foreign currency in exchange for domestic currency in the case of a balance-of-payments deficit to prevent the domestic currency from depreciating; and buy foreign currency with domestic currency in the case of a balance-of-payments surplus. In the first case the money supply will fall, and in the second case it will rise. Initial equilibrium is at *A*, where all three schedules intersect.

If there is an increase in the demand for money, the *LM* schedule will shift to the left. There will be an excess demand for real money balances which will cause interest rates to rise. Aggregate demand and income will fall because of the fall in investment. The fall in income will reduce the demand for imports and improve the balance of payments. The higher interest rates will also attract capital into the country, further strengthening the balance of payments. The latter two effects will put pressures on the currency to appreciate, necessitating a purchase of the excess foreign currency and an increase in the money supply, which will cause a shift to the right of the *LM* schedule, back to its initial position. Such a shock will have no effect in the level of income.

In contrast, under flexible exchange rates, the excess foreign currency will be absorbed by an appreciation of the exchange rate from e_0 to e_1. That will cause both the IS and the *FF* schedules to move to the left (see figure 12.2). The new equilibrium position is at B, where all three schedules intersect. The new equilibrium level of income is Y_1. Thus fixed exchange rates are more effective in stabilising the level of income when the shocks are financial and originate in the domestic economy.

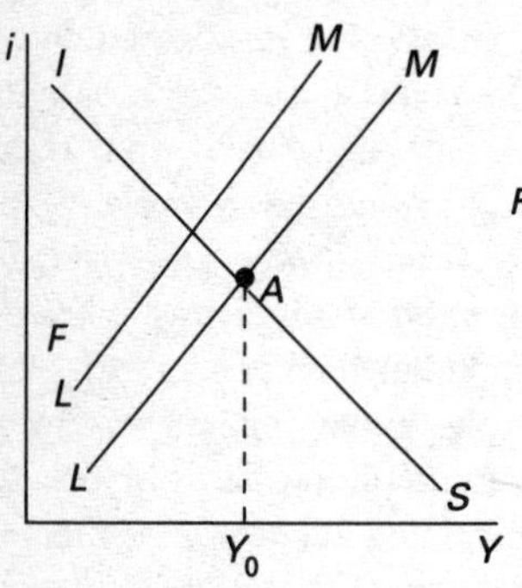

Figure 12.1

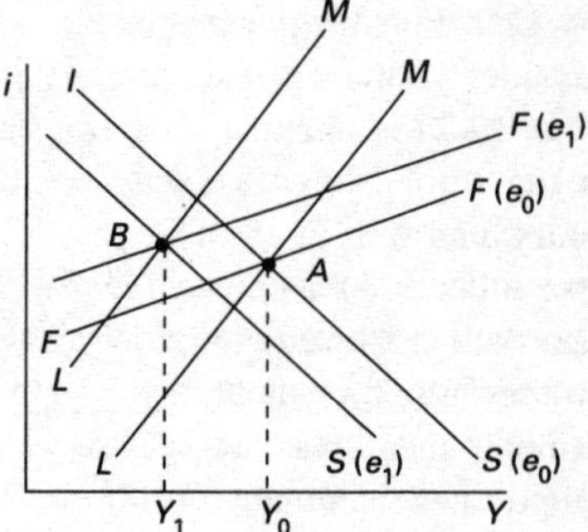

Figure 12.2

Box 12.2

Using the *IS–LM* framework for an open economy, an increase in the foreign price level makes the domestic goods relatively cheaper and cause an increase in exports. Figure 12.3 shows the effects of this shock for an open economy under fixed exchange rates. The increase in exports will shift the *IS* and the *FF* schedules to the right. At the same time, the improvement in the balance of payments will put pressure on the exchange rate to appreciate. The monetary authorities will intervene in the foreign exchange market to buy the excess foreign currency and the money supply will rise, shifting the *LM* schedule to the right. The new equilibrium position is at *B* and the level of income is Y_1.

However, if the country has flexible exchange rates, the exchange rate will be left to appreciate from e_o to e_1. The appreciation reduces the demand for exports and offsets part of the initial improvement in the balance of trade and the increase in the level of income. In figure 12.4, the *FF* and *IS* schedules shift to the left as a result of the appreciation. Thus, the flexible exchange rate regime has better insulating properties than the fixed exchange rate regime.

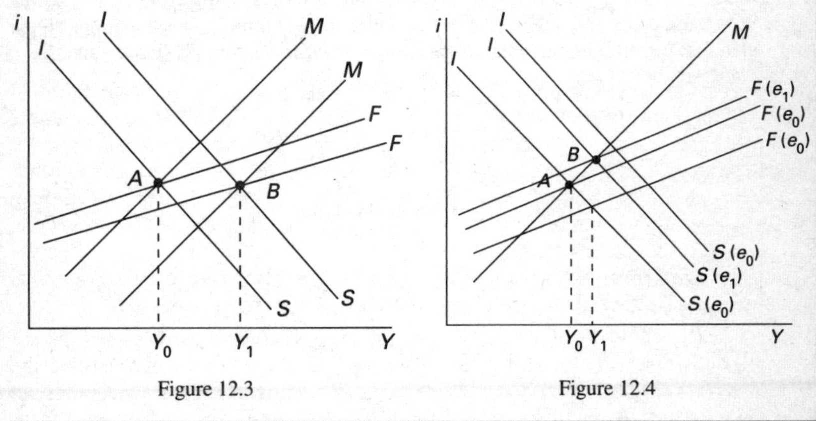

Figure 12.3

Figure 12.4

in Box 12.2. Flexible exchange rates will also have better insulating properties if we consider a domestic real shock, such as an increase in autonomous investment (see Box 12.3 for an explanation).[6]

On the whole, flexible exchange rates perform poorly when the shocks are monetary, and well in all other cases. This superiority of flexible exchange rates in these other cases is, however, diminished if capital mobility is low, a general characteristic of developing countries. For example, we have seen in Box 12.3 that in the case of a real domestic shock, for example, an increase in autonomous investment, there was an increase in output which was less under flexible exchange rates than under fixed ones because of the deflationary effects caused by the appreciation of the exchange rate due to net capital inflows. In the case, however, of reduced capital mobility or no capital mobility at all, there will be few or no capital flows and, instead of an appreciation, we will have a depreci-

Box 12.3

Once again within the framework of the Mundell–Fleming model, an increase in autonomous investment will increase aggregate demand and cause the *IS* schedule to shift to the right as in figure 12.5. The ensuing rise in income increases the transactions demand for money causing the interest rate to restore equilibrium in the money market. The increase in the level of income will increase the demand for imports, and the balance of trade will deteriorate. On the other hand, the capital account will improve because the higher domestic interest rates will encourage foreign investors to buy domestic assets. If there is sufficient capital mobility, the capital account surplus will more than offset the balance of trade deficit resulting in a balance-of-payments surplus and an increase in the money supply through the official purchase of foreign currency under fixed exchange rates. The new equilibrium will be at *B*, where the level of income will have risen to Y_1.

If, on the other hand, the country has flexible exchange rates, the balance of payments surplus will cause the exchange rate to appreciate from e_o to e_1, offsetting part of the initial favourable effect on the level of income. This is shown in figure 12.6. The *FF* and *IS* schedule shift to the left and the new equilibrium is at *B*, where the level of income is Y_1. The increase in the level of income is less than under fixed exchange rates. Flexible exchange rates have better insulating properties than fixed exchange rates.

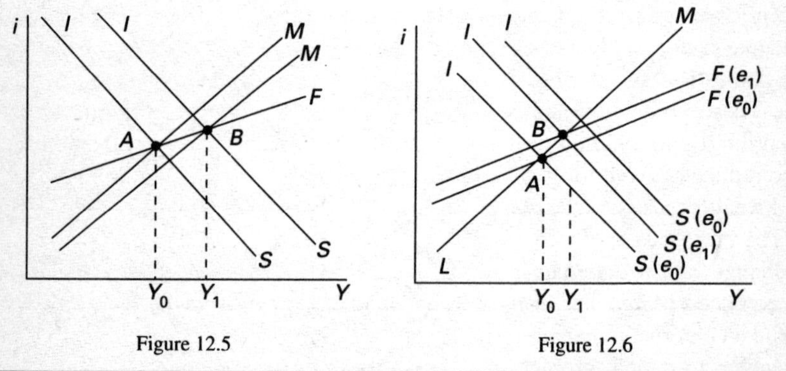

Figure 12.5

Figure 12.6

ation of the exchange rate caused by the increase in imports, which will lead to an enhancement of the initial increase in output.

Another factor which affects the insulating properties of the exchange rate regimes is the openness of an economy to international trade. Increased openness (i.e. a larger share of the traded goods sector), will under fixed exchange rates magnify the effects of certain disturbances and weaken the impact of others. For example, a given percentage change in *foreign* prices, or in *foreign* output, will have a larger domestic impact the more open the economy. By contrast, a given change in *domestic* expenditure, or in the demand for money, will have weaker domestic impact the more open the economy. The reason is that for any given change in *domestic* demand the leakage into imports is larger and hence the effect on domestic activity weaker. In summary, if *foreign* disturbances are dominant, the more open the economy, the greater the relative advantage of flexible exchange rates; while if *domestic* disturbances are dominant, the more open the economy then the greater is the relative advantage of fixed exchange rates. It is clear that openness *per se* does not unambiguously determine the choice of the exchange rate regime.

12.5 The real target approach to exchange rate policy

In this approach, the nominal exchange rate is a policy tool used by governments as part of their policy packages to attain internal and external balance. Changes in the nominal exchange rate affect the real exchange rate, that is, external competitiveness and the balance of payments. The real exchange rate was defined in section 12.1 as the ratio of domestic prices to foreign prices, when the latter is expressed in domestic currency (multiplied by the exchange rate).

An alternative, and theoretically more appealing, definition of the real exchange rate is the relative price of tradable to non-tradable goods, which provides a summary measure of the incentives guiding resource allocation between the two key sectors of the economy. Thus, when there is a nominal devaluation the price of tradable goods rises, creating incentives to divert resources to the tradable sector and increase its production. At the same time, there is a decline in the domestic demand for tradable goods because they are relatively more expensive. These production and consumption effects will improve the trade balance accordingly. In addition to this expenditure-switching effect, devaluation might also reduce demand for goods (both -tradable and non-tradable) through a fall in real wealth caused by the rise in the cost of living.[7]

Therefore one approach to exchange-rate policy is to manipulate the nominal exchange rate to maintain a target real exchange rate, which will prevent the emergence of large and sustained misalignments of relative prices and therefore avoid an external imbalance. The adoption of a real exchange-rate rule gives rise, however, to certain problems. The equilibrium real exchange rate may change over time because of different types of external and domestic shocks. For example, differential rates of technological progress have an important impact on the equilibrium real exchange rate. This is the well-known 'Balassa effect'. For example, if productivity rises faster in the tradable goods sector than in the non-tradable goods sector, the relative price of the non-tradables rises, because of the uniform increase in wages in the two sectors. With the price of tradable goods set in world markets, the equilibrium real exchange rate appreciates. Therefore, the equilibrium real exchange rate of countries with higher rates of productivity growth in their traded goods sectors tends to appreciate relative to that of countries with low rates of productivity.

A change in the equilibrium real exchange rate can also come from a tariff reform. When there is a tariff reduction it brings about a fall in import prices, creating an excess demand for these goods and an excess supply of both non-tradables and exportables. To restore equilibrium, the relative prices of non-tradables must fall. Thus, in response to a tariff reduction, the equilibrium real exchange rate tends to depreciate.

The above examples have shown how shocks can cause the equilibrium real exchange rate to change. The question arises of whether the monetary authorities can recognise these permanent changes in the equilibrium real exchange rate and adjust their real exchange rate rule.

There are, however, additional problems with a real exchange rate rule. The approach hinges on two other assumptions. First, it assumes that there must be some sluggishness in nominal wages and the prices of non-tradables. In particular, a reduction in real wages in terms of tradables brought about by nominal devaluation must not quickly be reversed by nominal wage increases. Thus, nominal devaluations should lead to prolonged real devaluations, though not necessarily to the same extent. Secondly, it assumes that real devaluations have significant effects, given time, on output and demand patterns; in particular, they must lead to increases in exports.

Such policies were adopted widely in the 1980s. Many countries achieved large real devaluations, especially during the period 1985–7, and in a number of them – for example, Turkey, Chile, Indonesia and Thailand – exports increased significantly, particularly of non-traditional or manufactured goods. In Box 12.4, we trace the experience of Indonesia.

Box 12.4

Indonesia from 1983 is a good example of a country which tried to maintain the competitiveness of its non-oil exports through devaluations of its currency, and succeeded in experiencing an export boom.

In understanding the policies followed by Indonesia, two factors have to be borne in mind. First, Indonesia has no restrictions on international capital flows. That implies that if the currency is under pressure to depreciate, speculative flows can put even greater pressure on official foreign reserves. Secondly, Indonesia exports oil and gas. Although the importance of these exports has declined over the years, at times the variations in the world prices of these goods have put pressures on the nominal exchange rate. This became evident in 1982, when the price of oil began to decline.

From 1983 onwards, and after a substantial devaluation, the monetary authorities embarked on an exchange rate policy of devaluing the rupiah to maintain competitiveness – maintain the real exchange rate constant – within the non-oil export sector, as well as raising the rupiah oil tax revenues. Up to 1986, the exchange rate was depreciated in line with the oil price decline. After 1986 the exchange rate was adjusted in order to maintain six months' official foreign currency reserves.

As a result of these exchange rate depreciations the non-oil export sector increased substantially in size and as a proportion of total exports. That reduced the vulnerability of the rupiah and of the Indonesian economy to oil price changes.

12.6 The nominal anchor approach to exchange rate policy

An important issue relating to the relative merits of fixed and floating exchange rate regimes is that of financial discipline. In particular, it is believed that the fixed exchange rate regime would facilitate the attainment of price stability. When a country fixes its exchange rate, say, to a single currency, it anchors its price level to that of the country to which its exchange rate is pegged. This can be seen from the purchasing power parity (PPP) proposition. Using the same symbols as before, PPP is given by $P = eP^*$, which implies that if e is fixed, P will have to move in accord with P^*.

If we look at the international parity condition for assets, which tells us that the rate of return of domestic assets is equal to the rate of return of foreign assets (with the same attributes) when both returns are expressed in the same currency, that is,

$$i = i^* + d \tag{12.3}$$

this implies that a country under fixed exchange rates cannot have a different interest rate from the interest rate that prevails in the rest of the world. The country gives up its discretion to have a monetary policy of its own choosing.

This financial discipline, however, depends on many conditions, some of which are detailed below. First, a fixed exchange-rate regime imposes a limit only on the *long-run* rate of growth of the money supply and inflation. In the short run, a country can pursue rapid credit expansion. The duration of periods of credit expansion – and thus the effective degree of discipline – depends on the initial stock of official foreign reserves. The financial discipline imposed by the reserve constraint may be weakened to the extent that the central bank can borrow abroad or impose controls on international capital flows. Borrowing abroad, however, has limits. Foreign creditors are not willing to lend to countries indefinitely, because they realise that as the debt increases the probability of default also increases.

The imposition of capital controls may delay in the depletion of official foreign exchange reserves because it interferes with the adjustment process of the economy by slowing it down. For example, a country can pursue a more expansionary monetary policy than its trading partners if it imposes controls to prevent domestic residents from investing abroad, as they are trying to benefit from the relatively higher rate of return on foreign assets. The imposition of controls can be thought of as a tax on the rate of return on foreign assets, which reduces it and equates it to the lower rate of return on domestic assets.[8]

However, capital controls, can only undermine financial discipline in the short run. Prices in the developing country will eventually increase in response to expansionary monetary policy as people find themselves with more real money balances and increase their purchase of domestically produced goods. That renders their exports uncompetitive and deteriorates the balance of trade. There will be further pressures on the balance of trade because some of the extra money balances will be spend on imported goods. These developments in the external sector will begin to drain official foreign reserves.

Furthermore, the mere existence of capital controls can add additional pressures to the official foreign reserves because it gives rise to black markets that cause the diversion of foreign currency from official to unofficial markets. When access to the official foreign exchange market is limited and there are various foreign exchange restrictions on international transactions, an excess demand for foreign currency at the official rate develops, which encourages some of the supply of foreign currency to be sold illegally, at a market price higher than the official rate. Other factors related to social and political unrest and economic malaise may support the black markets. For example, in the Philippines, black markets were supported by the outright theft of dozens of millions of dollars of foreign support and assistance payments, and by the funding of capital flight, which took place because of fear of dictatorship, of confiscation of assets and of blocking of bank accounts. In Thailand, the development of a black market for dollars was associated with narcotics-related activities. In other countries, such as South Korea and Indonesia, huge amounts of money from corruption fuelled the black market. In Box 12.5 we give an explanation of the operation of black markets and how foreign exchange controls affect the black market premium.[9]

Box 12.5

To understand the operation of a black market, it is useful to distinguish between stock transactions and current flow transactions. Let us look first at the stock transactions. The stock demand for foreign currency, which in our case we will take to be the US dollar, is influenced by the expected profitability of holding dollars rather than domestic currency, such as pesos, and thus depends on domestic interest rates, US interest rates and the expected exchange rate depreciation. In addition, it depends on wealth, which comprises domestic and foreign assets. The stock supply for black market dollars is determined by the flow market, which is associated with the international transactions of goods and services.

The supply of black market dollars comes from the following sources: smuggling of exports, underinvoicing of exports, foreign tourists coming to the domestic country, and diversion of remittances through non-official channels. The demand for black market dollars is determined by the smugglers of imported goods, especially manufactured goods, and by domestic residents travelling abroad but limited to a specific dollar allowance. Furthermore, the demand for black market dollars is a positive function of wealth.

The two markets can be represented by figures 12.7 and 12.8 below. Figure 12.8 shows the stock market for dollars. On the vertical axis we have the black market exchange rate (pesos/dollars), and on the horizontal axis the stock of black market dollars. The schedule *PP* shows the stock demand for black dollars for given domestic and US interest rates, expected exchange rate depreciation of the official rate, and domestic assets. The vertical schedule *BB* denotes the existing stock of black dollars at a given point in time. Short-run equilibrium occurs at the exchange rate e_o, when investors are happy to hold the existing stock of dollars.

Box 12.5 *cont.*

The stock of dollars depends on the flow market, which is represented by figure 12.7. On the vertical axis we have the black market exchange rate, and on the horizontal axis, the flow of dollars. The schedule SS shows the flow supply of dollars. It slopes upwards, because the higher the black market rate is in relation to the official rate, the higher will be the incentive for exporters to divert foreign currency to the black market. The schedule *DD* shows the demand for dollars to be inversly related to the black market rate. That is, the lower the black market rate in relation to the official rate, the cheaper it is to smuggle goods into the country, or to buy foreign exchange for travelling abroad.

The two markets are connected as follows. The black market rate is determined in the stock market for a given stock of black dollars. At that black market rate, there will be flow demand and supply for dollars which will give rise to a current account deficit or surplus. In the case of a surplus (deficit), there will be an increase (decrease) in the stock of dollars held in portfolios. In the figures below, the short-run black market rate is e_0. At that rate there is an excess supply of flow dollars equal to *AE*, causing the *BB* schedule in the stock market to shift to the right. The black market rate will be declining, reducing the current account surplus. The process will go on until the black market rate has fallen sufficiently to eliminate the flow surplus.

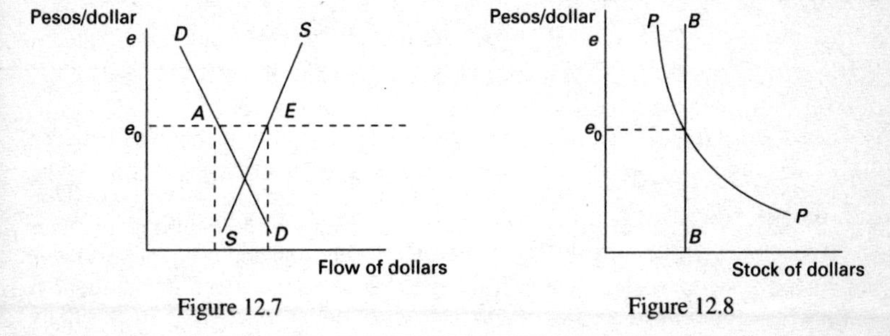

Figure 12.7

Figure 12.8

Now, when there is an expansionary monetary policy under a fixed exchange-rate regime, the fall in domestic interest rates will increase the demand for foreign currency in the black market as people switch to foreign assets. The black market premium rises and exporters have an incentive to under-report their true exports and to surrender their foreign exchange to the black market rather than to the central bank. Similarly, firms find a way to overstate the costs of authorised imports, diverting part of the foreign exchange obtained at the official rate towards the black market. These developments will be adding pressures on the official foreign reserves to the usual ones resulting from the deterioration in the balance of payments, calling for corrective measures to be implemented in the form of contractionary monetary policies, or in the form of a change in parity.

The following are some additional reasons why a fixed exchange-rate regime may not succeed in bringing about monetary and credit discipline. An unconstrained credit to the public sector will cause a continuous fall in foreign currency reserves leading to a crisis and devaluation. Furthermore, the exchange rate commitment must be credible in the foreign exchange market. If market participants have doubts they will engineer a speculative crisis. The exchange-rate commitment must also be credible to the labour market. If workers come to expect that the authorities will validate high inflation by devaluation, they will be taking that into account in demanding higher wages to accommodate the expected higher inflation.

An easy way to make the fixed exchange rate regime credible is for the authorities to surrender the power to change the exchange rate. This is the case when countries form a monetary union, with a common currency fixed to a major currency. Such an exchange rate regime has the disadvantage that devaluation cannot be used in response to permanent exogenous shocks, such as a terms-of-trade shock. The authorities will have to rely on financial policies to restore competitiveness, which might prove more costly than a one-off adjustment to the exchange rate. A good example of a monetary union is the CFA (Communauté financière africaine) franc zone. Box 12.6 gives an account of the problems the CFA franc zone has encountered.[10]

Can the historical record shed some light on the success of countries under fixed exchange rates in keeping down inflation? The experience of developing countries in the 1970s and 1980s suggests that the average rate of inflation has been lower in countries with fixed exchange rates than in countries with flexible rates. For example, the inflation-rate experiences of ten countries – Costa Rica, India, Indonesia, Kenya, Morocco, Nigeria, Pakistan, Sri Lanka, Thailand and Turkey – between 1970–2 and 1988–9, were studied by the IMF. In the first period, the ten countries had fixed rates; and in the second period, flexible ones. In three cases (Turkey, Nigeria and Costa Rica) the average inflation was much higher in the second period, suggesting that the regime switch caused a loss of discipline. In the other seven cases (five from Asia), while inflation was marginally higher, there was no loss of financial discipline.

The evidence, however, is not conclusive. Many countries under fixed exchange rates have experienced high rates of inflation by following expansionary financial policies, while many countries under flexible exchange rates have had low inflation by adopting prudent financial policies.

12.7 Summary and conclusions

In this chapter we have tried to highlight issues related to the exchange rate policy of developing countries. The purpose was not to arrive at one exchange rate policy suitable for all the developing countries; the optimum exchange rate policy could differ for each country depending on the monetary authorities' objective function, the nature of the exogenous shocks, and the structural characteristics of the country. Some general observations can be made, however, relat-

Box 12.6

The Union monétaire ouest africaine (UMOA) is a monetary union of fourteen sub-Saharan African countries, created in 1962. The member countries have a common currency, the CFA (Communauté financière africaine) which is fixed to the French franc at the rate of 100 CFA francs, following the massive devaluation of 50 per cent in January 1994. Within the monetary union there is harmonisation of banking and monetary legislation, and official foreign reserves are held centrally by the Banque centrale des états de l'Afrique Ouest (BCEAO). The BCEAO is obliged to deposit 65 per cent of its pooled foreign exchange reserves in French francs on an operations account at the French Treasury to ensure free convertibility of the CFA franc. As far as monetary policy is concerned, the BCEAO sets the amount of central-bank credit accorded to member states each year, and the discount rate, and decides on monetary policy changes to be made when appropriate. Monetary policy in each country is implemented by a local BCEAO agency.

There have been several problems with the exchange rate as a nominal anchor for monetary policy in the Franc Zone. These include persistent and substantial changes in real effective exchange rates because of price divergence and the inappropriateness of the French franc as the choice of nominal anchor.

During the 1970s and late 1980s some of the bigger economies, Ivory Coast and Gabon, have pursued weak monetary and credit control by overshooting their credit ceiling. This caused substantial overvaluation of their exchange rates and negative effects on trade performance. It should be noted, however, that part of the overvaluation during the 1970s was because of buoyant commodity export prices for such items as cocoa, which is the main export of Ivory Coast, and oil, which is the main export of Gabon. This highlights one of the disadvantage of this exchange-rate arrangement. By forgoing the use of the exchange rate instrument, the authorities are forced to rely entirely on financial policies to realign relative prices of traded and non-traded goods in the event of a permanent change in the equilibrium real exchange rate from, say, a terms-of-trade shock, which was the case in Ivory Coast and Gabon with the increases in commodity export prices.

Real-exchange-rate movements were also caused by the slow process of price convergence with France because of current-account restrictions. During the period of 1973 to 1980 the weakness of the nominal anchor and slow price convergence allowed Ivory Coast prices to rise 60 per cent above prices in France.

Another reason which created problems with the exchange rate as a nominal anchor for monetary policy in the Franc Zone was the inappropriateness of the French franc as the choice of nominal anchor. As the member countries developed and diversified their trade geographically, in particular to other European countries and to Japan, the relevance of French prices to Franc Zone inflation decreased.
For all these reasons, the CFA became increasingly overvalued until it was devalued by 50 per cent in January 1994.

ing to the role of exchange-rate arrangements in enhancing financial stability and adjustment in developing countries.

First, in a country with a well-established reputation for financial discipline, it is of small consequence whether a fixed or a flexible exchange-rate regime is maintained. In contrast, if the country does not have financial discipline, serious macro-economic problems would emerge, regardless of the exchange-rate regime adopted. A fixed exchange-rate regime would not of itself impose financial discipline, and would create further macro-economic problems because of the loss of external competitiveness resulting from high inflation. Secondly, most countries do not belong to these extreme cases and have to find a balance between restrictive financial policies and exchange rate arrangements. Finally, when the authorities are genuinely determined to establish financial discipline and price stability, but lack credibility because of their past record, commitment to fix the nominal exchange rate for an extended period would help to provide a strong anchor for price stability.

Notes

1. We assume here that the authorities do not sterilise the fall in the money supply by expanding domestic credit through the purchase of governments bonds from the private sector.
2. For an elaboration of this issue see Crockett and Nsouli (1977).
3. See Dornbusch (1993) for more information on the mechanics and costs of multiple exchange rates.
4. For more information on the factors which give rise to black markets, see Agénor (1992). For explicit examination of the effects of foreign exchange restrictions on the black market see Phylaktis (1991).
5. In other words, the Marshall – Lerner condition for devaluation to improve the balance of trade was not likely to be met. The sum of the price of the elasticities of demand for imports and exports was likely to be less than one.
6. For a more detailed explanation, see Argy (1981).
7. For the effects of devaluation using a traded/non-traded goods framework see Corden (1994).
8. See Phylaktis (1988 and 1990) for an explanation of the effects of capital controls on the domestic financial markets and an application to developing countries.
9. For a more detailed exposition of the operation of black markets, see, for example, Phylaktis (1991), and Phylaktis and Kassimatis (1994).
10. See also Page, (1993a and 1993b).

References

Chapter 1

Friedman, M. (1964) 'Post-War Trends in Monetary Theory and Policy', *National Banking Review*, **2** (1), September

Friedman, M. and Schwartz, A. (1969) 'The Definition of Money', *Journal of Money, Credit and Banking*, **1** (1), 1–14

Laidler, D. (1969) 'The Definition of Money: Theoretical and Empirical Problems', *Journal of Money, Credit and Banking*, **1**, 508–25

Morgan, V. E. (1969) 'The Essential Qualities of Money', *The Manchester School of Economic & Social Studies*, **37** (3), 237–48

Newlyn, I. W. and Bootley, P. R. (1978) *Theory of Money*, 3rd edn, Clarendon, Oxford

Pesek, B. and Saving, T. (1968) *The Foundation of Money and Banking*, Collier, Macmillan, New York

Pierce, G. D. and Shaw, M. D. (1977) *Monetary Economics*, Butterworths, London

Lord Radcliffe (1959) *Report of the Committee on the Working of the Monetary System*, Cmnd 827, HMSO, London

Yeager, B. L. (1968) 'Essential Properties of the Medium of Exchange', *Kyklos*, **21** (1), 45–68

Chapter 2

Abe, S., Fry, M. J., Min, B. K., Vongvipanond, P. and Yu, T. P. (1978) 'The Demand for Money in Pakistan: Some Alternative Estimates', *Pakistan Development Review*, **14**, 249–57

Adekunle, J. O. (1968) 'The Demand for Money: Evidence from Developed and Less Developed Economies', *IMF Staff Papers*, **15**, 220–66

Ahmed, S. (1977) 'Demand for Money in Bangladesh: Some Preliminary Evidence', *The Bangladesh Development Studies*, **5** (2), 227–37

Ajayi, S. I. (1974) 'The Demand for Money in the Nigerian Economy: Comments and Extension', *The Nigerian Journal of Economic and Social Studies*, **16** (1), 165–73

Akhtar, M. A. (1974) 'The Demand for Money in Pakistan', *Pakistan Development Review*, **13**, 40–5

Anon (1974) 'The Demand for Money', *The Banker*, 239–47

Artis, M. J. and Lewis, M. K. (1976) 'The Demand for Money in the United Kingdom', *The Manchester School*, **44** (2), 147–81

Artis, M. and Lewis, M. (1990), 'Money Demand and Suppy' in T. Bandyopadhyay and S. Ghatak (eds), *Current Issues in Monetary Economics*, Wheatsheaf (UK) and Barnes & Noble, Savage, MD.

Asilis, C. M., Honohan, P. and McNelis, P. D. (1993) 'Money Demand during Hyperinflation and Stabilisation: Bolivia, 1980–88', *Economic Inquiry*, 262–73

Baba, Y., Hendry, D. and Starr, R. (1992) 'US Money Demand, 1960–88', *Review of Economic Studies*, January, 25–61

Bank of England (1970) 'The Importance of Money', *Quarterly Bulletin*, **10** (2), June

Barro, R. and Grossman, H. J. (1976) *Money, Employment and Inflation*, Cambridge University Press, Cambridge.

Bhaduri, A. (1973) 'A Study of Agricultural Backwardness under Semi-feudalism', *Economic Journal*, **83** (329), 120–37

Bhaduri, A. (1977) 'On the Formation of Usurious Interest Rates in Backward Agriculture', *Cambridge Journal of Economics*, **1** (4), 335–52

Bhambri, R. S. (1968) 'Demand for Money and Investible Surplus', *The Nigerian Journal of Economic and Social Studies*, **10** (1), 87–93

Bhattacharyya, B. B. (1974) 'Demand and Supply of Money in a Developing Economy: A Structural Analysis for India', *Review of Economics and Statistics*, **56**, 502–10

Bottomley, A. (1971) *Factor Pricing and Economic Growth in Underdeveloped Rural Areas*, Crosby Lockwood & Son Ltd., London

Campbell, C. D. (1970) 'The Velocity of Money and the Rate of Inflation: Recent Experiences in South Korea and Brazil', in D. Meiselman (ed.), *Varieties of Monetary Experience*, University of Chicago Press, pp. 341–86

Charemza, W. W. and Ghatak, S. (1990) 'Demand for Money in a Dual-currency, Quantity-constrained Economy: Hungary and Poland, 1956–85', *Economic Journal*, 100: 1159–72

Charemza, W. and Deadman, D. F. (1993) *New Directions in Econometric Practice*, Edward Elgar

Chow, G. C. (1966) 'On the Long-Run and Short-Run Demand for Money', *Journal of Political Economy*, **74**, 111–31

Coghlan, R. T. (1978) 'A Transaction Demand for Money', *Bank of England Quarterly Bulletin*, **18** (1), 48–60

Davis, C. M. (1988) 'The Second Economy in Disequilibrium and Shortage Models of Centrally Planned Economies', Berkeley-Duke OP, no 12

Deadman, D. F. and Ghatak, S. (1994) 'The Demand for Money in Developing Countries'. University of Leicester, (mimeo)

Deaver, J. V. (1970) 'The Chilean Inflation and the Demand for Money', in D. Meiselman (ed.), *Varieties of Monetary Experience*, University of Chicago Press, pp. 9–67

Dornbusch, R. and Fischer, S. (1986) 'Stopping Hyperinflations Past and Present', *Weltwirtschaftliches Archiv*, 1–47.

Engle, R. F. and Granger, C. W. J. (1987) 'Co-integration and Error-Correction: Representation, Estimation and Testing', *Econometrica*, 251–276

Ezekiel, H. and Adekunle, J. O. (1969) 'The Secular Behaviour of Income Velocity: An International Cross-Section Study', *IMF Staff Papers*, **16**, 224–39

Fan, L. S. and Liu, Z. R. (1971) 'Demand for Money in Asian Countries: Empirical Evidence,' *Indian Economic Journal*, **18**, 475–81

Fisher, I., (1911) *The Purchasing Power of Money*, Macmillan, New York

Fisher, D. (1968) 'The Demand for Money in Britain: Quarterly Results 1951–67', *Manchester School*, **36**, 329–44

Friedman, M. (1959) 'The Demand for Money: Some Theoretical and Empirical Results', *Journal of Political Economy*, **67**, 327–51

Friedman, M. (1968) 'The Role of Monetary Policy', *American Economic Review*, **58**, 1–17

Fry, M. J. (1973) 'Manipulating Demand for Money', in M. Parkin (ed.), *Essays in Modern Economics*, Longman, pp. 371–85

Fry, M. J. (1976) 'Demand for Money in Afghanistan', *Journal of Political Economy*, **84**, 1133–8

Fry, M. (1988) *Money, Banking and Economic Development*, Johns Hopkins Press, Baltimore.

Ghatak, S. (1975) 'Rural Interest Rates in the Indian Economy', *The Journal of Development Studies*, 11, 3, 190–201

Ghatak, S. (1976) *Rural Money Markets in India*, Macmillan of India, Delhi

Ghatak, S. (1983) 'On Inter-regional Variations in Rural Interest Rates in India', *Journal of Developing Areas*, **83**, 21–34

Ghosh, D. and Kazi, U. (1977) '*Homogeneity, Expectation and Adjustment of Demand for Money in Nigeria*', Discussion Paper, Department of Economics, Ahmadu Bello University

Gordon, R. (1984) 'The Short-run Demand for Money: A Reconsideration', *Journal of Money, Credit and Banking*: 16: 403–34

Government of India – *Economic Survey*, 1991–2, Delhi, C.S.O. India

Gujarati, D. (1968) 'The Demand for Money in India', *Journal of Development Studies*, 59–64

Haache, G. (1974) 'The Demand for Money in the UK: Experience since 1971', *Bank of England Quarterly Bulletin*, 284–305

Hanson, J. S. and Vogel, R. C. (1973) 'Inflation and Monetary Velocity in Latin America', *Review of Economics and Statistics*, **55**, 365–70

Hendry, D. (1986) 'Econometric Modelling with Cointegrated Variables', *Oxford Bulletin of Economics and Statistics*

Hendry, D. and N. Ericsson, (1991) 'An Econometric Analysis of UK Money Demand', *American Economic Review*: 8–38

Hicks, R. J. (1937) 'Mr. Keynes and the "Classics": A Suggested Interpretation', *Econometrica*, **5**, 147–59

Hynes, A. (1967) 'The Demand for Money and Monetary Adjustments in Chile', *Review of Economic Studies*, **34**, 285–93

Johnston, J. (1992) *Econometric Methods*, 4th edn, McGraw-Hill

Karfakis, C, and Parikh, A. (1993) 'A Cointegration Approach to Monetary Targeting in Australia', *Australian Economic Papers*, 53–72

Kaufman, G. G. and Latta, C. M. (1966) 'The Demand for Money; Preliminary Evidence from Industrial Countries', *Journal of Financial and Quantitative Analysis*, **1**, 75–89

Khan, M. S. (1977) 'The Variability of Expectations in Hyperinflations', *Journal of Political Economy*: 817–27

Laidler, D. (1993) *The Demand for Money: Theories, Evidence and Problems*, 4th edn, Harper-Collins, New York.

Laidler, D. and Parkin, M. (1970) 'The Demand for Money in the United Kingdom 1956–67 Preliminary Estimates', *Manchester School*, **38**, 187–208

McKinnon, R. (1973) *Money and Capital in Economic Development, Oxford University Press, Oxford*

Melitz, J. and Correa, H. (1970) 'International Differences in Income Velocity', *Review of Economics and Statistics*, **52**, 12–17

Meltzer, A. (1963) 'The Demand for Money: The Evidence from Time Series', *Journal of Political Economy*, **171**, 1–34

Miller, S. R. (1991) 'Monetary Dynamics: An Application of Cointegration and Error-Correction Modelling', *Journal of Money, Credit and Banking*, 139–54

Myint, H. (1971) *Economic Theory and the Underdeveloped Country*, Oxford University Press

Nuti, D. M. (1986) 'Hidden and Repressed Inflation in Soviet-type Economies', *Contributions to Political Economy*, 5: 37–82

Page, S. (ed.) (1993), *Monetary Policy in Developing Countries*, Routledge, UK

Park, Y. C. (1970) 'The Variability of Velocity: An International Comparison', *IMF Staff Papers*, **17**, 620–37

Polak, J. (1957) 'Monetary Analysis of Income Formulation and Payment Problems', *IMF Staff Paper*, **6**, 1–50

Portes, R. and Santorum, A. (1987) 'Money and Consumption Goods Market in China', *Journal of Comparative Economics*, 11: 354–71

Portes, R. and Winter, D. (1978) 'The Demand for Money and Consumption Goods in Centrally Planned Economies', *Review of Economics and Statistics*, 60: 8–18

Ritter, S. L. (1977) *Principles of Money, Banking and Financial Markets*, 2nd edn, Basic Books, New York

Sharma, R. L. (1978) 'The Demand for Money in India: An Empirical Analysis', *Indian Economic Review*, **13** (1), 33–43

Shaw, E. (1973) *Financial Deepening in Economic Development*, Oxford University Press, Oxford

Teriba, O. (1974) 'The Demand for Money in the Nigerian Economy: Some Methodological Issues and Further Evidence', *The Nigerian Journal of Economic and Social Studies*, **16** (1), 153–63

Tobin, J. (1958) 'Liquidity Preference as Behaviour Towards Risk', *Review of Economic Studies*, **25**, 65–86

Wallich, H. C. (1971) 'Income Velocity', *Review of Economics and Statistics*, **53**, 200–201

Weston, C. R. and Towns, G. I. (1978) *The Short-term Demand for Money in Open Economics: Definition, Opportunity Costs and Stability*, Discussion Paper No. 24, La Trobe University

Wilford, W. T. and Villasuso, J. M. (1977) 'The Velocity of Money in Central America', *Indian Journal of Economics*, **5–7**, 173–83

Wong, C. H. (1977) 'Demand for Money in Developing Countries. Some Theoretical and Empirical Results', *Journal of Monetary Economics*, **3**, 59–86

Yi, G. (1993) 'Towards Estimating the Demand for Money in China', *Economics of Planning*, 243–70

Zwass, A. (1979) *Money, Banking and Credit in the Soviet Union and Eastern Europe*, Macmillan, London.

Chapter 3

Abe, S., Fry, M. J., Min, B. K., Vongvipanond, P. and Yu, T. P. (1978) 'The Demand for Money in Pakistan: Some Alternative Estimates', *The Pakistan Development Review*, **14**, 249–57

Aghevli, B. B., Khan, M. S., Narvekar, P. R. and Brock, K. (1979) 'Monetary Policy in Selected Asian Countries', *IMF Staff Papers*, **26**, 775–824

Akhtar, M. A. (1974) 'The Demand for Money in Pakistan', *The Pakistan Development Review*, **13**, 40–5

Alogoskoufis, G. and Smith, R. (1991) 'On Error Correction Models: Specification, Interpretation, and Estimation', *Journal of Economic Surveys*, **5**, 97–128

Arestis, P. (1988) 'The Demand for Money in Small Developing Economies: An Application of the Error Correction Mechanism', in P. Arestis (ed.), *Contemporary Issues in Money and Banking*, Macmillan

Arestis, P. and Demetriades, P. O. (1991) 'Cointegration, Error Correction and the Demand for Money in Cyprus', *Applied Economics*, **23**, 1417–24

Arize, A. (1984–5) 'Permanent Income, Inflation Expectations and Money Demand Functions in Nigeria, *The Indian Journal of Economics*, **65**, 289–305

Arize, A. (1989) 'An Econometric Investigation of Money Demand Behaviour in Four Asian Developing Countries', *International Economic Journal*, **3**, 79–93

Arize, A., Darrat, A. F. and Meyer, D. J. (1990) 'Capital Mobility, Monetization and Money Demand in Developing Economies', *American Economist*, **34**, 69–75

Asilis, C. M., Honohan, P. and McNelis, P. D. (1993) 'Money Demand during Hyperinflation and Stabilization: Bolivia, 1980–1988', *Economic Inquiry*, **31**, 262–73

Banerjee, A., Dolado, J. J., Galbraith, J. W. and Hendry, D. F. (1993) *Cointegration, Error Correction, and The Econometric Analysis of Non-Stationary Data*, Oxford University Press

Bank of England (1970) 'The Importance of Money', *Quarterly Bulletin*, **10**, June

Boughton, J. M. (1981) 'Recent Instability of the Demand for Money: An International Perspective', *Southern Economic Journal*, **47**, 579–97

Brown, R. L., Durbin, J. and Evans, J. M. (1975) 'Techniques for Testing the Constancy of Regression Relationships Over Time', *Journal of the Royal Statistical Society, Series B*, **37**, 149–63

Calomiris, C. W. and Domowitz, I. (1989) 'Asset Substitution, Money Demand, and the Inflation Process in Brazil', *Journal of Money, Credit and Banking*, **21**, 78–89

Cardoso, E. A. (1983) 'A Money Demand Equation for Brazil', *Journal of Development Economics*, **12**, 183–93

Charemza, W. W. and Deadman, D. F. (1992) *New Directions in Econometric Practice*, Edward Elgar, Aldershot

Chow, G. C. (1960) 'Test of Equality Between Sets of Coefficients in Two Linear Regressions', *Econometrica*, **25**, 591–605

Chow, G. C. (1966) ' On the Long-Run and Short-Run Demand for Money', *Journal of Political Economy*, **74**, 111–31

Darrat, A. F. (1985a) 'The Demand for Money in Brazil: Some Further Results', *Journal of Development Economics*, **18**, 485–91

Darrat, A. F. (1985b) 'The Demand for Money in a Developing Economy: The Case of Kenya', *World Development*, **13**, 1163–70

Darrat, A. F. (1986a) 'The Demand for Money in some Major OPEC Members: Regression Estimates and Stability Results', *Applied Economics*, **18**, 127–42

Darrat, A. F. (1986b) 'Monetarization and Stability of Money Demand in Developing Countries: The Latin America Case', *Savings and Development*, **1**, 59–72

Darrat, A. F. and Webb, M. A. (1986) 'Financial Changes and Interest Elasticity of Money Demand: Further Tests of the Gurley and Shaw Thesis', *Journal of Development Studies*, **22**, 724–30

Deadman, D. and Ghatak, S. (1981) 'On the Stability of the Demand for Money in India: Some Further Results', *The Indian Economic Journal*, **29**, 41–54

Deaver, J. V. (1970) 'The Chilean Inflation and the Demand for Money', in D. Meiselman (ed.), *Varieties of Monetary Experience*, University of Chicago Press, pp. 9–67

Diz, A. C. (1970) 'Money and Prices in Argentina 1935–62', in D. Meiselman (ed.), *Varieties of Monetary Experience*, University of Chicago Press, pp. 69–162

Doe, L. K. (1982–3) 'Demand for Money in Some Developing Economies', *The Indian Journal of Economics*, **53**, 91–114

Domowitz, I. and Elbadawi, I. (1987) 'An Error-Correction Approach to Money Demand: The Case of Sudan', *Journal of Development Studies*, **26**, 257–75

Domowitz, I. and Hakkio, C. S. (1990) 'Interpreting an Error Correction Model: Partial Adjustment, Forward-Looking Behaviour, and Dynamic International Money Demand', *Journal of Applied Econometrics*, **5**, 29–46

Evans, J. L. (1988) '*Adjustment Modelling and the Stability of the Demand for Money Function*', *British Review of Economic Issues*, **10**, 49–76

Fair, R. C. (1987) 'International Evidence on the Demand for Money', *The Review Of Economics and Statistics*, **69**, 473–80

Fan, L. S. and Liu, Z. R. (1971) 'Demand for Money in Asian Countries: Empirical Evidence', *Indian Economic Journal*, **18**, 475–81

Farley, J. V. and Hinich, M. J. (1970) 'A Test for a Shifting Slope Coefficient in a Linear Model', *Journal of the American Statistical Association*, **65**, 1320–9

Fisher, D. (1968) 'The Demand for Money in Britain: Quarterly Results 1951–67', *Manchester School*, **36**, 329–44

Fry, M. J. (1973) 'Manipulating Demand for Money', in M. Parkin (ed.), *Essays in Modern Economics*, Longman, pp. 371–85

Gerlach, S. and Nadal de Simone, F. (1985) 'A Money Demand Equation for Brazil: Comments and Additional Evidence', *Journal of Development Economics*, **18**, 493–501

Goldfeld, S. M. (1973) 'The Demand for Money Revisited', *Brookings Papers on Economic Activity*, **3**, 577–646

Gordon, R. J. (1984) 'The Short-Run Demand for Money: A Reconsideration', *Journal of Money, Credit, and Banking*, **16**, 403–34

Gujarati, D. (1968) 'The Demand for Money in India', *Journal of Development Studies*, **5**, 59–64

Gupta, S. (1978) 'Testing the equality between sets of coefficients in two linear regressions when disturbance variances are unequal', unpublished Ph.D dissertation, Purdue University.

Gupta, K. L. and Moazzami, B. (1990) 'Nominal vs Real Adjustment in Demand for Money Functions', *Applied Economics*, **22**, 5–12

Hendry, D. F., Pagan, A. R. and Sargan, J. D. (1984) 'Dynamic Specification', in Z. Griliches and M. D. Intriligator (eds), *Handbook of Econometrics*, volume II, chapter 18, pp. 1023–110

Hynes, A. (1967) 'The Demand for Money and Monetary Adjustments in Chile', *Review of Economic Studies*, **34**, 285–93

Johnston, J. (1984) *Econometric Methods*, 3rd edn, McGraw-Hill, New York

Kallon, K. M. (1992) 'An Econometric Analysis of Money Demand in Ghana', *The Journal of Developing Areas*, **26**, 475–88

Kamath, S. J. (1984) 'The Demand for Money in India 1951–1976: Theoretical Aspects and Empirical Evidence', *Indian Journal of Economics*, **65**, 131–72

Kamath, S. J. (1985) 'An Investigation of the Demand for and Supply of Money in India, 1951–1976', *Weltwirtshaftliches Archiv*, **121**, 501–23

Kulkarni, K. (1986) 'Empirical Evidence on Stability of Demand for Money in India', *Indian Journal of Economics*, special number, 18–34

Kaufman, G. G. and Latta, C. M. (1966) 'The Demand for Money: Preliminary Evidence from Industrial Countries', *Journal of Financial and Quantitative Analysis*, **1**, 75–89

Killick, T. and Mwega, F. M. (1993) 'Kenya, 1967–88', in S. Page (ed.), *Monetary Policy in Developing Countries*, Routledge, London

Laidler, D. E. W. (1993) *The Demand for Money; Theories, Evidence and Problems*, 4th edn, Harper Collins, New York

Leventakis, J. A. and Brissimis, S. N. (1991) 'Instability of the U. S. Money Demand Function', *Journal of Economic Surveys*, **5**, 131–61

Mangla, I. U. (1979) 'An Annual Money Demand Function for Pakistan: Some Further Results', *The Pakistan Development Review*, **22**, 21–33

Manning, N. and Mohammed, A. M. (1990) 'Money, Income and Prices in Singapore Reconsidered', *Applied Economics*, **22**, 653–68

Margaritis, D. and Maloy, F. J. (1990) 'An Intertemporal Error Correction Model of Money Demand for a Semi-Open Economy', *Journal of Macroeconomics*, **12**, 381–97

Meltzer, A. (1963) 'The Demand for Money: The Evidence from Time Series', *Journal of Political Economy*, **171**, 1–34

Metwally, M. M. and Abdel Rahman, A. M. M. (1990) 'The Demand for Money in the Economy of Saudi Arabia', *The Indian Economic Journal*, **38**, 89–102

Miller, S. R. (1991) 'Monetary Dynamics: An Application of Cointegration and Error-Correction Modeling', *Journal of Money, Credit, and Banking*, **23**, 139–54

Mills, T. C. (1990) *Time Series Techniques for Economists*, Cambridge University Press

Nickell, S. (1985) 'Error Correction, Partial Adjustment and All That: An Expository Note', *Oxford Bulletin of Economics and Statistics*, **47**, 119–29

Nisaer, S. and Aslam, N. (1983) 'The Demand for Money and the Term Structure of Interest Rates in Pakistan', *The Pakistan Development Review*, **22**, 97–116

Page, S. (1993) *Monetary Policy Developing Countries*, Routledge, London

Perera, N. (1988) 'Demand for Money in Sri Lanka, 1960–1984', *Indian Economic Journal*, **3**, 79–93

Psaradakis, Z. (1993) 'The Demand for Money in Greece: An Exercise in Econometric Modelling with Cointegrated Variables', *Oxford Bulletin of Economics and Statistics*, **55**, 215–36

Quandt, R. E. (1960) 'Tests of the Hypothesis that a Linear Regression System Obeys Two Separate Regimes', *Journal of the American Statistical Association*, **55**, 324–30

Ram, R. and Biswas, B. (1983) 'Stability of Demand for Money in India: Some Further Evidence', *The Indian Economic Journal*, **31**, 77–88

Wong, C. H. (1977) 'Demand for Money in Developing Countries: Some Theoretical and Empirical Results', *Journal of Monetary Economics*, **3**, 59–86

Chapter 4

Bardhan, P. and Rudra, A. (1978) 'Interlinkage of Land, Labour and Credit Relations: An Analysis of Village Survey Data in East India', *Economic and Political Weekly*, **13**, 6–7

Basu, S. and Ghosh, A. (1974) *A Review of Current Banking Theory and Practice*, 2nd edn, Macmillan, London
Furness, E. (1975) *Money and Credit in Developing Africa*, Heinemann, London/Nairobi
Ghatak, S. (1976) *Rural Money Markets in India*, Macmillan of India, Delhi
Gurley, S. G. and Shaw, S. E. (1967) 'Financial Structure and Economic Development', *Economic Development and Cultural Change*, **15** (3), 257–68
Iengar, H. V. R. (1962) *Monetary Policy and Economic Growth*, Vora, Bombay
Newlyn, Walter (1967) *Money in an African Context*, Oxford University Press, Lusaka/Addis Ababa
Newlyn, Walter and Bootle, R. P. (1978) *Theory of Money*, 3rd edn, Clarendon, Oxford
Reserve Bank of India (1979) *Report on Annual Currency and Finance*, Bombay
Sayers, S. R. (1957) *Central Banking after Bagehot*, Oxford University Press, London
Wai, U Tun (1957) 'Interest Rates Outside the Organized Money Markets in Underdeveloped Countries', *IMF Staff Papers*, **6**, 1
Wai, U Tun (1972) *Financial Intermediates and National Savings in Developing Countries*, Praeger, New York
Whittlesay, R. C. (1956) 'Relation of Money to Economic Growth', *American Economic Review*, **46**, 188–201

Chapter 5

Adekunle, J. O. and Hannan, E. (1969) 'The Secular Behaviour of Income Velocity. An International Cross-Section Study', *IMF Staff Papers*, **16**, 224–39
Adelman, I. and Morris, C. (1967) *Society Politics and Economic Development: A Quantitative Approach*, Johns Hopkins University Press, Baltimore
Bennett, R. (1965) *The Financial Sector and Economic Development: The Mexican Case*, Johns Hopkins University Press, Baltimore
Bhambri, S. R. (1968) 'Demand for Money and the Investible Surplus', *Nigerian Journal of Economic and Social Studies*, **10** (1), 87–93
Cagan, P. (1956) 'The Monetary Dynamics of Hyperinflation', in Friedman, M. (ed.), *Studies in the Quantity Theory of Money*, University of Chicago Press
Cameron R. *et al.* (1967) *Banking in the Early Stages of Industrialisation*, Oxford University Press, New York
Ezekiel, H. and Adekunle, J. O. (1969) 'The Secular Behaviour of Income Velocity: An International Cross Section Study', *IMF Staff Papers*, July 1969
Fan, L. S. (1970) 'Monetary Performance in Developing Economies: A Quantity Theory Approach', *Quarterly Review of Economics and Business*, Summer
Foley, K. Duncan, Shell, Karl and Sidrauski, M. (1969) 'Optimum Fiscal and Monetary Policy and Economic Growth', *Journal of Political Economy*, **77** (2), 698–719
Friedman, M. (1968) 'The Role of Monetary Policy', *American Economic Review*, **58** (1), 1–17
Fry, M. (1978) 'Money and Capital or Financial Deepening in Economic Development', *Journal of Money, Credit and Banking*, **10** (4), 464–75
Fry, M. (1988) *Money, Banking and Economic Development*, Johns Hopkins Press, Baltimore
Ghatak, S. (1995) *An Introduction to Development Economics*, Routledge, London
Gurley, G. J. and Shaw, S. E. (1960) *Money in a Theory of Finance*, Brookings Institute, Washington

Gurley, G. J. and Shaw, S. E. (1967) 'Financial Structure and Economic Development', *Economic Development and Cultural Change*, **15** (3), 257–68

Hanson, J. S. and Vogel, C. R. (1973) 'Inflation and Monetary Policy in Latin America', *Review of Economics and Statistics*, **55**, 365–70

Harberger, A. C. (1963) 'The Dynamics of Inflation in Chile', in C. Christ (ed.), *Measurement in Economics: Studies in Mathematical Economies in Honour of Yehuda Grunfeld*, Stanford

Johnson, H. (1966–67) 'Money in a Neo-classical One Sector Growth Model', in Harry Johnson (1978), *Selected Essays in Monetary Economics*, George Allen & Unwin, London

Jones, H. (1975) *An Introduction to Modern Theories of Economic Growth*, Nelson, Sunbury

Levhari, D. and Patinkin, D. (1968) 'The Role of Money in a Simple Growth Model', *American Economic Review*, **58**, 713–53

Melitz, S. and Correa, H. (1970) 'International Difference in Income Velocity;, *Review of Economics and Statistics*, **52**, 12–17

Metzler, A. (1969) 'Money, Intermediation and Growth', *The Journal of Economic Literature*, **7** (1), 27–56

McKinnon, R. (1973) *Money and Capital in Economic Development*, Brookings Institute, Washington

McKinnon, R. (ed.) (1976) *Money and Finance in Economic Growth and Development*, Dekker, New York

Moldonado, R. (1970–71) *The Role of the Financial Sector in The Economic Development of Puerto Rico*, Federal Deposit Insurance Corporation

Mundell, R. (1963) 'Inflation and Real Interest', *Journal of Political Economy*, **71**, 280–3

Newlyn, W. (1977) 'International and Credit Creation', in W. Newlyn (ed.), *The Financing of Economic Development*, Oxford University Press

Radcliffe Committee (1959) *Report of the Committee on the Working of the Monetary System*. Cmnd 827, HMSO, London

Shaw, E. (1973) *Financial Deepening in Economic Development*, Oxford University Press

Sijben, J. J. (1977) *Money and Economic Growth*, Martinus Nijhoff, Leiden

Sinai, A. and Stokes, H. (1972) 'Real Money Balances: An Omitted Variable in the Production Function', *Review of Economics and Statistics*, **54**, 290–6

Solow, R. (1956) 'A Contributionto the Theory of Economic Growth', *Quarterly Journal of Economics*, **70**, 65–94

Thirlwall, A. (1974) *Inflation, Saving and Growth in Developing Economics*, Macmillan, London

Tobin, J. (1965) 'Money and Economic Growth', *Econometrica*, **33**, 671–84

Vogel, R. and Buser, S. (1976) 'Inflation, Financial Repression and Capital Formation in Latin America', in R. McKinnon (ed.), *Money and Finance in Economic Growth and Development*, Dekker, New York

Wallich, H. (1969) 'Money and Growth: A Country Cross-Section Analysis', *Journal of Money, Credit and Banking*, **1**, 281–302

Chapter 6

Adekunle, J. O. (1968) 'The Demand for Money: Evidence from Developed and Less Developed Countries', *International Monetary Fund Staff Papers*, **15** (2), 220–66

Aghevli, B. B. and Khan, M. S. (1977) 'Inflationary Finance and the Dynamics of Inflation: Indonesia, 1951–72', *American Economic Review*, **67** (3), 390–403

Aghevli, B., Khan, M., Narvekar, P. and Short, B. (1979) Monetary Policies in Selected Asian Countries', *IMF Staff Papers*, **26**, 75–824

Argy, V. (1970) 'Structural Inflation in Developing Countries', *Oxford Economic Papers*, **22**, (1), 73–85

Bailey, M. (1956) 'The Welfare Cost of Inflationary Finance', *Journal of Political Economy*, **64** (2), 93–110

Barro, R. (1970) 'Inflation, the Payments Period, and the Demand for Money', *Journal of Political Economy*, **78** (6), 1228–63

Barro, R. (1972) 'Inflationary Finance and the Welfare Cost of Inflation', *Journal of Political Economy*, **80** (5), 978–1001

Betancourt, R. R. (1976) 'The Dynamics of Inflation in Latin America: Comment', *American Economic Review*, **66** (4), 688–91

Box,G. E. P. and Jenkins, G. M. (1970) *Time Series Analysis: Forecasting and Control*, Holden Day

Brown, R. (1984) *On Assessing the Effects and Rationale of the Stabilisation Programme in Sudan since 1978*, ISS Paper 12, The Hague: Money, Finance and Development Series

Bulmer-Thomas, V. (1977) 'A Model of Inflation for Central America', *Oxford Bulletin of Economics and Statistics*, **39** (4), 319–32

Cagan, P. (1956) 'The Monetary Dynamics of Hyperinflation', in M. Friedman (ed.), *Studies in the Quantity Theory of Money*, University of Chicago Press

Cavallo, D. (1977) 'Stagflationary Effects of Monetary Stabilization Policies', PhD thesis: Harvard University (unpublished)

Chakrabarty, S. (1977) *The Behaviour of Prices in India: 1952–1970*, Macmillan, Delhi

Chakrabarty, S. (1978) 'Money, output and price: guidelines for macro-cred planning', in Reserve Bank of India, *Recent Developments in Monetary Theory and Policy*, Bombay

Chandavarkar, A. (1977) 'Monetization of Developing Economies', *International Monetary Fund Staff Papers*, **24** (3), 665–721

Cole, D. (1976) 'Concepts, Causes and Cures of Instability in Less Developed Countries', in R. McKinnon (ed.), *Money and Finance in Economic Growth and Development*, Dekker, New York

Deaver, J. (1970) 'The Chilean Inflation and the Demand for Money', in D. Meiselman (ed.), *Varieties of Monetary Experience*, University of Chicago Press

Deggar, S. and Sen, S. (1983) Real shocks, output, growth and inflation: Marshall and Walras in the NICs. Paper presented to the Development Studies Association Meeting, Sussex, UK.

Dorrance, G. (1963) 'The Effect of Inflation on Economic Development', *International Monetary Fund Staff Papers*, **10** (1), 1 47

Dorrance, G. (1966) 'Inflation and Growth: the Statistical Evidence', *International Monetary Fund Staff Papers*, **13** (1), 82–102

Dutton, D. (1971) 'A Model of Self-Generating Inflation: The Argentine Case', *Journal of Money, Credit and Banking*, **3** (2), 245–62

Edel, M. (1969) *Food Supply and Inflation in Latin America*, Praeger, New York

Fitzgerald, E. V. (1984) *Problems in Financing a Revolution: The Case of Nicaragua*, ISS, The Hague.

Flemming, J. S. (1976) *Inflation*, Oxford University Press

Friedman, M. (1971) 'Government Revenue from Inflation', *Journal of Political Economy*, **79** (4), 846–56

Ghatak, S. (1976) *Rural Money Markets in India*

Ghatak, S. (1981) *Monetary Economics in Developing Countries*, Macmillan, London

Ghatak, S. (1987), Rural financial institutions in developing countries and implications for monetary policy'. Paper presented to the conference on 'Finance for Development', Kuala Lumpur, Malaysia, September: F. Shahadan and N. A. H. Idris (eds) (1987) *Financing for Development*, Oxford University Press

Ghatak, S. (1995) *An Introduction to Development Economics*, Routledge, London.

Granger, C. (1969) Investigating causal relations by econometric models and cross-spectral methods, *Econometrica*, **37**, 428–38

Greenberg, E. and Webster, C. E. Jr. (1983) *Advanced Econometrics: A Bridge to the Literature*, Wiley New York.

Harberger, A. C. (1963) 'The Dynamics of Inflation in Chile', in C. Christ (ed.), *Measurement in Economics: Studies in Mathematical Economies in Honour of Yehuda Grunfeld*, Stanford

Harvey, A. C. (1981) *Econometric Analysis of Time Series*, Addison-Wesley, Reading, Mass.

Hicks, G. L. (1967) 'The Indonesian Inflation', *Philippines Economic Journal*, **6** (2), 210–24

Howard, N. (1984) *Sri Lanka: The Post-1977 Economic strategy: A Comparative and Theoretical Overview*, The Hague.

Jacobs, R. L. *et al.* (1979) 'Difficulties with testing for causations', *Economic Inquiry*, **17**, 401–13

Jansen, K. (1984) *Stability and Stabilisation in Thailand*, ISS: MFD Paper No. 10.

Jansen, K. and Vos, R. (eds) (1985) *Finance in the Periphery: Report of a Policy Workshop, December 1984*, The Hague.

Kahil, R. (1973) *Inflation and Economic Development in Brazil 1946–63*, Oxford University Press

Kapur, B. (1976) 'Alternative stabilization policies for less developed countries', *Journal of Political Economy*, 777–92

Khan, M. (1977a) 'The Variability of Expectations in Hyperinflations', *Journal of Political Economy*, **85** (4), 817–28

Khan, M. (1977b) 'Variable Expectations and the Demand for Money in High Inflation Countries', *Manchester School*, **45** (3), 270–93

Kirkpatrick, C. H. and Nixson, F. I. (1976) 'The Origins of Inflation in Less Developed Countries: a Selective Review', in M. Parkin and G. Zis (eds.), *Inflation in Open Economics*, Manchester University Press, pp. 126–74

Kirkpatrick, C. and Nixson, F. (1987) 'Inflation and stabilization policy in LDCs'. In N. Gemmell (ed.), *Surveys in Development Economics*, Basil Blackwell, Oxford

Kirkpatrick, C. and Onis, Z. (1982) 'Structural determinants of inflation performance in IMF stabilisation programmes in less developed countries'. Paper presented to the DSA Conference, Dublin, September

Krugman, P. and Taylor, L. (1978) 'Contractionary effects of devaluation', *Journal of Development Economics*

Langoni, C. G. and Kogut, E. C. (1977) 'Development Policies and Problems: The Brazilian Experience', in K. Brunner and A. Meltzer (eds.), *International Organisations, National Policies and Economic Development*, North Holland, Amsterdam

Lemgruber, A. C. (1977) 'Inflation in Brazil', in L. B. Krause and W. S. Salant (eds), *Worldwide Inflation: Theory and Recent Research*, The Brookings Institute, Washington, D.C.

Lin, C. Y. and Siddique, A. K. M. (1978) 'Recent Patterns of Inflation in the Non-Oil Developing Countries', *Finance and Development*, **15** (4), 28–31

Logue, D. E. and Willett, T. D. (1976) 'A Note on the Relation between the Rate and Variability of Inflation', *Economica*, **43** (May), 151–8

McKinnon, R. (1973) *Money and Capital in Economic Development*, Brookings Institute, Washington, D. C.

Mathieson, D. (1979) 'Financial reforms and capital flows in a developing economy', *IMF Staff Papers*, **29**, 450–89

Meiselman, D. (1975) 'Worldwide Inflation: A Monetarist View', in D. Meiselman and A. Laffer (eds), *The Phenomenon of Worldwide Inflation*, American Enterprise Institute for Public Policy Research, Washington, D. C.

Mundell, R. (1965) 'Growth, Stability and Inflationary Finance', *Journal of Political Economy*, **73** (2), 97–109

Newlyn, W. T. (1977) 'International and Credit Creation', in W. T. Newlyn (ed.), *The Financing of Economic Development*, Oxford University Press

Nicholls, D. (1974) 'Some Principles of Inflationary Finance', *Journal of Political Economy*, **82** (2), 423–30

Parikh, A. (1984) 'Causality between money and prices in Indonesia', *Empirical Economics*, **9**, 217–32

Parikh, A., Booth, A. and Sundrum, R. (1985) 'An econometric model of the monetary sector in Indonesia', *Journal of Development Studies*, **21**, 3, 406, 421

Parikh, A. and Starmer, C. (1988) 'The relationship between the money supply and prices in Bangladesh', *Bangladesh Development Studies*, **3**, 59–70.

Parikh, A. and Starmer, C. (1993) 'An econometric model of the monetary sector of the Bangladesh economy', *Journal of International Development*, **5**, 1–21.

Saini, K. (1982) 'The monetarist explanation of inflation. The experience of six Asian countries', *World Development*, **10**, 10 871–84

Schofield, A. and Chatterji, M. *et al.* (1986) *Advanced Statistical Methods in Economics*, Holt, Rinehart & Winston, London, Ch. 6.

Shallan, A. S. (1962) 'The Impact of Inflation on the Composition of Private Domestic Investment', *International Monetary Fund Staff Papers*, **9** (2), 243–63

Shaw, E. S. (1973) *Financial Deepening in Economic Development*, Oxford University Press

Sheehey, E. J. (1976) 'The Dynamics of Inflation in Latin America: Comment', *American Economic Review*, **66** (4), 692–4

Silveira, A. (1973) 'The Demand for Money: the Evidence from the Bazilian Economy', *Journal of Money, Credit and Banking*, **5** (1), 113–40

Sims, C. A. (1972) 'Money income, casuality', *American Economic Review*, **62**, 540–52

Sjaastad, L. (1976) 'Why Stable Inflations Fail', in J. Parkin and G. Zis (eds), *Inflation in the World Economy*, Manchester University Press

Sunkel, O. (1960) 'Inflation in Chile: An Unorthodox Approach', *International Economic Papers*, (10), 107–31

Tanzi, V. (1977) 'Inflation, Lags in Collection and the Real Value of Tax Revenue', *International Monetary Fund Staff Papers*, **24** (1), 154–67

Tanzi, V. (1978) 'Inflation, Real Tax Revenue, and the Case for Inflationary Finance: Theory with an Application to Argentina', *International Monetary Fund Staff Papers*, **25** (3), 417–51

Taylor, L. (1980) 'IS-LM in the tropics: diagrammatics of the new structuralist macro critique'. In W. R. Cline and S. Weintraub (eds), *Economic Stabilisation in Developing Countries*, Brookings Institute, Washington DC

Taylor, L. (1983) *Structuralist Macroeconomics*, Basic Books, New York.

Taylor, L. (1991) *Varieties of Stabilisation Experience*, WIDER, Helsinki and Oxford University Press.

Thirlwall, A. P. and Barton, C. (1971) 'Inflation and Growth: the International Evidence', *Banca Nazionale del Lavoro Quarterly Review*, (98), 263–75

Thirlwall, A. P. (1974) *Inflation, Saving and Growth in Developing Economies*, Macmillan, London

Tower, E. (1971) 'More on the Welfare Cost of Inflationary Finance', *Journal of Money, Credit and Banking*, **3** (4), 850–60

Vandaele, W. (1983) *Applied Time Series and Box-Jenkins Models*, Academic Press, London

Vanderkamp, J. (1975) 'Inflation: a simple Friedman theory with a Phillips twist', *Journal of Monetary Economics*, **4**, 117–22

Van Themat, J. V. (1984) *Finance and Monetary Policies of Tanzania in the Present Economic Crisis*, ISS; MFD, 13, The Hague.

Vogel, R. (1974) 'The Dynamics of Inflation in Latin America, 1950–1969', *American Economic Review*, **64** (1), 102–14

Vogel, R. (1976) 'The Dynamics of Inflation in Latin America: Reply', *American Economic Review*, **66** (4), 695–8

Vogel, R. and Buser, S. (1976) 'Inflation, Financial Repression and Capital Formation in Latin America', in R. McKinnon (ed.), *Money and Finance in Economic Growth and Development*, Dekker, New York

Vos, R. (1984) *Financial Developments, Problems of Capital Accumulation and Adjustment Policies in Ecuador, 1965–1982*, ISS, MFD, No. 9, The Hague.

Wai, U Tun (1959) 'The Relation between Inflation and Economic Development: A Statistical Inductive Study', *International Monetary Fund Staff Papers*, **7** (2), 302–17

White, W. (1978) 'Improving the Demand-for-Money Function in Moderate Inflation', *International Money Fund Staff Papers*, **25** (3) 564–607

Wijnbergen, S. (1982) Stagflationary effects of monetary stabilisation policies: a quantitative analysis of South Korea, *Journal of Development Economics*, **10**, 133–69

Wijnbergen, S. (1983) 'Credit policy, inflation and growth in financially repressed economies', *Journal of Developed Economics*, **13**, 45–65

Wong, C. (1977) 'Demand for Money in Developing Countries: Some Theoretical and Empirical Results', *Journal of Monetary Economics*, **3** (1), 59–86

Wuyts, M. (1984) *Money and Balance of Payments in Mozambique*, ISS, MFD, No. 11, The Hague

Chapter 7

Baker, A. and Falero, F., Jr (1971) 'Money, Exports, Government Spending and Income in Peru, 1951–66' *Journal of Development Studies*, **7** (4), 353–64

Bolnick, B. (1975) 'Interpreting Polak: Monetary Analysis in Dependent Economics', *Journal of Development Studies*, **11** (4), 325–42

Ghatak, S. (1995) *Development Economics*, Routledge, London/New York

Gray, C. (1963) 'Credit Creation in Nigeria's Economic Development', *Nigerian Journal of Economic and Social Research*, **5**, 3

Khan, S. M. (1977) 'The Determination of the Balance of Payments and Income in Developing Countries', in IMF, *The Monetary Approach to the Balance of Payments*, Washington, D.C.

Newlyn, W. (1968) *Finance for Development*, East African Publishing House, Nairobi
Polak, J. J. (1957) 'Monetary Analysis of Income Formulation and Payment Problems', *IMF Staff Papers*, **6**, 1–50
Polak, J. J. and Boissonneult, L. (1959) 'Monetary Analysis of Income and Imports and its Statistical Application', *IMF Staff Papers*, **7**, 349–415
Polak, J. J. and Argy, Y. (1971) 'Credit Policy and the Balance of Payments', *IMF Staff Papers*, 1971, reprinted in IMF (1977), *The Monetary Approach to the Balance of Payments*, Washington, D.C.
Prais, S. J. (1961) 'Some Mathematical Notes on the Quantity Theory of Money in an Open Economy', *IMF Staff Papers*, **8**, 212–26
Schotta, C., Jr (1966) 'The Money Supply, Exports and Income in an Open Economy: Mexico, 1939–63', *Economic Development and Cultural Change*, **14**, 458–70

Chapter 8

Aschheim, J. (1961) *Technique of Monetary Control*, Johns Hopkins University Press, Baltimore
Basu, S. K. and Ghosh, A. (1976) *A Review of Current Banking Theory and Practice*, 2nd edn, Macmillan, London
Branson, H. W. and Litvack, M. J. (1986) *Macroeconomics*, Harper-Row International
Chacholiades, M. (1978) *International Monetary Theory and Policy*, McGraw-Hill, USA
Chandavarkar, A. G. (1971) 'Some Aspect of Interest Rate Policies in Less Developed Economies: The Experience in Selected Asian Countries', *IMF Staff Papers*, **18**, 1
Chick, V. (1978) *The Theory of Monetary Policy*, Gray Mills, London
Dernburg, T. F. and McDougall, D. M. (1976) *Macro-economics*, 5th edn, McGraw-Hill, New York
Eshag, E. (1971) 'The Relative Efficiency of Monetary Policy in Selected Industrial and Less Developed Countries', *Economic Journal*, **8**, 1
Fisher, D. (1976) *Monetary Policy*, Macmillan, London
Friedman, M. (1968) 'The Role of Monetary Policy', *American Economic Review*, **38**, 1–17
Furness, E. (1975) *Money and Credit in Developing Africa*, Heinemann, London/Nairobi
Ghatak, S. (1976) *Rural Money Markets in India*, Macmillan of India, Delhi
Hicks, J. (1937) 'Mr Keynes and the "Classics": A Suggested Interpretation', *Econometrica*, **5**, 147–59
Mundell, A. R. (1960) 'The Monetary Dynamics of International Adjustment Under Fixed and Flexible Exchange Rates', *Quarterly Journal of Economics*, **74**, 227–57
Sayers, R. (1957) *Central Banking after Bagehot*, Oxford University Press, London
Södersten, B. O. (1993) *International Economics*, new edn, Macmillan, London
Thorn, S. R. (1976) *Introduction to Money and Banking*, Harper-Row International, London/New York

Chapter 9

Bird, G. (1976) 'The Informal Link between SDR Allocation and Aid: A Note', *The Journal of Development Studies*, **12** (3), 268–73

Bird, G. (1978) *The International Monetary System and the Less Developed Countries*, Macmillan, London
Chow, G. C. (1960) 'Tests of Equality between Sets of Co-efficients in Two Linear Regressions', *Econometrica*, **28**, 591–605
Cline, W. R. (1976) *International Monetary Reform and the Developing Countries*, Brooking Institute, Washington, D.C.
Crockett, A. (1977) *International Money: Issues and Analysis*, Nelson, Middlesex
Grubel, H. G. (1977) *The International Monetary System*, 3rd edn, Penguin, Harmondsworth
Gupta, D. (1978) 'The Operation of the Trust Fund', *Finance and Development*, **15** (3), 37–40
Helleiner, G. K. (1974) 'The Less Developed Countries and the International Monetary System', *The Journal of Development Studies*, **10** (3), 347–71
Johnson, H. G. (1972) *Further Essays in Monetary Economics*, George Allen & Unwin, London
Leipziger, M. D. (1975) 'Determinants of Use of Special Drawing Rights by Developing Nations', *The Journal of Development Studies*, **11** (4), 316–24
Leipziger, M. D. (ed.) (1976) *The International Monetary System and the Developing Nations*, Agency for International Development, Washington, D.C.
Maynard, G. (1973) 'Special Drawing Rights and Development Aid', *Journal of Development Studies*, **9** (4), 518–43
Tew, B. (1977) *The Evolution of the International Monetary System, 1945–77*, Hutchinson, London
Triffin, R. (1960) *Gold and the Dollar Crisis*, Yale University Press, New Haven
Williamson, J. (1977) *The Failure of World Monetary Reform*, Nelson, Middlesex

Chapter 10

Bardhan, P. K. (1980) 'Interlocking, Factor Markets and Agrarian Development: A Review of Issues', *Oxford Economic Papers*, **32** (1), 82–98
Bardham, P. K. and Rudra, A. (1978) 'Interlinkage of Land, Labour and Credit Relations: An Analysis of Village Survey Data in East India', *Economic and Political Weekly*, **13**, 6, 7
Bathrick, D. and Gomez, G. G. (1983) 'Innovation Approaches to Agricultural Credit in the INVIERNO/PROCAMPO project in Nicaragua', in Von Piischke et al. (eds), *Rural Financial Markets in Developing Countries*
Bhaduri, A. (1973) 'A Study in Agricultural Backwardness in Semi-Feudalism', *Economic Journal*, **83**, 120–37
Bhaduri, A. (1977) 'On the Formation of Usurious Interest Rates in Backward Agriculture', *Cambridge Journal of Economics*, **1** (4), 341–52
Bliss, C. and Stern, N. (1982) *Palanpur: A Study of an Indian Village*, Oxford
Bottomley, A. (1971) *Factor Pricing and Economic Growth in Underdeveloped Rural Areas*, London
Bottomley, A. (1975) 'Interest Rate Determination in Underdeveloped Rural Areas', *American Journal of Agricultural Economics*, **57**, 279–91
Campbell, C. and Ahn, C. S. (1962) 'Kyes and Mujins – Financial Intermediaries in South Korea', *Economic Development and Cultural Change*, **xi** (1)

Chardavarkar A. G. (1971) 'Some Aspects of Interest Rate Policies in Less Developed Economies: The Experience in Selected Asian Countries', *IMF Staff Papers*, **18**, (1), 48–112

Charemza, W. and Ghatak, S. (1994) 'Financial Dualism and Virtual Interest Rates: The Case of India' *Economic and Political Weekly, April.*

David, C. C. and Meyer, L. R. (1983) 'Measuring the Farm Level Impact of Agricultural Loans', in Pischke Von *et al.* (eds)

Desai, B. M. (1983) 'Group Lending in Rural Areas', in Pischke Von *et al.* (eds)

Desai, S. (1979) *Rural Banking in India*, Bombay

Fry, M. (1988) *Money, Banking and Economic Development*, John Hopkins Press, Baltimore.

Fry, M. (1989) 'Financial Developmet, Theories and Recent Experience', *Oxford Review of Economic Policy*, 5, 4, 13–28

Gamba, C. (1958) 'Poverty and Some Socio-Economic Aspects of Hoarding, Saving and Borrowing in Malaya', *The Malayan Economic Review*, **III**, 2

Ghatak, S. (1975) 'Rural Interest Rates in India', *Journal of Development Studies*, **11**, (3), 191–201

Ghatak, S. (1983) 'On Inter-Regional Variations in Rural Interest Rates in India', *Journal of Developing Areas*, 21–34.

Ghatak, S. and Ingersent, K. (1984) *Agriculture and Economic Development*, Harvester, England and Johns Hopkins Press, USA

Graham, H. D. and Bourne, C. (1983) 'Agricultural Credit and Rural Progress in Jamaica', in Pischke Von *et al.* (eds)

Gupta, S. (1971) 'Interest Sensitiveness of Deposits in India', *Economic and Political Weekly*, **20**, 2357–63

Hoff, C. and Stiglitz, J. (1993) *The Economics of Rural Organization*, Oxford University Press.

Miracle, M. P. (1979) 'The ACAR Program in Minas Gerais, Brazil', in Bunting, A. H. (ed.), *Change in Agriculture*, London

Neary, P. and Roberts, K. (1981) 'The Theory of Household Behaviour under Rationing', *European Economic Review*, 13: 25–42

Nisbet, C. (1967) 'Interest Rates and Imperfect Competition in the informal Credit Market of Rural Chile', *Economic Development and Cultural Change*, **16**, October

Oug, L. M. Adams, D. W. and Singh, L. J. (1976) 'Voluntary Rural Savings Capacities in Taiwan, 1960–70', *American Journal of Agricultural Economics*, **58**, (3), 578–81

Patrick, H. (1966) 'Financial Development and Economic Growth in Developing Countries', *Economic Development and Cultural Change*, **14** (2), pp. 174–89

Pischke, J. D., von Dale, A. W. and Donald, G. (eds) (1983) *Rural Financial Markets in FD Developing Countries*, Johns Hopkins Press and the World Bank, USA and England.

Rahman, A. (1979) *Agrarian Structure and Capital Formation: A Study of Bangladesh Agriculture with Farm-Level Data*, unpublished Ph.D. thesis, Cambridge University

Reserve Bank of India (1956) *All India Rural Credit Survey*, vols. I, II, III, 1954–57, Bombay

Schulter, S. (1972) 'The Role of Co-operative Credit in Small Farmer Adoption of New Cereal Varieties in India', in *Small Farmer Credit in South Asia*, IAD, Washington D.C., USA

Shetty, S. L. (1978) 'Performance of Commercial Banks since Nationalisation of Major Banks', *Economic and Political Weekly*, special number, October–December

Srinivasan, T. K. (1979) 'Agriculatural and Backwardness under Semi-Feudalism – Comment', *Economic Journal*, **89**, 416–19

Stiglitz J. and Weiss, A. (1981) 'Credit Rating in Markets with Imperfect Information', *American Economic Review*, 71: 393–410

Taylor, L. (1983) *Structuralist Macroeconomics*, Basic Books, New York

Van Wijnbergen, S. (1982) 'Stagflationary Effects of Stabilisation Policies: A Quantitative Analysis of South Korea', *Journal of Development Economics*, 10: 133–63

Van Wijnbergen, S. (1983a) 'Interest Rate Management in LDCs', *Journal of Monetary Economics*, 12: 433–52

Van Wijnbergen, S. (1983b) 'Credit Policy, Inflation and Growth in a Financially Represses Economy', *Journal of Development Economics*, 13: 45–65

Vogel, R. (1983) 'Implementing interest Rate Reform', in Pischke Von *et al.* (eds)

Wharton, C. R. (1970) 'The ACAR Program in Minas Gerais, Brazil', in A. H. Bunting (ed.), *Change in Agriculture*, London

Williamson, J. (1968) 'Personal Savings in Developing Nations', *Economic Record*, **44**, 194–209

Wolfe, H. W. (1919) *Co-operation in India*, London

Chapter 11

Agarwala, R. (1983) 'Price Distortions and Growth in Developing Countries', *World Bank* discussion paper, Washington, DC, USA

Bhagwati, J. (1984) 'DUP Activities and Economic Theory', in D. Colander (ed.) *Neo-classical Political Economy*, Ballinger, Cambridge, Mass., USA

Bhagwati, J. (1988) 'Export-promoting Trade Strategy: Issues and Evidence', *World Bank Research Observer*, 3: 1

Bird, G. (1992) 'Ten Years Older and Deeper in Dept', *Economics*, XXVIII: 19–26

Buiter, W. H. and Patel, V. R. (1990) 'Debt, Deficits and Inflation: An Application to the Public Finances in India', CEPR Discussion Papers, 408, London

Deadman, D. and Ghatak S. (1981) 'On the Stability of the Demand for Money in India', *Indian Economic Journal*, **29** (1), 41–54

Dholakia, R. H. (1990) 'Extended Phillips Curve for the Indian Economy', *Indian Economic Journal*, **38** (1), 69–78

Eaton, J. (1989) 'Foreign Public Capital Inflows', in H. Chenery and T. N. Srinivasan (eds) *Handbook of Development Economics*, vol. II, North Holland, Amsterdam

Eaton, J. and Gersovitz, M. (1981) 'Debt and Potential Repudiation: Theoretical and Empirical Analysis', *Review of Economic Studies*, 48: 289–309

Eaton, J., Gersovitz, M. and Stiglitz, J. (1986) 'The Pure Theory of Country Risk', *European Economic Review*, 3: 481–513

Fry, M. (1988) *Money, Banking and Economic Development*, Johns Hopkins University Press, USA

Gaines, J., al-Nowaini, A. and Levine, P. (1989) 'The ACES Package for One Country Rational Expectation Models', Discussion Paper, CEF, LBS, London

Ghatak, A. (1985) *Consumer Behaviour in India*, D. K. Agencies, Delhi

Ghatak, S. and Levine, P. (1994) 'The Adjustment towards National Solvency in Developing Countries: An Application to India', *Journal of International Development, 6:4:399–41*

Ghosh, A. (1989) *Indian Economy*, World Press, Calcutta

Government of India (GOI) (1988–9) *Economic Survey*, Delhi

Government of India (GOI) Central Statistical Organisation (CSO) (1976, 1988) *National Accounts Statistics*, New Delhi

Healey, N. (1990) 'The International Debt Crisis Eight Years On: An Interim Report', *Journal of Regional Policy*, 10: 2

International Monetary Fund (IMF) (1980–91) *International Financial Statistics*, Washington D.C.

Krueger, A. (1978) *Foreign Trade Regimes and Economic Development*, Ballinger, Cambridge, Mass., USA

Krugman, P. (1988) 'Financing versus Forgiving a Debt Overhand', *Journal of Development Economics*, 10:2

Krugman, P. and Obstfeld, M. (1988) *International Economics*, Scott Foresman, Boston, USA, 2nd edn

Krugman, P. and Obstfeld, M. (1993) *International Economics*, Harper-Collins, New York, 3rd edn

Overseas Development Institute (ODI) (1993) *Developing Country Debt*, London

Ram, R. (1986) 'Comparison of Rates of Growth of GDP based on International and Domestic Prices for 104 Countries over the Period 1960–80', *Indian Economic Journal* **33** (4), April-June 1986

Sachs, J. (1986) *Managing the LDC Debt Crisis*, Brookings paper 397–443

Samanta, S. (1986) 'Prices Suprises and Real Output: The Indian Evidence', *Indian Economic Journal*, **34** (2), 49–58

Sen, Raj K. (1991), *The Changing Pattern and Distribution of Consumption Expenditure in India*, Rabindra Bharati University, Calcutta

World Bank (1988–9) *World Debt Tables: External Debt to Developing Countries*, vols. II & III, country tables Washington D.C., USA

World Bank (1993) *World Debt Tables, 1992–3*, Washington, USA

Chapter 12

Agenor, P. R. (1992) 'Parallel Currency Markets in Developing Countries: Theory, Evidence, and Policy Implications', *Essays in International Finance*, Princeton University, No. 188, November

Argy V. (1981) *The Postwar International Money Crisis: An Analysis*, George Allen & Unwin

Corden, M. (1994) *Economic Policy, Exchange Rates, and the International Economy*, Oxford University Press

Corden, M. (1993) 'Exchange Rate Policy for Developing Countries', *The Economic Journal*, **103**, 198–207

Crockett A. D. and Nsouli, S. M. (1977) 'Exchange Rate Policies for Developing Countries', *The Journal of Development Studies*, **13**, 125–43

Dornbusch, R. (1993) '*Policymaking in the Open Economy: Concepts and Case Studies in Economic Performance*', Oxford University Press

Lane C. E. (1993) 'Côte d'Ivoire, 1973–88', in S. Page (ed.), *Monetary Policy in Developing Countries*', Routledge

Lane C. E. 'Exchange Rates and the Effectiveness of Monetary Policy', in S. Page

Phylaktis, K. (1988) 'Capital Controls: The Case of Argentina', *Journal of International Money and Finance*, **7**, 303–20

Phylaktis, K. (1991) 'Black Market for Dollars in Chile', *Journal of Development Economics*, **37**, 155–72

Phylaktis, K. (1990) 'Capital Controls in Argentina, Chile and Uruguay', in Phylaktis, K. and Pradhan, M. (eds), *International Finance and the LDCs*, Macmillan, London

Phylaktis, K. and Wood, (1984) G. E. 'An Analytical and Taxonomic Framework for the Study of Exchange Controls', in Black, J. and Dorrance, G. S. (eds) *Problems of International Finance*, Macmillan, London

Phylaktis, K. and Kassimatis, Y. (1994) 'Black and Official Exchange Markets', *Applied Economics*, **26**, 399–407

Index

adjustment policies and problems 119–23
Africa, currency boards 73
aggregate net transfer (ANT) 201–2
agricultural credit programmes 189–90
Almon lag scheme 48, 49, 51, 52
Argentina 109
augmented Dickey–Fuller (ADF) tests 40
autoregressive distributed lag (ADL) models 30
availability of credit 26–7

Balassa effect 235
Bancor 162
Bangladesh 123–4, 193
bank accounts and deposits 3
bank deposit multiplier 66–7
  and criticisms 68–9
bank rate policy in LDCs 149–50
Banque centrale des états de l'Afrique Ouest (BCEAO) 241
barter economy
  defects 1–2
  and money 1–2
bilateral trade index 226
black markets 33, 34, 35, 227, 238–9
Bolivia 28–9, 61–2, 203–4
  borrowing by LDCs 195–6
Brazil 50, 61, 117-18, 188
Bretton Woods system 162, 205–6
  and the dollar standard 159
Burma 48
buy-back provisions 203–4

Cagan's study of hyperinflation 104, 108, 109
Cambridge demand for money, the cash-balance approach 12
'capital flights' 125
causality between money and prices 128–9
central banks
  and economic development of LDCs 64–5
  functions in LDCs 63–5
  interest rates 29–30
centrally planned economies (CPEs)
  credit facilities 34
  excess demand for goods 32–3
CFA franc zone 240, 241
Chile
  demand for money in 49
  inflation 98, 106, 124
Citicorp 201
classical quantity theory of money 11–12
classical savings, investments and interest rate 10–11
classical theory 8–12
co-integration 32
  demand for money in India 39–44
  error correction models 54–6, 58–9
commercial banks in LDCs 176
  and the changing pattern 69–71
  and the creation of bank deposits 65–9
  nationalisation 187
commodity money 3
competitiveness 225
complementarity hypothesis of McKinnon 89–91, 116
concerted lending 200
credit markets 176–9
credit policy 27
credit restraint 26–7
'curb' market rates 27
currency boards in Africa 73–4
Cyprus 58–9

debt crisis
  application of a model 199–200
  debt problems 196–7
  debt regulations 218–9
  managing debt crisis 200–2
  policy responses to debt crisis 202–5
  repayment of debt 218
debt–Laffer Curve 204, 205
debt repayment/repudiation 216–23
default theory 197–9
demand adjustments and lags 27
demand deposits 3
demand-following finance 189

demand for money
  and the Cambridge school 12
  in LDCs and empirical results 27–35
  for precautionary purposes 16
  recent developments 27–35
  for speculative purposes 16
  and stability 12
  for transaction purposes 16, 23
deposits, mobilisation 188
Dickey–Fuller (DF) test & 40
discipline, financial 237, 241–2
dollar standard 159
dual exchange rate system 227
dual money market
  and central bank 6
  and integration 6–7

East Germany 33
economic development and financial accumulation 86–8
economic growth
  and financial intermediaries 84
  and financial repression 88–91
  Gurley–Shaw Model 85–6
  Harrod–Domar model of 75–6
  McKinnon and Shaw Model 88–91
  money in 78–81
  in neo-classical theory 76-8
  Tobin Model 78–81
error correction method (ECM) 31–2, 37, 43–4
  demand for money functions 53–62
exchange rates 240–2
  alternatives 226–7
  arrangements in LDCs 227–31
  choice of 231–5
  in developing countries 227–31
  and the need for reserves 158
  nominal anchor approach 237–40
  real target approach 235–6
  role and influence 224–6
export-weighted index 226
Extended Fund Facility (EFF) 170–1, 207
Extended Structural Adjustment Facilities 207–9
external finance, in Gurley–Shaw model 87

Federal Reserve System 86
financial accumulation and economic development 86–8
financial 'dualism' in LDCs 6–7, 24–5, 72
financial intermediaries (FIs) and economic growth 84–6
financially repressed regimes (FRRs), characteristics 33, 34
fiscal policy 88–91
Fisher, Irving 11
fixed exchange rate regime 157–8, 226, 231, 241–2
floating exchange rate regime 226, 231–3, 241–2
free-rider problem 200, 201, 204
Friedman, Milton 2, 5, 8, 22, 106, 108
full employment equilibrium and the classical theory 8–9
fundamental disequilibrium 159

Gabon 241
general account 167
general equilibrium approach and the Hicksian analysis 18–21
Ghana 51, 124
'Goldfield Puzzle' 29
Grameen Bank 192
Greece 59–60
'green revolution' 192
Gujarati's model on demand for money in India 38, 41–3, 47, 48
Gurley–Shaw model 84–6

Harrod–Domar growth model 75–6
Hicksian *IS–LM* approach 18–21
Hong Kong 27
hyperinflation 28, 82
  in Cagan's study 104, 108, 109

import predeposit requirement (IPR) 154
import-substitution-industrialisation (ISI) policies 196
import-weighted index 226
India
  central bank 64
  commercialisation of national banks 71, 187
  demand for money in 37–45, 47, 48, 52–3
  inflation 100, 119, 129-30
  national solvency model 212–16
  rural money market 175, 185, 187, 188
  simulation results 219–23
Indonesia 108–9, 111, 124, 129, 236, 238

inflation
case against 115–18
causes of, in LDCs 96–103
characteristics in LDCs 94-5
demand for money 50
effects on growth 103–15
and exchange rates 225
in India 100
model of generation and stabilisation 125–32
and money and growth 94–118
and moneylenders 183–5
as a tax 103–15
uncertainty 28, 38, 43
interest rates
demand for money 50
determination of 179–86
in LDCs 25–7
policies 190–2
uncertainty 28
usurious 178–9
Interim Committee (IC) 169–70
internal finance in Gurley–Shaw model 87
International Bank for Reconstruction and Development (IBRD) 159
international debt crisis 194–5, 199–200
benefits and costs of default theory 197–9
debt policies after 1973 196–7
IMF adjustment policies 205–11
LDC borrowing before 1973 195–6
managing 200–2
policy responses 202–5
international liquidity
and the LDCs 159–62
problems of 159–62
International Monetary Fund (IMF) 159, 162, 163, 164, 170–1, 206–10
adjustment policies 118, 119, 120, 121, 201, 205–6, 210–11
debt crisis 200–1, 203
effectiveness of the IMF programmes 210–11
new critiques of IMF 209–10
response of IMF 206–9
international monetary reserves, need for 157–8
'invisible hand' 9
IS–LM framework 18–21, 232–3, 234
Ivory Coast 241

Jamaica 188

Keynes without money 15
Keynesian 'building blocks' 13–16
Keynesian income analysis 136–7
Keynesian remedies 14
Keynesian theory 12–16
and the 'monetarist' school 8, 121–2
'knife-edge' problem in Harrod–Domar model 76
Korea, South 131, 183, 192, 238

Latin America, inflation in 82–4, 116, 166–7
least developed countries 171
less developed countries (LDCs)
demand adjustment 27
and financial dualism 6–7, 24–5
nature and interest rate 25–6
money in LDCs' economies 1–7
recent developments in demand for money studies 27–35
and special characteristics 24–7
stabilisation policies of 118–21
liquidity crisis 199
liquidity preference schedule 13, 17
'liquidity trap' 13, 17–18

Malaysia 117, 131
Malta 59
Malthus, Thomas 9, 11
managed floating exchange rate 226–7
marginal efficiency of capital (MEC) 196
marginal propensity to consume (MPC) 14
Mauritius 59
McKinnon 84
hypothesis 35
and the limitations to neo-classical monetary growth theory 81–2
and Shaw model 88–91, 115–16
Mexico 135, 137–9, 199, 203
monetarists' case 22–4
monetarists' model of inflation 96–103
monetary and fiscal policy 21–2
monetary institutions in LDCs 63–74
monetary policy 21–2
instruments of, in LDCs 148–55
objectives 143–4
role of in LDCs 143–4, 155–6
theory of 144–8
monetary targeting 38
monetary union 240, 241

money, in a neo-classical growth model 78–81
 barter economy 1–2
 and credit creation 2–5
 definition 2–5
 and the interest rate 16–21
 as a medium of exchange 2
 money markets in LDCs 5–7
 role of money 1–7
 as a store of value 2
 as a unit of account 2
money markets 5–7
 the dichotomy in the 6–7
 functions of 5–6
 in LDCs 5–7
money supply 3, 4, 5, 12, 16, 29–30, 35–7
moneylenders in LDCs 176–86
moneyness 4
moral suasion 155
multiple exchange rate regime 227
Mundell–Fleming model 232–3, 234
Mundell model 104, 106

national solvency condition 212–13
near monies 85
near money assets 3
neo-classical growth model 76–8
 and money 78–81
neo-classical monetary growth theory, and the application to LDCs 81–4
neo-structuralism 91–3
Nicaragua 188
Nigeria 40, 52, 82, 140
nominal exchange rate 224, 237–40
non-banking financial intermediaries (NFIs) 3
non-monetised economy 2
Nuti hypothesis 35

official market (OM) money 33, 34, 35
Oil Facility, and the IMF 171
open market operations 150
 and the central bank 5
 in LDCs 150–1
openness of economies 234–5
optimum rate of growth of money supply 83
 in Asian countries 83
Organisation of Petroleum Exporting Countries (OPEC) 171
organised money market 71
 and the links with unorganised money markets 72–3

Pakistan 48, 124–5
partial adjustment model 51, 56
pegged exchange rates 226, 228
Peru 139–40
Philippines 130–1, 238
Polak–Boissonneult (PB) model 133–5
 application of 135–6
 and the Keynesian income analysis 136–7
 limitations of 141–2
 and Mexico 135, 137–9
 and Nigeria 140
 and Peru 139–40
 policy implications 140–1
 and Uganda 140
Poland 33
Policy Framework Paper (PFP) 209
production function 83
 in neo-classical theory 77
Puerto Rico 91
purchasing power parity (PPP) proposition 237

quantity theory of money 11
 and the classical view 11–12
quota system
 criticisms of 164, 169–70
 and the SDRs 163

Radcliffe Committee in Britain 3, 86
real bills doctrine 70
real exchange rate target 224, 235–6
reconstitution obligation 169
Regulation Q, in USA 86
Regulation W, in USA 165
remonetisation 28
reserves, need for 158
rural interest rates in LDCs 179
rural financial institutions in LDCs 175
 imperfect rural credit markets 177
 policies 187
rural money markets in LDCs 71–3, 175–6
 Bangladesh 193
 evaluation 186–7
 integrated development policy 187–91
 interest rates 25, 179–86
 money demand 27–8
 policy implications 191–3
 unorganised 176–9

Saudi Arabia 51
savings gap 195, 200
Say's law 8
seigniorage 161, 162, 165
selective credit controls (SCCs) 153
  in LDCs 153–5
share-cropping 177
Singapore 27, 60
South Korea 131
Special Drawing Rights (SDRs) 157, 160, 162, 228
  and aid: 'the link' 167–9
  allocation of 163, 167
  further changes in allocation of 169–70
  implications of 164–5
  interest rate on 163
  nature and role of 162–70
  recent value of, in basket of currencies 170
  and transfer of resources 167
  use of, by the LDCs 165–7
Sri Lanka 123, 132
stabilisation 118–25
steady-state equilibrium 77
Structural Adjustment Facilities 207–9
structural adjustment lending (SAL) 208
structural adjustment programmes 201, 205–11
structuralism 191–2
structuralists' view of inflation 96–103
student-*t* tests 53
Subsidy Account, for the least developed countries 171
subsistence economy 2
Sudan 60
supply-leading finance 189

Tanzania 121, 124
tariffs 235–6
term lending, by the commercial banks in LDCs 70
Thailand 238
Tobin model 78–81
trade gap 195
'transmission mechanism' 27
Triffin Plan 159
Trust Fund, and the least developed countries 171
Turkey 130

Uganda 140
unemployment equilibrium 13
Union monétaire ouest africaine (UMOA) 241
unorganised money markets 175
  and consequences 176–9
  in LDCs 6–7, 26, 71–3

Van Wijnbergen–Taylor model 92–3
variable reserve ratios (VRRs) 151
  in LDCs 151–3
velocity 11–12
  income 26
  and inflation 109–10

'war chest' 158
world liquidity 159